Anglican Communion in Crisis

Anglican Communion in Crisis

How Episcopal Dissidents
and Their African Allies
Are Reshaping Anglicanism

Miranda K. Hassett

PRINCETON UNIVERSITY PRESS

PRINCETON AND OXFORD

Copyright © 2007 by Princeton University Press
Published by Princeton University Press, 41 William Street,
Princeton, New Jersey 08540
In the United Kingdom: Princeton University Press, 3 Market Place,
Woodstock, Oxfordshire OX20 1SY

Library of Congress Cataloging-in-Publication Data

Hassett, Miranda Katherine
Anglican Communion in crisis : how Episcopal dissidents and
their African allies are reshaping Anglicanism / Miranda K. Hassett.
p.   cm.
Includes bibliographical references and index.
ISBN-13: 978-0-691-12518-3 (hardcover : alk. paper)
ISBN-10: 0-691-12518-X (hardcover : alk. paper)
1. Anglican Communion—Forecasting. I. Title.
BX5005.H37   2007
283.09'0511—dc22
2006029030

British Library Cataloging-in-Publication Data is available

This book has been composed in Sabon

Printed on acid-free paper. ∞

pup.princeton.edu

Printed in the United States of America

10   9   8   7   6   5   4   3   2   1

*For Phil, companion on this journey
and many others*

Contents

Acknowledgments

I OWE MANY DEBTS of gratitude to those who have helped me in the researching and writing of this book. This research could not have been undertaken without the kind welcome and assistance of two communities: the congregation I have called St. Timothy's, and the staff and people of Uganda Christian University. Other consultants within the Episcopal Church in the United States and the Anglican provinces of Uganda and Rwanda also provided invaluable help by sharing their perspectives on our global church. I also deeply appreciate several individuals who offered me access to their personal archives of relevant documents, including James Thrall, who shared his excellent collection of Lambeth 1998 materials. I thank James Peacock, Margaret Wiener, Glenn Hinson, and David Newbury, for all the ways they pushed my thinking and improved this work; I am especially grateful for the mentoring and guidance provided by Dorothy Holland. Brooks Graebner and Ian T. Douglas, as fellow scholars and fellow Anglicans, also encouraged me in this work and helped me to put it in its broader context. My writing group, the DangerGirls, deserves significant credit for keeping me on task and clarifying my prose—thanks to Jill DeTemple, Celeste Gagnon, Cheryl McDonald, Marsha Michie, and Quincy Newell. Thanks also to Joel Robbins and the readers who reviewed this manuscript on behalf of Princeton University Press and another press; their feedback particularly aided my theoretical conceptualization of this material. Fred Appel, my editor, has been a kind and straightforward guide through the process of preparing a book for publication. My preparation for this research was supported by a Foreign Language and Area Studies grant from the University of North Carolina, while my field research was funded by a grant from UNC's University Center for International Studies and a William Rand Kenan, Jr., fellowship. My writing was funded by a fellowship from the Louisville Institute. I deeply appreciate all those agencies that provided financial support for my research and writing. The Centre for Basic Research in Kampala offered me useful archival resources and connections with a Ugandan scholarly community. Finally, I thank my parents, Eliot and Pamela Smith, for their help with polishing this manuscript and their unwavering confidence in me, and my husband, Philip, for coming along for the ride, picking me up when I wore myself out, being a fellow observer and a sounding board for my ideas, and generally making the whole thing possible.

Abbreviations

AAC	American Anglican Council (conservative American organization)
AACOM	Association of Anglican Congregations on Mission (conservative American organization)
ACC	Anglican Consultative Council (governing body in world Communion)
ACiNW	Anglican Church in New Westminster (conservative Canadian organization)
ACNS	Anglican Communion News Service (offical Anglican news agency)
AMiA	Anglican Mission in America (conservative American organization)
CMS	Church Missionary Society (Church of England missionary agency)
ECUSA	Episcopal Church in the United States of America
EkkSoc	Ekklesia Society (conservative American organization)
ESA	Episcopal Synod of America (conservative American organization)
EU (EURRR)	Episcopalians United for Revelation, Renewal, and Reformation (conservative American organization)
FIF-NA	Forward in Faith, North America (conservative American organization)
FSC	Franciscan Study Centre (facility at Lambeth 1998)
NGOs	Non-governmental organizations
PECUSA Inc.	Protestant Episcopal Church in the United States of America (conservative American organization)
REC	Reformed Episcopal Church (separated Anglican church in America)
TESM	Trinity Episcopal School for Ministry (conservative American seminary)
UCU	Uganda Christian University (Anglican seminary and college in Uganda)

See figure 1 in chapter 1 for additional information on the relationships between many of these organizations.

Anglican Communion in Crisis

A Communion in Crisis?

THE WELCOMING RED DOORS of St. Timothy's Episcopal Church face onto the main street in a small southeastern town. Arriving at the church for the first time at 11 A.M. on a Sunday in mid-2001, I join the stream of members entering the nave, receiving bulletins and warm greetings from the ushers. Sitting among the parishioners of St. Timothy's, I observe what looks to me like a typical Episcopal congregation: some diversity in age, but largely white and middle-class. The worship service, too, is familiar to me as a cradle Episcopalian. Apart from the addition of some praise and worship music, it closely follows the order of service from the Episcopal Book of Common Prayer and takes its music from the Episcopal Church's *Hymnal 1982*. There is little here to suggest an international identity—until the people of St. Timothy's begin to talk about who they are. In the sermon and in the announcements, in the fine print on the bulletin that proclaims that this church is under the authority of the archbishop of Rwanda, in the sign on the lawn that informs passersby that St. Timothy's is a member parish of the Episcopal Church of Rwanda, come the surprising clues that all is not as it seems.

What looks at first glance like an ordinary Episcopal church is actually part of a challenging and unprecedented global movement that has brought American Episcopalians into relationships with Anglicans in the global South—Africa, Asia, and Latin America. Although St. Timothy's congregation and liturgy are in many respects typical of the national Episcopal Church to which the parish once belonged, St. Timothy's has rejected its American denomination and affiliated with a poor African church. A growing socially conservative and religiously evangelical orientation among the leaders and members of St. Timothy's, along with moves to the left by the larger Episcopal Church, created a divide that eventually proved irreconcilable. In mid-2000 the leadership of St. Timothy's decided to separate the parish from the Episcopal Church in the United States of America (ECUSA) and formally join the Anglican Church in the African country of Rwanda. In so doing, St. Timothy's became one of approximately fifty churches making up a new church organization called Anglican Mission in America (AMiA). AMiA's head bishops are themselves Americans and former Episcopal priests, who were consecrated as bishops in January 2000 by the archbishops of the Anglican provinces of Rwanda and South East Asia in order to lead and serve conservative Episcopal dissidents in the United States.

Nor are AMiA's member parishes the only Episcopal or formerly Episcopal churches with newfound international connections. On November 26, 2000, a festival Evensong service filled the Episcopal Church of the Good Shepherd, in Rosemont, Pennsylvania. Seventy people were confirmed, affirming their commitment to the faith of the church and receiving the laying on of hands by a bishop. Usually the rite of confirmation is performed by the local bishop, the church leader who holds authority over priests and church members within a given region or diocese. At the service at Good Shepherd, however, the two bishops who performed the confirmations came from far beyond the nearby diocesan headquarters in Philadelphia. These bishops came from South America and Africa to lay their hands upon the bowed heads of American Episcopalians, at the invitation of the leaders of Good Shepherd, who believe their American bishop is so radically liberal that he is not qualified to administer the sacrament of confirmation.

GLOBAL CONSERVATIVE ANGLICAN DISSIDENCE

These two examples hint at the contours of a diverse and dispersed movement opposing liberal policies and leaders in the Episcopal Church in the United States. This movement brings together theologically and socially conservative Episcopalians with those of the same faith elsewhere in the world, especially in the global South. The Episcopal Church in the United States is a member province of a worldwide federation called the Anglican Communion, consisting of Anglican and Episcopal national and regional churches in Europe, Africa, Asia, and North and South America. These churches, though sharing a common bond of Anglican heritage, are diverse in their histories, their worship styles, their spiritual concerns, and their social and political orientations. Church services in Uganda, where I conducted part of my fieldwork for this book, differ from those at St. Timothy's in everything from the music style to the dominant sermon themes. An increasing sense of alienation within the Episcopal Church, however, has motivated Episcopal conservatives like the people of St. Timothy's and the Church of the Good Shepherd to seek allies in the global South who might share their positions and concerns.

Signs of tolerance for gays and lesbians in the national Episcopal Church, beginning in the early 1990s, made conservative Episcopalians feel increasingly oppressed and embattled.[1] As a result, in the late 1990s they began looking for help from the Anglican world beyond the Episcopal Church, building a network of relationships and a common agenda with Southern Anglican leaders from Africa, Asia, and Latin America. Some Southern bishops have responded to these calls, moved by a complex assortment of motives that include anger at the Episcopal Church, concern about Western morality and cultural dominance, and eagerness for strengthened relationships with American Christians and stronger roles in the worldwide Communion. Some speak out against the Episcopal Church, asserting that the Bible condemns homosexual practice and that churches may not condone immorality. Some assist by offering the rites that only a bishop can provide—confirmation, ordination to the priesthood, consecration as a bishop—to Episcopalians unwilling to accept those rites from their own bishops. Some claim jurisdiction over conservative Episcopal parishes, enabling these churches to declare their independence from the Episcopal Church. In all these ways, Southern Anglican leaders and their churches have become more and more intimately involved in struggles over morality and orthodoxy within the Episcopal Church.

Together, these Southern Anglicans and Episcopal dissidents constitute a profoundly influential movement within world Anglicanism. Their collaborative activism aims to establish conservative sexual morality within the Episcopal Church and to increase the influence of Southern Anglicans in the Anglican Communion, a goal attractive both to formerly marginalized Southern leaders and to American conservatives, who hope Southern Anglicans will exert a conservative moral influence on the global church. Working across national and provincial boundaries and through diverse channels and tactics, this transnational religious movement seeks to challenge policies and power structures—not those of particular nation-states, but of national and global Anglican institutions.

In this book, drawing upon textual sources, interviews, and fieldwork with Anglicans in the Church of Uganda and Episcopal dissident groups in the United States, I explore the history, dynamics, and implications of this transnational movement, focusing largely on the formative period of 1997–2002 with some attention to more recent events. I challenge the tendency among conservatives and liberals alike to explain the increased global activism of Southern church leaders as part of a long-term global historical shift in the center of gravity of world Christianity to the global South—a theory expounded by scholar of religion Philip Jenkins and widely invoked by observers of the current Anglican scene. I question whether such global-shift arguments constitute an adequate or helpful account of recent developments in the Anglican Communion. Working from my analysis of inter-Anglican North/South alliances, I argue that the globalization of Episcopal Church conflicts is not primarily due to the inevitable rise to prominence of conservative and zealous Southern Christianity.[2] Rather, the increasing involvement of Southern Anglicans in the

Episcopal Church and the global significance now widely ascribed to Episcopal Church events result primarily from the cooperative globalizing work of American conservative dissidents and a number of sympathetic Southern Anglican leaders since the mid-1990s. The Episcopal Church's dissidents and their Southern allies are not merely carried along by global trends, but have actively shaped the character and impact of globalization on the Episcopal Church and the Anglican Communion.

A GLOBALIZING CONSERVATISM

Conservative in its agenda and outlook yet global in its membership and scope of action, this movement presents an intriguing challenge to common views of globalization and global movements. Globalization is a term of great currency and great complexity. The late 1990s and early 2000s were characterized by the proliferation of *globalisms*, or "endorsements of the importance of the global," in economics, politics, culture, and religion.[3] The terms "globalization" and "global" are invoked to refer to many different developments, including the worldwide spread of cultural elements, the domination of the world economy by transnational corporations, the increasing speed and accessibility of transport and communication technologies, and the new and subtle forms of domination of poorer countries by wealthier ones. Those of liberal or multiculturalist commitments are attracted to visions of globalization promising opportunities for cross-cultural sharing and increased self-determination for minorities and the poor.[4] Capitalist elites around the world look favorably on globalization because it presents opportunities for flexibility, cost-cutting, and market-opening; defenders of cultural diversity and economic self-determination fear it for the same reasons. Some apologists for globalization argue that the persistent inequities of the global order are holdovers from the era of colonialism and that globalization will eliminate such problems; critics suspect that inequality is perpetuated and even produced in new ways by the processes of globalization.

Corresponding with this heightened public interest, scholars have taken an increasing interest in the global and globalization. Sociologists Zsuzsa Gille and Sean O Riain find that the number of sociological studies listing "globalization" as a keyword increased from 29 between 1985 and 1990 to 985 in 1998 alone. Similarly, anthropologist Susan Brin Hyatt, reviewing anthropological studies of globalization, observes that "globalization" has virtually replaced "culture" as anthropology's "master trope."[5] Academic approaches to globalization are diverse, but most scholars agree that the term refers to transnational flows of capital, people, commodities, images, and/or ideologies.[6] Moreover, the term suggests that such flows are increasing in speed and density.[7] These processes mean that the world is becoming in some sense smaller, with remote encounters and relationships becoming increasingly important relative to more traditional face-to-face interactions.[8]

This increased networking has enabled the proliferation of global social and religious movements. A substantial scholarly literature examining such movements has developed. This literature, however, provides few parallels to the case I examine here. Studies of global religious movements or the impact of globalization on religious communities tend to focus on religious traditions defined as "other" by scholars in the Northern academy, such as fundamentalist Islam and Pentecostal Christianity. Few scholars examine globalization in the context of a mainline, Northern-headed religious body like the Episcopal Church or the worldwide Anglican Communion.

Furthermore, the conservative globalism of this Anglican movement challenges the assumptions of much of the existing scholarship. Recent years have witnessed increased scholarly and public attention to conservative religious movements that are worldwide in their scope and orientation. Yet observers of these movements tend to treat conservatives' globalism as if it were merely a rhetoric or veneer over an underlying reactionary antiglobalism. In the theoretical literature, conservative religious movements are often explained as a retreat from the radical openness and interconnectedness of the global world into faith-based fundamentalism or, at least, parochialism. Globalization scholar John Tomlinson associates religion with security and locality, as against the insecurity and openness of globalization.[9] Peter Beyer, in his book *Religion and Globalization*, identifies the conservative religious response to globalization as a retrenchment, a return to absolutes in the face of the relativization of identities brought about by increased intercultural contact.[10] Sociologist Manuel Castells likewise argues that evangelical Christianity is essentially a reactive movement seeking a return to traditional values in the face of "the threat of globalization."[11] Castells contrasts such reactive movements "against the new global order" with "proactive" movements that engage productively with globalization, like the environmental movement.[12] These scholars acknowledge that conservative religious responses to globalization reflect the forces and forms of globalization. But they, and many others who deal with these issues in depth or in passing, assume that the content of such conservative religious movements is always fundamentally antiglobalist, opposing the increased networking and exposure to difference that globalization brings. This conception of the relationship between religion and globalization may be summed up in Benjamin Barber's dualism "Jihad versus McWorld"—

with religion placed firmly on the side of reactionary resistance to globalization's cultural and economic currents.[13]

At the same time, scholars examining global social movements tend to focus on progressive movements, such as the environmental and feminist movements and the movement against economic globalization. Compendia of case studies of transnational activism rarely include conservative movements, and if they are touched upon, they are usually described as reacting against globalization, rather than embodying it.[14] This limited focus reflects the widespread assumption that progressive agendas are closely, even inevitably, linked with globalist orientations and movement structures. This literature, too, seems dominated by a dualism—that between corporate globalization (viewed negatively) and activist globalization within progressive social movement networks, a dualism epitomized by the clash between the World Trade Organization and anti-(corporate) globalization protesters.

In either the Jihad versus McWorld view of globalization or the WTO versus protesters view, no room seems to exist for a conservative religious movement that is substantively or, in Castells's term, proactively globalist in its outlook and actions. Yet the transnational Anglican movement I focus on is both explicitly conservative and explicitly globalist. Simon Coleman, who has studied the globalism of Swedish Pentecostals, notes that movements can be conservative in fixing certain identities, doctrines, or behaviors while in other respects embracing global flows.[15] Similarly, James Peacock observes that movements can simultaneously be conservative in their content and positively oriented toward the global context.[16] This global Anglican movement's fixed conservative content consists in its strong opposition to the acceptance of homosexuality. This position is literally conservative, both socially—in that the historical norm in movement members' host societies has not been public acceptance of homosexual identities—and scripturally, in that the Church has traditionally not read scripture as permitting such acceptance. Furthermore, opposing the acceptance of homosexuality is associated with the conservative side both in American public debate and, increasingly, in many Southern societies.

Simultaneously, this globalizing conservative movement is engaged with the flows of the global context in many respects: its use of transportation and communication technologies, its efforts to build cross-cultural solidarity, its denial of the relevance of distance and geographical boundaries, and its express goal of replacing the Anglican Communion's Eurocentric structure with transnational networks. This movement has had at least two distinctly proactive effects, heightening African Anglicans' sense of importance and empowerment within the worldwide Anglican Communion and heightening American conservatives' awareness of those living in the world's poorer countries. These changes not only affect movement leaders but have also shaped the identities and thoughts of ordinary Anglicans and Episcopalians globally, in both the North and the South.

The mix of fixity and flow, of conservative content and global orientation, in this movement casts new light on scholarly debates about globalization. Many scholars describe globalization as merely a refinement of Western/Northern imperialism, but in analyzing this movement, the useful question is not simply whether or not it spreads Northern hegemonies. Rather, this movement's hybrid nature demands attention to where and how it has extended or left intact Northern dominance, and where and how it has unsettled the old patterns of the Northern-headed global Communion. The fact that the alliances constituting this movement are largely initiated and maintained by the Northern partners, by virtue of their greater wealth, suggests that Northern dominance is one dynamic of these relationships. Northern conservatives' need for the assistance of poor and globally marginal Southern Anglicans, however, creates a situation of surprising reciprocity.

Participants often describe these North/South relationships in terms of exchange: the Northerners share material resources, while the Southern partners lend their ecclesiastical rank, moral authority, and general spiritual wealth to Northern dissidents. This vision of exchange, which was the most commonly voiced description of North/South relationships I encountered in my fieldwork, encapsulates the widely shared model of a bifurcated world Christianity and the presumed characteristics of its Northern and Southern "halves." One example of exchange talk comes from the website of the Ekklesia Society, a conservative American organization devoted to creating networks among bishops around the world:

> Each Member, Each Region Shares Its Strength: . . . . Materially wealthy US parishes can be greatly enriched by contact with (and exposure to), preaching and evangelists from Asia and Africa. At the same time, sharing even a small percentage of the relatively opulent Western parish budgets can provide resources that will make a tremendous difference in areas of great poverty in the under developed nations which make up what is called the "two- thirds world."[17]

An understanding of these relationships as fundamentally reciprocal views the materially poorer partners as sharing spiritual resources of equal or greater value than any material resources they may receive. The exchange model therefore represents an innovative solution to the common problem of asymmetry within global activist alliances, and may well be a significant reason these relationships are attractive to Southern Anglicans, who want to feel like partners rather than petitioners.

GLOBALIZATION AS PROCESS AND TACTIC

In my analysis I focus on the ways movement leaders and members not only have taken advantage of general processes of globalization but have also undertaken globalizing work themselves in the context of the Episcopal Church and the Anglican Communion. Certain aspects of globalization theory are useful in framing this analysis, particularly those addressing cultural and religious aspects of globalization, though inevitably economic and political aspects are intertwined with the circulation of ideologies, cultural products, and people in these Anglican networks. Approaches to globalization that focus on the lessening importance of geographic and cultural distance and the increase in long-distance relationships and global awareness are relevant to this analysis as well, to help explain the dynamics and conditions of possibility for these relationships. But although I take up some threads of globalization theory in the chapters that follow, I differ from many theorists in my fundamental approach.

I approach globalization neither as a defined process or teleology nor as primarily something that happens to people, but as something people do. In her 2000 article "The Global Situation," anthropologist Anna Tsing called for greater scholarly attention to the production and propagation of particular global visions. Susan Brin Hyatt likewise argues that many scholars apply the concept of globalization too loosely and uncritically, thereby masking particularities and processes and perpetuating conceptual oppositions between the cosmopolitan, "globalized" North and the "local" societies of the global South. She suggests that the notion of globalization ought to be "textually resisted" or "written against," rather than accepted and reified.[18] Anthropologists have examined the concepts of "modernity" and "culture," not by taking them for granted, but by critically analyzing how they are defined, circulated, and deployed; a similar approach should be taken with "globalization."[19]

Such an approach involves looking at people fundamentally as authors of globalization, not as subjects or victims. As Coleman notes, "processes of globalization do not simply happen to believers; they also create them in their own image."[20] These Anglicans, Northern and Southern, are globalizing both the Episcopal Church, by insisting that its policies are globally significant, and the Anglican Communion, by challenging the historical dominance of the Northern provinces. My analysis of this movement's development, based on ethnographic and textual data, demonstrates the effectiveness of globalizing as a strategy to change the balance of power in a situation of conflict. Globalization also serves here as a mobilization tactic in which, as Hilary Cunningham observes, "social actors appropriate distinctive kinds of global imagery and rhetoric to create new forms of activism."[21] Tracing the development of conservative Anglican globalism as a strategic response to particular circumstances of church conflict leads away from understanding "globalization" as a known process and into an examination of the relationships and motives of particular Anglican agents and groups, Northern and Southern, as they collaborate or clash in globalizing the Anglican world.

This movement has globalized the Episcopal Church by arguing for the relevance of the whole Anglican Communion as the appropriate frame of reference for events in the American church. Globalist discourses frequently involve the assertion, explicit or implicit, of the global scale—the whole world—as the appropriate frame of reference for whatever is at stake. Much of the globalist discourse among Episcopal dissidents and their Southern allies asserts that Episcopal Church policies are not only that province's business but the world's. Understanding the significance of this discursive move requires a basic understanding of worldwide Anglican polity. The Anglican Communion consists of nested jurisdictional structures.[22] An individual Episcopalian belongs to a particular parish church; churches are aggregated into geographical jurisdictions called dioceses, overseen by a bishop. The Episcopal Church, for example, has roughly one hundred dioceses. Dioceses belong to national or regional churches, or provinces, such as the Episcopal Church in the United States of America, or the Anglican Church of Uganda. These provinces are constituent bodies of the worldwide Anglican Communion. Provinces have a high degree of autonomy in governance and are not normally involved in one another's affairs, nor are the decisions of individual provinces usually held up for the approval of the worldwide church.

In arguing that the worldwide Communion should be considered and consulted in Episcopal Church policies, Episcopal dissidents are challenging the historical modus operandi of the Anglican Communion. The movement's globalist assertions raise questions over matters of scale and authority that formerly had clear answers. Is a conflict between a priest and the bishop who oversees her or him contained by the boundaries of that bishop's diocese, or can bishops from other dioceses in the province, or even from other provinces, legitimately intervene? Do individual Anglican provinces have the authority to separate themselves from another province in response to a decision made by that province affecting only its own constituents? The relevance of the global scale has itself become a contested strategic issue.[23] The recent history of the Episcopal Church and the Anglican Communion can be seen as a history of contention over what people, places, and connections have a role in resolving particular church conflicts.

In this book, drawing on my critical reading of recent Episcopal Church and Anglican Communion history and my fieldwork with Anglicans in the United States and Africa, I offer an account of conservative claims for the global scale as the appropriate frame for events in the Episcopal

Church.[24] This process of asserting the relevance of the global has had both discursive and practical aspects. Tsing and Coleman each distinguish between two aspects of globalization: ideas and discourses about the global, and material connections and flows or movements.[25] My study of movement documents and my conversations with participants both reveal the articulation and circulation of discourses describing events in the Episcopal Church as of global relevance. Likewise, my research also casts light on the proliferation of networks physically connecting Anglican leaders from outside the United States with dissident groups and parishes in the Episcopal Church. The most symbolically powerful of these globalizing projects are interventions cutting across jurisdictional boundaries, which assert the global relevance of Episcopal Church events in visible and concrete terms—for example, in the form of a bishop from Congo, Uganda, or Rwanda laying hands on a dissident Episcopalian to confirm, ordain, or consecrate. In the chapters that follow, I trace the parallel development of projects and discourses as this Anglican globalism has taken shape. I analyze the evolution and outcomes of these globalist ideas and tactics from 1997, when this movement first coalesced, through 2002, though I also touch on later developments. In this task of description and analysis, I "write against globalization" by revealing how this Anglican globalism works—how it has developed and spread and how it has been enacted, negotiated, and challenged along the way.

A note on terminology may be helpful here. My use of the term "discourse" in describing the spread of globalist vocabulary does not mean that these things are just talk. As used by scholars in the social sciences and humanities, the term "discourse" does not imply that something is not "real." Rather, discourses can be powerfully constitutive of reality. Widely accepted discourses can shape and even determine what people count as salient problems and rational solutions. Perspectives and actions that do not make sense in terms of a dominant discourse may be misinterpreted or ignored altogether. To refer to globalization as a discourse (or, more accurately, as a set of interrelated discourses) is not to suggest that globalization is not real. It is, instead, to indicate that the reality of globalization is located in the ways people and institutions think and talk in global terms, as well as in the myriad ways that thinking and talking produce projects making globalization manifest.

A GLOBAL VISION: NORTH/SOUTH SHIFT

Central to the globalist discourse of this Anglican movement is the idea of a shift in world Christianity from North to South, and I examine the use and implications of this vision of the globe. The idea of global shift is often invoked by movement members and observers as an explanatory framework for collaborative North/South activism opposing the Episcopal Church. This vision of global Christian reconfiguration consists in a narrative of the decline of the churches of the North (Europe and North America), beset by modernism and secularism, and the concomitant rise in vitality and influence of the churches of the global South, characterized by a zealous, conservative scriptural faith. According to this narrative, this rising Southern Christianity—what Philip Jenkins names as the "inexorable" coming of "the next Christendom"—constitutes *the* force with which Northern Christians must reckon.[26]

This view of North/South division subsumes the rhetoric of "culture wars," the language of conservative/progressive polarization prevalent in the 1980s and early 1990s. In the past, Episcopal Church conflicts were often described in the culture wars discourse of polarization then common in American society.[27] Today similar conflicts are instead described in terms of a new vision of *global* moral polarization. American conservatives describe themselves as a "faithful remnant" struggling to survive the North's moral decline, and thus as natural allies of Southern Christians. In addition, travelers and scholars often describe Southern Christians as "conservative," inviting the assumption that their conservatism corresponds to that of American dissidents. Conservative Episcopalians, in identifying with Southern Christians, seek to minimize the significance of geographic distance and cultural difference, exemplifying the growing irrelevance of national boundaries seen by some scholars as a central dynamic of globalization. American dissidents hope to transcend their Northernness and ride the rising wave of Southern Christianity to a renewed and realigned Anglicanism that reflects their values and convictions.

The global-shift vision, propagated by conservative dissidents and popularized by Jenkins's work, has become widely accepted in the Episcopal Church and other mainline American bodies. But although it is true that Christianity in the global South has grown dramatically in recent decades, the character of these churches and the implications of this growth are more complex than the global-shift model suggests.[28] Anthropological analysis shows that "North" and "South" as categories bear little descriptive or explanatory value. Yet preconceived ideas about the North and South play an important role in shaping North/South relationships such as those between Episcopal dissidents and Southern Anglicans. I offer here not a further reification of these categories, but an illustration of how their logic is propagated and becomes part of people's understandings of the world.

The extent to which global-shift language has become dominant in talk within and about the Episcopal Church was vividly illustrated in the controversy surrounding the Episcopal Church's decision to consecrate a gay man as a bishop a year after I finished this research. In the summer of

2003, the national General Convention of clergy and lay (nonordained) leaders of the Episcopal Church voted to accept Gene Robinson, an openly gay and partnered man, as the next bishop of the Diocese of New Hampshire. This decision, and Robinson's subsequent consecration in November 2003, drew an intense outcry from Anglican leaders around the world.[29] Several Anglican provinces broke off relations with the Episcopal Church, and the Archbishop of Canterbury, formal head of world Anglicanism, convened a commission to examine the implications of Robinson's consecration for Anglican unity. Even the secular press gave the situation considerable attention; the New York Times and National Public Radio carried frequent updates on Anglican news during the summer and fall of 2003.

The vocal international response to Robinson's consecration led many Episcopalians and observers to conclude that this event had unprecedented global implications. Conservatives argued that the international outrage proved that the Episcopal Church had abandoned "the Global Anglican tradition" and that permitting homosexual clergy was an absolute moral error, qualitatively different from previous changes that eventually became widely accepted (such as the full inclusion of racial minorities and the ordination of women).[30] Liberals in the church, too, saw the controversy in global terms. One liberal Anglican source stated, "The threat of [global] schism over the election of a gay bishop is like nothing the Church has ever seen before. The response isn't just larger and more organized. It's also global."[31]

This global response to Robinson's consecration was widely attributed, in both church-related and secular sources, to the worldwide reconfiguration of Christianity. In such sources, Episcopal Church events are described as of global significance because they represent the waning of Northern Christianity and thus demand the intervention of the orthodox, zealous Christian South. An editorial in the Dallas Morning News, covering a meeting of conservative Episcopalians to plan their reaction to Robinson's consecration, makes reference to this global-shift narrative: "[Conservatives] may be on the losing end of [the debate over homosexuality] within the Episcopal Church, but their meeting is worth considering in the context of a worldwide struggle that may transform Christianity in this century." Conservative Episcopalians called for a "dramatic realignment" of worldwide Anglicanism, separating the "archbishops of the dynamic Global South and the archbishops of the disintegrating Old West."[32]

The response to Gene Robinson's election and consecration is truly unprecedented in scope. Past seasons of conflict in the Episcopal Church's history have not been accorded such global significance. In the late 1970s a group of conservative Episcopalians broke from the Episcopal Church in response to the national church's revision of its liturgical manual, the Book of Common Prayer, and the decision to ordain women to the priesthood. The dissidents of that era issued no global appeals for help and received no global responses. Yet although the scope of the controversy over Robinson was unprecedented, it should not have been unexpected, given growing ties between American conservatives and Southern Anglicans.

The outrage of African, Asian, and Latin American bishops concerning Robinson's consecration may be due in part to a large-scale historical process in which Northern Christianity's traditional dominance is giving way to Southern Christianity. Such an assertion is difficult to prove or refute without the long-term perspective that only time can bring. But it is clear that the global response in the Robinson case was also due to the recent history of alliance building and globalizing carried out by American conservatives and sympathetic Southern Anglicans.[33] This globalizing work has profoundly entangled two processes: first, the growing power and assertiveness of Southern Anglicans in an Anglican Communion still struggling with the implications of decolonization; and second, American conservatives' search for Southern allies to help discipline the Episcopal Church. As a result, Episcopal Church politics over doctrine and morality have become wrapped up with Anglican Communion politics over inclusion, decolonization, and power. This entanglement, in large part, constitutes the conditions under which the Episcopal Church's vote to accept a gay bishop is seen as having—and, perhaps, actually has—the potential to provoke a total realignment of the worldwide Anglican Communion.

In exploring how we arrived at this point, I am laying out a history that, though recent, seems now in danger of being forgotten. The vision and language of "global shift," of rising Southern Christendom and worldwide realignment, so pervades perceptions of current events in the Episcopal Church and the Anglican Communion that it is difficult to step back and recall that this interpretation is not inherent in the events themselves. The degree to which this vision of the Anglican Communion now seems self-evident masks another perspective from which it appears quite surprising. I first undertook this research because I was intrigued, as both an anthropologist and an Episcopalian, by developing alliances between some unlikely allies: American social conservatives, commonly stereotyped as having little interest in including the marginalized, and Southern church leaders, whose demands for greater influence threaten the Northern-dominated status quo. When these groups first began to collaborate, many observers expressed perplexity or cynicism at the puzzling convergence of interests between these constituencies. Today, however, the naturalization of these alliances through the language of global shift has muted curiosity about how they came about.

The premise that the Anglican Communion has reached a moment of crisis in North/South relationships primarily as a result of a global shift in world Christianity deserves critical scrutiny. Instead of explaining the Communion's predicament on the basis of large-scale historical trends, I present here some of the particular people, places, interests, and motivations involved in bringing about the current situation. This story is both more complex and more interesting than the oft-invoked grand narrative of Northern moral collapse and Southern Christian triumph, which is compellingly simple and dramatic, yet largely bereft of historical or ethnographic grounding.

METHODS FOR A CRITICAL ACCOUNT OF GLOBALIZATION

The complex entanglement of Northern and Southern aspects, and of Episcopal Church–level with Anglican Communion–level dynamics and implications, demands a multifaceted analytical approach incorporating ethnographic fieldwork. The empiricism and potential for nuanced qualitative analysis of ethnographic study make it ideal for exploring processes of globalization and moving beyond a reductionist North/South model of contemporary Anglicanism. Rather than taking the categories of Northern and Southern Christianity as given, my approach, based on participant-observation, interviewing, and reading of relevant texts, allows an analysis of how ideas about Northern and Southern Christianity play into these relationships, sometimes challenged, sometimes confirmed; sometimes enabling, sometimes constraining. I demonstrate that these new transnational alliances are best understood not as by-products of a global moral shift but as the work of particular people and groups striving to live their faith, achieve their strategic aims, and create new ways to be Anglican together.

The fieldwork component of my research was multi-sited in order to capture the complexity of this situation. Anthropologists, qualitative sociologists, and others have remarked upon the need for multi-sited research designs for studies of global institutions and relationships.[34] In their review of ethnographic approaches to the global, Gille and O Riain describe such research: "Multisited research is designed around chains, paths, threads, conjunctions, or juxtapositions of locations. . . . What ties together fieldwork locations is the ethnographer's discovery of traces and clues, her logic of association. The methodological imperative of *being there* is replaced by that of *chasing things around*" (emphasis added).[35] Whereas in traditional ethnographic research, the anthropologist would spend extended time in one site, "being there," I divided my time between two sites and structured my research questions around tracing connections between American and African people and places. In anthropologist

Ulf Hannerz's terms, I explored one field that consists of a network of localities—a network including my primary fieldsites, domestic and international conferences, and other interconnected sites.[36]

The central set of connections I followed were those between an American parish, now under African ecclesial leadership, and one of its African associations. At the first service I attended at St. Timothy's, my American fieldsite, the visiting preacher was an American priest and former conservative Episcopalian activist who had since moved to Uganda to work for the church there. The presence of this American priest, bringing greetings from Uganda to an American parish under the authority of the archbishop of Rwanda, is one direct connection between the sites of my ethnography. This conjunction of people and places also hints at the much wider circulations of people, objects, and discourses that connect the Church of Uganda—together with a number of other African, and some Asian, Anglican provinces—with conservative Episcopal dissidents.

When I heard that sermon at St. Timothy's, I had already chosen the Church of Uganda as the site for my African fieldwork because the names of Ugandan bishops, Ugandan sites, and even Ugandan martyrs often came up in textual materials associated with Episcopal conservative activism. Although the Province of Rwanda is the African province best known for its involvement with the conservative Episcopal cause (see chapter 5), the Church of Uganda has multiple lines of connection to the conservative Episcopal movement as well. A 2001 analysis of conservative Americans' growing relationships with African Anglicans commented that "Ugandan bishops make up the largest contingent in [the Episcopal Church's] right wing's growing international network."[37]

In moving between St. Timothy's and my central sites in Uganda, both literally in the course of my fieldwork and now metaphorically in my writing and analysis, I follow North-South trails in order to clarify the meanings, dynamics, and implications of such connections. What I "chased around," as the uniting theme in this multi-sited research, was talk and ideas about the Northern (or American) and Southern (or African, or Ugandan) Anglican churches, their respective strengths and weaknesses, and how they do and should relate to each other as sister churches in the worldwide Anglican Communion.

FIELDSITES AND DATA SOURCES

The American component of my fieldwork consisted of four months with St. Timothy's Church, a parish in the southeastern United States that broke from the Episcopal Church and placed itself under the authority of the archbishop of Rwanda. I chose St. Timothy's because I wanted to focus on a parish that had broken from the Episcopal Church in the

United States and formed new African associations. I contacted the rector, asking permission to do research on the congregation, and he and the vestry agreed to welcome me. At St. Timothy's I participated in worship services, prayer groups, discussions, and other events, paying particular attention to the congregation's self-understanding in relation to the Episcopal Church, the Anglican Communion, the Anglican Church in Rwanda, and American and African Christianity more generally. I also interviewed approximately sixty leaders and members of this congregation face to face and several leaders in other conservative parishes and organizations by phone. In these interviews, I focused on how these individuals see their relationships with Southern churches as solutions to their conflicts with the Episcopal Church.

In addition to my work in this American fieldsite, my husband and I spent almost six months in central Uganda, where I studied the Anglican Church of Uganda. Working in Uganda gave me the opportunity to explore the character of lay support for Southern leaders' involvement in global church politics, as well as Southern laypeople's ideas about Northern and Southern churches and their relationship. This fieldwork was particularly essential because Southern perspectives on these alliances are underrepresented in movement documents, partly owing to Southern Anglicans' limited access to the Internet. The extent to which the Church of Uganda is truly "typical" of other Southern Anglican churches in these matters could be ascertained only through much more extensive field research, but my work in Uganda nonetheless offers at least a limited look at the realities of Southern Anglicanism, and my occasional quotations of other African bishops demonstrate that church leaders in many other African countries have much in common with their Ugandan colleagues.

I focused my attention on the services and other events, teaching, and talk at Uganda Christian University (UCU), an Anglican seminary and university located twenty miles outside the capital city of Kampala.[38] I chose UCU because many Americans and other Northerners visit the campus, making it a nexus of North/South relations. In addition, the academic community provided a comfortably familiar atmosphere, and the location permitted easy access to churches and provincial offices in Kampala. In Uganda, my fieldwork was less focused on a single site than it was in the United States, though UCU provided both a home and a primary site for my day-to-day learning about Ugandan Anglicanism, and I interviewed many of its staff and students. I took a broader approach in Uganda because I sought the kind of general familiarity with the Ugandan church that I had with the American church. Furthermore, the small size of Uganda (and my status as an American researcher) made it relatively easy to travel to different dioceses and meet with different bishops.

In addition to UCU and the adjacent cathedral, I observed and interviewed at other Anglican parishes in the Kampala area, including Namirembe Cathedral. I interviewed a number of provincial officials and bishops, usually by traveling to their offices. My husband and I also traveled to dioceses in Rwanda and western Uganda that had significant contact with transnational Anglican dissident networks, and I interviewed laity and leadership in these locations. I found little regional variation among Ugandans in views regarding North/South relationships; hence, I offer my findings as generally descriptive of the Church of Uganda as a whole.[39] Although I sometimes targeted particular individuals (especially leaders involved with these alliances) for interviews, in both Uganda and the United States my search for consultants usually followed the pattern of "snowball sampling," asking each consultant for recommendations of other people I ought to talk with. I completed about seventy interviews in my Uganda research, including interviews with bishops from nine of the Church of Uganda's twenty-two dioceses.

The Ugandans quoted in this text represent a broader range of positions in the church than those of the Episcopalians quoted. My Episcopal consultants were largely actively involved in the dissident movement, with the exception of a few moderate or liberal leaders I also interviewed for their perspectives. I quote a wider range of Ugandans partly to provide a fuller perspective on the Ugandan church, less familiar to many of my readers, but also to illustrate that the Ugandan church is not sharply divided on questions of morality or the relative merit of Northern and Southern Christianity in the way the American Episcopal church is divided. Although I discovered a range of opinion on these issues among Ugandans, a generally coherent sense of the quality, position, and power of African Christianity emerged from my Ugandan interviews. My account of Ugandan attitudes thus integrates the views of Ugandans of various liturgical and social ranks and leanings, while my account of American attitudes is focused only on the dissident conservative wing of the Episcopal Church.

In approaching prospective consultants in both countries, I told them that I was an anthropology student at the University of North Carolina, working on a research project for my dissertation. I explained that I wanted to learn about relationships between Anglicans in the United States and Africa, about conflicts within the Episcopal Church and the Anglican Communion, and about similarities and differences between churches in the United States and Africa. Nearly everyone I approached was willing to talk with me, and most had thoughts about some or all of these issues. I suspect the facts that I was engaged, and then married, during my year of field research helped me to be accepted comfortably by my consultants and communities; it reassured people that, though inquiring about issues surrounding homosexuality, I myself was safely hetero-sexual. In Uganda, when my husband was with me, a few consultants were so much more comfortable in his presence that we had a hard time convincing them that I was the one to talk to. My acceptance into my field sites was also eased by the fact that I am a practicing Episcopalian and was willing to participate in worship with my consultants, which was a tremendous help in establishing rapport. My Episcopalian identity also raised the question of my position vis-à-vis current church conflicts. How-ever, few of my consultants in either the United States or Uganda ever asked my opinion. Some probably assumed I shared their views, though I suspect that my status as a woman pursuing higher education at a secular university led others to guess that my personal sympathies were with the liberal side. In explaining my work and framing my interview questions, I endeavored to convey my commitment to conducting this research, not as any sort of ecclesio-political exposé, but as a search for fuller under-standing of dissidence within my own church and Communion. Appar-ently my consultants were satisfied with this, and willing to help.

All the names of individuals quoted in the chapters that follow (as well as the name of St. Timothy's parish) are pseudonyms.[40] The atmosphere of division and mistrust surrounding the issues I was concerned with in the Episcopal Church and abroad complicated the issue of citing my consultants. Anthropologists normally use pseudonyms to protect the privacy of the community and individuals studied; the conflictual context of my research made such protection all the more important. For Ugan-dans to speak frankly about their experiences with American visitors, sponsors, and hosts; for members of a dissident Episcopal parish to talk freely about the details of their long struggle with their former bishop; and for leaders in the dissident movement to discuss matters of past and present strategy that other leaders might not wish disclosed, I had to be able to make assurances about the protection of my consultants' identi-ties. I have tried to provide readers with some details about the consul-tants I quote—age, gender, position in the church, placement in terms of larger debates and divisions. In the cases of some prominent church and organizational leaders, however, I have altered details to further protect identities, while still seeking to retain some sense of such individuals' sig-nificance as leadership voices.

My consultants in both the United States and Uganda included both laity and clergy. Although many of the controversial actions and relation-ships I focus on primarily involve a limited number of church leaders and activists (both Northern and Southern), I have found lay perspectives to be an important part of the whole picture of how and why these new transnational Anglican relationships developed and what they mean for the present and future of the Anglican Communion. Local church commu-nities are tied together in various ways through this movement's globalizing projects, and they participate in the circulation and elaboration of globalist visions.

Although my consultants represent a diversity of ecclesiastical roles, they are less diverse in terms of gender proportions. The vast majority of the consultants quoted here, both American and Ugandan, are male. This reflects not a bias of my fieldwork but the reality that lay and clerical leadership in both the American and the Ugandan churches is predominantly male. This is less true in the United States, but the American conservative movement is more male-dominated than the church at large. Evangelical Episcopalians do not all oppose women's ordination, but these churches tend to be more socially conservative and thus maintain a tradition of male spiritual leadership. Female voices, both American and Ugandan, do appear in this book, but almost all are those of laypeople.

In addition to the interview and observational data I gathered, textual data sources have also been central to my research. Hannerz has observed that "text and media studies take up a central space in many contemporary field studies," because of the character of today's information-based society and the multi-sited fieldworker's need to utilize all available data sources.[41] My analysis integrates a critical reading of a variety of texts dealing with Episcopal Church, Church of Uganda, and Anglican Communion politics, produced by sources of various leanings (conservative, moderate, or liberal within the church, as well as the outside press) and in various genres (expository, persuasive, and declaratory). These texts have been used both as sources of historical data, to fill in the record of events from the years preceding my research, and as sources of data concerning the development and contestation of particular discourses about homosexuality and morality, the Episcopal Church, the Anglican Communion, and the global North and South. I draw extensively on the wide range of texts produced and distributed by conservative Episcopal individuals and organizations, frequently by means of the Internet, though also as mailings, press releases, and so on. As a vocal minority seeking wider support, conservative Episcopalians have been prolific in producing and circulating such texts, not only among their immediate allies but also, where possible, to larger audiences, including Southern Anglicans. These conservative Northern sources provide a vast body of data for tracking the development of particular ideas and discourses as conservative Anglican globalism has evolved and spread.

PLAN OF THE BOOK

In chapter 1, I present relevant background and history for understanding the rest of the book. I describe the history, character, and current concerns in the Church of Uganda and the Episcopal Church in the United States, respectively, and use the issue of homosexuality to illustrate the divergent perspectives of moderate/liberal Episcopalians, and conservative Episcopalians, regarding scripture, orthodoxy, and morality.

Chapter 2 presents an account of the development of conservative Episcopalians' globalist discourses and projects, in cooperation with Southern Anglican leaders. Frustrated by their failure to maintain or restore orthodoxy, as they understood it, in the Episcopal Church, certain Episcopal conservatives began in 1996 and 1997 to reach out to Southern church leaders. At meetings before and during the 1998 worldwide conference of Anglican leaders in Lambeth, England, American conservatives and Southern church leaders developed networks, shared their concerns, and strategized to pass a conservative resolution on sexual morality at that conference. In chapter 3, I take up questions of Northern hegemony within this movement as I continue my analysis of Lambeth 1998, exploring Southern views of homosexuality and Lambeth's other central issue of international debt forgiveness.

In chapter 4, I recount the ways in which the Lambeth Conference of 1998 was experienced and portrayed as a North/South battle, despite efforts by organizers to stress themes of global inclusiveness and unity in diversity. I describe and analyze Northern conservative "accountability globalism," an ideology of global scale first fully articulated in talk about Lambeth immediately following the Conference. This globalist discourse served as the foundation for Northern conservatives' post-Lambeth efforts to seek international assistance in enforcing the Lambeth sexuality resolution.

Chapter 5 begins with a brief account of the founding of the transnational dissident organization Anglican Mission in America and its implications and reception. I then broaden the picture, describing several other globalizing projects—in the form of activist North/South alliances, parallel to AMiA—that developed in the period following Lambeth 1998. I explore the depth of the impact of such globalizing projects through an account of how these transnational relationships are talked about in the congregational life of St. Timothy's, a member parish of the AMiA. This chapter completes my analysis of how, from the late 1990s through 2002, the Anglican globalist ideologies and projects endorsed by conservative Northerners and many Southern Anglicans developed, spread, and mutually reinforced one another.

In chapters 6 and 7, I take up the ways in which this innovative conservative Anglican globalism, in its discourses and practices, transforms or re-creates established patterns of Northern dominance within the worldwide Anglican Communion. Chapter 6 examines the discourses used to explain and justify such transnational Anglican relationships, especially images of the churches of the global North and South. An analysis of assumptions about the degree, character, and source of African Christian moral authority, or spiritual capital, provides the substance for this chapter. I lay out the common arguments that African Christian moral authority derives from African Christian youth, zeal, numbers, suffering, and poverty, giving particular attention to the ways Ugandan Christians both use and question these discourses, and to the continuity of this language with colonial constructions of the global South.

Money, power, and influence are the topic of chapter 7. In this chapter, I start with an account of mutual accusations exchanged between Northern liberals and conservatives that the other side is trying to use money inappropriately to influence Southern bishops. I then turn to the implications of such accusations in the African context, and in Uganda in particular. I describe the general cultural-economic predicament of the Ugandan church and society in relation to American cultural and economic power. I use the case of the controversy over Integrity-Uganda, a Ugandan Anglican gay-rights organization, to explore the dimensions and dynamics of influence and agency that emerge in Ugandan talk about North/South relationships. I argue that the question Americans tend to ask—*Are African leaders doing this for money, or not?*—is too stark and simplistic a question in the Ugandan context; and that, in spite of the best efforts of many, the material inequality between Northern and Southern partners in these transnational alliances continues to subtly determine patterns of thought and relationship.

In chapter 8, I return to the North/South conflict and the global-shift thesis, particularly to the ways that Philip Jenkins's work has been taken up by conservatives in the Episcopal Church as a description and justification of current developments in the Episcopal Church and the Anglican Communion. I look ahead to the implications of widespread acceptance of this polarized global vision, questioning whether this view of the world-wide church, even as it has undeniably made Anglicans around the world more aware of one another, may also have undermined the potential for greater global mutual understanding.

PERSONAL NOTE

Throughout this project, I have often thought of a line by Agha Shahid Ali, from the introduction to Faiz's *The Rebel's Silhouette*, which I noted down long ago: "Someone of two nearly equal loyalties must lend them, almost give them—a gift—to each other and hope that sooner or later the loan will be forgiven and they will become each others'."[42] I began this research as I complete it, as someone with two nearly equal loyalties: to the analytical perspectives and central questions of my discipline as an anthropologist, and to the Anglican tradition to which I belong.

I took up what would become the first threads of this project during my first year of graduate study in anthropology, as a project for an ethnography class. I had then only recently learned of the existence of the Continuing Church movement—the body of small breakaway American Anglican churches formed in the late 1970s. I decided to try my ethnographic skills at a local Continuing Church congregation in order to reach an understanding of why people would want to leave the church in which I had been raised. Now, after following those threads of discord from the Continuing Churches to the study of more recent divisions and alliances, after reading countless documents, holding countless conversations, hearing countless sermons and discussions, I have arrived at some understanding of why people are angry at, and choose to leave, the Episcopal Church. But I have also gained a greater understanding of why people love it, and choose to stay.

Both burdened and enlightened by all that I have learned of loyalty and loss, I offer this account of recent conflicts in the Episcopal Church. This work is too partial, no doubt, in both senses of the word—in some areas, too incomplete; in others, too much informed by one or another of the contested positions in the current Anglican world. But I have tried, sometimes with conscious struggle against my eagerness to offer my own solutions or conclusions, to avoid adjudicating on matters of debate. Instead I have striven to cast light on the terms of debate themselves: how Episcopalians and Anglicans came to be arguing about these particular issues, in these particular ways, among these particular parties. In his incisive piece on the anthropology of Islam, Talal Asad concluded with a note on the challenges of writing about contemporary religion: "There clearly is not, nor can there be, such a thing as a universally acceptable account of a living tradition. Any representation of tradition is contestable."[43] My account of current debates in the Anglican tradition will no doubt be contested; my hope is that people on all sides of current debates will find an equal measure in this text with which to take issue. I ask that my readers, especially those with hearts and minds invested in these disputes, will accept this work in the spirit in which it has always been intended—as a gift.

CHAPTER ONE

Renewal and Conflict: The Episcopal Church and the Province of Uganda

A YOUNG ADULT praise team kicks off the English-language Sunday service at Mukono Cathedral, the church near our home in Uganda. Today one young man fires up the synthesizer, while another takes up a microphone and reminds us all to praise God for the day and for all our blessings. The keyboardist plays quietly behind his words and picks up the tune immediately when the man at the microphone begins to sing: "What a mighty God we serve, what a mighty God we serve . . . ." A young woman shakes a tambourine, and two little boys keep the rhythm on traditional drums. The congregation sings and claps enthusiastically along with the music.

Praise music is one of the biggest draws of this particular service, an example of the lively, English-language, less Prayer-Book–bound services that are becoming common in Ugandan Anglican churches. Such services, described to me by one young clergyman as the "renewed Charismatic Anglican" style, appeal to many young people (and some adults) more than traditional Ugandan Anglican worship, which is based on the seventeenth-century English prayer book and nineteenth-century English hymnal, translated into local languages during the colonial period. Anglicans who attend traditional services defend the solemn tone of the traditional worship, often remarking, "Our God is a God of order." But many young people describe the older style as boring, preferring the freedom in prayer and music that they find in the "renewed" English services.

"What a mighty God we serve . . . " Standing in a pew among Ugandan worshipers, I sing along gamely, recalling that I learned this song in praise and worship sessions at my American fieldsite, St. Timothy's Church. Finding myself singing the same *traditional* Anglican hymns in Ugandan churches and at St. Timothy's would not be particularly surprising. After all, both American and Ugandan Anglicanism are offshoots of the Church of England, and both the Luganda hymnal and the Episcopal hymnal have roots in English hymnody. But this song is not in either hymnal. "What a mighty God we serve" is an example of contemporary praise music, a genre of Christian music that is pop-influenced in melodies, rhythms, and instrumentation, is usually lyrically simple, and stresses themes like submission to God and personal faith experiences. Praise music has entered both American and Ugandan Anglicanisms in the relatively recent past.

Even without the development of the alliances I examine here, Mukono Cathedral and St. Timothy's would be connected through certain global networks. Both are member parishes of provinces of the worldwide Anglican Communion; both owe their identity to the historical global formations of British colonialism; and both are influenced by the global circulation of praise music and other Northern evangelical cultural products. Yet such connections link these sites only as points in a complex network, with no direct links or mutual awareness. And if these sites share features in common, they differ in many ways as well. True, in both American and Ugandan Anglican contexts, praise music helps define a "renewed" Anglicanism over against traditional Anglican liturgy and hymnody. The implications of this renewal, however, differ significantly between these Northern and Southern contexts. Singing the same song may carry quite different meanings, depending on one's location within global Anglicanism.

CONTEMPORARY ANGLICANISMS: ROOTS OF A TRADITION

The Episcopal Church in the United States of America and the Church of Uganda are both branches of the worldwide Communion of Anglican churches. The Anglican Church, or Church of England, was founded when the English church broke from Roman Catholicism in 1534. The Anglican reformation made the liturgy more accessible to the laity through the development of an English-language liturgy and prayer book, while retaining much of the Catholic pattern of worship.[1] Anglicans also carried on the Catholic understanding of Christian identity as rooted in participation in the sacramental rites of the church, rather than viewing church membership as primarily a matter of doctrinal belief, as in most Protestant traditions. The Church of England also maintained the doctrine of apostolic succession. Each bishop is consecrated by bishops who are part of an unbroken succession of ordinations traced back to the first Christian bishops.[2] The Anglican tradition shares this sense of the sacredness of church polity with the Orthodox and Roman Catholic traditions.

Anglicanism spread around the globe with British colonialism. English missionaries planted churches wherever British political or economic involvement opened a path, and sometimes even beyond. As colonialism waned, these Anglican missions grew into independent Anglican churches and provinces. The Anglican Communion today is a worldwide communion of national or regional provinces united by their roots in the Church of England; their common loyalty to the Archbishop of Canterbury; their common faith and practice embodied in their prayer books; and their common participation in the decennial Lambeth Conference of bishops from throughout the Communion. Yet despite this shared heritage, Anglicanism today is far from a globally uniform tradition. Local cultural, political, and economic factors, and particular histories of missionization and revival, have created significant diversity among Anglican provinces.

Anglicanism possesses a dual character as both a *tradition* and a *polity*. As a tradition, Anglicanism consists of an interrelated set of meaningful elements: institutions (such as parishes and dioceses), practices (baptism, consecration, Lambeth Conferences), artifacts (prayer books, albs), roles (primate, rector), and discourses (of Anglican tradition, of liturgical order). Identification with the Anglican tradition indicates that (at least some of) these elements are held as essential aspects of a person or group's spiritual, social, or ecclesiastical identity. Nevertheless, there is no guarantee that any two individuals or groups who hold to the Anglican tradition will be alike in practice or conviction. I define Anglicanism as a tradition because it is an indigenous terminology—Anglicans often cite the "Anglican tradition" in argumentation and explanation. I also apply, by analogy, Talal Asad's argument for the term *tradition* as the most useful and flexible way to conceptualize Islam, which encompasses a tremendous variety of doctrines and practices.[3]

A person or group who identifies with the Anglican tradition, however, is not necessarily "officially" Anglican in terms of worldwide Anglican polity. In a 2003 interview, Episcopal priest and scholar Ian Douglas described the Anglican provinces as "autonomous . . . sibling churches," and offered this explanation of their relationship:

> Our organizational structure stands somewhere between . . . Protestant churches as federations [and] a strong, centralized church like the Roman Catholic Church. . . . The Archbishop of Canterbury does not have canonical authority or the power to tell any one church of the 38 churches in the Anglican Communion what to do, [but] who's in or who's out of the Anglican Communion depends on who the Archbishop of Canterbury wants to recognize as being in communion with him.[4]

The distinction between belonging to the Anglican tradition and belonging to the official Anglican polity (that is, being recognized by the Archbishop of Canterbury and included in gatherings of the global church) is significant in understanding the contemporary Episcopal dissident movement. Unlike earlier dissident groups, who identified strongly with the Anglican *tradition* but, in breaking away from the Episcopal Church, broke (albeit unwillingly) from the global Anglican *polity*, the dissidents of the 1990s have sought ways to leave the Episcopal Church while maintaining a defensible claim to membership in the global body through their ties with African and Asian provinces.

ANGLICANISM IN UGANDA

The first Anglican missionaries to Uganda, from the Church Missionary Society, arrived in Buganda, a kingdom in what is today central Uganda, in 1877. These British Anglicans came in response to explorer Henry Morton Stanley's call for missionaries to come convert the Baganda people.[5] Roman Catholic missionaries from France arrived in 1879; Islam had entered Buganda in the 1840s. Two decades of struggle ensued between Christian converts and a coalition of Baganda Muslims and adherents of traditional religions; when the Christians triumphed, conflicts between Anglicans and Catholics followed. The dominance of Anglicanism was assured when British troops arrived in 1891 to claim Buganda and surrounding regions as the British protectorate of Uganda.[6] Ugandan Christianity continued to grow in the wake of these conflicts. Louise Pirouet, a scholar of Ugandan Christianity, observes, "Probably in few areas [of Africa] was there an indigenous expansion of Christianity comparable to that in Uganda between 1890 and 1914."[7]

Although British colonial officials refused to treat Anglicanism as an established religion in the colonial state, Anglicanism has from the start served as the de facto established church, as even the church's name suggests: simply "the Church of Uganda." The Church of Uganda has been both helped and hurt by its association with governmental power and especially with the Baganda people, who, favored by the British, were educated and sent to neighboring peoples to help spread British rule and British religion throughout Uganda. These Baganda leaders were resented by those they were sent to instruct or rule, and the resultant taint of domination associated with Anglicanism may account for the slight but consistent majority held by Roman Catholicism in Uganda from the early twentieth century onward.[8] Today members of the Church of Uganda come from all regions, ethnic groups, and socioeconomic positions. Figures from the 1990s suggest that approximately 35 percent of Uganda's population were Roman Catholic, about 25 percent Anglican, 8 percent other Protestants, 15 percent Muslim, and the rest nonreligious or adherents of indigenous or minority religions like Hinduism.

The Church of Uganda was founded on evangelical theology and a low-church liturgical style of relatively simple worship.[9] Much of East Africa was missionized by the Church Missionary Society, which had been strongly influenced by evangelical revivalism in the Church of England that stressed spreading the gospel and encouraging all to seek a relationship with Jesus Christ as Savior. Pirouet describes the society:

> Its members, as well as distrusting ritual, set less store by the sacraments [and] the apostolic succession in the episcopacy. . . . For evangelicals, the distinguishing mark of a true, as opposed to a nominal Christian, is not good works or habits of devotion, but the ability to look back to some definite moment in life when the person became overwhelmingly aware of himself as a sinner and of God's complete and undeserved forgiveness.[10]

A low-church approach to liturgy was reinforced by the African context. As one Ugandan priest pointed out to me, austere and simple worship becomes a practical necessity for a poor parish that cannot afford many liturgical accoutrements. Further, British missionaries at times restricted access to the sacraments in order to encourage Ugandans to conform to British cultural practices. For example, communion was denied to couples who had not had church weddings, which were expensive and inaccessible for many. Under such circumstances, the Church of Uganda grew to see Christian identity as based less on sacramental participation than on knowledge of scripture and personal piety.

The evangelicalism of the nascent Church of Uganda was strengthened by the East African Revival of the 1930s and 1940s, which began in Rwanda and rapidly spread into Uganda. The East African Revival emphasized conviction of one's sins and conversion from being a "nominal" Christian or non-Christian. Revivalists stressed seeking to correct one's past sins, sharing one's ongoing struggles with sin with a fellowship group, and clean living. In spite of clashes with Anglican leaders, the Balokole or "saved ones," as those affected by the Revival were called, have staunchly remained within the Church of Uganda, devoting their energies to its revival.[11] This loyalty has been rewarded; East African Revival spirituality has by now thoroughly permeated the Church of Uganda as well as the Rwandan church. Kevin Ward, a British historian and former professor at Bishop Tucker College (now Uganda Christian University), writes, "While only a minority of Church people actually belong to [Balokole] fellowship[s], the Balokole movement has tended to provide the criteria by which all Ugandan Anglicans judge themselves as faithful Christians."[12] Many clergy and lay members of the Church of Uganda told me the East African Revival is the key to understanding today's Church of Uganda and the strength and vitality it has to offer the world.

One significant feature of the Church of Uganda (and of many African churches) is its involvement with its members' well-being. The Episcopal Church in the United States, an affluent church in an affluent society, carries no particular burden for the health and material development of its members. The context and obligations of the Church of Uganda are markedly different. Christian churches in Uganda have been involved from the early colonial period with the education, health, and general welfare of the Ugandan people—people who were, from the start, both members of these churches and beneficiaries of their services. Colonial-era underdevelopment, international debt, periods of active strife, and the regulations imposed on government operations by agencies like the IMF and World Bank have produced a nation with very little in the way of social, health, or development programs to serve its population.[13] Non-governmental organizations (NGOs), including churches, have filled in the gaps as best they can in Uganda and in many other countries in the same predicament. The Church of Uganda, itself seriously underfunded, works for the physical welfare of its members both on its own and in partnership with other NGOs and outside church organizations (such as sister parishes or mission teams). Lay and clergy leaders, in describing their church, often stressed to me the importance of "developmentalism" and "holistic ministry," meaning the church should improve people's situations as well as sharing the gospel with them. Michael, a young northern Ugandan priest studying at UCU, shared his concern for his church with me as we chatted under a spreading mango tree on campus one sunny afternoon: "It is very difficult for a person to be happy, even if the person is saved, if there are no medical facilities, if there are no schools for literacy, if there are no developmental programs."

In addition to greater involvement in the welfare of its members compared with the Episcopal Church, the Church of Uganda also has a much greater public role as one of the country's largest faith bodies. The Episcopal Church appears in the secular press only when some conflict or major change of leadership takes place, but Church of Uganda leaders and events are regularly covered in Ugandan national media. As might be expected of an institution as numerically strong and nationally visible as the Church of Uganda, the church is neither particularly conservative nor particularly liberal vis-à-vis the surrounding society; in fact, the American categories of "liberal" and "conservative" do not readily apply to this context. The Ugandan church is relatively progressive concerning the role of women, having women priests but no women bishops—paralleling Ugandan society, in which women are accepted in some positions of power, but are still expected to fulfill traditional roles. The church's active commitment to the poor and powerless might sound to American ears like the liberal Christian denominations, who in the United States inherited the Social Gospel tradition of concern for, and activism on behalf of, the needy and oppressed. But the Church of Uganda is also strongly committed to its stand on sexual morality; it opposes divorce, abortion, and homosexuality, positions corresponding with those of American conservatives.

TRENDS IN THE CONTEMPORARY CHURCH OF UGANDA

Unlike some African churches, the Church of Uganda does not face serious competition with expansionist Islam. The relatively small Muslim community in Uganda is not especially aggressive or politicized. Competition with other Christians, however, has become an increasingly pressing issue for the church. After the oppressive Idi Amin regime of the 1970s and a subsequent period of instability and war, Uganda experienced a great influx of Pentecostal and other Protestant groups. Pentecostal churches have proved a particular challenge to the Church of Uganda. Their free style of worship and lively music appeals to Ugandan youth and young adults, as does the use of English, which many young people prefer. The popular television channel Lighthouse TV, which broadcasts many American and other foreign Pentecostal programs, is an additional influence.

Growing competition for members with these churches and the related movement toward a more Pentecostal worship style were the two trends most often mentioned when lay and clergy Ugandans spoke to me about the Church of Uganda. Charles, a middle-aged parish priest, described the situation: "There is a lot of challenge from these other mushrooming churches around. . . . The only way out [for] the Church of Uganda . . . is also to take that direction of the charismatic movement. Which, I am indeed happy, it is already done in the Church of Uganda. . . . We also are dancing and clapping." As Charles suggests, many Anglican churches—encouraged by their archbishop and other leaders—have added or altered services to lure back straying members, offering them (some of) the strengths of Pentecostalism combined with the institutional and doctrinal stability of a traditional denomination. An increasing number of Anglican churches now offer English-language "renewed" services, responding to the demand from young people for services featuring spontaneous prayer, a high degree of lay leadership, and Northern-style praise music like that heard in Pentecostal churches and on Lighthouse TV. Evangelical Anglican and nondenominational missionaries from Britain and the United States have in many cases facilitated and supported such changes.

These shifts in liturgical style are a source of conflict and worry for some. Anglicans (mostly, but not all, in their forties or older) who prefer the quieter, traditional style of prayer-book worship feel alienated by the new styles and belittled by advocates of the new ways. Tensions have arisen between some adherents to the older ways of worship, who see the renewed style as a "new sect" and fear their church is losing its Anglican heritage, and adherents of the renewed style, who see nonrenewed Anglicans as spiritually "dead" and in need of conversion. Further objections to the renewal trend come from some who support changes in the Church of Uganda's liturgical style, but would prefer Ugandan Anglicans to renew their church through greater indigenization—the development of new liturgies and songs based on local idioms and styles, rather than, or at least in balance with, the adoption of Northern Pentecostal and evangelical worship and music styles.

These tensions over liturgical styles, however, play out primarily at the individual or parish level, rather than polarizing the church on a larger scale. The use of songs like "What a Mighty God We Serve" in a given service tells you little about that church, because renewal in the Church of Uganda is not consistently tied to other ecclesiastical or theological positions, nor to societal divisions on moral, social, or political issues. Indeed, the Church of Uganda suffers little from such divisions. There is heterogeneity within the church, to be sure, but there is no defining division—unlike the Episcopal Church's division between the moderate and liberal majority and the renewal-oriented minority who oppose tolerance of homosexuality.

ANGLICANISM IN AMERICA

The Episcopal Church's liturgical character, public role, and current contentious politics are notably different from those of the Church of Uganda. Like its sister church, however, its roots lie in British colonialism. English settlers brought the Church of England to North America, where it re-formed after the Revolutionary War as an independent province, the Protestant Episcopal Church (or, as it is known today, the Episcopal Church/USA or ECUSA).[14] For the next two centuries the Episcopal Church for the most part carried on peacefully and successfully, though it was always, and remains, a relatively small denomination. The nineteenth century brought tensions between waves of evangelicalism within the church, inspired by revivals around the country, and a movement of liturgically oriented, traditionalist Episcopalians that influenced the church strongly in the direction of Anglo-Catholicism.[15] From that time on, the Episcopal Church has been dominated by what historian Allen Guelzo characterizes as an "Anglo-Catholic hegemony," meaning that the Episcopal Church places substantially more emphasis on liturgical aesthetics and performance than do many other Anglican provinces or Protestant churches.[16] Episcopal historian David Holmes notes, "Of all American Christians, Episcopalians may be the most interested in the structure, language, music, colors, and millinery of worship."[17] One evangelical Episcopalian I interviewed described the Episcopal Church's contemporary leadership as largely "liberal Catholics"—the "Catholic" referring to this heritage of liturgical traditionalism.[18]

Liberalism, too, has fairly deep roots in the Episcopal Church. Holmes writes, "Instead of a common theology, [Anglicanism] has found its identity in a tradition of common worship and prayer."[19] This permits broad variation in political, theological, social, and ecclesiastical views among Episcopalians.[20] Most of the Episcopal Church accepted Darwinism and the new biblical criticism from the late nineteenth century on without controversy, suggesting that the Episcopal Church had already become a relatively modernist and doctrinally relaxed denomination. A Baptist minister who became an Episcopal priest in 1925 wrote of his new denomination, "It is the roomiest church in Christendom, in that it accepts the basic facts of Christian faith as symbols of transparent truths, which each may interpret."[21]

The Episcopal Church's membership numbers, like those of other mainline denominations, peaked in the 1960s and have slowly declined in the decades since.[22] Today the church has approximately 2.4 million members, concentrated in the East, Southwest, and in urban areas elsewhere.[23] Church members are primarily white (92 percent, according to a 1987 Gallup poll), though with some primarily minority congregations and some minority membership in largely white congregations.[24] In contrast with the Church of Uganda, whose membership represents a cross section of Ugandan society, the Episcopal Church is a notably elite denomination. The Episcopal Church consistently ranks third, after Unitarian-Universalists and Jews, on "all the status indicators—education, family income, occupational prestige, and perceived social class."[25] The church has been traditionally associated with wealth and prestige. Kit and Frederica Konolige's 1978 book *The Power of Their Glory* (1978) details the history of America's Episcopalian elite—including more presidents in the twentieth century than any other denomination, in spite of the denomination's small size.[26]

Today the Episcopal Church retains its reputation as the church of the wealthy elite, while also becoming known as one of the most socially and theologically liberal of the mainline denominations.[27] Since World War II, the church has shifted its policies to engage with pressing social issues and accommodate social changes, as part of a general leftward shift in American mainline Protestantism.[28] The Episcopal Church's move to the left has been dominated by four main issues: the question of civil rights for minorities in American society; revision of the Book of Common

Prayer; the ordination of women; and the conjoined issues of ordination of "practicing" homosexuals[29] and blessing of same-sex unions by the church. On all of these issues, the position at which the church has eventually arrived has corresponded with liberal or progressive views in secular society.

The Episcopal Church first took up the issue of civil rights for black Americans and other minorities in the 1950s. The 1964 General Convention, the triennial governing conference of the church, prohibited racial discrimination in Episcopal churches, and the 1967 Convention made a controversial decision to give $9 million to minority advocacy groups.[30] The question of the role of women in the church's leadership first arose in the 1940s, when several dioceses sent women as lay deputies to General Convention. Nevertheless, women deputies were not accepted by General Convention until 1967. By this time the controversial liberal bishop James Pike had already ordained a woman as a deacon, an ordained role oriented toward service and without all the sacramental duties of the priesthood.[31] With the encouragement of the women's movement in the larger society, other breakthroughs followed quickly. The General Convention of 1970 accepted female deacons, and the 1976 Convention admitted women to the priesthood, following the unauthorized 1974 ordinations of eleven women as priests.[32] The first Episcopal woman bishop, Barbara Harris, was consecrated in 1989. In 2006 there were twelve female bishops in the Episcopal Church (out of approximately three hundred living bishops, around half of whom are currently serving a diocese). One of these, Katharine Jefferts Schori, was elected presiding bishop (primate, or head bishop, of the American church) in 2006.

In 1964, inspired by the Second Vatican Council of 1962, the Episcopal Church undertook a major revision of its prayer book. From 1967 to 1976, trial rites were shared with parishes around the country to elicit responses and suggestions. The draft revised Book of Common Prayer (BCP) was passed at the 1976 Convention and fully authorized at the 1979 Convention, by strong majorities in both cases. The revised prayer book included both traditional and contemporary language options for the most commonly used services and prayers, as well as additional new materials and practices, such as increased lay involvement in the liturgy. This process caused great distress to some Episcopalians. Some older worshipers felt anger and loss at the changes to a beloved liturgy they had been performing every Sunday since childhood. Other Episcopalians objected to the 1979 BCP on ideological, rather than practice-based, grounds. They felt, as Holmes notes, that "the addition of gender-free language and prayers for social concerns was troubling. . . . [and] seemed to show that the same liberals who had led the church into social action and women's ordination were now forcing their views on its worship life."[33]

Following the 1976 General Convention, a small but vocal contingent of concerned clergy and laity formed a separate Anglican body outside the Episcopal Church (and not recognized by the worldwide Anglican polity).[34] This break was a surprise for a church with relatively little experience of schism. The doctrine of apostolic succession presents the church as a sacred body, not lightly to be broken, and Anglican freedom of conscience has tended to mitigate tensions. As a result, Episcopalians had an image of their church as schism-free, even schism-proof.[35] John Krumm, in his book *Why Choose the Episcopal Church?*, praises the church's "success in avoiding endless divisions and schisms over relatively obscure points of theology or because of geographical and cultural differences."[36] In the late 1970s and early 1980s, however, differing views of how the church should accommodate changing cultural mores meant that some Episcopalians felt they had to leave the Episcopal Church in order to maintain true Anglicanism.

Many of the Episcopal Church's most adamant Anglo-Catholics, those who demonstrate "conservatism . . . in relation to church tradition," left the church at this time.[37] As the 1980s and 1990s advanced, it was the growing party of *evangelical* conservatives in the Episcopal Church that increasingly came into conflict with Episcopal Church leadership over the issue of attitudes towards homosexuality, reflecting "evangelical conservatism . . . in relation to interpretation of Scripture."[38] Tensions over homosexuality in the Episcopal Church go back to the 1970s, when the movement for gay and lesbian rights first began to develop in American society and the Episcopal gay and lesbian advocacy group, Integrity, was founded. In 1977 an acknowledged lesbian was ordained as a priest in the Diocese of New York, provoking the 1979 General Convention to affirm heterosexual marriage.[39] Still, strong disciplinary measures were not undertaken and occasional ordinations of gay or lesbian candidates continued. The issue of church-sanctioned blessings of same-sex unions was often linked, by both supporters and opponents, to the ordination issue as twin aspects of the question of including gays and lesbians in the life of the church.[40]

In 1995 a group of conservative Episcopal bishops, both Anglo-Catholics and evangelicals, brought heresy charges against Bishop Walter Righter for knowingly ordaining a noncelibate gay man as a deacon. The resulting highly publicized heresy trial ended early in 1996 with dismissal of the case, when the committee of bishops hearing the case concluded that the Episcopal Church's doctrine and discipline did not prohibit the ordination of a homosexual person living in a committed relationship. The election in 1997 of Frank Griswold as presiding bishop further signaled a broad, if quiet, consensus on the sexuality issue, since Griswold had ordained openly homosexual candidates to the priesthood during his tenure as bishop of Chicago. The 2003 affirmation by the General Convention of the election of Gene Robinson, a gay man living with a partner, as bishop of New Hampshire made acceptance the clear direction of the church, though barriers to full inclusion still remain.

EVANGELICALS IN THE EPISCOPAL CHURCH

During the same decades that the Episcopal Church was moving gradually to the left regarding homosexuality, the constituency that would most adamantly oppose this trend was taking shape: the Episcopal conservative charismatic/evangelical movement. Following conflicts with the Anglo-Catholic movement in the nineteenth century, evangelical Anglicanism virtually died out as an active force in the Episcopal Church in the United States.[41] As in other mainline denominations, however, the 1960s and 1970s brought a wave of evangelical/charismatic activity in the Episcopal Church, involving both evangelical elements such as emphasis on personal conversion and biblical authority and charismatic elements such as speaking in tongues, healing, and prophecy.[42] At the same time, Anglican evangelicals from England, where evangelicalism was a stronger presence, were encouraging the evangelical renewal movement in the Episcopal Church.[43] Andrew, one of my American consultants, talked with me extensively by phone about his involvement with the conservative American Anglican Council (AAC), his well-informed interest in the churches in Africa, and his views on the state of the Episcopal Church. He told me that his own position in current church conflicts owes much to the influence of these earlier developments, and described the charismatic/evangelical movement of the sixties and seventies as "the most formidable movement in the church in the last fifty years."

Nearly all of the leaders and organizations involved in the conservative dissident movement of the late twentieth and early twenty-first century are products of this Episcopal charismatic and evangelical renewal movement.[44] In their theology and understanding of the church, these dissidents emphasize the authority of scripture and the importance of personal conversion and relationship with Jesus Christ, key themes of the evangelical tradition in American Protestantism. These groups also accept or encourage seeking the gifts of the Holy Spirit, a central charismatic theme. One prominent conservative leader characterizes Episcopal renewal as "radically Biblical in theological emphasis, gently charismatic in worship, strongly mission-and-evangelism-oriented, integrating clergy and laity in joint ministry, and fuelled by a desire to expound Scripture and proclaim the gospel."[45] I describe these individuals and groups as evangelical, using the word "charismatic" only where it is useful to distinguish between the two streams. This usage follows that of many conservative Episcopalians, who use "evangelical" as a blanket term for all those Episcopalians who identify themselves variously as charismatic, evangelical, renewal, or orthodox, but find unity in basic theological positions and shared identification of themselves over against liberalism. Most often, however, I will use the term "conservative," which I intend to encompass both those evangelical Episcopalians who are mobilized against the Episcopal Church and those of explicitly nonevangelical orientation (for example, Anglo-Catholic groups) who share those convictions and concerns.

EVANGELICAL RENEWAL AT ST. TIMOTHY'S EPISCOPAL CHURCH

The life story of the parish of St. Timothy's illustrates the rise of evangelicalism in the Episcopal Church and the growing tensions between this constituency and the national church's leadership. In 1980 St. Timothy's was a mainstream Episcopal parish, perhaps a little on the traditionalist side. During the 1980s and 1990s, under the guidance of strong clergy and lay leaders who had been influenced by the currents of renewal moving through the national Episcopal Church, the church developed a marked evangelical and charismatic identity. St. Timothy's today remains solidly Episcopal in its basic liturgical expression, following the 1979 Book of Common Prayer in all three Sunday morning services, but with the addition of evangelical and charismatic elements in worship (such as praise music and occasional altar calls and speaking in tongues) and a new emphasis on evangelical understandings of Christian identity and life. For example, a brochure about the parish describes the Parish Purpose as "to teach Jesus Christ, preach Jesus Christ and Him Crucified, acknowledge Him as Lord and Savior and seek a personal relationship with Him; we actively seek the anointing of the Holy Spirit to equip us for ministry." This statement, with its evangelical stress on a personal relationship with Jesus Christ (the authority of scripture occupies another page of the brochure) as well as on the gifts of the Holy Spirit, hints at the parish's slightly less pronounced charismatic bent.

Over the past two decades, this shift at St. Timothy's has attracted many non-Episcopalians as new members. St. Timothy's grew from about one hundred members in 1980 to around six hundred at the time of its break from ECUSA. As I learned from the life stories I collected in the course of my interviewing, many of these new members came from evangelical churches and brought that orientation to St. Timothy's. While the Episcopal Church in general is characterized by a high proportion of adult converts, coming from Roman Catholicism, from other mainline denominations, and from evangelical and charismatic churches, most of the last contingent enter the Episcopal Church with a sense of leaving their earlier religious identity behind, rather than seeking to find it again or anew within Episcopalianism. In contrast, many new members at St. Timothy's left their former denominations or parishes because the latter were not sufficiently committed to evangelical principles. One account of these new members' impact came from one of those who left St. Timothy's when the parish broke from the ECUSA. With the help of referrals from the rector, I interviewed six of these Episcopal loyalists, in order to expand my knowledge of the parish's history. This consultant, a middle-aged man and lifelong Episcopalian, told me, "There seemed to be a shift in the makeup. A lot of people came into the church who are not in my opinion familiar with the Episcopal Church. . . . There seemed to be a change also in the direction of a more fundamental or evangelical program," led by the clergy, whom he described as "more evangelical than what you would find in a mainline Episcopal church."

Lifelong Episcopalians and longtime members of St. Timothy's like this consultant found renewal and change in the parish much more challenging than those newer members who were less invested in traditional Episcopal worship and identity. These long-standing members found it difficult, for example, to accept an evangelical understanding of Christian identity based on a specifically dated, personal experience of accepting Christ as savior, in contrast with the general Episcopal tendency to define Christian identity through regular participation in the sacraments and in the church's life of fellowship and outreach. During one conversation about the congregation's history, the rector, Joe, a jocular man in his early sixties, told me, "We've had a lot of Episcopalians who've become Christians." Such a statement makes it clear that Episcopalians who remained at St. Timothy's had to come to terms with a new faith identity.

Although the journey out of the Episcopal Church for parishes like St. Timothy's began with a shift to a more evangelical worship style, it rapidly moved into the terrain of social and moral issues. Evangelical Episcopalians like those at St. Timothy's, reading the Bible through the lens of faith commitments to its literal truth, plain sense, and authority, often arrive at conclusions that are different from those of moderate and liberal Episcopalians who see the Bible as a historically situated document and feel freer to interpret its meaning and relevance. As in Uganda, renewal has swept through the Episcopal Church and caught up a sizable minority of individuals and congregations. But unlike the situation in Uganda, divisions in the American church between evangelical renewed Episcopalians and nonevangelicals tend to line up with divisions over theological and social positions. In the American setting, evangelicalism has become enmeshed with polarized intrachurch politics.

THE DEVELOPMENT OF AN EVANGELICAL OPPOSITION

In the late 1980s, Episcopal evangelicals began to form organizations that not only propagated evangelical theology, as in the past, but now also sought to engage the Episcopal Church's leadership more directly on issues of doctrine and morality. Although some parishes, like St. Timothy's, have shifted toward evangelicalism, evangelicals have remained a minority within the Episcopal Church and have felt increasingly unable to change the church's direction.[46] John Rodgers, a prominent evangelical priest and scholar, stated in the mid-1990s that evangelicals in the Episcopal Church are "alarmed and frustrated."[47] *In Church on Fire: The Story of Anglican Evangelicals*, Roger Steer observes, "Evangelicals feel, and probably are, relatively powerless in the wider structures of the Episcopal Church, in many dioceses, in General Convention, and in the committees and staff of ECUSA generally."[48]

Accordingly, evangelicals began to seek more actively to change the Episcopal Church's direction in order to restore the church to Anglican orthodoxy as they understood it—or, failing that, to establish an alternative, orthodox Anglican province in the United States.[49] In 1996 the Rt. Rev. Alden Hathaway, then bishop of the Diocese of Pittsburgh, organized the American Anglican Council to serve as a mutual support network for conservative Episcopalians and as a voice for evangelicalism at the national church level.[50] The AAC issues press releases and commentaries on events in the Episcopal Church and the Anglican Communion, with the hope of gaining more support for the conservative constituency. The AAC was rarely actively combative and remained committed to working within the Episcopal Church until the Gene Robinson controversy of 2003. Another evangelical organization, Episcopalians United for Revelation, Renewal, and Reformation (EURRR, or just EU), founded late in the 1980s, was described by liberal Episcopal journalist Jack Taylor as "the biggest and often the most vocal of the anti-progressive right wing of the Episcopal Church in terms of wealth, power, influence, longevity and unabashed homophobia," though by the mid-1990s its dominance had waned considerably.[51] Like the AAC, EU published a newsletter (through 2000), United Voice. (See figure 1.)

Some Episcopal conservatives who are more traditionalist or Anglo-Catholic, rather than evangelical, in their orientation have also joined the evangelicals' struggle to reform or replace the Episcopal Church. The

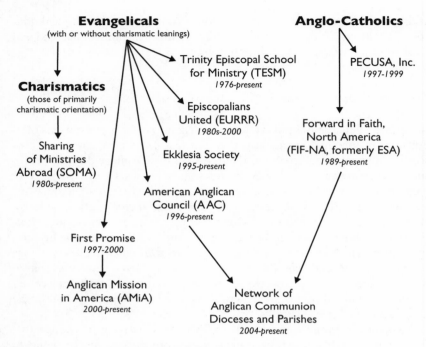

Figure 1. Conservative Episcopal dissident organizations.

Episcopal Synod of America (ESA), an Anglo-Catholic–leaning group, was founded in 1989 and has been active on and off in Episcopal Church politics since then. It is the sister organization of an English group named Forward in Faith, and in recent years changed its name to Forward in Faith–North America (FIF-NA). The ESA was initially organized to oppose the ordination of women and to lobby to protect the rights of those bishops, clergy, and parishes who shared this position. But the ESA has also spoken out about homosexuality; ESA leaders, for instance, called the Righter trial decision "an open rejection of the clear teaching of Holy Scripture."[52] Another contentious organization was PECUSA Inc. This body received widespread attention in late 1997 when it became known that William Wantland, the bishop of Eau Claire, Wisconsin, with a board of other conservative leaders, had claimed the Episcopal Church's historical name and incorporated it in forty-five states.[53] In Wantland's words, PECUSA Inc.'s purpose was to ensure there would always be an orthodox Anglican province in the United States. A lawsuit against PECUSA Inc. for fraud, unfair competition, and trademark infringement was settled in January 1999.[54] By late 1999 what was left of PECUSA Inc., the final effort to reform the Episcopal Church with only domestic resources and personnel, had been absorbed into a new organization, First Promise, which explicitly sought international help. Finding themselves unable to influence the Episcopal Church on their own, conservatives reached out to find global allies in a process whose initial steps I describe in the next chapter.

HOMOSEXUALITY: TOLERANCE VERSUS ORTHODOXY

Homosexuality has become the defining issue in contemporary Episcopal Church (and, arguably, Anglican Communion) conflicts. My account of these conflicts demands some attention to the main competing discourses—what Asad calls "the kinds of reasoning and the reasons for arguing"—surrounding this central issue.[55] Homosexuality serves as a symbolic focus in these Episcopal and Anglican conflicts, and is constructed by those involved as standing for a number of other positions.[56] For example, people who hold a conservative view on homosexuality—believing it should not be accepted as an orientation morally equivalent to heterosexuality—are generally presumed, by themselves and others, to also share pro-life beliefs, Republican political loyalties, and often evangelical or fundamentalist religious identities. But homosexuality also has enough salience to unite relatively diverse constituencies on the basis of positions on this single issue. For example, in spite of past antagonisms between Anglo-Catholics and evangelicals in the Episcopal Church, Anglo-Catholic groups support the current evangelical-led movement against Episcopal Church tolerance of homosexuality.

Within the Episcopal Church, homosexuality as an issue defines a conservative camp more clearly than a liberal camp. This conservative camp consists of evangelical and some Anglo-Catholic priests and bishops, lay leaders, congregations, and other dispersed laypeople, who feel strongly that acceptance of homosexuality threatens the moral order of society. People in this camp tend to be highly motivated, since opposing homosexuality has become the minority position and thus demands more activism from its supporters. Further, the evangelical view of homosexuality as a social and moral threat calls for vehemence in defense of conservative Christian values.

In contrast, the majority of Episcopalians seem to lean toward tolerance on this issue. For instance, Gene Robinson's election was affirmed by a majority of bishops, priests, and lay deputies, who apparently did not fear censure from their home congregations. In this predominant tendency toward tolerance, Episcopalians reflect the slow leftward shift on this issue in American society, as evidenced by widespread negative reactions to the Boy Scouts' discriminatory policies; the proliferation of gay characters on network television; and President George W. Bush's hesitance to express explicitly antigay sentiments. Most Episcopalians, however, are not particularly mobilized on the issue of gay rights. Public, outspoken activism for the full inclusion of gay, lesbian, bisexual, and transgender (GLBT) Episcopalians in the church is largely limited to the leaders in the Episcopal GLBT rights group, Integrity, and a few outspoken bishops, other church leaders, and scholars. [57] However, many Episcopal parishes quietly welcome gays and lesbians as members and leaders, and the leftward movement of the national church implies at least moderate lay support for this inclusive practice, since lay representatives are involved in church policymaking at the parish, diocesan, and national church levels.[58]

The group of Episcopalians who are mobilized and vocal in favor of gay rights is not at all equivalent to the conservative camp, which encompasses a large number of at least moderately mobilized laypeople. But the mobilized liberal camp also represents a position with the general support of a majority of Episcopalians, whereas the conservative camp includes most of those who hold strong conservative views on homosexuality. I will thus use the adjectives "conservative" and "liberal" when opposing positions on this (or another) issue are in question. However, I will also often contrast "conservative" with "liberal/moderate" positions, denoting with the latter term the moderate or left-leaning, but generally nonactivist, majority of the Episcopal Church's membership.

In their conflicting positions on homosexuality, both sides view their positions on this issue as part of their religious identities and faith commitments. Although conservatives sometimes describe the liberal position as an adoption of secular humanist values from the surrounding culture, proponents of both the conservative and the liberal positions ground their arguments in understandings of God, scripture, and the church. Following this lead and my own inclinations as an anthropologist of religion, I, too, treat these faith commitments and social convictions as profoundly interrelated, separating "social" from "religious" issues only for the sake of clarity and not because that separation has subjective meaning for my consultants.

LIBERAL CHRISTIAN VIEWS OF HOMOSEXUALITY

The liberal Episcopalian perspective on homosexuality, generally speaking, rests on several basic concepts. First, liberals often frame homosexuality within a discourse of civil rights and social progress. In this view, as ethnic and racial minorities and women have been recognized, included, and elevated to positions of (theoretically) full participation in society, so will and should gays and lesbians be recognized and included. Liberals often point out that the Bible was used to defend slavery and the oppression of women, as it is today used to argue against tolerance of homosexuality. Liberal Christians generally do not take a literalist view of Scripture and offer less condemning readings of the biblical passages that conservatives take as denouncing homosexuality. One example comes from the book *What the Bible Really Says about Homosexuality*, by Roman Catholic priest David Helminiak. Helminiak writes: "Somehow God must be behind the fact that some people are homosexual. Then why should God's word in the Bible condemn homosexuality? . . . There must be another answer. *The mistake must be in how the Bible is being read.*" [59]

Helminiak's statement hints at a second liberal argument, based on humanistic ideas about the naturalness and goodness of human nature. This argument holds that since some people experience themselves as homosexual, and since presumably God made them that way, then expressing their sexual orientation cannot be inherently wrong. Such views also rest on an incarnational theology that sees Jesus Christ's taking on human form as validating humanity in a fundamental way. Human nature is seen not as negative and inimical to faith and purity, but as God's gift, sanctified by Christ's sharing in it. An element of liberation theology is present here as well, in the conviction voiced by many liberal Episcopalians that the gospel's central message concerns freedom from oppression.

CONSERVATIVE CHRISTIAN VIEWS OF HOMOSEXUALITY

The most basic argument for conservative (and especially evangelical) Episcopalians is found in certain biblical texts that appear to prohibit homosexual behavior. These Episcopalians believe that the fundamental truths laid down in scripture do not change and should not be reinterpreted to accord with contemporary mores. Many evangelicals believe that scripture speaks plainly concerning sexual morality and that a tolerant position on homosexuality is tantamount to disregarding the authority of the Bible. As Joe, the rector at St. Timothy's, told me when explaining the reasons for his parish's break from the Episcopal Church, "the homosexual issue and all the others are just lightning rods. They got an awful lot of press, but that's not the issue. The issue is, either the Scripture is God's word and God's authority for the church, or it's not." None of my consultants at St. Timothy's talked about knowing gay or lesbian people, and there were no openly gay members in the congregation. Homosexuality seems to be in many respects a relatively abstract issue for this community, and most members describe their opposition as arising from their biblical beliefs rather than from any firsthand knowledge of the lives and habits of gays and lesbians.

Evangelical Episcopalians see tolerance of homosexuality as a symptom of a general tendency on humanity's part to ignore God's word and will.

Steer expresses the evangelical tendency to assume that a liberal position on the sexuality issue stands for many other theological errors: "People who accept the homosexual agenda in the USA often also deny the essence of the Trinity, the deity of Christ, the authority of Scripture, any doctrine of eschatology, any idea of transcendence or revelation."[60] In addition, conservative Episcopalians sometimes argue that homosexuality is unnatural.[61] Such arguments are often couched in the discourse of science, but for these Christians the issue of naturalness, too, leads back to the authority of scripture. The unnaturalness of homosexuality is linked to theological understandings of creation and the complementarity of male and female. Anthropologist Constance Sullivan-Blum explains how this understanding makes homosexuality such a significant issue for evangelicals: "The Genesis narrative presents gender as one of the primary ways by which God orders creation. As such, the possibility that Christianity might embrace same-sex marriage is profoundly destabilizing to the Evangelical worldview."[62]

Most conservative Episcopalians accept that homosexuality does exist, but for them the reality of homosexuality does not mean that homosexuality is in accord with God's created order. Rather, they point out that all Christians must set aside sinful urges and submit themselves to God's law, and argue that for gays and lesbians their sexual desires must be part of what is set aside. Evangelicals also stress the possibility of transformation, arguing that such renewal of life is possible for homosexuals as for any other sinners. This emphasis is seen in evangelicals' positive attitude toward "ex-gay" groups and ministries aimed at "healing" people of homosexuality (defined as an affliction) so that they can lead heterosexual lives. Those who hold liberal views about homosexuality hear only condemnation in evangelicals' calls for gays and lesbians to change their orientation, but evangelical Episcopalians I talked with describe the temptation to sin as something they share with homosexuals. Although homosexuality is often singled out for particularly vehement opposition, my time at St. Timothy's showed me that evangelical Episcopalians' responses to homosexuals are framed in the same language of sin and the need for transformation through a relationship with Jesus Christ that they apply to their own lives.

THE AUTHENTICALLY ANGLICAN VIEW?

Liberal Episcopalians and Anglicans often assert that their position on homosexuality is an authentically Anglican position, in keeping with their church heritage. They point to a tradition of breadth or "latitudinarianism" in the Anglican tradition, arguing that Anglicanism has never been a confessing tradition—that is, a tradition which demands that its members assent to some common set of doctrinal beliefs—but is, rather, a tradition in which members find their unity through the practice of common prayer. They find support in the idea of the "three-legged stool" upon which the Anglican tradition is said to rest: scripture, reason, and tradition. Liberals accuse conservatives and especially evangelicals of overemphasizing scripture to the detriment of the role of tradition and human reason in guiding the church. An Episcopal writer offers an example in an article critical of conservative activism in the church:

> By insisting on a particular understanding of Holy Scripture, the conservatives have also abandoned a broad tolerance of different positions that goes back in the Church of England to the Elizabethan Settlement of the 16th Century. . . . Ironically, the Episcopal conservatives, so determined to go forward in a doctrinally pure church, call themselves defenders of tradition. They should take another look at the roots of their church.[63]

Conservatives, too, assert the authenticity of their position on homosexuality. Conservatives are more likely than liberals, however, to describe their position as the authentic and historic Christian, rather than Anglican, position. These arguments are implicit in the very adjectives conservatives use in naming their position as the "scriptural" or "traditional" view of homosexuality. Their stance is grounded, as many of my consultants describe it, in the clear message of the Bible on sexual morality and in two thousand years of Christian tradition in which openly gay church leaders were never accepted, nor gay unions celebrated. Such descriptions imply literal and monolithic readings of both scripture and tradition that many liberals find more problematic. Some conservatives also assert that theirs is the authentically Anglican perspective. For example, Canon David Anderson of the conservative American Anglican Council, at a 2003 meeting of conservative dissidents, stated: "We are the rightful heirs of all the cultural legacy and faith of the Episcopal Church. We are walking in the footsteps of the apostles. . . . We are true heirs of Anglicanism in the United States."[64]

Conservatives also often describe their position, and themselves, as "orthodox." Indeed, they use "orthodox" much in the way that I use "conservative": as an encompassing term for people, groups, or statements opposing church tolerance of homosexuality and other trends in the Episcopal Church. This invocation of orthodoxy has as much to do with power as it has with doctrine. Asad has observed that orthodoxy is not "a mere body of opinion" but is centrally concerned with "the power to regulate, uphold, require, or adjust correct practices, and to condemn, exclude, undermine, or replace *incorrect* ones."[65] Although the word *or-*

thodoxy means "right doctrine," it is not only, or not even primarily, about doctrine. Rather, orthodoxy names the power to define the boundaries of right practice and belief. This power may lie primarily in a group's ability to command or persuade. As Catherine Bell has noted, "power refers less to physical control of people than to social prestige or the concern to secure the dominance of models of reality that render one's world coherent and viable."[66]

Doctrinally, this conservative Anglican orthodoxy is rather minimally defined. The only doctrinal issue uniting the broad coalition of Northern Episcopal conservatives and Southern Anglicans is opposition to church acceptance of homosexuality. But the concept of orthodoxy is nonetheless rhetorically potent. In claiming the ground of orthodoxy, these allies strongly assert the rightness of their position. The deployment of this vocabulary represents a claim to possess the power to establish and maintain boundaries and to secure the dominance of a particular model of Christianity and morality.

No direct equivalent to the concept of "orthodoxy" exists in liberal discourse. The liberal view of the church as unified in common worship and community feeling is inimical to the idea of orthodoxy. This is not to say that there is no "liberal orthodoxy" or hegemonic position in the Episcopal Church; it would not be difficult to argue that such a position does exist, characterized by such nigh-on obligatory liberal Episcopal themes as community, inclusion, and social justice. But this liberal orthodoxy is propagated and policed implicitly and indirectly, not named or defined as an orthodox position. Liberals tend not to engage with conservative claims of orthodoxy; instead, they shift the debate to values and priorities other than correct doctrine. These different approaches help make the conflict over homosexuality so intractable. Liberals, relatively uninterested in doctrinal questions per se, see conservatives as overly obsessed with the letter of the law, while conservatives see liberals as having abandoned any concept of right and wrong. The two sides speak different languages and focus on different aspects of Christian life and morality, making communication, let alone compromise, extraordinarily difficult.

Struggles in the Episcopal Church may therefore be described in a peculiar sense as struggles over orthodoxy, not because competing orthodoxies are at issue, but because those committed to a particular orthodoxy are struggling to establish their understanding as the Anglican orthodoxy, and to find means to maintain and enforce that orthodoxy. In so doing, they have secured the assistance of African Anglicans for whom the most pressing issues in their home churches are issues of orthopraxy, or right liturgical practice, in the context of growing Pentecostal influences. But as the following chapters show, once invited by American conservatives to step into the role of representing Southern Anglican orthodoxy, many African leaders were ready and willing.

The Stage Set for Developing Global Ties

The Church of Uganda and the Episcopal Church in the United States share a history of British colonization and missionization, a common Anglican heritage, and membership in the worldwide Anglican Communion. They also both possess constituencies committed to renewal in spirituality and worship style. Although none of these factors linked these churches very directly, they provided foundations for the alliances that developed in the late 1990s. Common Anglican identity made African connections desirable and useful for American conservatives frustrated with the liberalism of the Episcopal Church. In addition, a shared sense of themselves as renewed Anglicans helped create a sense of solidarity between American conservatives and Anglican leaders in Uganda and in other African provinces. The trajectories and implications of these renewal movements are not equivalent in these Northern and Southern contexts, since renewal has become associated with polarized church politics in the Episcopal Church. However, shared tastes in music and worship style have undoubtedly eased the development of relationships between renewal-minded Ugandan Anglicans and their American partners. Members from these two convergent renewal traditions, like members accustomed to the more traditional liturgies of each provincial church, feel at home in the services held in their sister province. When an East African Anglican visits an American evangelical church or vice versa, hearing familiar music is not the least of the factors contributing to a sense of connection and solidarity.

Such preexisting global ties have opened pathways for stronger and more direct links to grow. The motivation for the development of such links came from evangelical Episcopalians' increasing frustration with their powerlessness in the Episcopal Church. The Episcopal renewal movement has come into increasing conflict with the rest of the church over movement toward the full inclusion of noncelibate homosexuals. By 1997 there existed a significant body of lay and clergy Episcopalians who felt the Episcopal Church's recent history was a story of increasing apostasy. Groups like the AAC, EU, ESA/FIF-NA, and PECUSA Inc. saw the church as in desperate need of spiritual renewal and doctrinal reform— which they lacked the power to implement. The choice for such dissenters in the past had always been either to compromise their convictions and stay within an errant church, or to split off and become yet another small, unofficial Anglican body, unrecognized by the Anglican Communion.

This option was unattractive to the 1990s generation of dissenters, who could easily see the fragmentation and stagnation of the Continuing Church movement since the late 1970s. In the late 1990s, this generation of dissenters invented a new option, an untried path: involving other Anglicans, with the authority of the larger Anglican Communion, in their efforts to reform the Episcopal Church. The word was spreading among conservative Episcopalians that there was a world out there beyond ECUSA full of evangelical, renewed, orthodox Anglicans. Unprecedented experiments in Anglican polity and politics would follow, and the Communion would never be the same.

CHAPTER TWO

Taking Africa Seriously: The Globalization of Conservative Episcopalians

ONE EVENING during our stay at Uganda Christian University, my husband and I were chatting with some campus friends and acquaintances after a Bible study meeting at a faculty member's campus home. A dozen people, mainly senior divinity students, sat around the comfortable living room decorated with photos of relatives and plaques spelling out pious mottoes. Our friend Peter, a divinity student in his thirties and one of the many at UCU who had come to earn his master's of divinity after spending some time serving rural parishes, had some news to share which he found quite disturbing. He had just learned that the archbishop of the British province of Wales, Rowan Williams, was scheduled to speak at UCU—coincidentally, right in the middle of the university's upcoming Mission Week, a week of special preaching, music, and evangelizing programs intended to convert non-Christian students and renew those already committed to Christ. At the time, Williams was a strong candidate to become the next Archbishop of Canterbury, formal head of the Church of England and the entire Anglican Communion. Peter feared that the archbishop's presence and presentation, far from contributing to Mission Week, would detract from it. He explained to the group that he had heard (probably from some of the UCU faculty) that Williams was "the kind of liberal who would happily accept homosexuality." Hearing this, most of the others present agreed that it was totally unacceptable for Williams to speak on their campus. Peter went on to suggest that in welcoming Williams, the Church of Uganda's provincial officials were motivated by the access to power and resources such a friendship might bring. He remarked, "It's hard to resist such people when they come with inducements, with a carrot."

Peter's objections and those of other UCU students and staff were of no avail. On May 2, 2002, Archbishop Williams spoke to a crowd packed into the UCU chapel. Williams's address elucidated some early developments in Christian beliefs about Jesus, ending with a discussion of contemporary challenges to the faith. Both the atmosphere in the room and the subsequent discussions I had with people suggested that members of the audience, perhaps expecting to be shocked or angered, were surprised and pleased at the Christ- and Bible-centeredness of this address. The occasion did not pass, however, without some interrogation of the orthodoxy of the Northern church and of Williams himself. As soon as he finished speaking, one young man shot out of his seat to ask, "Homosexuality is becoming a problem for Anglican Christology. What is your view about it?" Another questioner also challenged Williams as a Northerner to reveal his own orthodoxy or lack thereof: "Many Western Christians and bishops no longer believe in the virgin birth of Christ. Do you? And do you believe that he had no biological father?"

Williams responded to the latter question first, replying that he believed personally in the virgin birth, but explaining the thinking of those who do not. In answering the even more loaded question concerning homosexuality, Williams began, "This question is not directly relevant to the topic of the afternoon, but I feel I must answer it because it preoccupies many people." He went on to reveal that his personal view is that "what the church has said about homosexuality through the ages does not reflect our current understandings," and expressed his wish that he could "more wholeheartedly" agree with "the traditional teachings and official beliefs of the church." He expressed regret that this issue has been so divisive in the Church, and stressed that he would not want to impose a view from Europe or America on any other Anglican province. A murmur went through the crowd, but no one denounced the archbishop or walked out in protest. Perhaps because of Williams's soft-spoken personal style or the orthodoxy of his presentation, he came through his visit to UCU without any significant eruptions of controversy. Williams soon left Uganda to return to the UK, his African tour completed; four months later, he was chosen as the next Archbishop of Canterbury.

Ugandan clergy often joke about the widespread practice of sending Ugandan bishops-elect to England before their consecrations to visit the "mother church" and obtain her blessing—a pattern dating back to before Uganda's political and ecclesiastical independence in 1962, when the Church of Uganda was still a mission church subordinate to the Church of England. Archbishop Williams's visit to Uganda represents almost the reverse, a British churchman visiting Uganda preparatory to his own elevation to higher office. His visit can be interpreted as an effort simultaneously to enrich his knowledge of the Anglican Communion and to solidify relations with some of those African Anglican leaders who had caused such a stir in the Communion of late. The trip also arguably enabled him to demonstrate to those in England who would choose the next Archbishop of Canterbury that he had good relations with African bishops, a characteristic that by 2002 had become centrally important for Anglican Communion leaders. It is hard to judge whether Williams's African tour helped him appear the best candidate for the See of Canterbury, but it can hardly have hurt his chances, and it is notable that the other frontrunner for the position also had strong global South connections: Bishop Michael Nazir-Ali, a Pakistani immigrant to Britain.

This rather remarkable reversal is only one of many clear indicators that much of the Northern church has lately come around to "taking Africa seriously." I borrow this phrase from Abner, a young Ugandan Anglican layman, who used it in describing the distinction he saw in the American church between conservatives, who were building ties with dioceses like his own, and liberals, who seemed less interested in the African churches' needs or opinions. How did African leaders and their churches become some of the most important agents and most powerful tools in developments and debates within the Anglican Communion? How has the shape of world Christianity changed, such that African divinity students feel comfortable challenging the orthodoxy and authority of a British archbishop? And what role did alliances between disaffected Americans and African church leaders play in all these changes? Searching for allies in their struggles to alter the Episcopal Church's course, American conservatives took the consequential step of beginning to take the global South seriously as a potential force in world Anglicanism. American dissidents increasingly stressed the global scale in their indictments of the Episcopal Church, and began to speak of themselves not just as an oppressed minority within ECUSA, but as in solidarity with Anglicans around the world. At the same time they reached out to develop relationships with Anglicans in the global South, transcending distance and cultural difference to forge a shared global identity. These relationships were initially developed as preparation for the global meeting of Anglican bishops at Lambeth in 1998, but just as important, the willingness of many Southern Anglicans to collaborate with American conservatives supported conservatives' assertions that they had the backing of the worldwide Anglican Communion in their struggles with Episcopal Church leadership.

INITIAL INTERNATIONAL CONNECTIONS

The earliest roots of current transnational inter-Anglican alliances lie in missionary relationships between Northern and Southern churches. Never a major missionary-sending church, the Episcopal Church in the United States nevertheless sent its share of missionaries to Africa, Asia, and South America, to educate, heal, and preach. In 1965 the Episcopal Church supported 459 overseas missionaries and spouses.[1] The church's growing evangelical constituency, more missions-oriented than the mainstream church, became active in missions in the 1970s and 1980s. Although involvement with missions provided some sense of global Christian context for Episcopalians of all stripes, this early engagement was particularly significant for evangelicals and laid the groundwork for the later globalization of evangelical Episcopal concerns.[2] As my consultant Andrew put it, "engagement with mission has brought American conservatives and traditionalists into contact with a community of interest in the Two-Thirds World."[3]

These early missionary relationships, however, carried little weight in church politics. Overseas Anglicans were not brought, rhetorically or literally, into debates over prayer book revision, the ordination of women, or other Episcopal Church conflicts of the 1970s and 1980s. One exception was the January 1978 consecration of four bishops to lead the dissident Continuing Church movement. Because not enough Episcopal bishops could be persuaded to participate, one of the consecrating bishops came from the Philippine Independent Church, a small non-Anglican denomination.[4] Still, involving the Filipino bishop was simply a pragmatic move, and engaging with overseas bishops did not become a strategy for the Continuing Church movement. Continuing Church literature stresses this movement's sense of itself as continuing or maintaining a traditional orthodoxy, defined almost exclusively in relation to an idealized ecclesiastical past, not (as would become the case among Episcopal dissenters of the 1990s) in relation to the beliefs of other contemporary Anglican provinces. Involving international bishops was not yet a significant tool in the repertoire of the Episcopal Church's conservatives.

THE MID-1990s: THE RIGHTER TRIAL INSPIRES GLOBAL APPEALS

Before the Righter heresy trial of 1995, the idea of appealing to overseas Anglican leaders to intervene in Episcopal Church politics had begun to be mentioned among Episcopalian conservatives but still was not a common idea; little direct action had been taken. The failure of the presentment against Bishop Righter indicated to Episcopal conservatives that the Episcopal Church could clearly not be reformed from within. Texts critical of the Righter decision argued that the Episcopal Church had departed from its own traditional teachings on matters of doctrine and sexuality, with little reference to a wider context of worldwide Anglican belief and practice. However, it was the Righter decision, among other events, that motivated evangelicals unhappy with ECUSA's tolerance of homosexuality to look beyond the Episcopal Church for orthodox leadership.

A further indicator that social and theological conservatism were fast losing ground in the Episcopal Church was the August 1997 election as presiding bishop of Frank Griswold, who, the American Anglican Council noted at the time, "has ordained non-celibate homosexuals and encourages the blessing of their unions."[5] Andrew recalled for me the growing sense of helplessness and despair among AAC members and other evangelicals through the mid-1990s: "[The move to appeal to overseas Anglican leaders] came out of, I think, a sense in the 1990s that the Episcopal Church and its bishops were unwilling and unable to discipline themselves, in terms of credal or moral orthodoxy. . . . And so I think there were those in the Episcopal Church who said, Well, it's unreformable, it's going to go this way."

Faced with these clear signs that the mind of the Episcopal Church would not easily be changed from within, a few conservative and evangelical leaders began to seek new structures and new ways to reach out to bishops outside the United States in search of potential allies. Sanjeev Khagram, James Riker, and Kathryn Sikkink observe of contemporary global movements that "it is [often] blockage in the domestic society that sends domestic social [in this case, religious] movement actors into the transnational arena."[6] Transnational support for one party in a domestic conflict tends to change the direction of the struggle. In their article "Space and Contentious Politics," Deborah Martin and Byron Miller examine contests over scale as a tactic of contemporary social movements. They point out, "Shifts in the scalar definition of the conflict inevitably entail changes in the . . . relative power and standing of contestants. Thus scalar definitions of a conflict may themselves be a locus of contention."[7] When American conservatives first looked to the Anglican Communion, they began to shift the ground of conflict within the Episcopal Church from the morality of homosexuality to the right of Anglicans from other provinces to intervene in the American church.

THE MID-1990S: NEW ORGANIZATIONS AND NEW PROSPECTS

Members of the American Anglican Council experienced a move from despair to hope, according to one chronicler, at their 1995 founding meeting as the possibilities of international alliances began to become clear: "[We realized that] our collective despondency over the state of the Church was somewhat unjustified. . . . If we looked at the health and vitality in much of the Anglican Communion, we had much reason to hope for healing and restoration in the Episcopal Church."[8] The AAC began to build networks "to bring Anglican bishops from around the world for teaching missions in the USA," in order to "provide opportunities for AAC parishes to broaden their experience of our global Anglican fellowship."[9] These networks could serve political purposes as well. The 1998 Lambeth Conference of all the bishops of the Communion was drawing near, raising conservatives' hopes that bishops in the wider Anglican world could be informed of their situation in the Episcopal Church. If, at Lambeth, some of these bishops were to advocate for the orthodox position on sexuality and for the disciplining of the Episcopal Church, then might there not, after all, be hope for orthodoxy?

The Ekklesia Society (often abbreviated EkkSoc), also founded in 1995, rapidly became influential through the work of its general secretary, the Rev. Bill Atwood of Texas. Atwood founded EkkSoc after coordinating an international conference on missions and evangelism held by the Archbishop of Canterbury. Following that conference, with the endorsement of a few foreign bishops, Atwood traveled the world asking Anglican leaders for prayers, support, and visits to the United States to witness and minister there. But at the time of EkkSoc's founding, few American conservatives were interested in Atwood's work. A colleague whom I interviewed characterized the reaction of most American conservatives to Atwood's early efforts: "Who cares what a bunch of Africans think?" Such indifference would not last long; a new global vision was taking shape.

One explicit aim of EkkSoc from the start was to provide encouragement and support to disaffected Americans who felt there was little space left for them in the Episcopal Church. EkkSoc's home page explains: "The ability to identify with others who share the orthodox historical faith of the church is a great encouragement to those in the portions of the communion which are straying from historic, Biblical Christianity."[10] Leonard, a member at St. Timothy's who has been active in the larger conservative Episcopal movement, articulated that sense of encouragement and recognition in recalling his thoughts the first time he attended a conference with overseas Anglicans: "Ah! I'm an Anglican!" Atwood was concerned, however, with the situation of impoverished Southern Anglicans as well as with that of disaffected Northern ones. He hoped to connect the spiritual resources of the global South with the materially rich global North by building networks of orthodox Anglicans and coordinating various small-scale development projects in Southern provinces.

Although EkkSoc's vision was eventually sidelined by more assertive forms of transnational networking, Atwood's work linking Southern bishops with one another and with Northern conservatives played a central role in the development of conservative Anglican global relationships. A significant catalyst for the rapid development of these relationships was the approach of the 1998 Lambeth Conference. Daniel, a priest active in the conservative movement whom I interviewed by phone, told me it was due in large part to Atwood's networking that by the time of Lambeth, American conservative bishops and many Southern bishops felt they knew each other and could work together.

Anticipating Lambeth 1998: Official Anglican Communion Preparations

The decennial Lambeth Conferences both embody and maintain the unity of the worldwide Anglican Communion. Episcopal scholar John Wall, in his *Dictionary for Episcopalians*, defines the Conference as follows:

> [A] meeting of all bishops in the Anglican Communion . . . convened every ten years by the Archbishop of Canterbury, who chairs the sessions at Lambeth Palace in London [the traditional site] or at the University of Kent in Canterbury [used in recent decades]. As well as maintaining relationships among the member churches of the Anglican Communion, the conference also studies questions of mutual concern and passes resolutions. The conference has only advisory power, but its opinions do have great influence on the decisions of member churches of the Anglican Communion.[11]

At Lambeth, bishops formulate and vote on resolutions that express the common mind (or at least the majority view) of the worldwide church on a spectrum of social, political, ecclesial, and theological issues, ranging from calling for peace in particular world regions to untangling doctrinal details. Because of the relatively loose structure of the Anglican Communion as a federation of related churches, the Lambeth Conference (like the Archbishop of Canterbury) cannot set policy, but can only "advise" and "influence" member provinces. Still, resolutions passed by the bishops at Lambeth carry significant moral weight for the Communion's provinces.

Lambeth Conferences, like the Communion itself, have long been dominated by the Northern provinces. The Anglican Consultative Council (ACC), the Anglican Communion's leadership body between Lambeth Conferences, has sought for decades to make Lambeth accessible to all the bishops of the Communion, ending Anglicanism's traditional association with colonial power. During the 1960s, the ACC began working to involve bishops from the churches of the newly independent nations of the global South in Communion affairs.[12] Anglican leaders sought to re-create the Communion as an egalitarian and multicultural worldwide institution, trading cultural and religious Eurocentrism for the complexities of managing diversity.[13] Bishop Michael Marshall, in his analysis of Lambeth 1988, explains:

> Until very recent times (and largely because of language difficulties) Lambeth Conferences have been dominated by the English bishops, with the American bishops coming in a close second. Big bucks and large representation can easily tempt a spirit of imperialism to take

over. Hence the need to make sure that what was to be discussed at Lambeth represented the heartfelt concerns and issues coming out of five continents.[14]

Simultaneous translation facilities were provided at Lambeth 1978 so that non-Anglophone bishops could better understand the proceedings, but this helped little in furthering Southern participation. Marshall quotes an analysis of Lambeth 1978 that highlights the alienation felt by Southern bishops, unfamiliar with the formal rules of debate employed. "Some Third World bishops lost hope, both in listening and speaking. . . . One Ugandan said . . . , "This is not our way of doing things, so we just leave you to it.'"[15] Marshall notes, "With a few notable exceptions much of the drafting [of resolutions] was the work of the English and American bishops, who still (almost inevitably) tended to dominate, especially in the plenary sessions."[16]

In preparation for the 1988 Conference, the ACC went much further than in 1978 in preparing bishops for informed participation. The 1988 gathering was the first Lambeth at which a majority of the bishops attending were from Southern churches. The ACC held advance meetings all over the world and distributed study materials to help bishops and their churches prepare for Lambeth. Marshall states, "The preparation was on a scale hitherto unrealized at any of the earlier Lambeth Conferences."[17] This preparation was almost exclusively organized by the ACC; apparently few other church organizations held preliminary meetings before Lambeth 1988, in contrast with preparations a decade later.

These 1988 efforts by Northern Anglican leaders to encourage the participation of formerly marginalized Anglican provinces were rewarded. Northern church leaders were at pains not to dominate as much as in the past, and Southern leaders indeed played a comparatively strong role at that Lambeth.[18] With the help of the ACC, which held several pre-Conference meetings specifically to explore the concerns of the African churches, African bishops spoke out strongly on polygamy and poverty.[19] In addition, Southern bishops were credited with one major outcome of Lambeth 1988: the resolution to name 1990–2000 as a Communion-wide "Decade of Evangelism." The African voice in 1988, however, seems to have been limited for the most part to issues that were not relevant for the Northern provinces. The African message (articulated with the involvement of the ACC) at Lambeth 1988 was, essentially, "Africa has these problems, and the rest of the Communion and the world needs to respond to them." In 1998, with respect to homosexuality, the Southern message would be more challenging: "The rest of the Communion has a problem, and Africa and the global South are going to respond to it."

The Anglican Consultative Council's preparations for Lambeth 1998 saw a new round of efforts to come to grips with the Communion's diversity—now, in the dominant discourse of the 1990s, termed "global." The Anglican Communion's concern with defining itself as global reflected wider ideological trends in the Northern world in the 1990s. This term was used in a humanistic sense by Anglican leaders, to imply a complex whole in which diverse members, representative of different cultures and parts of the world, work together in mutual understanding, appreciation, and cooperation. Affirming the Communion's globalness at Lambeth 1998 was particularly pressing, because this was to be the largest Lambeth Conference ever, due largely to church growth in Southern provinces.[20] As in 1988, bishops from the global South would be in the majority. Anglicans around the world looked toward Lambeth 1998, on the cusp of Christianity's third millennium, as a great opportunity to come together as a global Communion shaped and owned by all its members. Hoping to bring this vision to fruition, ACC officials again held advance meetings and distributed materials to help bishops around the world prepare, at a level even exceeding the preparations for Lambeth 1988.

ANTICIPATING LAMBETH 1998: CONSERVATIVE GROUPS PREPARE

The ACC was not the only Anglican body anxious to encourage Southern participation in Lambeth 1998. Some conservative Anglican evangelicals found, in Lambeth 1988's proclamation of a Decade of Evangelism, hope for new calls to faith from the global South in 1998. Archbishop Maurice Sinclair wrote in 1997, "The voice of the South has already been heard at Lambeth bringing us the Decade of Evangelism. Could it be heard again reaffirming vital orthodoxy in the midst of social change?"[21] American conservatives, in particular, saw Lambeth 1998 as pivotal because the fight for orthodoxy within the Episcopal Church seemed all but lost. The Episcopal Church was known to be among the most liberal provinces of the global Communion (in company with Canada and New Zealand), so the global church was unlikely to endorse ECUSA's liberal moves. Conservatives feared that the Lambeth agenda and the outcome of debates would be dominated, as in the past, by moderate and liberal Northern provinces and by the ACC, seen by many conservatives as controlled by liberals. But conservatives also hoped that, with sufficient preparation and strategizing, a conservative resolution on homosexuality might be passed at Lambeth 1998. Such a resolution would be a powerful rebuke to the Episcopal Church, far more so than any tool of protest wielded by earlier waves of disaffected Episcopalians.

Northern conservatives' interest in building alliances with Southern Anglicans to influence Lambeth exemplifies the tendency within global movements to seek to minimize difference and distance. Globalization, whether economic, cultural, or religious, is often described as making the world smaller and concomitantly bringing far-flung people closer together. Some scholars of globalization argue that modern transport and communication technologies render geographic distance irrelevant, or at least much less relevant than in the past. Roland Robertson has observed that local communities and places are increasingly incorporated into one global society, in a process he describes as the compression of the world.[22] Other prominent scholars of globalization, modernity, and postmodernity have also identified globalization as a process that results in events in one place having an immediate impact on another and in our daily lives being increasingly dominated by remote, rather than face-to-face, encounters.[23]

Analytical questions about these trends focus on the depth and impact of these processes of deterritorialization. Does all this increased interaction make the global geography of difference less real, less relevant? Does it blur the lines between North and South, the West and the Rest?[24] Do the continuing concrete realities of distance, difference, and inequality continue to matter in certain ways, and if so, how is that in tension with the increased sense of global proximity, connectedness, and likeness created by globalization?[25] In later chapters, I will address some of the ways the global orthodox Anglican movement reinscribes North/South divisions, as cultural difference, distance, and inequality continue to matter in relationships between American conservatives and African Anglicans. In this chapter, however, I explore how the movement's early leaders sought to blur North/South distinctions by developing a common set of convictions and goals and a shared vision of an Anglican Communion in which geography no longer mattered, subsumed completely to ecclesial connections based on moral and spiritual affinity.

E-mail and the Internet were important tools for conservative Americans seeking to build a global movement. These communication technologies were in very limited use in 1988, but by the late 1990s they had become central to conservatives' efforts to persuade and mobilize, domestically and internationally. Even more important than electronic communication, however, were a number of pre-Lambeth meetings held or attended by American conservatives. These preparatory gatherings became important sites for the development of a common global vision and for initial exploration of shared global projects among conservative American dissidents and Anglicans from the global South. Hannerz notes that in a global age such meetings are often important ethnographic sites: "It is often precisely these kinds of temporary meeting places . . . which contribute critically to the formation and enduring cohesion of translocal networks."[26] These conferences brought people together, spread ideas, and asserted the relevance of the global scale by making the global concrete and local—in the form, for example, of a Texas plenary hall full of African and Asian bishops.[27] The very names of the sites of significant conferences held in this period—Kuala Lumpur, Dallas, Kampala—not only illustrate the scope of the nascent transnational orthodox movement but evoke a sense of broadened horizons, of global scale.

These gatherings brought Northern and Southern Anglicans together, but also made evident the disparity in their material resources. At least two of these gatherings (Dallas and Kampala) had extensive financial support from Northern conservative groups and individuals. Significant financial resources were necessary not only to book conference centers and remunerate speakers but to bring together large numbers of African, Asian, and Latin American bishops, few of whom can afford nonessential international travel. These facts highlight the unusual character of this transnational movement. Clifford Bob has noted the familiar pattern of transnational advocacy in which a disempowered group in a particular domestic context—a political, ethnic, or sexual minority whose livelihood or life is threatened—appeals for assistance from transnational NGOs or other bodies, who are usually relatively resource-rich and powerful in comparison.[28] In contrast with this pattern, Episcopal conservatives, though ecclesiastically disempowered, are relatively wealthy in world terms, and have the resources to import potential foreign allies (who in this case are ecclesiastically powerful, as church leaders, but have limited material wealth). These relationships from their inception have thus taken the form of the exchange envisioned by Atwood (and subsequently taken up as a theme by many movement members, Northern and Southern): Northern material resources traded for Southern spiritual resources. Conservative Americans did not simply use money to recruit Southern allies; chapter 7 discussed the complex role of money in these relationships. Still, these alliances probably would not have developed without conservative Episcopalians' ability to bring Southern Anglicans together to involve them with the dissidents' cause.

PRE-LAMBETH MEETINGS: KUALA LUMPUR

The first pre-Lambeth conference significant for the development of Southern alliances with dissident conservative Northerners took place far from the United States and apparently with little Northern involvement. In February 1997, eighty delegates, mainly Southern bishops and archbishops, gathered in Kuala Lumpur, Malaysia, to talk about the Southern agenda for Lambeth 1998. This meeting represented an important moment for the political development of Southern Anglican leaders. Jonathan, an AAC member who has been actively involved in building connections between American conservatives and Southern bishops, told me about the history of such relationships when I interviewed him at his hotel in Kampala, where he was visiting Ugandan colleagues. Before Kuala Lumpur, he said, "there had been some loose theological fellowships of Third World leaders, but in terms of a political force that would actually organize itself to achieve some goal, there hadn't been much of that."

Those gathered in Kuala Lumpur concluded their meeting by issuing a statement, the "Second Trumpet from the South," a wide-ranging document covering such topics as "prophetic and redemptive witness, mission, people of other faiths, youth, contextualization, the family and human sexuality, church unity, and practical next steps in South-to-South relationships."[29] A study group at the meeting also produced a "study document" on human sexuality, which explicitly addressed some Northern Anglican provinces' increasing liberalism in matters of human sexuality: "We are deeply concerned that the setting aside of biblical teaching in such actions as the ordination of practicing homosexuals and the blessing of same-sex unions calls into question the authority of the Holy Scriptures. This is totally unacceptable to us. . . . This leads us to express concern about mutual accountability and interdependence within our Anglican Communion."[30]

The study document, which came to be called the "Kuala Lumpur Statement," was eagerly received by Northern conservatives—so much so that the full Second Trumpet document was quickly forgotten.[31] The Kuala Lumpur Statement was rapidly incorporated into Northerners' talk and lobbying efforts. In May 1997, the Episcopal Synod of America, claiming to represent "thousands of orthodox Episcopalians," expressed strong support for the Kuala Lumpur Statement; the American Anglican Council and Ekklesia Society similarly praised the document.[32] Conservative bishops presented a resolution to endorse the Kuala Lumpur Statement at the Episcopal Church's national General Convention in July 1997. The resolution failed, but in spite of that disappointment, the statement opened new possibilities for appeals to the authority of Southern Christian leaders in American conservative discourse.[33] Conservatives were beginning to imagine that Anglicans might work together, even across vast geographical and cultural differences, on the basis of a sense of shared doctrinal orthodoxy concerning human sexuality. A new politics was being born, one of making connections with other Anglicans who shared key convictions, which would transform the older dissident politics of breaking connections between Anglicans of different convictions.

Pre-Lambeth Meetings: Dallas

With growing hopes for cooperating with Southern Anglican leaders at Lambeth, the AAC, Ekklesia Society, and a like-minded English institution, the Oxford Centre for Mission Studies, convened the "Anglican Life and Witness" conference in Flower Mound, Texas, in September 1997, six weeks after ECUSA's General Convention. The conference brought American conservatives together with overseas Anglicans to share ideas and begin to plan collaborative actions. Doug LeBlanc, the head journalist of Episcopalians United's publication United Voice, writes, "The conference united 45 bishops and four archbishops [of Kenya, Sudan, Sydney, and the Southern Cone] from 16 nations in Africa, Asia, Australia, the Caribbean and North and South America."[34] In addition to the overseas bishops, a wide array of American evangelicals, charismatics, and traditionalists attended the event, including representatives of Episcopalians United and the Episcopal Synod of America.

The core purpose of the Dallas conference was to spread the vision of its organizers: that Anglicans from around the world could cooperate to reform the Episcopal Church and establish clear moral standards at Lambeth 1998. And indeed, the conference seems to have led both American conservative Episcopalians and Southern Anglicans to take seriously the idea that Southern church leaders could be an effective force in the worldwide Communion. Although the aim of spreading this vision among Episcopalians was generally implicit in the events of the Dallas conference, the aim of encouraging and equipping Southern leaders to be such a force was often explicit. American conservative leaders knew from long experience how easy the rest of the Episcopal Church found it to ignore their opinions. But if Southern bishops could be mobilized to speak out at Lambeth against tolerance of homosexuality, Episcopal leaders might feel more obligated to listen.

The conference schedule therefore devoted considerable time not only to networking and sharing perspectives through Bible study and other small-group meetings but also to preparing Southern bishops for Lambeth. This aim was accomplished by providing information and strategizing tips to Southern bishops through teaching and plenary sessions—including a plenary discussion entitled "Empowering Others' Voices." One particularly significant presentation was given by the Rev. Dr. Stephen Noll, then of the evangelical seminary Trinity Episcopal School for Ministry (TESM). His talk, entitled "The Handwriting on the Wall: Why the Sexuality Conflict in the Episcopal Church Is God's Word to the Anglican Communion," addressed the question of why bishops from the global South should care about the Northern church's increased tolerance of homosexuality:

The fact is, problems in the Episcopal Church tend to become symptomatic. As one African bishop put it: when America sneezes, the whole world catches a cold. In the case of the sexuality virus, it has already spread to most Western churches of the Communion, and Southern hemisphere churches will be exposed more and more because of the financial, educational, and media influence of the West. . . . It is crucial for the rest of the Anglican Communion to take notice and "come over and help us." It has frequently been said in recent years that Third World Anglicans are in a much stronger place spiritually than Westerners. . . . In particular, I believe the Lambeth Conference in 1998 offers a decisive opportunity for the wider body of Anglicans to speak clearly on the question of Christian sexual norms.[35]

Noll thus explained to Southern leaders that although homosexuality was not a matter of current public debate in most of their home contexts, they must engage with the issue in order to help beleaguered Northern brethren and to protect their own churches from the spread of negative Northern influences.

Noll and others sought to motivate Southern Anglicans; other elements of the program sought to equip them to be an effective force at Lambeth. Gerald, a retired Episcopal bishop with strong ties to several Southern Anglican churches developed through past involvement with the AAC and his own travels, shared his recollections of the Dallas meeting with me. He explained how American conservatives began the work of empowering Southern bishops' voices:

They were simply briefed. And they were also given to get to know each other and to get to understand how a strategy had to be put together. So that when they did get to Lambeth, they had some caucuses in place and they learned how to work that parliamentary structure so that the things they were interested in got a proper hearing, and also got supported. . . . They simply began to learn how to play the game.

Northern and Southern attendees at the Dallas conference also planned collaborative global projects. Support groups met on the conference's last day to deal with two main concerns of this nascent transnational orthodox Anglican movement. One session, entitled "The North American Context," focused on how to support and help orthodox parishes in the United States, perhaps through the development of transnational relationships. The second session, "Lambeth Resolutions and Strategy," dealt with plans for the allies at Lambeth.[36]

Southern Anglican leaders responded positively to the conference's content and tone. They heard in the pleas of Northern conservatives a call to claim a stronger, determining role in world Anglicanism. Many Ugandan

bishops and others whom I interviewed agreed that they had been ignorant of the gravity of the worldwide situation and insufficiently organized
to address it, before American conservatives set out to inform, encourage,
and mobilize them. Thomas, the bishop of a central Ugandan diocese,
met me at his office for an interview about his thoughts on international
Anglican relationships. He had attended the Dallas conference, and told
me what he thought its effect was:

> It gave us [African bishops] understanding of what in the Communion
> was going on . . . [so that] when we went to Lambeth, we were more
> or less aware of the background information. . . . During Lambeth you
> meet for so short a time, you're a big body of people, everything can
> be skimmed through and you won't understand. But the people who
> called us in Dallas did give us a lot of information about that, so we
> were able to help ourselves to understand what was going on in the
> Episcopal Church.

For Southern leaders the message of the Dallas conference was an affirmation that their voices mattered, and were needed, in the worldwide
Communion—as well as some welcome training in having an effective
common voice.

One outcome of the conference was the "Dallas Statement," a six-page
document focusing on the problems of international debt and homosexuality. These two issues were explicitly connected: "It is precisely unbridled
economic individualism that has led both to the breakup of families and
the escalation of international debt."[37] These issues were thus bound together into a sort of hybrid agenda, asserting that concerns usually associated with the global South (international debt) and issues more dominant
in Northern societies (human sexuality) are related. The statement
thereby asserts a natural convergence of interests behind the coalition of
Northern conservatives and Southern Anglican leaders taking shape at
Dallas and beyond.

The Dallas Statement, like the Kuala Lumpur conference, called for
greater mutual accountability in the Anglican Communion and hinted
that this might require intervention across church boundaries: "The bishops express concern for Anglican bodies that are "oppressed, marginalized, or denied faithful episcopal oversight by their own bishops. . . . In
such situations, a way must be found to provide pastoral support, oversight and formal ecclesiastical relationships for faithful people," the bishops write."[38] This suggestion of the potential for making new alliances
among orthodox Anglicans was accompanied by acknowledgment of the
necessity of breaking relationships with nonorthodox believers. The statement notes: "Those who choose beliefs and practices outside the bound-

aries of the historic faith must understand they are separating themselves from communion, and leading others astray."[39]

Such talk about breaking off ecclesiastical relations with insufficiently orthodox church bodies was not new. Evangelical, charismatic, and traditionalist Episcopalians have debated since the 1970s whether they should stay and fight within the Episcopal Church or leave it to join or create other church bodies. The new element, unspoken as yet but taking shape, was the prospect of involving foreign bishops in alternative networks of orthodox Episcopalians and Anglicans, thereby replacing broken ties to heterodox leaders with new ties to orthodox ones. The further development of these transnational relationships was, however, a longer-term project. The more immediate work was the pre-Lambeth preparation that went on in Dallas—and continued at a third international meeting, in Kampala, Uganda.

Pre-Lambeth Meetings: Kampala

The Kampala conference continued the work of informing and mobilizing Southern leaders for Lambeth. It was attended by bishops from Uganda, Kenya, Rwanda, Burundi, Tanzania, the Democratic Republic of Congo, and Sudan, and focused on the two central issues that had emerged at Dallas, sexuality and international debt. This meeting was intended both as Lambeth preparation and as an occasion to foster unity among the bishops of East and Central Africa, including many who had not attended the Dallas conference. The few Northerners present were described as presenters and facilitators. One of the African bishops who planned this meeting, George, visited Kampala during my stay in Uganda. We met for an interview at Namirembe Guest House, the church-sponsored hostel perched on a hill in Kampala just below Namirembe Cathedral, the Church of Uganda's elegant flagship cathedral. Over bottles of soda at an outdoor table with a view out over the city center, we talked about the Kampala meeting, and he described its purposes:

> I was seeking to bring the awareness to the African church that we are in trouble. . . . You need to realize that what happens to the American church does not leave us unaffected. . . . [Also,] we were going to Lambeth. And Lambeth has been a kind of a cheat on Africans. Because [Northern church leaders] know the parliamentary procedures. They know how they debate things, they know how they pass resolutions, they know how they propose and second, they know how they change resolutions, they know how they amend resolutions, and Africans do not. So you get the African church, which is much bigger than . . . other

parts of the world. . . . But because they don't know the procedures, the parliamentary procedures of Lambeth conference, [Africans] go just to rubber-stamp what the West is doing. And I wanted that to come to an end. I wanted the Africans to be prepared to face what's going on to happen there. I wanted them to be able to handle the agenda with worth and merit.

George strongly articulated the goals he shared with the Northern conservatives who joined him in planning this meeting: convincing African bishops that there was a problem demanding their attention, and that they could make a difference by working together to shape the outcome of Lambeth 1998.

Some Northern liberals criticized the Kampala and Dallas meetings as attempts by Northern conservatives to indoctrinate or subvert Southern leaders. African bishops I interviewed, however, described these meetings in different terms. Limited funding in many African churches makes it difficult for African bishops to travel and consult together, so the resources provided by Northerners to support the Kampala meeting made a substantial difference by allowing East and Central African bishops to talk and plan before heading to Lambeth. Mark, bishop of one central Ugandan diocese, stressed to me that this meeting's most valuable outcome was the chance to find a common mind among African bishops:

> Some of us were beginning to become very seriously concerned about what was happening in the church in America particularly. . . . [At the Kampala meeting] we took a unanimous position decision, that when we are in Lambeth, we are going to stand firm and tell the whole Lambeth and the rest of the world that for us, here, our position is that homosexual practice, and especially when it comes to marrying people of the same sex, we really say no.

Bishop Mark and other Ugandans who attended this meeting emphasized the opportunity it offered for conversation and strengthening of unity around an existing consensus, rather than any sort of indoctrination by Northerners.

FOSTERING UNITY ELECTRONICALLY

Southern Anglicans' eagerness to become better informed about the global church was answered by Northern conservatives' eagerness to respond. During the months preceding Lambeth, in addition to holding international meetings, Northern conservative organizations circulated conservative Northern reporting and commentary to Southern Anglicans—

via some of the same e-mail lists that helped St. Timothy's members develop identities as conservative evangelical Episcopalians. The widespread availability of publications carrying Episcopal conservatives' news analyses and opinions, in hard copy as well as electronically, was brought home to me while I was interviewing a moderate Ugandan bishop with minimal involvement in international Anglican politics. At one point, he casually picked up and gestured with a copy of the conservative Episcopal publication *Christian Challenge*, which had been lying on his desk. I subsequently learned that the publishers of *Christian Challenge* try to send the magazine to as many overseas bishops and other leaders as possible.[40]

E-mail and the Internet have been key tools in exposing Southern Anglicans to conservative Northern perspectives. In a 2003 article in the conservative publication *Mandate*, Ekklesia Society head Bill Atwood accuses liberal Northern leaders of trying to keep the Anglican world ignorant of their revisionist moves, and states that such tactics will no longer work: "Now it is possible for people in far-flung portions of the communion to be well informed about events from the other side of the globe. News that used to take months to travel from continent to continent now zips across cyber-space in seconds."[41] Atwood's picture is somewhat optimistic; for example, my fieldwork in Uganda showed that while many Ugandan church leaders and members do have access to the Internet and e-mail, the access of most laity is indirect or nonexistent. Still, the wide circulation of American conservative accounts of ECUSA is hinted at by the frequency with which African church leaders I met mentioned American bishop John Spong as the epitome of what is wrong with the Episcopal Church. Some African bishops had direct contact with Spong through Lambeth 1998, but many more have heard of him, and all tended to use his name to stand for all the perceived ills of Northern Christianity—as is often the case in Northern conservative writings. Thus electronic communication, print publications like *Christian Challenge*, and face-to-face meetings like those held in Dallas and Kampala have all shown to African and other Southern Anglicans conservative Episcopalians' vision of the Episcopal Church as in crisis and demanding global attention.

THE GLOBALIZATION OF EPISCOPAL CONSERVATIVES

The Kuala Lampur, Dallas, and Kampala meetings and the dissemination of information and opinion by other means during this period spread globalist thinking among two constituencies: Southern Anglican leaders, who were encouraged to think of themselves as a global force, and Episcopal conservatives, who were taught that it might be worth their while to pay attention to "what a bunch of Africans think." This shift in conservative American Episcopal thought and action—from a domestic orientation through the mid-1990s, to an international or global orientation by the end of 1997—represents a process of conceptual and strategic globalization. This alliance-building work included a great deal of "globalization" in the sense of moving people and ideas from place to place in order to build transnational networks. But this movement can also be seen as the outward and physical sign of an ongoing inward globalization process in the discourse of American conservative Episcopalians, as they have shifted from a focus on domestic struggles and solutions to vehement insistence that their problems are of global relevance and require global responses. The development of this globalism can be tracked in the growing occurrence, in conservative Episcopal documents, of invocations of the "global," the "Two-Thirds World," the "worldwide," and a heightened level of talk about the Anglican Communion. The rhetorical use of the global scale as a way of talking about what is wrong with the Episcopal Church (by accusing it of parochialism, arrogance, or other insufficiently global mind-sets) is now so well established that a shorthand has developed. On one conservative Episcopal e-mail list in mid-2003, one member asked the relevance of recent events in the Episcopal Church for the "WWAC," which I quickly realized stood for the "World-Wide Anglican Communion."

This newly developed global-mindedness of the conservative Episcopal camp is surprising to many other Americans, who do not generally expect socially conservative white people to think, talk, and work in terms of greater relationship with the global South across racial and cultural boundaries. Social and moral conservatism in the United States tends to correlate with American exceptionalism, a view of the United States as a special nation with a unique global role—usually one of leading, teaching, and intervening in other nations. In contrast, Episcopal conservatives in the late 1990s were increasingly arguing that the Episcopal Church, and the United States in general, had a problem that needed intervention and correction from other nations—and not just any other nations, but the poor and marginalized nations of the global South.

This newfound globalism was primarily domestically oriented, in that conservative Episcopalians sought international assistance in order to correct the situation in the American church. The transnational movement that developed from these first steps also remained primarily America-focused, since the Southern leaders who became involved did so to support American dissidents, and not because they needed help with parallel conflicts or movements in their provinces. Many, perhaps the majority, of global movements have a similar focus on particular domestic contexts. Sidney Tarrow, in his study of social movements, has noted that the primary impact of transnational movements is usually on domestic politics.[42]

Hilary Cunningham observes that such movements engage in a particular and limited way with the tendency to subvert geographic boundaries, one often-cited aspect of globalization. Cunningham writes, in reference to another American-based but globally minded religious movement, "The global or transnational sensibility of Sanctuary participants was not a broad deterritorialization based on the growing irrelevance of a series of borders . . . but a more specific kind of deterritorialization that renounced the U.S. state as a central source of authority."[43] Although for Episcopalians the authority in question is the national Episcopal Church rather than the U.S. government, the conservative movement, like the Sanctuary movement, has been engaged in "crossing a sovereign border and creating a transnational anti–Americanism."[44]

By the late 1990s most conservative Episcopal groups recognized the potential benefits of creating a transnational anti–Episcopal Church movement. Accordingly they adopted the tactic of arguing that not the diocesan scale, not the provincial scale, but the global scale was the correct frame of reference for Episcopalians and other Anglicans. Even as Lambeth 1998 approached, a peerless opportunity to bring local church conflicts into a global context, two significant projects bringing the global into local contexts were taking shape: the First Promise organization and the parish of St. Andrew's, Little Rock, Arkansas.

First Promise/AMiA

During the weeks following the 1997 ECUSA General Convention, while final preparations were being made for the Dallas conference, a much smaller meeting of Episcopal clergy and laity was held at All Saints' Episcopal Church in Pawley's Island, South Carolina.[45] This meeting gave birth to a new organization, First Promise, which by March 1998 had grown to a network of at least two hundred clergy.[46] The leader of the First Promise organization was the Rev. Chuck Murphy, the evangelical rector of All Saints' Church. An article in the AAC publication *Encompass* explains the new body's rationale: "The "First Promise" [founders] declared that when the Church itself departs from the faith it has received, their first loyalty must be to apostolic faith rather than the authority of canons, institutions, and bishops."[47]

First Promise's initial declaration made it clear that its leaders saw transnational alliances as a fruitful route to maintaining "apostolic faith." The First Promise document declared, in part:

6) We will not be bound, in the exercise of our priestly or diaconal ministries, by the legal or geographical boundaries of any parish or diocese. . . .

7) We pledge to remain under the ecclesiastical jurisdiction of faithful bishops who uphold our heritage in the gospel, seeking alternative episcopal oversight if necessary. . . .

9) We appeal to the bishops of the Anglican Communion, to reassert the apostolic truth and order which we have received in the gospel of Jesus Christ, to affirm and support theologically orthodox Anglicans in America, and to discipline those members who have departed from it.[48]

The language of this declaration, in denying the relevance of geographical boundaries in the search for faithful ecclesial leadership and especially in the call to outside bishops to "support theologically orthodox Anglicans in America," both affirms a global frame of reference for Episcopal Church conflicts and foreshadows what would soon become a reality, the claiming of jurisdiction over an American parish by a foreign bishop. Three years later, First Promise would fulfill this vision itself by becoming the new transnational church body Anglican Mission in America.

First Promise absorbed momentum and personnel from several earlier conservative organizations and was welcomed by many conservative clergy and parishes. The leadership at St. Timothy's Episcopal Church greeted the news of First Promise's founding with pleasure. During the 1990s, their evangelical orientation had led them into increasing conflicts with their bishop and diocese. At the same time, church members were hearing through Episcopal dissident news sources about other parishes' struggles with liberal bishops, and they began to see themselves as one of many beleaguered orthodox parishes. Gradually, St. Timothy's lay and clergy leadership developed strong ties to the wider conservative movement within the Episcopal Church. These leaders subscribed to e-mail lists and publications and attended conferences, and shared what they learned with other parishioners. One St. Timothy's couple I interviewed, Nancy and Bud, showed me a sheaf of e-mail printouts from conservative lists like Virtuosity. Laying out the pages on their kitchen table where we sat, Nancy told me that subscribing to such lists has helped them to know what's going on in the Episcopal Church: "We're looking at the national level." Indeed, almost every conversation about St. Timothy's situation that I participated in or observed included some statement placing St. Timothy's in a national frame—such as comments about parallel developments at other churches, or generalizations about the Episcopal Church's leadership—and even in a global frame, such as remarks about the relative weaknesses of Northern Christianity as compared with Southern.

Increased awareness of wider Episcopal Church and Anglican Communion issues led St. Timothy's to join First Promise in early 1998. First Promise and its successor organization, AMiA, shared and affirmed St.

Timothy's independently developed evangelical and charismatic character. Ted, a middle-aged doctor who joined St. Timothy's after finding another mainline church insufficiently biblical, told me First Promise was exciting because it embodied "what we've been doing here at St. Timothy's" for many years now, as "an orthodox Episcopal church that is a bunch of evangelicals." But beyond a general shared outlook, First Promise was also exciting to people at St. Timothy's—and to other Episcopalians in similar situations—because of the possibilities it presented for escape from ongoing conflicts with the Episcopal Church. As I was told by Frieda, a member of St. Timothy's since 1957 and one of the rare long-term members who had happily gone along with changes in the parish, St. Timothy's was "ready for First Promise."

St. Andrew's, Little Rock

Shortly after the founding of First Promise, one conservative Episcopal parish found its own escape route from perceived oppression within the Episcopal Church. St. Andrew's Church, in Little Rock, Arkansas, was founded by a small group of conservative Episcopalians who, as one member explained to me, wanted to worship in Episcopal liturgical style in a theologically orthodox parish. The group began meeting once a month in homes, inviting priests from all over the country and even beyond to preach and minister to them.[49] By January 1998 the group had around sixty members and was ready to meet more regularly and call a priest. Their bishop, Larry Maze, denied the group permission to become a recognized Episcopal parish, reportedly claiming that the group was motivated only by opposition to homosexuality and that this was a poor reason to found a congregation.[50]

Undeterred by Maze's refusal, St. Andrew's called a rector—T. J. Johnston, formerly an assisting priest at All Saints' Church, Pawley's Island, and an original member of First Promise. Maze opposed this call and threatened to file charges against Johnston if he came to the unauthorized parish. Johnston, however, was not concerned; one article quotes him as stating, "I'd rather face the wrath of a bunch of cranky old bishops than to see Jesus eyeball to eyeball one day and have him ask, 'What did you do to bring in the Kingdom?'" This article further noted, "Johnston had reason to be joyous in adversity. Johnston expected to soon come under the episcopal authority of an African bishop, which would diminish his chances of facing a trial for breaking church canons."[51] An Episcopal bishop has the authority to inhibit (prohibit from serving) or depose (remove) a priest in his diocese. However, Maze's authority to take such action would become uncertain, once Johnston was under the authority of an African bishop.

The African bishop who took on the responsibility of protecting and overseeing Johnston was John Rucyahana, then newly elected bishop of the Diocese of Shyira in northwestern Rwanda. Rucyahana was well connected with American conservatives owing to his studies at Trinity Episcopal School for Ministry. He had met Johnston at the Dallas conference, and when Johnston found himself on ecclesiastical thin ice only months later, he appealed to Rucyahana. Johnston's American bishop, the conservative-leaning Ed Salmon of South Carolina, agreed to transfer Johnston's letters dimissory to Bishop Rucyahana—the official means of moving a priest to another bishop's jurisdiction.[52]

This arrangement was an extraordinary departure from Episcopal and Anglican polity, and its legality was, and remains, uncertain. In a letter addressed to Bishop Rucyahana in July 1998, Archbishop of Canterbury George Carey wrote, "It is my clear view that what you are doing is completely illegal and I hope you will quickly disentangle yourself from something that is quite unconstitutional."[53] However, as with future moves along similar lines, the legality of transferring an American priest to the jurisdiction of an African bishop was apparently not questionable enough for punishment to be possible. Johnston and St. Andrew's, though dogged by controversy, were able to use this loophole in Anglican polity to escape the authority of the Episcopal Church and its bishops. Illegal perhaps, irregular indeed, surprising for certain—but it worked. Johnston quipped in the Arkansas Democrat-Gazette, "It's like setting up an offshore corporation for protection."[54]

The arrangement brought stability and growth to St. Andrew's. By February 2002, the church had four hundred members and was planning to build its own sanctuary. More significantly, the connection between Bishop Rucyahana and St. Andrew's pointed the way forward for other dissident Episcopalians. This new relationship connected two far-distant sites, the Diocese of Shyira and the congregation of St. Andrew's, in a relationship of proximity and protection. It also brought the global church into a specific local situation, escalating a conflict between a bishop and a small would-be congregation into an affair with global implications for issues of geographical jurisdiction, episcopal authority, and worldwide Anglican polity.

The placement of Johnston and his church under an African bishop, which one conservative Episcopal journalist called an "unprecedented development,"[55] opened the door to a whole new world of possibilities for Episcopal dissidents, who were fast learning the value of "taking Africa seriously." First Promise leaders were delighted by these events, which in the words of one reporter gave the organization a "test case for their growing conviction that other Anglican avenues must be explored to pre-serve the biblical message they set out to preach and embody at the time of their ordination."[56] They trumpeted the news of St. Andrew's new African patron at their March 1998 conference, which was attended by nearly six hundred people.[57] Subsequent developments have amply proved *United Voice* reporter England right when he predicted, "The battle of Little Rock could turn out to be only the first skirmish in a full-fledged global confrontation."[58] St. Andrew's revolutionary alliance with a Rwandan bishop may have brought peace to its members, but for the rest of the Episcopal Church and the wider Anglican Communion, the excitement was just beginning.

CHAPTER THREE

"White Hands Up!" Lambeth 1998 and the Global Politics of Homosexuality

THE 1998 Lambeth Conference began on July 19 with a grand showing of the Communion's multicultural colors. A British reporter described details of the opening litugy: "The Archbishop of Canterbury, Dr. George Carey, . . . welcomed 800 bishops and 600 spouses with a greeting in Swahili. The Epistle was in Portuguese and the service set to the Kenyan rite with a South African spiritual and Argentinian chorus."[1] This liturgy reflected the determination of conference planners and Anglican Communion leadership to show the world an Anglican Communion unified in its diversity, celebrating its global breadth at the largest Lambeth Conference yet. Lambeth 1998 was attended by nearly 750 bishops, including 224 from Africa, 177 from the United States and Canada, 139 from the United Kingdom and Europe, 95 from Asia, 56 from Australia, 41 from Central and South America, and 4 from the Middle East.[2] Joining this already diverse crowd of bishops on the campus of the University of Kent, near the town of Canterbury and its historic cathedral, were Conference and campus staff, observers from various countries and from other Christian traditions, and a wide variety of journalists and church activists, including a number of American clergy and lay leaders representing both conservative and liberal interest groups. Searching for Anglican unity in a changing global Communion among these diverse, lively, and numerous Conference participants would be one of the great themes and tasks of Lambeth 1998. The outcomes were by no means guaranteed to conform to the happy model of the opening liturgy's showy celebration of multiculturalism.

Another vignette from much later in the Conference became in many people's minds more typical of the dynamics of cross-cultural conversation at Lambeth 1998. This scene took place outside the plenary hall on the day of the plenary debate over a Lambeth resolution on homosexuality, two and a half weeks into the three-week-long conference. One reporter set the scene: "On Wednesday the breadth of the Anglican Communion was unforgettably demonstrated by the Nigerian Bishop Emanuel Chukwuma attempting to exorcise the English deacon Richard Kirker on the campus of the University of Kent. Kirker's sin, or distinction, was to be a homosexual."[3] Another British reporter described the repeated confrontations between the Nigerian bishop and the gay English activist as "scenes of unprecedented vitriol, near violence and . . . the prolific and unsolicited laying on of hands."[4] James Solheim, in his account of Lambeth 1998, reports Bishop Chukwuma's words to Kirker: "God did not create you as a homosexual. That is our stand. That is why your church is dying in Europe—because it is condoning immorality. You are killing the church. This is the voice of God talking."[5]

Not surprisingly, this public and dramatic confrontation caught the attention of the secular press, who interpreted the incident as a prime illustration of North/South antagonisms. Conservative Episcopal reporter Robert Stowe England observes: "Photographs and videos of Bishop Chukwuma holding a Bible, preaching and shaking his finger only inches from Richard Kirker . . . became a symbol in the British press and on television of the culture clash between the moral clarity of the South and the moral laxity of the North."[6] The Kirker–Chukwuma face-off became an icon of what many came to see as the central theme of Lambeth 1998: righteous Southern rebuke to a cowering North. Despite the best efforts of the Conference's organizers to have Lambeth 1998 remembered for multicultural warmth and unity, the meeting came to be experienced by many participants, and described by even more observers, as a site of tension. In examining Lambeth 1998's contentious politics, this chapter will also explore Ugandan views of homosexuality, not only to help explain Ugandans' votes at the meeting but to address critics' charge that African Anglicans' concern with the issue constitutes an example of Westernization posing as globalization.

"Us Uneducated, Bought-Out Third Worlders": North/South Tensions as Lambeth Begins

Even before Lambeth's opening liturgy, controversy over statements by American bishop John Spong had heightened a sense of North/South antagonism. Spong, then bishop of the Diocese of Newark, is an outspoken proponent of accepting homosexuality and a prolific writer of modernist theology. Many conservative Episcopal and Anglican leaders regard Bishop Spong as the essence of what is wrong with liberal Episcopalianism. Nine days before Lambeth began, Spong was quoted in the conservative-leaning *Church of England Newspaper* as stating that African Christians are "superstitious, fundamentalist Christians" who have "moved out of animism into a very superstitious kind of Christianity . . . [and have] yet to face the intellectual revolution of Copernicus and Einstein that we've had to face in the developing world; that is just not on their radar screen."[7] These comments, and Spong's unwillingness to apologize until nearly two weeks had passed, infuriated Southern Christians and heartily embarrassed other American bishops.[8]

Southern responses to Spong's remarks were indignant and defensive. Some responded to Spong by using his terms themselves, sarcastically. A Hispanic missionary commented, "Given the [recent ruling on homosexuality] for United Methodists in the USA, I would suggest that it is not just us poor, superstitious, uneducated and bought-out Third Worlders who appear to think that the blessing of same-sex unions is not particularly Biblical."[9] Other Southerners defied Spong's characterization of Southern Christians. I heard such a response from Ezekiel, a Ugandan bishop who is outspoken in his opposition to homosexuality and who attended Lambeth 1998. His hearkening back to Spong's remarks four years after Lambeth, during our conversation in mid-2002, suggests that Spong's words still rankled: "Some of us have so many degrees, we have gone to the same school [as American church leaders], yes? . . . [We have] the same training. . . . But they are saying we have not gone very far, we are still primitive, untrained, because we supported an orthodox teaching."

Spong's remarks and the resultant bad feelings toward Northern liberals gave Northern conservatives an opportunity to strengthen their own alliances with Southerners. Word of Spong's remarks spread rapidly through a pre-Lambeth charismatic leadership retreat in Canterbury, hosted by several Anglican charismatic-renewal groups sympathetic to the American conservative cause. Photocopies of the offending Spong article were circulated among the approximately 450 Anglican bishops, priests, and lay leaders present. The Americans at the retreat, including many leading conservative Episcopal activists, decided to make a public apology, which was welcomed by their Southern colleagues with embraces and tears.[10] Todd Wetzel of Episcopalians United described the moment as "one of the American Church's finest moments in decades."[11] Besides emphasizing their own respect for Southern Christians in this apology and other contexts, American conservatives also used Spong's remarks to depict the whole Episcopal Church as condescending and racist. Doug LeBlanc, for example, asserted that Spong's comments "expose a certain arrogance that lies beneath the surface of some liberal circles in the Episcopal Church."[12]

Between Spong's words and American conservatives' efforts to identify Spong closely with the Episcopal Church in general, the 1998 Lambeth Conference began with Africans and other Southern bishops already feeling insulted and defensive. These North/South tensions and suspicions constituted a significant step away from the increased global understanding and cooperation that were a hoped-for outcome of the conference. As one Ugandan bishop described it to me, "When we met at Lambeth, the church was not at oneness. Each church . . . we dismissed each other."

Lambeth: Global South Rising

As at the 1988 Conference, African, Asian, and Latin American bishops were in the majority, and as Lambeth 1998 opened, the Communion's Southern provinces appeared poised to play a much more pivotal role than they had in the past. Encouraged both by Northern multiculturally minded liberals and moderates and by conservative would-be allies, and further incited by Spong's remarks, African and other Southern bishops were prepared to be assertive. Expectations were high among all parties that African, Asian, and Latin American bishops would wield unprecedented and decisive force. Religion columnist Larry Stammer observed in an article written early in the Conference that many expected Lambeth 1998 to be dominated by concerns like international debt "that reflect the increasing importance of Asians and Africans in the church that once was run by their former colonial overlords."[13] A *United Voice* editorial written just before Lambeth further illustrates the expectations of Southern influence at the Conference, and shows that the hopes of American conservatives rested heavily upon the idea of an ascendant orthodox South:

> We believe the 13th Lambeth Conference needs to witness the arrival of Southern Hemisphere Anglicanism as a compassionate rebuke to an uncertain and confused North. . . . Orthodox Anglicans in the North, exhausted as they sometimes are, know in their souls that they stand with the vast body of orthodox Christians in the Worldwide Anglican Communion. May the South rise to this occasion to ask just what the North thinks it is doing to Scripture, reason and tradition.[14]

But until the day of the sexuality debate, late in the Conference, many observers felt such expectations had gone unfulfilled. During the first two weeks, the bishops met in groups organized around particular topics, preparing reports and resolutions for the Conference to vote on during the plenary sessions of the third week.[15] These two weeks of committee discussions passed in relative quiet. Several accounts note that by the conference's halfway point, African or other Southern protests or actions had not played much public role. Lamin Sanneh remarked upon the lack of a strong African presence or voice by midway through the gathering in an interview with Alistair Macdonald-Radcliff: "Professor Sanneh . . . made it clear that he was aware of deep pain felt among his African and Caribbean brethren at the Lambeth Conference: 'They feel they haven't been given a hearing.' "[16] Seven Southern archbishops, including the primates of Rwanda, Uganda, the Southern Cone, and Southeast Asia, issued a "Midpoint Letter" to the other bishops present asserting that their concerns (including human sexuality and the authority of the Bible) had not yet come to the fore.

Some Northern conservatives blamed the weak Southern impact in the Conference's first weeks on liberal bias and draconian control by organizers and staff.[17] Yet Northern moderates and liberals, too, were wondering when the much-heralded Southern voice would be heard. An article drafted by the official Lambeth press team near the end of the second week raised the question of why Southern Anglican leaders hadn't yet played their predicted assertive role. Most Conference attendees and observers anticipated, with hope or dread, that the sexuality debate would be Lambeth 1998's defining event, and that there, if nowhere else, the voice of the Anglican South would be heard.

Energetic preparations for the coming sexuality debate continued in the form of lobbying and strategizing by activists and allied bishops on either end of the spectrum of opinion. Conservative activism included the wide circulation of literature intended to persuade the bishops and others not to support gay rights in the church. Gay and lesbian rights activists were also a visible presence at Lambeth; representatives of several gay and lesbian Christian groups distributed literature and demonstrated outside plenary sessions. Meetings and presentations were held to support both the antihomosexuality and the pro-tolerance positions.

The scheduling, and subsequent cancellation, of one such presentation was surrounded by controversy, which newspaper articles described as the first rift in Lambeth's appearance of unity. South African bishop Duncan Buchanan, the head of the group of sixty bishops in charge of discussing and producing a resolution on human sexuality for the whole Conference to vote on, scheduled an informational presentation by gay and lesbian Christians.[18] On July 22, after an acrimonious debate, that presentation was canceled by a two-thirds majority vote by the group.[19] Several African bishops spoke to the press at this time about their opposition to homosexuality. Both these bishops and the press coverage described the controversy over the scheduled presentation as a case of African Christians revolting against liberal Northern agendas. The cancellation strengthened the general perception of North/South confrontation that had been circulating since the Conference began—despite the fact that Bishop Buchanan, who had scheduled the presentation, is a white South African, and that the "hour-long brouhaha" which resulted in the presentation's cancellation was started, not by a Southern bishop, but by conservative American bishop James Stanton.[20]

After the cancellation of this presentation, two American bishops decided to host an open session giving British and American church-affiliated gay and lesbian groups another opportunity to present their points of view.[21] Meanwhile, those opposed to church acceptance of homosexuality countered with their own informational session, an event on July 29 entitled "An Evening to Understand More about Homosexuality and the Reality of Change." The invitation to this meeting, officially extended by seven African and Asian archbishops and eighteen bishops, mainly African and American, read in part: "We are calling for a meeting in order to signal the intention that the majority of this Lambeth Conference accepts a resolution that clearly and unambiguously affirms the biblical position on marriage and the church's traditional teaching that genital sexual behavior belongs within the context of heterosexual, monogamous lifelong marriage."[22] The site of this event and for other conservative strategizing and lobbying efforts was the Franciscan Study Centre (FSC) on the campus of the University of Kent. A coalition of conservative organizations used the FSC to provide a gathering and resource center for overseas bishops. Free long-distance phone calls, e-mail, and copying were reportedly offered. Meetings, dinners, presentations, and other events, social, informational, and strategic, were held at the center. Several liberal and moderate leaders and commentators criticized the use of the FSC, accusing Northern conservatives of using the facility to bribe, organize, and generally inappropriately influence the views and votes of Southern bishops, as we shall see in chapter 7. Conservatives argued, in response, that they were merely providing information and resources to enable Southern bishops to participate fully at Lambeth. The Southern bishops themselves, as with the pre-Lambeth meetings, seemed appreciative of the assistance. One Ugandan bishop told me, "They were very, very, very helpful."

The program for the FSC evening event on homosexuality included brief statements by several bishops and a conservative expert on homosexuality, testimonies from "ex-gay" men and women who said they had been cured of homosexuality through faith, a moderated discussion period, and then a "time for the Bishops to reflect on appropriate steps to be taken during this Lambeth Conference."[23] As suggested by this final period of reflection, the goal of the evening was not only to present an alternative to analogous presentations promoting the liberal view on homosexuality, but to plan for the passing of a conservative sexuality resolution. A document entitled "Observations on the Politics of Passing a Sexuality Resolution," shared with me by an American activist who helped plan this event, makes it clear that part of this plan was to develop a single strongly worded antihomosexuality resolution that would be "promulgated" at this evening meeting. This single resolution was then to be presented to the Conference during the sexuality debate and backed by all orthodox bishops present, a strategy intended to ensure that the conservative vote would not be split between competing resolutions.[24]

Conservatives' concerns over resolution texts were heightened by one more controversy arising during the last day before the sexuality debate.

A confusion over what text would be used as the basic resolution on human sexuality to be debated and amended in the plenary session heightened fears among those opposed to church acceptance of homosexuality that savvy liberal leaders would trick them out of the conservative resolution they sought. The titles of conservative articles covering this matter demonstrate this feeling: "Lambeth Uproar over Liberals' 'Dirty Tricks,'" by Robert Stowe England of the ESA, and "How the Liberals Have Schemed to Get Their Way," by Stephen Noll of the AAC. Although the controversy was resolved in a way that settled conservatives' fears, the confusion further increased the atmosphere of hostility and distrust.

LAMBETH: THE SEXUALITY DEBATE

The Lambeth debate on human sexuality has been well documented by a number of sources; all agree that the proceedings fulfilled most, if not all, of conservatives' hopes.[25] The effort to unite opponents of homosexuality behind one resolution text was largely successful. Although several regional groups (including West Africa and East Africa) had composed sexuality resolutions, these were quickly put aside and a strong bloc coalesced around the main resolution text produced by the sexuality study group. However, this text, in its original form, did not make a strong enough statement against homosexuality to satisfy many Southern bishops. Tanzanian Archbishop Donald Mtetemela proposed an amendment stating that the Anglican Communion "rejects homosexual practice as incompatible with Scripture." In speaking for this amendment, Mtetemela said that without it the resolution would be weak and would "not state the position of the African communion." After some debate, Mtetemela's amendment passed by 389 to 190 votes. That strong majority gave confidence to orthodox bishops, and several more amendments strengthening the resolution's statements against homosexuality were quickly proposed and voted in. A clause condemning homophobia was altered to a condemnation of "irrational fear of homosexuals," since some conservative bishops felt "homophobia" implied any objections to homosexuality, including their own. A clause recommending "chastity" for any unmarried Christian was changed to "abstinence" when Bishop John Sentamu, a Ugandan serving in England, argued that this was unclear because it is possible to define some sexual relationships as chaste.

The tone of this debate, according to several bishops who were present, was notably less cordial than other Lambeth debates. One commentator describes a bishop who spoke in favor of softening the resolution's language being hissed and booed. Bishop William Swing of the Diocese of

California wrote later, "The feeling level in the debate was actually a lot worse than the final resolution. It was worse than liberal vs. Conservative; it was Black vs. White, Imperialists vs. The natives, North vs. South. It was raw."[26] But despite the hostile atmosphere and the apparent strong support for a clear conservative statement on homosexuality, two amendments were passed that limited the harshness of the resolution text. First, Canadian Archbishop Michael Peers proposed an amendment stating that the Conference "notes the significance of the Kuala Lumpur Statement on Human Sexuality," hoping to forestall the proposing of an amendment which would fully adopt the harshly antihomosexual Kuala Lumpur Statement as the normative Anglican position.[27] Another amendment added a commitment on the part of the Lambeth bishops to "listen to the experience of homosexual people."

The final text of Resolution 1.10 read:

This Conference:

(a) commends to the Church the sub-section report on human sexuality;

(b) in view of the teaching of Scripture, upholds faithfulness in marriage between a man and a woman in lifelong union, and believes that abstinence is right for those who are not called to marriage;

(c) recognizes that there are among us persons who experience themselves as having a homosexual orientation. Many of these are members of the Church and are seeking the pastoral care, moral direction of the Church and God's transforming power for the living of their lives and the ordering of relationships, and we commend ourselves to listen to the experience of homosexual people. We wish to assure them that they are loved by God and that all baptised, believing and faithful persons, regardless of sexual orientation, are full members of the Body of Christ;

(d) while rejecting homosexual practice as incompatible with Scripture, calls on all our people to minister pastorally and sensitively to all irrespective of sexual orientation and to condemn irrational fear of homosexuals, violence within marriage and any trivialization and commercialization of sex;

(e) cannot advise the legitimizing or blessing of same-sex unions, nor ordaining of those involved in same-gender unions;

(f) requests the Primates and the ACC to establish a means of monitoring the work done on the subject of human sexuality in the Communion and to share statements and resources among us;

(g) notes the significance of the Kuala Lumpur Statement and the concerns expressed in resolutions IV.26, V.1, V.10, V.23, and V.35 on the authority of Scripture in matters of marriage and sexuality and asks the Primates and the ACC to include them in their monitoring process.[28]

The amended text passed with 526 votes in favor, 70 opposed, and 45 abstentions. Lambeth 1998 had accomplished what it would be known for around the world and through the years: for "rejecting homosexual practice as incompatible with Scripture" by a landslide vote, to the delight of many and the horror and grief of many others. Although the resolution, like all Lambeth resolutions, is nonbinding on the Communion's provinces, such an overwhelming vote carried considerable moral authority.

The landslide vote demands some explanation. Nearly all Southern bishops voted for the resolution, as well as all Northern bishops who opposed church acceptance of homosexuality. These numbers, however, do not fully account for the overwhelmingly favorable vote—many moderate and even liberal bishops from North America, Europe, and elsewhere voted for the resolution as well. Several explained later that they realized they were outnumbered by conservative bishops and feared that if this resolution did not pass, something more condemnatory might be passed instead. This resolution text was restrained enough for liberals and moderates to focus on a few bright spots, such as the clauses about listening to the experience of homosexuals and ministering pastorally to all people regardless of sexual orientation.

As expected, African bishops played a major role in the Lambeth plenary debate and vote on the sexuality resolution. Many participants and observers noted the diversity of support for the sexuality resolution, in contrast with the almost exclusively Anglo opposition (probably including some bishops from North America, Europe, Australia, New Zealand, and possibly South Africa). Robert Stowe England points out the rather weak participation in the sexuality debate by American bishops, and observes of the final vote, "When [plenary chair Archbishop Eames] called for those favoring the resolution, a multiracial sea of hands went up across the plenary hall. The no votes were scattered and nearly all white. Finally, the abstentions, mostly white, were sparser still."[29] Ezra, a Ugandan bishop, made a similar observation in recalling the scene for me four years later, as we sat discussing Anglican Communion politics in his office: "Those who are supporting [homosexuality], all of them, we saw their white hands up! . . . . But when they said, those who are opposed, those who are not supporting those things, those supporting Resolution 1.10 [the amended resolution]: Black, Asian, white—I mean, all of them. There were many." This racial division was widely interpreted as further evidence of North/South division in the Anglican Communion—and of the greater legitimacy of the position endorsed by Southern leaders, due to their diversity and numbers.

Is Globalization Really Westernization?

What are the realities behind this apparent overlap of moral and global polarizations? Is Southern Anglicanism fundamentally opposed to homosexuality? Or, as some Northern liberals have argued, have Northern conservatives simply persuaded Southern Anglicans to take up their own views on homosexuality?

These questions reflect one major debate over globalization: whether it constitutes Westernization or Western neocolonialism—whether the processes of globalization are fundamentally about the spread of Western cultural and economic hegemony or dominance.[30] Scholarly critics point out that the transnational flows of globalization are asymmetrical, biased in the direction of West-to-Rest or North-to-South. The dynamics of globalization, some argue, are thus the dynamics of cultural imposition and adoption, and corresponding loss of diversity, as explored in the literature on "McDonaldization" and related phenomena.[31]

Other scholars and activists argue that this focus on Westernization is too simple a view of global cultural and economic practices, and makes non-Western peoples seem passive receivers of Western culture. Many ethnographic studies explore the processes of indigenization, or local interpretation, by which societies around the world grasp international commodities, media images, and ideologies and make them their own—as in the appropriation of American praise music by some Ugandan Anglicans as "authentically African." Furthermore, some argue that globalization can create differentiation as well as sameness, through the relativization of identities that can cause groups to set themselves apart more sharply, as well as by offering people and groups more cultural alternatives to choose from in constructing their identities and shaping their lives.[32] In addition, the flows of globalization, while tending to asymmetry, are not all one-way; some non-Western ideas, products, and people enter global circulation and affect the West. Some observers go so far as to argue that these processes may actually unsettle the West's traditional position of power, disrupting "the cultural certainties and fixities of the metropole."[33] In their recent review of theories of globalization, Jonathan Xavier Inda and Renato Rosaldo argue that unchallenged Western cultural dominance no longer exists in the world; instead, the West now has to compete with other cultural centers.[34] Such developments bring hope to the many people—both scholars and ordinary citizens, both left- and right-leaning in social and moral commitments—who share the view that the West (or global North) has been dominant long enough.

The same debates over the cultural implications of globalization appear in the literature on global religion. In *Exporting the American Gospel: Global Christian Fundamentalism*, Steve Brouwer, Paul Gifford, and Susan Rose argue for the Westernization view, casting the rise of fundamentalist and especially prosperity-gospel movements in the global South as primarily the result of American neocolonialism.[35] Joel Robbins offers an extensive review of the literature on the globalization of Pentecostalism, including some works describing this trend as Westernization and others describing it as indigenization. He writes, "[Pentecostal/charismatic Christianity] appears to weigh in both for theories that stress processes of Western cultural domination and homogenization and those that emphasize the transformative power of indigenous appropriation."[36]

Most Anglicans, Northern, Southern, liberal, or conservative, express hopes that globalization will bring greater affirmation of cultural diversity, not greater homogeneity. Consequently, one of the major debates over the transnational alliances between Northern conservatives and Southern Anglicans concerns whether such alliances serve primarily to spread Northern hegemony by colonizing the Southern churches with Northern moral debates, or, alternatively, strengthen indigenous Southern Anglican voices by providing resources and outlets for sharing Southern perspectives with the global church. Few dispute that there are now many more Anglicans in the global South than in the global North, and that the power structures of the Anglican Communion ought to shift and give these Southern provinces a greater role in worldwide Anglican affairs. But is such a process actually occurring? Or are these alliances and activism better understood, as some critics have argued, as the result of Northern exploitation of the moral authority of Southern Anglicans to advance one side in what is essentially a Northern debate? Many Northern liberals and moderates fear that Northern conservatives are co-opting and using Southern Anglicans for their own goals. In contrast, Northern conservatives and Southern church leaders argue that their alliances represent the development of more cosmopolitan, globally aware Anglican identities and a profound unsettling of traditional Northern dominance in the Anglican Communion. Conservative Episcopal commentator Richard Kew wrote following Lambeth 1998, "The older provinces might still have more than their fair share of material resources, but it is the churches of Africa, Asia, and Latin America, who are now easing themselves into the driver's seat."[37]

The reality is more complex than either of these perspectives suggests. In Anglicanism as in the world at large, both Westernization and de-Westernization processes often occur simultaneously—at different levels, in differing sites, or from different angles of observation. The processes of globalization in the Anglican Communion that brought Southern bishops to such influential involvement at Lambeth 1998 did not merely consist in the exporting of American views of, and conflicts over, homosexuality. The Northern and Southern parties in the global orthodox Anglican movement have collaborated in creating shared identities and agendas that articulate the particular concerns, ideas, and situations of Anglicans in Africa as well as in the United States. African bishops' responses to issues arising in international contexts like Lambeth are most fundamentally shaped, not by the convictions of their Northern conservative partners, but by the concerns of their own churches, their primary responsibility. An understanding of Southern bishops' Lambeth votes must therefore begin, not from the polarized politics of the Lambeth debate, but from the more complex cultural and political contexts of the churches in Uganda, Tanzania, South East Asia, and other Southern provinces.

African Anglicanisms: The Martyrs of Uganda and Ugandan Views on Homosexuality

Every year on June 3, the Martyrs of Uganda are honored with services and celebrations at separate Catholic and Protestant shrines in the town of Namugongo, near Kampala. Martyrs' Day commemorates the deaths of forty-some Baganda converts to Christianity, young men who served in the royal court and were killed in 1885 and 1886 at the command of the kabaka or Baganda king. The Ugandan paper New Vision estimated that half a million pilgrims, from Uganda, Tanzania, Kenya, and even Europe, attended the Martyrs' Day celebrations in 2001.[38] When I visited the Catholic shrine on Martyrs' Day of the next year, I found the crush of people so intense that it was almost necessary to step over the omnipresent vendors' blankets, spread with Martyrs' Day memorabilia. The shrine for the Protestants had a similarly bustling, carnival atmosphere. The hillside facing the Namugongo Anglican church was thick with worshipers, seated on mats to listen to the four-hour-long service held in the Martyrs' honor. There was plenty to see apart from the service: food, drink, and religious books for sale; people playing music on the sidelines; and an opportunity to tour the reproduction Executioner's Hut and life-size plaster model of the Martyrs on the pyre, ready for burning.

In recent years, as public conversation about homosexuality has taken shape within Ugandan society and the worldwide Anglican Communion, the Martyrs have often been invoked as icons of African resistance to homosexuality. British historian Kevin Ward gives an account of how the Martyrs became the victims of Kabaka Mwanga: "The trigger for this purge was the refusal, at the urging of older Christian pages, by one of the youngest boys . . . to submit to the sexual demands of the Kabaka Mwanga."[39] Ward stresses, however, that homosexual practice should be seen as, at most, a trigger, and not as the central issue in conflicts between the Kabaka and the nascent Christian community: "Fears that Baganda Christian converts were disloyal and were acting as spies, and that Europeans were poised to undermine the state, were much more important."[40] Detailed accounts of the martyrdoms tend to stress other factors, treating the sexual issue as only one conflict among many. Both *Namugongo: From Shame to Glory*, an English/Luganda booklet by an Anglican priest, and a Catholic account, Francis Marion's *New African Saints: The Twenty-Two Martyrs of Uganda*, offer many reasons for the executions and stress the martyrs' faith as the central message of the episode.[41]

Other discussions of the Martyrs' significance in Ugandan society take a very different approach, also not focused on sexuality. The Martyrs' heroism has been questioned in the context of wider societal debates over nationalism, outside influences, cultural authenticity, and power. Features on the Martyrs in Ugandan newspapers regularly question whether Kabaka Mwanga is the real hero, rather than the Martyrs, for resisting foreign cultural and political intrusions. Ward notes that such themes have been central in conversations about the Martyrs for decades.[42] Given the fact that the Martyrs are not infrequently held up as cultural traitors for accepting Christianity, it is ironic that in the context of Anglican debates over sexuality they have come to symbolize African resistance to Western cultural encroachment, in the form of tolerance toward homosexuality.

TALKING ABOUT HOMOSEXUALITY IN AFRICA

Since the early 1990s Uganda, like many Southern societies, has seen the rise of both liberation movements for sexual minorities and overt oppression against them. Scholars Elizabeth Povinelli and George Chauncey note the global spread of gay and lesbian movements: "Postcolonial nations [are] witnessing the emergence of sex-based social movements whose political rhetoric and tactics [seem] to mimic or reproduce Euro-American forms of sexual identity, subjectivity, and citizenship."[43] In part this trend is due to media globalization; Northern television and movies depict and normalize identities and behaviors that are viewed, marked, learned, and inwardly digested as potential identity resources by people in contexts outside the global North. The Internet, too, provides access to new information, images, and discourses. Sexual identities, including gay and lesbian identities, are part of this dispersion of Northern cultural roles and mores. Rudolf Gaudio, in a conference paper on homosexuality in Nigeria, noted that media globalization gives people many resources for cross-cultural identification and self-fashioning.[44]

Another factor in the rise in public debates over homosexuality worldwide is increased international activism regarding homosexuality as a human rights issue. The activism of (largely Northern-led) bodies like the International Lesbian and Gay Association (ILGA), the International Gay and Lesbian Human Rights Commission (IGLHRC), smaller gay-rights–focused bodies, and human-rights organizations who occasionally take up gay-rights issues (such as Human Rights Watch) has created greater international awareness of gay and lesbian identities and greater political tensions over their acceptance or suppression.[45]

Joseph Massad introduces a useful concept, borrowed from Michel Foucault, regarding the impact of all this in Southern societies: that of "incitement to discourse." Activism or interventions by Northern NGOs, formation of a local gay-rights group inspired by Northern media or sibling organizations, or politicians' public statements about homosexuality in response to the issue's rising salience elsewhere may all serve to incite an intensification of discourse over homosexuality within a given society. Massad explains that, prior to the incitement to discourse on homosexuality of the mid-1990s, "same-sex contact between men has not been a topic of governmental or journalistic discourse" in the Arab world for two centuries.[46]

Likewise, same-sex sexual contact had not generally been the subject of governmental and journalistic discourse in much of Africa until the 1990s. In the mid-1990s, this lack of attention began to change. Zimbabwe, under Robert Mugabe, was one of the first African states where homosexuality became the subject of public debate. Antihomosexual language appeared in the state-sponsored Zimbabwean press in 1994 and 1995, in relation to a controversy over whether the organization Gays and Lesbians of Zimbabwe (GALZ) could have a booth at a national book fair.[47] The outspokenness of Mugabe and his government and press inspired "international imitation" in neighboring countries, including Zambia, Namibia, and Botswana.[48] Governmental and journalistic antihomosexuality rhetoric, along with the coalescing of political gay identities, thus spread from country to country.

Uganda's public debate over homosexuality arose relatively late in terms of this larger picture, but nonetheless emphatically. Homosexuality became a recurring issue in the Ugandan press and government statements in mid-1998—the same time that the issue was being discussed and debated at Lambeth 1998, likely no coincidence. President Yoweri Museveni made several strong antihomosexuality public statements that summer. Discourse on the issue quieted somewhat in early 1999, before re-erupting with the publication of news stories on an alleged gay wedding in Kampala. Museveni again spoke out strongly, calling for the police to find, arrest, and jail homosexuals. The Anglican archbishop of Uganda proclaimed his full support for Museveni's antigay position.[49] In late 2000 and early 2001, the formation of a group for gay and lesbian Anglicans brought the debate over the place of homosexuality in Uganda to the headlines again.

Stating that same-sex sexual expression was not publicly discussed prior to the 1990s is not the same as stating that such sexual expression did not exist. A growing body of literature traces the elusive contours of diverse African sexual identities and desires, past and present.[50] It is difficult, however, to come to any clear conclusions about the character of same-sex-oriented sexual practices in Africa before the colonial period. Much of the writing on this topic is polemical, either discovering or denying indigenous African same-sex desires—a polemicism made all the easier by the paucity of sources.

Ward notes that the silence in African history on the matter of same-sex desire could indicate either absence or unspoken tolerance.[51] On the basis of his reading of the available literature, Ward concludes that various forms of same-sex relations have always been part of many African societies, though usually defined in terms of behavior or stage in life, rather than as stable individual identities (on the model of contemporary Northern gay and lesbian identities). Ward cites an elderly Ugandan who told a questioner that "people with homosexual tendencies have always been there," though they were regarded as misfits. I encountered a few such remarks in my own interviewing—for example, in the course of my conversation with Ephraim, a Ugandan bishop whom I met when he visited UCU for a ceremony opening a new campus building. Ephraim voted with the majority at Lambeth 1998, and is convinced that homosexual behavior goes against the teaching of scripture, but he does not feel strongly on the matter and was honestly curious about my point of view. Concerning homosexuality in Africa, he told me, "We cannot deny these things. . . . I don't think we can say we have learnt it; it is part of us. Part of us."

Even Ugandans who believe that there has always been homosexuality in Africa share the perception that there is growing pressure from the global North to accept homosexuality as an equally valid alternative lifestyle. Many Ugandans perceive the incitement to discourse over homosexuality in their country—the dramatic increase in talk about homosexuality since the late 1990s—as due largely to the influence of outside forces, including outright activism, the implicit values propagated by donor agencies, media images of Northern sexual liberation, and Northern evangelists preaching against sexual liberation. Accordingly, in Ugandan public discourse the growth in talk about homosexuality in Uganda (which is undeniable) is often glossed as a growth in the actual phenomenon of homosexuality in Uganda (which is unverifiable). For example, several Ugandans voiced to me the belief that Ugandan youth in boarding schools learn homosexuality from Northern propagandistic mailings. These statements suggest an epidemiological view of homosexuality as an acquired or learned trait, at both the individual and the societal level: as individuals are exposed to these practices and "converted," Ugandan society as a whole is also increasingly influenced. In a 2001 interview Archbishop Nkoyooyo used such epidemiological language about homosexuality: "I don't know what the cause of this disease [homosexuality] is. I just pray it does not hit epidemic levels."[52]

Whether it is homosexual practice that is seen as spreading throughout Ugandan society, or the idea of homosexuality as an acceptable alternative orientation, matters little to those who oppose homosexuality, since both are viewed negatively. The debate over homosexuality in Uganda is as much over outside influences and the cultural and economic power of the North as it is about the morality of same-sex desire. Massad writes about the arrest of several gays in Egypt, "it is not same-sex sexual practices that are being repressed by the Egyptian police but rather the sociopolitical identification of those practices with the Northern identity of gayness and the publicness that these gay-identified men seek."[53] President Museveni spoke along much the same lines in 2002. Responding to worldwide public outcry over his claim at an international meeting that there are no homosexuals in Uganda, Museveni softened his stance, acknowledging the existence of gay Ugandans but expressing his desire for them to keep to themselves: "In an apparent U-turn Museveni now says he does not have a problem with his queer countrymen, as long as they 'did it quietly' the news agency quoted him as saying. He blamed the west for Ugandan gays and lesbians asserting themselves 'in the open.'"[54] I heard many Ugandan church leaders express the same view: that the real issue is not sexual practice or desire per se, but the rise in Uganda of a politicized gay identity with strong Northern associations. Homosexuality has thus become one of the key points at which Ugandan leaders seek to express their ideological independence from Northern cultural influences.

In Africa and other formerly colonized settings, resisting homosexuality is often tied to nationalism and cultural nativism. Homosexuality is perceived or at least described in such contexts as a form of corruption or degradation associated with the colonizing power (in spite of the fact that antihomosexuality attitudes and laws were often adopted from colonizing powers). In a piece entitled "A Lambeth Background Guide," the Rev. You-Leng Lim, a liberal priest in the Diocese of Los Angeles who was born and raised in Singapore, argues that heterosexism and condemnation of homosexuality are reactions against Singapore's colonial past, not elements of its traditional culture.[55] The rejection of homosexuality is thus understood, in Singapore and in many other postcolonial societies, as a reassertion of the value and purity of indigenous culture and a rejection of continued neocolonial influences. Appearing to reject Northern cultural influence can be even more important for Christian leaders, since Christianity itself is criticized in some postcolonial contexts as a negative Northern cultural influence.

Blaming the North for propagating homosexuality in African nations is often quite politically effective, because it ties the homosexuality issue to deep-seated concerns and resonant discourses over neocolonialism and the maintenance of authentic African culture and morality. Further, cases in which Northern NGOs, governments, and journalists have pressured African leaders or institutions to be more tolerant of homosexuality—for example, the clamor in the world press over Museveni's assertion of the absence of homosexuals in Uganda—provide apparent substantiation for such leaders' assertions that homosexuality is being forced on Africa by Northern gay interests.

Ugandan and other African bishops' votes for the sexuality resolution and their willing adoption of homosexuality as an issue before Lambeth should be understood in light of the rising discourse over homosexuality in many of their home countries. Many African bishops came to Kuala Lumpur, Dallas, Kampala, and Canterbury with some sense of homosexuality as a looming threat encroaching on their societies and churches. Northern conservative Episcopalians presented these leaders with a picture of the worldwide Anglican Communion, through the influence of ECUSA, as one more channel through which the rising tide of homosexuality might creep into their countries. Taking a strong stand against homosexuality at Lambeth may have appeared to many African leaders as an opportunity to set clear standards on an issue of growing urgency, even if homosexuality had not yet or had only recently become politically salient in their home societies.

It is in the context of such growing concerns about homosexuality in Uganda and elsewhere in Africa that the sexual aspect of the Martyrs' story took on a new prominence, in new, global settings. The Martyrs were mentioned at Lambeth during the flare-up over the canceled presentation by gay and lesbian Christians. The secular press quoted Bishop Mutebi of Uganda speaking out against homosexuality, and cited the Martyrs as if in explanation of Mutebi's stand. The *Daily Telegraph*, for example, explained: "Uganda has 22 Christian martyrs who were killed in 1885 by their king because they refused to be sodomised by him."[56] The point of the Martyrs' story, as invoked in such pieces, is not that Uganda has a history of committed Christian faith, but that Uganda has a history of saying "no" to sodomy. Other Africans, too, invoked the

Martyrs at Lambeth as symbols of antihomosexual sentiment. The West African proposed sexuality resolution read in part: "This Conference, noting that . . . . (iv) some African Christians in Uganda were martyred in the 19th century for refusing to have homosexual relations with the king because of their faith in the Lord Jesus and their commitment to stand by the Word of God as expressed in the Bible on the subject; stands on the Biblical authority and accepts that homosexuality is a sin."[57] This resolution was quickly abandoned in favor of the resolution text that was ultimately amended and passed. So ended the Martyrs' brief appearance on the central stage of world Anglicanism, but while there they had carried the message with which they had been entrusted: that African Christians will never accept homosexual practice.

UGANDAN PERSPECTIVES ON HOMOSEXUALITY

The realities of Ugandan (and other African) perspectives on homosexuality, however, are more complex than this image of stark zero-tolerance. The issue of homosexuality in Uganda is more like the Martyrs' story as it has traditionally been told, and debated, in Uganda: complicated, ambiguous, rife with questions of outside cultural influence and power, and characterized by broad differences of opinion among people of conscience and conviction.

In his article on East African opinions about homosexuality, Ward argues that homosexuality has not historically been a central moral concern in Ugandan society, and that even today there is no societal consensus on the issue: "When it is discussed, a range of popular attitudes are forthcoming, symptomatic of an issue about which there is, as yet, no clearly established norm."[58] My own observations during my fieldwork tend to confirm Ward's picture. Ward cites the range of views represented in the Ugandan papers as one piece of evidence of the lack of social consensus. I noted the same phenomenon while in Uganda, through my archival newspaper research and tracking ongoing news and editorial coverage. Articles in the Ugandan papers during Lambeth 1998 covered a range of views, including a short piece entitled "Gays, just come out, fame awaits," arguing that what Uganda lacks is not gays but gay pride; an anonymous letter to the editor entitled "I'm gay! And it's my right to be!," observing that people argue against the writer's "acquired Western un-African practice" by referring to Christianity, another acquired Western practice; and an editorial column praising the role of African bishops in the passage of the Lambeth sexuality resolution and saying that Ugandans now need to face the "scourge" of homosexuality in Uganda.[59]

Newspaper coverage, of course, does not provide a direct index of societal and individual sentiments, but articles, opinion pieces, and letters to the editor give some indication of the main positions on the issue, and interviews and other data have enabled me to fill out this picture. The debate over homosexuality in Uganda, as in many Southern contexts, borrows its contours and content to a significant degree from the parallel Northern debate. Advocates of gay and lesbian rights adopt and adapt language and arguments from the Northern gay rights movement; opponents draw on Northern conservative, especially religious conservative, resources.[60] However, the homosexuality debates in Uganda or elsewhere are not simply imports or duplications of Northern debates. Ugandan pro-gay rights and antihomosexuality positions may line up roughly with Northern liberal and conservative positions, but the correspondence is far from complete.

The Ugandan strong antigay position can be summed up in the words of a Zimbabwean I once heard quoted on BBC Network Africa: "It's not natural, it's not moral, and it's not African!" The argument that homosexuality is "not natural" is common in Uganda. Like Northern evangelicals, Ugandans argue that homosexuality goes against the created order. But rather than the scientistic arguments about genes and psychology often heard in Northern debates, Ugandans' arguments tend to be earthier, relying on birds-and-bees analogies—perhaps not surprising in a church in which many bishops own cattle and goats. Bishop Ezekiel, for example, turned to the natural world when explaining his opposition to homosexuality to me: "We are asking: is the God who created human beings, is he the God who created other creatures? If he's the God who created people, the same God who created animals and birds and insects, why is it that . . . he did not put in those creatures those ingredients that persuaded them to have sex with the same sex?" As well as being unnatural, homosexuality is "not moral," in the view of many Ugandan and other African leaders. This argument closely parallels Northern evangelical assertions that homosexuality is clearly prohibited in scripture and that biblical truth cannot be bent or changed.

Finally, an important argument for African church leaders is that homosexuality is "not African," an argument with no direct analogue in the American debate. This argument is implicit, for example, in the assertion that there are no words for "homosexuality" or "lesbianism" in African languages. I heard this assertion from several Ugandan consultants, and have seen it in conservative Northern texts as well; it serves more as an ideological assertion than as a linguistic observation. Such "it's not African" statements have taken their place in Uganda's developing public antihomosexuality discourse. The "not African" argument gains much of its potency from the broader context, in Uganda and across the postcolonial world, of ambivalence about Northern influences and suspicion of Northern power. Questions about Northern influence on African churches, particularly in reference to homosexuality, can become particularly loaded in parts of Africa (unlike Uganda) where competition with Islam is intense. Accusations of Northern influence have become weapons in the competition between Christianity and Islam for converts, and Christianity faces a tougher struggle to shake off its image as the "white man's religion."

Although some Ugandans hold passionately to a strong antihomosexuality position, my observations and interviewing gave me the impression that a majority of Ugandans held a milder antihomosexuality view. Many people are ambivalent toward what they see as hedonistic Northern cultural values, but implicit in statements rejecting Northern values is often a sort of cultural relativism. Such relativism can be heard even in strong statements like that of a Nigerian bishop at Lambeth: "We are being oppressed with this issue of homosexuality, which is a Western problem. If the Western Churches want to be homosexual, they should not make us change as well."[61] More generally, many Ugandans spoke as if the question for them is whether homosexuality should be allowed or encouraged in Uganda or Africa, not whether homosexuality should be permitted anywhere.

But even in contemplating homosexuality within their own society, many Ugandans seemed to lack personal emotional investment in the issue—unlike many Americans, for whom it is a hot-button issue of social polarization. Most of my consultants raised the issue of homosexuality spontaneously during our interviews; apparently it came readily to mind when we began talking about the Anglican Communion and the Episcopal Church. The majority expressed opposition to homosexuality, but many didn't show strong feeling about it. One man told me calmly, "Oh, we don't accept homosexuals here. We stone them." Although it was chilling to hear this statement made so coolly, his calm tone probably reflected the fact that my consultant was simply telling me the way things were, not expressing any passionately felt personal position. The relatively free debate in the newspapers, too, shows that while general social sentiment (and Ugandan law) may oppose homosexuality, there is not such unanimous opposition to homosexuality that there is no space for public debate. There are known gay hangouts in Kampala, also suggesting a limited degree of tolerance.

In addition to postcolonial ambivalences about Northern cultural influences, other factors shaping the Ugandan Anglican mildly negative view of homosexuality likely include attitudes toward sexual "misfits" carried over from the country's traditional cultures; the evangelical biblicism of the missionaries who evangelized the area; and the East African

Revival stress on sexual purity.[62] However, the heritage of the East African Revival may actually be a moderating influence on antihomosexuality sentiment. East African Revival spirituality, while heightening sensitivity to sin, seems also to increase tolerance of the sinner. I found that some Balokole (Revival adherents) were surprisingly tolerant, perhaps because Balokole fellowships stress that everyone has sin to overcome. One Mulokole (Revivalist) I interviewed, a middle-aged layman and a leader in his home parish, told me his opinion of the Lambeth sexuality debate: "Those who were for not practicing homosexuality in the church ended on a good note which I liked, that they should not condemn them. Instead they should be pastoral, . . . talk to them, counsel them, love them, but not condemn them, say, 'Out of my church!' "

Two Balokole were among the handful of Ugandans who asked me about my views on homosexuality.[63] One of these, an older layman who had been active in his Balokole fellowship for decades, sat and drank soda with me in the cafeteria of the Namirembe guesthouse. We talked at length about the cultural trends he found puzzling in the world today, and the changes in cultural mores he had witnessed in Uganda; within the context of this broader conversation, homosexuality was clearly not a huge issue in his mind. The second of these Mulokole was Bishop Ephraim, who questioned me closely concerning why Northern heterosexuals would support the cause of tolerance and rights for gays and lesbians, a puzzle which he assured me had caused himself and his colleagues a great deal of perplexity. A few other consultants indicated to me that they felt they did not understand the issue well enough to have a firm opinion. Ward suggests that another moderating influence on Ugandan attitudes about sexuality in general may have been the strain of living up to European Christian ideals in an impoverished colonial context, which he argues may have inculcated a degree of tolerance in Ugandan Christians with respect to matters of sexual morality.[64]

Besides some emphatic antihomosexuality positions, and a wide range of milder or less-formed antihomosexuality positions, Ugandan society also possesses a nascent liberal position regarding homosexuality. Ward observes, "In urban settings, more recognisably modern forms of [homosexual identity] have begun to emerge. . . . [but] so far in East Africa the emergence of a self-consciously gay community of people is in its infancy."[65] While in Uganda, my husband and I had the opportunity to get to know one such newly formed community: the small Anglican gay-rights group, Integrity-Uganda. This group was formed in 2001, with some help from the American Episcopal Integrity group, in order to reach out to and advocate for Ugandan gays and lesbians. The controversy surrounding its founding is discussed in chapter 7.

When I made e-mail contact with one of the group's leaders, a young Anglican priest whom I will call Frank, he invited me and my husband, Phil, to a meal at his home. A week later we shared a meal of fish stew, fresh avocado, and fruit with Frank, his wife Alice, and another young couple—Edward, a layman also involved with the group, and his girl-friend. Frank and Edward both got involved in gay and lesbian issues through pastoral work with young people. They found some were coming to them with questions about their sexual orientation, and through these encounters, they began to rethink their own understandings of sexuality. Edward asked us whether left-handed people used to be punished in our society. When we answered affirmatively, he told us the same was true in Uganda, and that he now sees homosexuality as a natural variation within a population, just like left-handedness. Increasingly convinced that gay youth should be not treated as sinners but instead welcomed and coun-seled, Frank found a retired bishop willing to help, and so the organiza-tion Integrity-Uganda was born. Frank noted the irony that the first public gay-rights organization in Uganda was founded by straight people: "It's even been a surprise to the international [gay] community. They didn't know we would be willing to walk into deep waters for them."

The setting for our meal and conversation was Frank and Alice's small village home. Not far away, on a small dirt road outside the village, mem-bers and sympathizers of Integrity-Uganda were volunteering their efforts to build a tiny office and chapel for the group. Frank hoped that situating the office in the countryside would protect it; he and Alice moved out to this area themselves after leaving their larger house in Kampala when the controversy and media attention became too intense, and both lost their jobs due to their association with a gay group. Alice has found work again, but no one in the Church of Uganda will employ Frank. As we rode back into Kampala together, squeezed close in the back seat of a public taxi van, Edward told us that all the publicity was actually good for their cause because it raised so much awareness. The Integrity-Uganda post office box got many letters from gay Ugandans saying they wished they could find others like themselves, and even from straight people wish-ing they could help. Edward concluded, "We used to think, in Uganda, there were only heterosexuals. We are learning, learning so much."

As more Ugandans, heterosexual and homosexual, take the risk of nam-ing their sexual identities or voicing acceptance of homosexuality in the Ugandan public sphere, the liberal Ugandan position continues to take shape. Arguments and statements in newspaper articles suggest elements of this Ugandan liberal position, which in some ways reflects Northern rhetoric and in others represents a particularly African and Ugandan form of pro–gay-rights positioning. For example, the assertion of the natural-ness of homosexuality (and the denial that it is a Northern innovation or imposition) parallels Northern arguments, but the differentiation made by the liberal Ugandans we met between "situational" homosexuals (influenced by prison or single-sex schools) and "essential" homosexuals has little parallel in American pro–gay-rights discourse.

Thus although discourse about homosexuality has gained more in public prominence in Uganda since 1998, the issue is still not central in Ugandan society—or in the other African societies that reflect a roughly similar situation. Homosexuality commands medium-tier headlines when issues arise, and shows up on editorial pages periodically, but was not mentioned, for example, in one UCU class's recent assemblage of essays about the most pressing concerns for Ugandans today. Contrary to the impressions of many Northerners, and despite its salience in international contexts, homosexuality is not a driving concern of Ugandan and other African Christians on a daily basis.

GLOBALIZATION: DIFFERING MOTIVES FOR TRANSNATIONAL ALLIANCES OVER HOMOSEXUALITY

The views of Ugandan Anglicans—including Ugandan bishops—on homosexuality are not uniform, and even Ugandan antihomosexuality views are shaped by Uganda's history and context and do not directly reflect American conservative views. Nevertheless many American liberals accuse conservatives of co-opting African Anglicans, persuading them to support their views and thereby perpetuating the cultural colonization of the global South. In contrast, Northern conservatives defend these alliances against charges of spreading Northern hegemony. They insist instead that the interests they share with Southern Anglicans are signs of a new global order in which cultural difference and geographical distance are rendered irrelevant by shared convictions. From this point of view, the North's traditional position of superiority is radically decentered by these alliances, as Northern conservatives find allies and even leaders among Anglicans in the global South.

Examining the range of issues surrounding homosexuality in one Southern society, contemporary Uganda, allows us to move beyond these polarized positions and into a more grounded look at how and why particular constituencies come to collaborate cross-culturally on an issue—or not. Although alliances with Southern Anglicans have served the interests of Northern conservatives at Lambeth and beyond, these alliances are not therefore simple cases of cultural colonization or exploitation. Nor does it make sense to attribute these alliances to a basic similarity between the Northern and Southern constituencies involved; clearly much about Ugandan and other African cultural situations and moral discourses is quite distinct from those of the contemporary United States.

Ugandan church leaders' willingness to collaborate with Northern conservatives was due both to generally shared views on homosexuality and to Ugandans' concerns with asserting cultural purity and Christian orthodoxy in the face of Northern influences. Many Africans and Americans share perceptions of homosexuality as unnatural and immoral. Further, testimonies by American "ex-gays," who define themselves as having been healed of homosexuality, carry weight with African Christian leaders, perhaps because confessing sin and testifying to transformation through faith are important speech genres in many African churches (including the East African Revival tradition). Because of such commonalities, Northern conservatives have been successful in cultivating alliances with African church leaders. Stephen Noll's call at the Dallas conference for Southern leaders to help prevent the acceptance of homosexuality in the Anglican Communion resonated with what many Southern church leaders had heard of homosexuality as an encroaching trend in their home countries. Many Southern church leaders accepted Northern conservatives' assurances of the urgency of this issue and began to articulate stronger negative views. American and African Anglicans have thus managed to develop a sense of unity regarding homosexuality sufficient to encourage and sustain relationships across considerable differences and distances—relationships that would probably never have developed, certainly not to their current extent, without that unifying and motivating issue.

The exchange model, often cited by those involved in these relationships, also helps explain this cross-provincial collaboration. In the case of Lambeth, Northerners provided material resources by funding meetings and informational materials to help African bishops prepare for Lambeth, while African bishops placed the weight of their voting bloc behind Northern conservatives' push for a conservative sexuality resolution—which most likely would have supported in any case, but perhaps with less vehemence and unanimity. This collaboration had benefits for all concerned: Northern conservatives were satisfied with the resolution, while African Anglicans were pleased to have been a dominant force at a gathering of the worldwide Communion.

As for liberal Episcopalians, their success in building rapport with Southern Anglicans around the issue of homosexuality has been limited. Liberal Americans tend to see homosexuality as a liberation issue and thus as akin to the struggle of other marginalized peoples, including people of the global South, to be recognized by those in power in the current social, economic, and political order. One liberal Episcopal scholar told me that as he sees it, African Anglicans actually have a great deal in common with

Northern gays in their common experience of being excluded from the structures of religious institutions. Such common experiences, however, only have the power to produce feelings of solidarity if they are recognized as such. The scholarly literature on sexuality and postcolonial theory tends to focus on discovering local queer identities in Southern societies as part of an interpretive project focused on liberation—the voicing of the doubly suppressed identities of the queer and colonized.[66] However, the gay liberation/colonial liberation analogy does not resonate with many Southern Christians' thinking. The rejection of Northern influence in Ugandan society cuts the other way from Northern liberals' liberationist projects. Tolerance of homosexuality is seen as a Northern agenda, probably the single biggest factor in its *dis*favor. American liberals find this rejection of their proffered solidarity dismaying and confounding, and often react by explaining away African views and blaming Northern conservatives for indoctrinating Southern Anglicans, rather than seeking to understand how homosexuality functions as an issue in other cultural and political contexts around the world.[67]

LAMBETH AND UGANDA: THE AMAZING VANISHING DEBT ISSUE

At Lambeth 1998, the contrast between the "white hands up" in support of tolerating homosexuality and the broad multiracial support for a resolution opposing homosexual practice created the appearance of a South-versus-North vote, with a conservative Northern minority siding with the South. This vote was widely interpreted as a rebuke from the orthodox Anglican South to the liberal/moderate Northern churches. Such a view of Lambeth's dynamics as fundamentally defined by North/South tensions was influential at the Conference itself, shaping participants' perceptions of their fellow bishops and the Conference's events. But although some events at Lambeth did play out in North/South terms, others did not. In fact, most Southern Anglicans sided with the liberal/moderate North (and against many conservative Northerners) regarding the other dominant issue at Lambeth 1998, international debt. Probably because the debt issue never attracted as much press as the sexuality issue, that blurring of the liberal North/conservative South lines apparently did not shake the general sense that Lambeth was dominated by North/South tensions—a view that became even more entrenched in subsequent descriptions of Lambeth's implications, as the next chapter will make clear.

Leading into Lambeth, there was a strong consensus that international debt was one of two main issues, or even the main issue, for Lambeth 1998. An Episcopal Life headline stated, "Sexuality, Debt Loom as Concerns of World Bishops," and a Lambeth organizer commented before the

Conference, "The number-one concern to come from all the provinces, whether First World or Third World, is international debt."[68] The prominence given to debt in many pre-Lambeth articles reflects an assumption among Northern Anglicans that the new Southern Anglican majority would care deeply about this issue, because of its Southern impact and because some Southern leaders, like South African archbishop Njongonkulu Ndungane, had been outspoken on the need for debt forgiveness.

Given Northern expectations that Southern votes would be of central importance in the outcomes of Lambeth 1998, and assumptions that debt would be a motivational issue for Southern leaders, it was inevitable that the debt issue should become involved in bids for Southern loyalty by various Northern constituencies. Some Northern liberals and moderates hoped to keep the Conference's focus on issues of international debt, where they had a record of concern and activism—support for the Jubilee 2000 debt forgiveness initiative was particularly strong among Northern liberals—and felt on solid ground in terms of their engagement with Southern Christians. Accordingly, liberals were suspicious when Northern conservatives began to show interest in international debt by including it on the agenda at the pre-Lambeth Dallas conference. Some critics accused the American conservatives who hosted the conference of buying the loyalties of Southern bishops on the homosexuality question by declaring their support on the debt issue. In an article on Lambeth 1998, Ian Douglas gives one such account of the Dallas conference:

> Third World bishops, who were enjoying a free trip to the U.S. at the expense of the Ekklesia Society and the Diocese of Dallas, had more pressing concerns than the West's hang-up on sex, namely the sinfulness of Western capitalism and the international banking system. In a classic case of money for sex, the bishops from the Southern hemisphere traded their concern about international debt relief for the Americans' statement regarding traditional, "biblical" norms of sexuality.[69]

This view of the Dallas conference as a site of quid pro quo arrangements assumes that Southern Anglicans had to be persuaded to support the conservative position on homosexuality. But as I have argued, the task before American conservatives at the Dallas conference was not one of convincing Southern bishops to share their views—which many already did—but of persuading them that the homosexuality issue was *not* only a Northern problem, but had serious enough implications to deserve attention at the Lambeth Conference. Some Northern conservatives felt they should take up Southern concerns, in turn.

Evangelical Episcopalians' historical involvement in international missions may have given them a better awareness of Southern poverty than many mainstream Episcopalians, but engaging with poverty through missions is not the same as having a developed position on the issue of global poverty. During 1997 and 1998, American conservatives began to develop such a position. Rather than supporting the Jubilee 2000 initiative, which called for large-scale unconditional debt forgiveness in the year 2000, many conservatives felt they needed their own distinctive proposal for easing the debt burden. Episcopalian conservatives may have been partially motivated by a desire to differentiate themselves from Northern liberals, but they also had substantive problems with the Jubilee 2000 concept. Some objected to Jubilee 2000 as a shallow engagement with the problem of poverty.[70] Others objected to Jubilee 2000 on ideological grounds based in their social and economic conservatism, preferring market-based reforms to debt forgiveness, which they likened to welfare.[71]

In April 1998, Diane Knippers, a conservative Episcopalian and head of the Institute on Religion and Democracy, invited a number of conservative leaders to gather and develop their own approach to world poverty. Her letter makes it clear that a significant motivation for this engagement with international debt was the fear that American liberals would be able to use their demonstrated commitment to debt forgiveness to attract the loyalties of Southern Anglicans.

> There are signs that some left- leaning western bishops are trying to use the debt and poverty relief issues as a trade-off to persuade the African bishops to be more accepting of their homosexual agenda. We believe it is essential that several of the AAC bishops are able to engage the international debt and poverty issues knowledgeably and compellingly both because these are intrinsically important, but also because these issues are related to our ability to persuade two-thirds world bishops to address our moral and spiritual poverty.[72]

Conservatives like Knippers feared liberals would use the debt issue to push for acceptance of homosexuality (or at least avoid censure). Conservatives also realized they needed a strong position on the undeniably pressing issue of global poverty in order to make any credible argument for the urgency of the sexuality issue. Robert Miclean spoke about the interconnectedness of debt and homosexuality at the May 1998 meeting on debt:

> The Worldwide Anglican Church must effectively address two issues this summer: spiritual poverty in the West and material poverty in the South. . . . To only address the material needs of Africa, as some western liberals apparently prefer, suggests that the Church in the West has nothing to learn from its brethren in the rest of the world. . . . Likewise, to solely focus on the growing immorality and even apostasy found in parts of the western Church would lead to gross neglect of the sufferings of our brothers and sisters in the poorest of the developing countries.[73]

In Dallas, Stephen Noll told Southern bishops explicitly why they should care about Northern liberal heterodoxy; in Knippers's letter and Miclean's talk, Northern conservatives were told why they should care about Southern debt. Following this meeting, conservatives launched their own poverty reduction program, Five Talents, a micro-enterprise program providing small loans to people in poor countries to start small businesses. Five Talents was officially launched during Lambeth with a reception at the Franciscan Study Centre and was apparently well received. Within the space of a year, conservatives had developed and presented their own alternative approach to the problem of global poverty, in order to demonstrate their commitment to the well-being of Southern Christians.

As it transpired, the Lambeth resolution on international debt can be claimed as a modest triumph for Northern liberals. Julie Wortman writes that the Conference "strongly ratif[ied] and committ[ed] itself to the Left's Jubilee 2000 call for immediate debt relief for third-world nations."[74] The passage of this strongly pro–debt-forgiveness resolution in part reflects the fact that the Jubilee 2000 approach to international debt was quite popular with those Southern bishops who were mobilized on this issue. Five Talents simply did not have as much public support as Jubilee 2000. Furthermore, few people besides conservative Episcopalians saw Five Talents as necessarily an alternative to Jubilee 2000, rather than a potential addition, operating on a level different from that of debt-forgiveness–based solutions.

The support by Southern bishops for an approach to debt primarily associated with Northern liberals did not, however, mean that Southern bishops chose to restrain their views on homosexuality in order to please Northern liberals when the sexuality debate rolled around. Nor did the relative lack of interest in Five Talents prove to be any barrier to cooperation between Northern conservatives and Southern church leaders. Ultimately the debt issue did not turn out to be a particularly effective political tool in North/South relationships for either Northern liberals or conservatives.

Uganda: Differing Salience of Debt and Sexuality

Why did debt turn out to be a weak issue in terms of making or breaking North/South alliances or voting blocs at Lambeth 1998? No doubt one reason was that debt simply didn't draw the same attention in the press as the sexuality issue.[75] But there are also substantive reasons why debt was a less motivating issue for African bishops.

Many African church leaders and members are not very aware of international debt. This reality dawned on me when I noticed that, after four months of attending Church of Uganda events, reading Church of Uganda documents, and talking with bishops, priests, and laypeople about the Church of Uganda's issues, virtually no one had mentioned international debt. People talked about poverty and the need for development, and for donors and sponsors to help with these problems, but nobody talked about debt. Nor was it a frequent subject in the newspapers or other domains of Ugandan public life.

James is a young UCU professor and priest with a keen critical eye for Anglican Communion events and politics. When I interviewed him in his campus office and asked him about this strange invisibility of the debt issue in Uganda, he replied, in essence, that people have to be told that debt is having an impact on their lives in order to see that impact:

Many of the African Christians actually are not part of the whole process of this borrowing, and they don't know when it is done and who does it. So it does not easily come into their daily vocabulary, because it is beyond their imagination. . . . It affects them, [but] . . . it doesn't come anywhere, in the reports or even in the newspapers or even anywhere . . . and somehow the governments, they shelter information from the population of Africa. So the population of Africa cannot be concerned with something that is not coming to them. . . . It's not within the thinking of many Africans. Nobody knows what's happening.

Margaret, Bishop Ephraim's wife, talked with me about a session on international debt at a pre-Lambeth meeting she attended, and provided some confirmation of James's explanation. Margaret is middle-aged, well educated, and lives in the central, urbanized region of Uganda; she is well aware of her country's problems. Yet her account suggests that she had never thought of Uganda's problems in terms of its international debt, though once the problems of indebtedness were explained to her, she recognized them instantly as Uganda's problems: "Mainly they were talking about this debt burden, and its effect. Because it was one of the issues which was to be discussed at Lambeth. How poor countries like Africa come up [to] accumulate such debts, and they become a burden for the nation . . . . I had never thought of such as debt burden. It was never an issue. But when the man talked, I said, 'Oh, yes.'" Although the degree to which international debt is a subject of public knowledge may vary a great deal among indebted countries, James's and Margaret's words suggest one reason why the issue of international debt may have had minimal motivating power for African bishops at Lambeth. If many bishops knew relatively little about the problem of international debt, they still may have willingly voted for the debt-relief resolution. But coming from contexts where debt is hardly a subject of conversation, let alone a pressing politico-economic concern, they may not have developed sufficient engagement with the issue to be more generally motivated by it—for example, to form enduring alliances with liberal Northerners who shared their pro–debt-forgiveness stance.

Furthermore, African leaders may have engaged more readily and deeply with homosexuality than with debt because they believe scripture speaks more directly to homosexuality than to debt.[76] Margaret raised this issue in our conversation: "I remember asking the facilitators, 'Where does God talk about debt burden and how it affects us?' . . . Debts are . . . there to stay, and we shall try to do our best to tell our countries. But . . . sexuality was in the church and killing the church." Her words express a kind of fatalism about debt in contrast to the conviction that sexuality is a core life-or-death issue for the church. Bishop Thomas, talking with me about his priorities as a Ugandan church leader, made much the same point:

> I think there is a big difference between this kind of indebtedness and the doctrinal issue of homosexuality. . . . The question of debt, OK, we have to address it as a church, and we have to plead with people whom we owe money to help us, so that . . . our economies also may take off. But as a church leader, that does not bother me as much as a doctrinal issue. Because however much Africa or Asia might be indebted to First World countries, that will not kill the church. What will kill the church is for people to begin dismantling the Christian doctrine and beginning to undermine and to remove the foundation.

In contrast with some Northern, and a few Southern, church leaders who describe international debt as a faith issue and homosexuality as a cultural and contextual issue, most Ugandans seem to view the appropriate expression of sexuality as a central faith issue and define international debt as a political and economic issue outside the scope of the church. Further, Ugandan Anglicans seem to regard debt as something they can do little about; they see no point in taking it up as a major concern. Both Margaret and Bishop Thomas stated that they would try to talk about debt with those in power ("we shall try to do our best to tell our countries," "we have to plead with people whom we owe money"), but then both immediately turn to sexuality as an issue that can and should be addressed in and by the church. Sexual behavior, too, unlike the large-scale structural issue of international debt, is under an individual's voluntary control, and thus may seem a better target for moral teaching.

Many factors may account for the relative weakness of the debt issue at Lambeth 1998: lack of media coverage, insufficient awareness and mobilization among African leaders, and the perceived status of debt as a temporal, rather than spiritual, concern. Whatever the explanation, Northern liberals' successful championing of international debt met with wide approval among Southern Anglicans but did not turn the hearts of Southern bishops toward them more generally. Nor did it shake the general perception of Lambeth as a site of conflict between Northern liberals and Southern Anglicans. Conservatives' concerns about the debt issue were ultimately unnecessary. Whatever resolution Lambeth passed on debt, whether conservative or liberal, challenging or bland, revolutionary or ineffectual, would perhaps inevitably be lost in the anticipation of the sexuality debate and the subsequent outcry over the sexuality resolution. The media, the churches of the Communion, and the world were listening for one thing only from Lambeth 1998: what the Conference would say about homosexuality. And indeed the resolution on debt was quickly forgotten, while the sexuality resolution has dominated the way Lambeth 1998 is remembered and invoked as the Communion's complex and conflicted history rolls on.

CHAPTER FOUR

From African/Asian Juggernaut to Global Orthodox Majority

THE HOTEL AFRICANA is one of the most expensive hotels in Kampala. Widely used by international business travelers and other wealthy visitors, it perches on one of Kampala's many hills, its airy balconies and lush, well-tended gardens beckoning from behind high iron gates. In these elegant surroundings, in November 1999, Anglican primates and American conservative leaders held a secret meeting to consider the fate of the Episcopal Church.

Lambeth was over a year past and, American conservatives argued, there was no sign that the Episcopal Church would change its policies in response to the Lambeth resolution on human sexuality. These Americans, with the help of some African Anglican allies—most notably, Rwandan bishop John Rucyahana and archbishop Emmanuel Kolini—had organized this meeting to seek the assistance of the other Anglican primates present: the heads of the provinces of Uganda, Congo, Burundi, Tanzania, Sudan, Kenya, and the Southern Cone of the Americas. Several conservative Episcopal bishops were also present—an indicator of the seriousness of the occasion, since bishops have much to lose by breaking from the national church structure and thus are somewhat notorious for their hesitance in conservative Episcopal circles. Also present in Kampala were the Rev. Dr. John Rodgers, a priest and retired theology professor, and the Rev. Chuck Murphy, rector of All Saints, Pawley's Island, where First Promise was founded.

For the African leaders present, the goal of the Kampala meeting was to learn more about the Episcopal Church's alleged apostasy.[1] George, a conservative African bishop who was involved in the planning of this meeting, told me that one central objective was to bring together leaders from different American conservative groups, to get as much clarity as possible about the situation in the Episcopal Church in order to know how best to respond: "We wanted to know whether the bishops in American Anglican Council confirm the pleas and demands of the First Promise, of Forward in Faith, of all these lay and presbyters' organizations. . . . We wanted to make sure that when we intervene, we intervene with enough information from different [groups] before the Primates."

From the perspective of the Americans involved, however, the meeting's purpose was to solicit a response to the unbearable situation in which they found themselves. The talk by Rev. Geoffrey Chapman of First Promise presented the essential request:

> We believe that it is essential that much of the Episcopal Church be rebuked by the international communion and called to repentance. . . . [Therefore,] we ask for a new jurisdiction on American soil, under the temporary oversight of an overseas province. We believe that such a jurisdiction would provide the best hope for supporting those who are being persecuted for biblical faith and values. . . . Such a jurisdiction would also provide visible restraint and warning to those who oppose the Gospel.[2]

First Promise leaders were ready for such a jurisdiction to be established immediately. They had brought a draft constitution for a proposed "Anglican Missionary Province," and an African priest I interviewed who was present, assisting his bishop, told me he heard that several First Promise priests were ready to be consecrated as bishops for this proposed province. No such immediate solution emerged from Kampala, but nevertheless this meeting—both the renewed calls for help from the Americans and the African leaders' increasing conviction that the American church was seriously astray—opened the door for the next contentious chapters in the Communion's history.

The Kampala meeting of November 1999 carried echoes of the earlier Kampala meeting held before Lambeth. In 1999 as in 1998, conservative Americans gathered to tell African Anglican leaders about the problems in the Episcopal Church; in 1999 as in 1998, these Americans sought the African leaders' assistance in altering the situation. In spite of the passing of the Lambeth sexuality resolution, little had changed. The nonbinding character of Lambeth resolutions and the lack of clear authority structures within the Anglican Communion for enforcing such a resolution meant that the sexuality resolution did not, could not, settle anything. The sexuality resolution's implications for the Episcopal Church could only be hammered out through argument and persuasion. Lambeth did, however, alter the contours of the debate; as Sidney Tarrow has noted, "where international organizations can make decisions that are . . . even semibinding on member states, they offer domestic challengers institutional opportunities to transcend their national arenas for consultation [and] collective action."[3] The passage of the sexuality resolution allowed conservative Episcopalians to shift to a new set of projects. No longer was their goal to secure a clear orthodox statement on homosexuality, a bar against which to measure and judge the Episcopal Church's policies. That statement had been secured, from the highest possible levels of Communion leadership and with a surprisingly strong mandate. The overarching goal now became, as conservatives knew from the moment of the resolution's passage, to bring it to bear on the Episcopal Church.

Much of this work took place through conservatives' discursive insistence on the relevance of the sexuality resolution for the Episcopal Church, thereby applying a global frame to the American province. This increasing globalist orientation of conservative Episcopalians challenges the assumption of many scholars of globalization that conservative religious movements are a form of reaction against globalization. Manuel Castells describes Christian conservatism as "an attempt to reassert control over life . . . in direct response to uncontrollable processes of globalization that are increasingly sensed in the economy and in the media."[4] Peter Beyer argues that the goals of the American religious right include "limit[ing] the inclusive tendencies of the global system by asserting the exclusive validity of a particular group culture."[5] Conservative Episcopalians, however, combined their desire to maintain traditional sexual morality with a radical inclusiveness with regard to global relationships. Their efforts since Lambeth have created a transnational Anglican movement that is conservative in its content, focused on sexual morality and biblical authority, while proactively engaged with the global context through a networked structure and the tactic of establishing relationships that transgress the Communion's geographical boundaries.

These post-Lambeth developments are best understood by comparing Southern, Northern liberal/moderate, and Northern conservative reactions to the Conference, then tracing the contours of the conservative globalist discourses that took shape in this period. In parallel with this discursive struggle, American conservatives were planning and pursuing projects to involve outside Anglican authorities in subverting the Episcopal Church's intransigent authorities and making the American church take the Lambeth resolution seriously. The 1999 Kampala meeting just described hints at the projects embodying conservatives' globalist discourses that were also taking shape in this period. Lambeth 1998's official word on homosexuality was sealed in the moment of the vote on the sexuality resolution; but what this resolution meant for the American Episcopal Church was—and remains—contested.

THE AFRICAN/ASIAN JUGGERNAUT: INITIAL VIEWS OF LAMBETH 1998

The Archbishop of Canterbury had closed the sexuality debate with this fervent but fruitless hope: "I fully believe with all my heart that if this Conference is known and named by what we have said about homosexuality we will have failed."[6] But Lambeth 1998 is indeed "known and named" by the resolution on sexuality—in fact, the resolution on sexuality is often "named" by the very words "Lambeth 1998." In both interviews and texts, the word "Lambeth" often serves as shorthand for the sexuality resolution passed at that Conference—as in one conservative commentator's division of the Episcopal Church into "Lambeth-abiding dioceses and Lambeth-rejecting dioceses."[7]

In the days and weeks following Lambeth 1998, not only was the Conference's meaning reduced to the sexuality resolution, but the sexuality resolution's meaning was reduced to the idea of a rebuke to the North by the righteous bishops of the global South. Ian Douglas wrote about the Kuala Lumpur document, "Conservative media [in the West] soon misrepresented Kuala Lumpur as an authoritative, unanimous statement from all of the bishops in the Third World chastising the Church in the U.S. for ordination of gay and lesbian people and blessing of same-sex unions."[8] Much the same could be said of the way Lambeth was interpreted by reporters, commentators, and church leaders in the period following the Conference.

In an article written soon after the Conference, analyzing the sexuality vote, conservative Episcopal commentator David Virtue wrote, "All the African bishops vigorously opposed any attempts to legitimize homosexuality at Lambeth. . . . [Northern liberals] failed . . . to stop the African/ Asian juggernaut towards a resolution supporting a Biblical understanding of human sexual behavior."[9] In attributing the sexuality resolution primarily to African and Asian bishops, Virtue was certainly not alone. Despite the fact that 526 bishops voted for the sexuality resolution, far more than the combined number of African and Asian bishops at the Conference, secular press coverage widely credited the sexuality vote to the "Third World," "Africa and Asia," or often just "Africa" or "African bishops." Both British and American papers carried the message of Southern dominance. Elaine Storkey of the *Independent* wrote:

> The time has long gone since Third World bishops were token representatives. Theirs has been the voice that has prevailed on most of the agenda, whether in discussions on international debt or human sexuality. . . . The overwhelming vote for the Church's traditional sexual morality and against the "marriage" or ordination of practising homosexuals illustrated the Third World empowered.[10]

Likewise, a *Wall Street Journal* article described Lambeth 1998 as characterized by "debate [which] pitted a left-leaning American establishment against their more orthodox brethren from Africa and Asia."[11] Indeed, scholar Philip Jenkins was inspired to conceive and research his "Next

Christianity" thesis after observing Lambeth 1998, at which, as he explains it, "African bishops created a stir by outvoting their Northern brethren on key moral issues."[12]

AFRICAN VIEWS OF LAMBETH: A VICTORY FOR THE SOUTH

Most Ugandan Anglicans seem to share similar views of Lambeth as the site of North/South conflict and, especially, of African victory. An editorial in the *New Vision* the day after the sexuality debate praised the role of African bishops. Nearly four years after Lambeth, many Ugandans and other Africans still describe the Conference in similar terms. Jonah, a fiftyish priest and professor I met at UCU and interviewed about Anglican Communion affairs, described Lambeth 1998 to me as "when the African bishops stood against homosexuality." Similarly Emile, a young Rwandan priest studying at UCU, described Lambeth to me as: "a meeting in Canterbury where there was a dispute between African and Western bishops over homosexuality . . . [and] Africans were able to stand firm for [the] moral position, though some Western clergy and bishops were angry, even threatening an embargo on resources." Many of my African consultants described Lambeth 1998 in the same way, and with pleasure. These positive feelings result in part from the strength of the African voice in 1998 versus past Lambeth Conferences where, in the words of Bishop George, Africans just "rubber-stamped" whatever the Northern churches did. My consultants' agreement on the need for pre-Lambeth preparatory meetings and resources like the FSC reveals a sense of past disempowerment that needed to be overcome. And many Ugandans, laity as well as bishops and priests, spoke to me about the need for African bishops to know what is going on in the Anglican Communion and to have their say in Communion affairs. No wonder that the idea of Lambeth 1998 as a site of African triumph (over the liberal Northern homosexual agenda, and also over procedural obfuscations that have limited African participation for decades) is so widely and favorably held in Uganda and elsewhere in Africa.

The significance of this moment of African triumph on a global stage is underscored by the contrast between this image of Africa—faithful, strong, commanding—and the image, often dominant in the Anglican Communion, of Africa as a place of perpetual crisis. The Anglican Communion's official website, some time back, featured a handsome color image of Archbishop Carey holding a Rwandan child on his lap.[13] Whoever chose the picture probably felt it showed the Communion's global interdependence, but the image is also overwhelmingly paternalistic, symbolically identifying Africa as a nameless child in the lap of the white

Englishman who represents the worldwide church. Such imagery is not uncommon in the Anglican Communion, nor are depictions of Africa as a continent of chaos and lack.

The stories that the Anglican Communion News Service (ACNS) releases and circulates to any interested and e-mail–equipped Anglican serve as one source of such images. For example, the Africa-related stories for June 2002 were headlined: "Tutu leads formation of charity to aid farmers in Zimbabwe" (June 18); "Archbishop [of the Sudan] crosses [military] front-line to visit Nuba Mountains" (June 18); "Archbishop of Canterbury calls on governments of the G-8 countries to boost poverty reduction in Africa" (June 27); "Mission to AIDS orphans [in South Africa]" (June 30); "Filing of international legal claims for apartheid reparations" (June 30); and "Train accident in Tanzania" (June 30). In presenting such stories, the ACNS increases awareness across the Communion of the needs of Anglicans who are most troubled by poverty, disease, and war. But these accounts also perpetuate a familiar image of Africa as the eternally troubled continent, rarely, if ever, the source of good news. Well might an ACNS subscriber be led to wonder, "Can anything good come out of Africa?"[14] As for Lambeth 1998, Africans may have played unprecedented leadership roles in the Conference's politics, but in resolution texts Africa was treated in the same familiar ways. Nearly all the resolutions touching on Africa focus on crises, citing such problems as civil war and landmines in Uganda, the "exceptional circumstances" associated with the Rwandan genocide, and the "human disaster in the Sudan.'"[15]

African church leaders stepping forward to act on the global stage of the Anglican Communion do so against the backdrop of the widespread representation of Africa—in Anglican publications and in the mainstream Northern media—as a site of constant crisis and desperate need. Most Africans never see such ACNS headlines, but they are well aware that the rest of the world tends to see Africa as a place of trouble, disease, and conflict. The assertiveness of African leaders at Lambeth and beyond was in part a rejection of this image. Part of the appeal of seeing Lambeth 1998 in terms of African triumph lies in the way that interpretation runs against other images and holds up Africa as a bastion of morality and courage.

EXPLAINING AND EXCUSING AMONG NORTHERN LIBERALS AND MODERATES

Similar views of Lambeth as a site of Southern victory were widely articulated during and after Lambeth by Northern Anglicans, including both those with both positive views and those with negative views of the rising influence of Africans in the worldwide Communion. Many Northern liberals and moderates reacted negatively to Lambeth's results and to the role of Southern bishops in those outcomes. Philip Jenkins writes, "Western reactions to the [Lambeth] sexuality statement can best be described as incomprehension mingled with sputtering rage."[16] Immediately after the sexuality vote, explanations and dissociations began on the part of bishops who wanted to soften the blow or explain their votes to their home constituencies. ACNS stories from shortly after the sexuality vote reveal liberal leaders struggling to recover their composure and restate their message of tolerance:

> At a press conference organized by the Lesbian and Gay Christian Movement immediately following the plenary session, several bishops shared their disappointment. . . . Primus Richard Holloway of Scotland said he "never felt this depressed and so close to tears in my life,'" but said he would continue his efforts as an advocate for gay and lesbian Anglicans. "I feel gutted, I feel betrayed, but the struggle will go on,'" he said. . . . Bishop Duncan Buchanan, chair of the sexuality subsection, insisted that "nobody's existing ministry will be invalidated by this development."[17]

Over 100 bishops, including several primates, signed a statement released the day after the sexuality vote that expressed a commitment to dialogue with gays and lesbians in the church and called on all Anglicans to continue "prayerful, respectful conversation on the issue of homosexuality."[18] This statement, entitled "A Pastoral Statement to Lesbian and Gay Anglicans from Some Member Bishops of the Lambeth Conference," was eventually signed by nearly 180 bishops—far more than had voted against the sexuality resolution.

Many bishops wrote pastoral letters to their dioceses soon after Lambeth concerning the sexuality resolution. Northern bishops who had voted for the resolution or abstained sought to reassure gays, lesbians, and sympathizers within their dioceses by reaffirming their support for gays and lesbians in the church. Bishop Winterrowd of Colorado, who voted for the sexuality resolution,[19] provides one example of after-the-fact apology and explanation. He told a reporter from his home diocese that he had made a "strictly pragmatic" decision to vote for the resolution: "Frankly, the African church needed that vote to take back with them. . . . They are under a great deal of pressure politically because the Muslims are watching."[20] Explanation and an apologetic tone are also evident in a letter written by the suffragan bishop of the Diocese of North Carolina, explaining his vote: "My abstention was a vote for unity within diversity. I am sure that some will disagree with me and I honor that."[21]

While these bishops were apologetic, bishops who voted against the sexuality resolution expressed anger and reassurance. A typical example of the tone of such letters comes from the bishops of the Diocese of New York: "We want to make it plain to the members of this Diocese, and especially to our gay and lesbian members, that the resolution passed at Lambeth will not change the character of our life together."[22] Bishop Catherine Roskam wrote to her gay and lesbian clergy: "Do not identify a gaggle of bishops behaving badly as The Church. . . . You are the church, an integral part of the Body of Christ. Period. . . . Keep the faith. Stay the course. Say your prayers. We're in this thing together. And God *will* prevail."[23] This outpouring of episcopal epistles of explanation, apology, and reassurance testifies to the urgency with which many bishops felt they had to address and calm their constituents following the contentious events of Lambeth.

In talking about the Lambeth sexuality resolution, many Northern moderate and liberal leaders sought the silver lining in the resolution's text. Bishop Swing of the Diocese of California, in his response letter to his diocese, wrote: "Ten years ago the slightest mention of homosexuality brought howls of protest from 98% of Lambeth. This time there were sizable numbers of bishops who could make sure that a livable compromise resolution was presented. . . . There is every reason to believe that more progress will be made in the next decade before Lambeth 2008."[24] The presiding bishop (who abstained from the sexuality vote) falls into this category, reminding Episcopalians that the Lambeth bishops had committed themselves "to listen to the experience of homosexual persons," and that "the fruits of such listening, particularly in parts of the Anglican world where sexuality is seldom if ever publicly discussed, cannot be predicted."[25]

Northern moderates and liberals' negative reactions to much of the content of the sexuality resolution put them in a difficult spot, given the strong identification of the sexuality resolution with the historically marginalized churches of the global South. Accustomed to seeing themselves as advocates for the marginalized, these Northerners struggled to come to terms with what many experienced as a betrayal. Conservative activist Diane Knippers commented on the discomfiture Lambeth caused for many Northern moderates and liberals: "One result [of Lambeth 1998] is dismay for those who long championed multiculturalism and Third World causes. Picture these liberal American bishops, who . . . once fancied themselves on the progressive edge of every noble cause. The 'oppressed' whose plight they so long championed have taken over their church and rejected their liberal legacy."[26] As Knippers noted, many Northern liberals and moderates apparently felt dismayed and perplexed by the vehemence of sentiment against Northern culture and Northern church leaders manifest at Lambeth. The South-versus-North dynamic was new and troubling. Northern liberals and moderates, in talking and writing about Lambeth 1998, often tried to excuse or explain away Southern bishops' support for the sexuality resolution. Critical reading of documents produced in this post-Lambeth period reveals much about how these Northerners perceived their Southern colleagues.

The desire of formerly colonized peoples for self-assertion was one common explanation for Southerners' sentiments. Bishop Hays Rockwell's reflections on the sexuality debate included this observation: "The African and Asian churches are quite freshly indigenous. Now nearly every African bishop is an African, and they are understandably eager to assert themselves in the presence of their former 'masters.'"[27] Bishop Swing explained the African vote to his diocese as a result of the indignant assertiveness of marginalized Southern leaders who had been "stirred" by Bishop Spong's remarks with their echoes of paternalism and racism; he likened the result to that of "whack[ing] a beehive with a long stick."[28] Swing also, as noted earlier, described the dynamics of the debate as "Imperialists vs. The natives," and Bishop Frederick Borsch of Los Angeles wrote, "There was . . . a measure of anti-colonialism still evident in the Communion."[29] Other observers and commentators have offered similar explanations; I have several times heard Lambeth 1998 described by Episcopal leaders as "The Empire Strikes Back." While these attributions of the strong antihomosexuality sentiment at Lambeth 1998 to lingering postcolonial antagonisms do carry some negative evaluation of the Southern churches, they serve nonetheless to absolve the Southern churches of any fundamental blame. By this logic, Southern bishops were reacting against a history of oppression and cannot really be held responsible.

Other common explanations included competition with Islam in Africa and Asia and the idea that African bishops were essentially bought out or won over by American conservatives. Bishop Swing wrote, "The African bishops, as well as Pakistani, Indonesian, Malaysian, and others, are indeed facing great competition and persecution from radically militant Islam. Islam gains a big upper hand on the field of battle when Christians are seen in newspapers as supporting homosexuality."[30] Bishop Rockwell likewise observed, "Many of these bishops live in close quarters with growing Moslem populations, in which attitudes towards homosexuality are punitive. It is clear that some of the voting was influenced by that fact."[31] As for the influence of Northern conservatives, Scottish primate Richard Holloway was outspoken about this idea: "There was a lot of American money from a very traditionalist diocese and a lot of entertaining of bishops from the two-thirds world [the global South]."[32] Swing agreed: "The Bishop of Dallas, James Stanton . . . . [and] his colleagues invested a lot of time, money, and recruiting energy in rallying troops around this amendment. They did their homework, and the fight on the floor was like a rugby match."[33] One liberal Episcopalian compiled a list of "Nine Reasons Why the Lambeth Resolution Has Little Credibility," including this point: "The influence of the American Anglican Council and its affiliates was enormous. They produced mountains of paper the bishops received nearly every day. They paid for a major pre-Conference meeting of African bishops. They held seminars and barbecues throughout the Conference. Their Executive Director described their work as 'facilitative.'"[34] Such explanations were a way to attribute the outcomes of Lambeth to familiar enemies. The explainers may not have realized how condescending they sounded to many Southerners, who noted the lack of agency and judgment attributed to themselves by these explanations.

All of these arguments—postcolonial/racial antagonisms, competition with Islam, and Northern conservative influence—represent liberal and moderate efforts to excuse Southern leaders for siding with the enemy, Northern dissidents. These explanations offered Northern moderates and liberals a way out of the double bind of seeking to include one historically marginalized group (gays and lesbians) and running into head-on conflict with the expressed convictions of another historically marginalized group (Southern Anglicans).

The "New Xenophobia": Liberal Constructions of Africa after Lambeth

Some Northern liberals and moderates, however, expressed more hostility toward Southern Anglicans in arguing why Southern views should not influence the wider Communion. Several posited Southern Christian leaders' lack of education, sophistication, or thoughtfulness as the prime causal factors in the sexuality vote.[35] One English bishop, David Jenkins, stated: "[Lambeth] has voted to face the moral issues of the 21st century on the basis of an unreflective return to the traditions of the 16th and 17th. Those who are more moved by fear than full of faith, together with Third World bishops who have not yet faced up to irreversible developments in biblical, historical and scientific criticism, have prevailed."[36] Martin Smith, an Episcopal priest who attended Lambeth, labeled the Southern churches as "appallingly repressive authoritarian societies . . . which do not allow even the concept of gay and lesbian people, patriarchies that have no way of admitting into consciousness the realities we know here."[37] Smith attributes some of this division to a global gap in training and subtlety of understanding: "Anglicans have always claimed that truth emerges from a strenuous process of intelligent reflection and interpretation of scripture and tradition. But . . . literally hundreds of bishops in the newly expanded churches have had no more theological education than a few months of bible school, and the only form of discourse they know is a very simple form of biblical literalism."[38] Bishop Borsch also hinted at a lack of sophistication in Southern bishops' approaches to scripture, and described Southerners' reactions to gays and Northern liberals as the "new xenophobia."[39] He was among many liberal-leaning Northern bishops and other Lambeth observers who attributed Southern support for the sexuality resolution at least in part to unexamined patriarchalism and to a lack of education and critical thought among Southern bishops.

One conservative commentator, referring to accusations that conservative Northerners bought the loyalties of Southern leaders, wrote, "These exemplars of liberal arrogance are so convinced of their moral superiority that they really believe anyone opposing them must either be stupid or cynical."[40] Although such comments are obviously hostile criticism, the evidence of quotations like those given above make the point difficult to dismiss. In the post-Lambeth period, some Northern liberals and moderates were indeed moved to speak about the global South in derogatory terms. These ideas were widely expressed and represent a real struggle with the painful experience of Lambeth 1998. In such remarks, American Episcopal liberals and moderates were giving voice to their fear, anger, and sense of alienation from the Southern church, for whom they had previously seen themselves as advocates.

PRAISE FOR THE SOUTHERN ROLE FROM NORTHERN CONSERVATIVES

Northern conservatives, not surprisingly, were positive in their reactions to the sexuality vote. Those who had lobbied for the sexuality resolution, or hoped for such an outcome, initially joined the secular press in crediting Southern leaders with the victory for the conservative side. *United Voice* ran an article entitled "Africans Strengthen Sexuality Resolution."[41] The conservative British paper *Church Times*, describing the sexuality debate, attributed (unlike many liberal sources) considerable political savvy to the "Southern axis": "During the homosexuality debate, the Southern axis was fully in control. . . . By every reckoning, it was a pivotal moment in the life of the Anglican Communion. The Provinces in the South have been numerically stronger than those in the North for many years, but until now the political power and influence have stayed where the money is."[42]

Northern conservatives described Lambeth joyfully as heralding the shift of world Christian power to the global South. The American Anglican Council's newsletter *Encompass*, in its August 1998 issue, illustrated the language of global shift in a front-page letter to readers from its president, Dallas bishop James Stanton, who observed, "I think this Conference will be known as the moment when the voice of the 'South,' i.e., the

Two-Thirds World Anglicans, became the voice of the Communion."[43] Richard Kew similarly concluded, "Anglicans are the first worldwide family of Christians in which the baton of leadership has passed to the younger, dynamic churches of the global South."[44] Diane Knippers wrote for the *Weekly Standard* in early September:

> What Westerners on the right and left are learning is that Anglicanism has been geographically and demographically transformed. Today's statistically typical Anglican is not drinking tea in an English vicarage. She is a 26-year-old African mother of four. . . . The Western churches were vastly overrepresented at Lambeth; Stephen Noll of Trinity seminary near Pittsburgh noted that the average American bishop represented up to 10,000 lay men and women, the average Nigerian bishop up to 200,000. Despite the imbalance, the orthodox Anglicanism espoused by Africans, Asians, and South Americans carried the day at Lambeth. The center of Anglicanism is now in the southern hemisphere.[45]

"THE VOICE OF THE SOUTH BECOMES THE VOICE OF THE COMMUNION"?

Immediately following Lambeth 1998, Northern conservatives made much of what David Virtue described as the "African/Asian juggernaut" that had won the day in the sexuality debate. But attentive reading of post-Lambeth conservative commentaries reveals a significant shift to a more global account of the sexuality vote. As two conservative commentators wrote in early 1999:

> While Lambeth revealed that the strength of Anglicanism does now lie in the "global South" . . . further analyses found that most western bishops had voted with global South prelates on the sexuality resolution, making it a genuine expression of the Anglican common mind. . . . Lambeth's results vindicated the claim of conservative [Episcopal] bishops that they—not liberal revisionist American leaders—represent the Anglican mainstream.[46]

A short article entitled, "Sex Resolution Didn't Need Africans, Bishop Says," in the same issue of *Christian Challenge*, describes an analysis of Lambeth written by Bishop Herbert Thompson, Jr. of southern Ohio. The article explains that Thompson's analysis "further combats the notion that African Anglican bishops were solely or chiefly responsible for the adoption of the Lambeth Conference's orthodox sexuality resolution": "Further analysis [of the vote on the sexuality resolution] indicates that if all the African bishops had been present and voted 'no,' with

45 abstentions, the resolution still would have passed by a vote of 302–294. The Africans did not do it! We did it. The resolution represents the mind of the Anglican Communion as expressed by the bishops of the Communion around the world."[47] When Bishop Stanton stated that the voice of the South had become the voice of the Communion, he meant that the voice of the South had become more central in Communion affairs. But his words proved prophetic in another way, for in Northern conservative discourse an emphasis on the voice of the South was quickly displaced by discourse describing Lambeth as the voice of the whole Anglican Communion.

Although Northern conservatives and their African allies continued to share the agenda of changing the Episcopal Church's liberal policies, the Americans' shift to a globalist discourse represents a revealing difference between Northern conservatives and African Anglicans. The Africans I interviewed still, several years after Lambeth 1998, describe the Conference using the language of African victory, a language that resonates with their past experiences of marginalization and present concerns about favorable representation of the African church in the worldwide Communion. American conservatives, however, rapidly moved away from that language of African victory in favor of discourse about global consensus. In so doing, they performed a sort of reverse metonymy, naming part of the Communion (the churches of the global South who had supported the resolution) as the global whole.

This shift served conservative Americans' primary desire to challenge Episcopal leaders, many of whom apparently found it relatively easy to dismiss the views of African leaders, but who might find it harder to ignore "global" opinion. American conservatives frequently hold up African Anglicans as moral exemplars; their shift to global language in describing Lambeth implied not an overall rejection of Africa as a source of moral authority, as we shall see, but rather a shift to a potentially more persuasive discourse. The difference between Africans' and Americans' talk about Lambeth has had no negative consequences for their relationship. Nonetheless, it reveals yet again that these constituencies, though united enough on certain key issues to constitute a momentous movement within world Anglicanism, are grounded in very different realities, motivations, and concerns.

A GLOBAL ORTHODOX MAJORITY?

One key aspect of Northern conservatives' new discourse about the global Communion was the idea that the Lambeth sexuality vote represented the view of a global orthodox Anglican majority. This idea can be read in the Thompson argument cited above and in many other examples, such as Stephen Noll's analysis of Lambeth 1998. Noll casts the sexuality vote as mere "individuals" voting against the resolution versus the entire Anglican Communion, who supported it: "While individual bishops voted against the resolution, the official position of the Anglican Communion is a clear and unequivocal reaffirmation of the biblical teaching."[48] The strong vote in favor of the sexuality resolution convinced Northern conservatives that they had the support of a doctrinally orthodox Anglican majority that was ready and willing to hold errant provinces accountable to Lambeth's decisions. This inferred global orthodox majority became a central feature of scale-making arguments and conservative discourse urging Episcopal Church leaders and members to take seriously the Lambeth resolution on sexuality. Noll presents one example: "The Lambeth Conference cannot force member churches to conform, but the resolution was clearly intended to be heeded and responded to. . . . [The bishops of the Communion] . . . expect the leaders of the Episcopal Church to answer to the formulation of Anglican teaching in this resolution. *Ultimately, they are calling for conformity.*"[49] The threat of enforcement or punishment behind that expectation of conformity remained unstated, but the image of a worldwide majority of Anglican bishops watching for the American church's compliance with the Lambeth sexuality resolution is intended to give authority to Noll's call. In many other conservative sources in the post-Lambeth period, the discourse of a watchful orthodox majority waiting upon the American church's reformation was used similarly to lend persuasive weight to conservatives' arguments that the American church should, indeed must, change its policies on homosexuality.

Does this global orthodox majority exist, or is it only a rhetorical construction? A full answer to this question must wait upon subsequent chapters in the Communion's life, as it remains to be seen whether a majority of global bishops will finally rally around Northern conservatives and recreate the Communion united around orthodox understandings of biblical morality. But it is clear that, in many respects, conservative Episcopalians were as much constructing or imagining a global Anglican orthodox majority as aligning themselves with some existing entity approximating that description.

The global majority in conservatives' discourse was based upon the evidence of the 526–70 vote for the orthodox sexuality resolution at Lambeth 1998, but this vote provides only a limited warrant for inferring such a global majority. Most likely, a majority of Anglican bishops at Lambeth 1998 did support the passage of a resolution advising Anglicans against the ordination of noncelibate gays and lesbians and the blessing of same-sex unions; but this majority may have been both narrower and less vehement than the vote for the sexuality resolution suggests. Various bishops' accounts of their own votes suggest that many bishops voted for (or did not vote against)[50] this resolution because it was clearly going to pass anyway, and because this resolution (which had some softening clauses) was preferable to a sterner antihomosexuality resolution that could have been passed by a smaller majority. The overwhelming 526 votes for the sexuality resolution thus did not represent a lasting, cohesive orthodox bloc.

Further, Northern conservative discourse implies that this majority is "orthodox"—that is, committed to (Northern) evangelical understandings of biblical doctrine and morality in some generalized and lasting way. Yet the overwhelming success of an essentially liberal approach to international debt issues shows that there was no solid orthodox bloc at Lambeth that would reliably support Northern conservatives' views. As I argued in chapter 2, Northern liberal/conservative positions and distinctions do not correspond with the salient political issues and divisions in, for example, Uganda's church and society. The fact that a majority of Southern bishops shared the Northern conservative position on human sexuality does not mean that the same majority would support other Northern conservative beliefs and concerns across the board.

These qualifications notwithstanding, American conservatives' shift from describing the Lambeth sexuality vote as a Southern victory to a global victory was a discursive shift that strengthened arguments urging the Episcopal Church to change its policies. The success of this discourse is evident in the fact that Episcopal liberals and moderates rarely questioned it, instead arguing for their province's freedom to ignore the will of such a majority. American conservatives also used the discourse of global majority for mobilization purposes, to try to persuade conservative-leaning Episcopal laity, clergy, and congregations to join First Promise or other conservative organizations. Members of St. Timothy's described joining First Promise, which seemed to be backed by a majority of Anglican bishops worldwide, as much more appealing than joining such an organization when it appeared to be out on a limb, challenging the American church without a global safety net of sympathizers and supporters.

GLOBAL COMMUNION: COMPETING VISIONS

American conservatives' use of global language in discussing Lambeth 1998 and its potential consequences for the Episcopal Church illustrates the evolution of a conservative Episcopal global vision: conservative in its strong assertion of social and moral norms understood as deriving directly from a literal reading of scripture; globalist in both its transnational scope and its vision of the Anglican Communion's ideal character. Such a conservative global vision clashes with the more widespread liberal/moderate vision of globalism as based on diversity and autonomy.

The possibility of competing, radically different visions of the global Anglican Communion owes much to the Communion's loose political structure. The shape and character of Anglican globality—the range of diversity permitted among provinces, and how they ought to relate to one another—is not determined by a solid hierarchical structure. Yet the Communion's polity and unity are not so loose that member provinces, finding themselves out of accord with sister churches, easily shrug off their membership and become fully independent. In a sermon given in the months before Lambeth, Archbishop Carey outlined the indeterminacy of international Anglican polity: "We are not a monolithic church which dictates to our members precisely what shall and shall not be the package of faith. But nor are we simply a collection of independent churches, doing what we will regardless of the effect we have on others."[51] As differences between the provinces—over women's ordination in the 1980s, over responses to homosexuality in the late 1990s—have become increasingly politicized, the pressure to clarify the nature of the unity of the Anglican Communion has increased. Some Anglicans advocate affirming anew the tradition of provincial autonomy, arguing that provinces with sharply differing policies should simply agree to disagree, and continue to celebrate the elements of Anglican heritage they do share. Others feel that the loosely defined unity of the past was based upon theological and moral convictions shared around the Communion, a common base that no longer exists. These Anglicans argue that recent conflicts point to a need to strengthen authority and disciplinary structures within the Communion.

Torn between these opposing impulses, the Communion's leaders and member provinces have grappled with the nature of the Communion's unity, the degree of autonomy permissible, and who or what has the authority to establish and police the limits.[52] The Anglican Communion possesses four "Instruments of Unity" charged with the work of managing the Communion's common life: the primates (or provincial head bishops), as gathered in their periodic consultative meetings; the Archbishop of Canterbury; the Lambeth Conference itself; and the Anglican Consultative Council, a body of bishops, priests, and laity from around the world who help run the Communion between Lambeth Conferences and plan the Conferences themselves.[53] As the Communion grows ever more diverse and complicated, the uncertainty of the Anglican Communion's authority structures becomes more problematic and pressure to define the powers of these Instruments of Unity increases.

At Lambeth 1998, those pressures resulted in the passing of several resolutions dealing with matters of authority and autonomy in the Anglican Communion. Yet these measures offered no clear direction, but rather illustrated the opposing impulses to protect autonomy and strengthen accountability. Several resolutions seemed intended to affirm the self-determination of Anglican provinces. One resolution stated that each province should have discretion on the issue of women's ordination, implying a concept of the Anglican Communion as a loosely defined federation characterized by mutual regard rather than by establishment of uniform policies. Another resolution affirmed the principle of "subsidiarity" as fundamental to Anglican polity, meaning that Anglican polity includes a predisposition against giving any central body powers to do things that can be done effectively by the provinces, dioceses, or parishes of the Communion.[54] A third resolution reaffirmed the integrity of diocesan boundaries, and was proposed by the North American bishops in response to Rwandan bishop John Rucyahana's claiming of jurisdiction over St. Andrew's, Little Rock. These three resolutions suggest a trend in the direction of affirming autonomy and clear boundaries within the Anglican Communion.

However, one important resolution took a distinctly different tack. This resolution called for a dramatic strengthening of the roles of the primates, urging them to meet more often and exercise greater leadership, through their "moral authority," in defining the limits of Anglican diversity on "doctrinal, moral, and pastoral matters"—including possible intervention in internally troubled provinces. Reactions to this resolution were divided. Liberal priest and scholar Ian Douglas, for example, viewed it negatively, writing that it "gives the Primates' Meeting . . . unheard of extra-metropolitical authority to intervene in the life of Anglican provinces locally, while eviscerating the sharing of power with lay people and priests in the old Anglican Consultative Council."[55] In contrast, many Northern conservatives expressed pleasure at this strengthening of the primates' power, and optimism about its implications. Many conservatives and Southern leaders believe Northern liberals and moderates still exert a disproportionate influence at the Lambeth Conference, because the wealthy Northern provinces can afford a higher ratio of bishops to church members. For example, the 7 million Anglicans in Uganda had about 20 bishops at Lambeth 1998, while the 2.4 million American Anglicans had over 100. However, in the context of the Primates' Meeting, the Episcopal Church and the Church of Uganda each have one vote, and provinces with a clear liberal leaning are a distinct minority among the world's 38 Anglican provinces. Thus Northern conservatives hoped this strengthening of the primates' role would provide new avenues for protecting Anglican orthodoxy. American Anglican Council staff member

Alistair Macdonald-Radcliff, writing in 2000, argued that more frequent Primates' Meetings "will speed up the process by which Primates are acquiring a greater role with in the Communion, and it will also inevitably entail a much higher degree of mutual accountability."[56]

Autonomy and Accountability in Opposing Global Visions

The divided reactions to this resolution on the primates' role suggest differing visions of the ideal structure of the Anglican Communion that correspond with liberal and conservative positions in the debate over homosexuality and related issues. Northern liberals and moderates hold a vision of the Anglican Communion as embracing diversity within a loose and noncoercive unity of shared heritage and goodwill. Once the sexuality resolution had passed, protecting the diversity and autonomy of the Communion's provinces became all the more important to these Anglicans and Episcopalians, since strengthening the structures of the Communion might force member provinces to comply with Lambeth resolutions. For the same reason, Anglicans who oppose church acceptance of homosexuality favor stronger unifying and disciplinary structures within the Anglican Communion that would force provinces to be more accountable to the will of the worldwide church, as expressed in Lambeth resolutions.

These divisions were strengthened by the opposing resolutions on authority emerging from Lambeth 1998. Liberal bishops returned home armed with resolutions on subsidiarity and diocesan boundaries, prepared to cry "Foul!" at the next international trespass. But conservatives made it plain that their willingness to observe ecclesiastical boundaries was contingent on the Episcopal Church's willingness to submit itself to the authority of the Lambeth Conference. At the same time, they expected that the Episcopal Church would in fact *not* fall into line with the sexuality resolution—thus, as they saw it, opening up the errant American province to all manner of outside intervention, especially from the primates whose authority Lambeth had also affirmed.

These concerns with provincial autonomy and global accountability are foundational to the respective global visions advocated by proponents and opponents of church acceptance of homosexuality. In their post-Lambeth talk and actions, liberal/moderate and conservative Anglicans articulated visions of the global Anglican Communion's ideal structure and character that built upon profoundly differing concepts of how the provinces relate to one another as sister churches in a worldwide body. To analyze these clashing perspectives, I rely on the many relevant texts produced during and after Lambeth 1998. Useful in part because these developments took place before my ethnographic fieldwork, these documentary materials were also important in themselves in the circulation of these two models, especially the newer conservative globalism—still taking shape in 1998 and 1999, but recognizably the same as the globalism I heard voiced by my consultants in 2001 and 2002. A close reading of post-Lambeth sources' use of the key concept of "global Communion" reveals the contours of competing understandings of the nature of Anglican globalness. Many Anglicans endorsed what I will call *diversity globalism*, founded on principles of tolerance within a federation of loosely unified provinces. Advocates of diversity globalism insisted that if the Communion would not fully welcome diversity, at least it should not also impose conformity. At the same time, other Anglicans, especially conservative Northerners, articulated a vision of the Anglican Communion founded on what I call *accountability globalism*—the idea that the dawning global era calls the Anglican Communion to establish clearer doctrinal standards and more accountability between provinces.

Diversity Globalism

Moderate and liberal Anglican Communion leaders who planned Lambeth 1998 shaped the Conference to uphold a particular vision of global Communion, characterized by acceptance of and engagement across differences of culture, experience, and belief. Similar definitions of globalness as synonymous with multiculturalism and unity in diversity have become common in most Northern societies and in many Southern societies as well. This vision of globalism posits encounter across difference as beneficial in and of itself, and the innate value of cross-cultural encounter is often described as the central, motivating good to be obtained from striving for unity across difference. Diversity is the primary focus of this vision, while the unity that encompasses diversity often consists in nothing more clearly defined than general mutual goodwill. Moderate and liberal Anglicans often add a theological aspect to this humanist value; as one priest I know puts it, humans know God more fully in the encounter with other humans who are different from themselves.

The high value placed upon diversity within community by Anglican Communion leaders is easily found in statements describing Lambeth using the vocabulary of globalness or other related terms: worldwide, multicultural, local, diverse. In one of many examples, Archbishop Carey, addressing Lambeth 1998, expressed the idea that diversity contributes to the greater unity: "I have often said, jokingly of course, to those provinces influenced by the English church in the last century: 'Be less English! Be more African or Asian or South American. Let your own tradition, music and ways of devotion enrich your life!' . . . By empowering and celebrat-

ing the local, we enrich the whole."[57] This liberal/moderate Anglican globalism envisions globalness as diversity in unity, in which each party brings
its culture, experience, and perspective to the common table in a grand
global sharing, and each party is enriched and broadened (though not,
usually, seriously challenged, unsettled, or changed) by hearing others'
stories. James Thrall commented on the weaknesses of this approach:
"Liberal forces at Lambeth seemed at times to seek . . . an acceptance of
plural viewpoints and practices, without wanting to engage in the conflictual power relations that would seriously address the challenges those
practices posed for each other."[58] In this globalism, the implications of
difference are downplayed in favor of autonomy and cordiality. Each Anglican province is a separate entity; these autonomous bodies gather into
a whole as equals; and every perspective contributes equally to the collective sharing.[59]

Following Lambeth, many understood its tensions as a struggle over
globalness. Ian Douglas wrote, "[At Lambeth 1998] for the first time ever,
the Anglican Communion has had to face head-on the radical multicultural reality of a global Christian community."[60] As Douglas's phrasing
indicates, liberal/moderate diversity globalism was profoundly challenged
by the events of Lambeth. Having come with a vision of a global Communion characterized by the affirmation of cultural and experiential diversity, many bishops and observers left the Conference feeling that this vision had been betrayed by the Conference's events. The multicultural
liturgies had been colorful and joyful, the cross-cultural small group discussions had been warm and broadening, but the Anglican Communion
gathered at Lambeth had failed to affirm the diversity of its churches'
cultures. Many liberals and moderates from Northern provinces where
homosexuality is tolerated saw the sexuality vote as a double betrayal:
not only had the global South turned upon Northern liberal and moderate
would-be allies, but the ideal of affirming diversity had been rejected.

Few Northern liberals had realistically expected the passing of any resolution that would have affirmed the acceptance of homosexuality, but
many did expect, or at least hope, to have their views on homosexuality
heard and tolerated, just as they saw themselves, as good diversity globalists, as hearing and tolerating others' culturally informed views. The bishops of New York, in a statement issued soon after Lambeth, are explicit
that their experience with the issue of homosexuality constituted their
cultural witness to the rest of the Communion: "What we encountered
. . . in the debate over [the sexuality] resolution was a profound clash of
cultural assumptions. . . . As Bishops in New York, we feel that we can
offer Christians elsewhere in this global Communion an opportunity to
hear voices that they have not heard before. We can give personal testimony to our own experiences of ministry with gay and lesbian people."[61]

These bishops voice their hope that intercultural dialogue will continue—implying that they felt American views were not truly heard at Lambeth. Bishop Borsch's phrase describing the sexuality debate as the "new xenophobia" expresses his feeling that Northern conservatives and Southern bishops had refused to hear the voices of those of differing views.[62] Northern liberals such as the bishops quoted here experienced the passing of the sexuality resolution as not only a political defeat but a turning away from what they deeply believed the Communion should be.

Given the Conference's perceived rejection of the diversity globalist value of inclusiveness, it became all the more important for these Anglicans and Episcopalians to affirm the diversity globalist value of autonomy. Starting immediately after the sexuality vote, a strong chorus of American voices emerged, saying, "This resolution doesn't affect us!" Many leaders pointed out that Lambeth resolutions are nonbinding, and that their effect in any given province depends on that province's decision to abide by the resolution or not. Liberal American leaders also stressed the Anglican tradition of provincial autonomy. Bishop Swing's letter to his Californian diocese began, "Dear Friends, The most important thing to know about the resolution on homosexuality passed at the 1998 Lambeth is that it is not binding. It only 'advises.' Thus the Diocese of California and its bishop are duly advised but nothing will change in our practice."[63] The leaders of the Episcopal gay-rights group Integrity were likewise quick to reassure their members that the "issue of reception" would work in their favor: "The chances of this resolution's positive reception by the majority of US Episcopalians are slim to none. And since this resolution is only advisory, . . . such reception is absolutely necessary to its authority. . . . The life of the Church in the US is not going to come to a halt because bishops from other parts of the world refused to even listen to the stories of their gay and lesbian brothers and sisters and even denied their existence".[64] Over the next year, a significant number of Episcopal dioceses passed resolutions distancing themselves from the condemning language of the sexuality resolution—effectively declaring their freedom to take Lambeth or leave it.

It is an interesting irony that, following Lambeth 1998, American liberals and moderates found themselves insisting that Lambeth and the wider Communion had no jurisdictional authority in the American church, because "No jurisdiction!" had been the rallying cry of American conservative dissidents defying Episcopal bishops whom they saw as heretical. Disinviting a "revisionist" bishop from his annual parish visitation, refusing to pay the diocese the customary yearly sum from a parish's budget, and other forms of ecclesiastical civil disobedience have long served as common weapons for American dissident parishes. At St. Timothy's, relations with their bishop had been strained for several years before their break from the diocese. The rector of St. Timothy's once wrote to the bishop to explain that all the young adults in his confirmation class had decided they did not want the bishop to confirm them, so there was no need for the bishop to visit St. Timothy's for the scheduled confirmation service. Such actions represent more or less overt assertions that leaders whose convictions differ from those of the parish are not welcome and have no authority.

Following Lambeth, however, American conservatives began to augment these strategies of dissociation with a new politics of appealing to the global church, arguing for a higher-level jurisdictional authority over the leadership of the Episcopal Church. This shift increasingly pushed moderates and liberals toward their own politics of dissociation from the global Communion and its asserted moral authority. David Virtue noted this growing tendency in the talk of liberals at Lambeth, though he seems unconscious of how recently separatism had been a primary conservative strategy: "A new word is being heard to describe former liberals and revisionists. It is Separatist, says a thoughtful observer of the Lambeth scene. The opposite of separatism is unity, which is what we are all striving for."[65] Calls for continued discretion for each province to set its own policies are central to liberal/moderate visions of global Communion as welcoming diversity without imposing conformity.

ACCOUNTABILITY GLOBALISM

Meanwhile, Northern conservatives built upon the victory in the sexuality debate to elaborate an alternative vision of global Communion. They opposed liberal/moderate diversity globalism, which they described as relativist and profoundly threatening to authentic Christianity. Most American conservatives were convinced by the events of Lambeth that the global scale, the worldwide Anglican Communion, was indeed relevant to Episcopal Church struggles. From the point of view of the national Episcopal Church, these conservative Episcopalians were an embattled minority; but the sexuality vote at Lambeth gave them a sense of solidarity with a like-minded worldwide majority. During Lambeth, Doug LeBlanc wrote, "Orthodox Anglicans in the North, exhausted as they sometimes are, know in their souls that they stand with the vast body of orthodox Christians in the Worldwide Anglican Communion."[66] Post-Lambeth commentaries make it clear that conservatives felt their international support strengthened them in domestic conflicts. Such sources argued that the "global shift" of world Christianity to the "suffering and vibrant" churches of the Third World put American conservatives and traditionalists on the "moral high ground" when they challenged the Episcopal

Church's leadership.[67] Thinking and talking about global scale was both comforting and rhetorically advantageous for American conservatives. Following Lambeth, their new strategy was to impress the relevance of the global scale upon the Episcopal Church's liberal and moderate majority.

This emergent global vision, far from being a reactionary retreat from an increasingly complex global context into some narrow and protective biblicism, was global in its reliance on the support of a worldwide Anglican majority, in its perspective on scripture, and in its ideal of global interdependence and mutual accountability. Simon Coleman, a student of global Christianity, notes that one question to raise in looking at transnational religious movements concerns how new global flows are "articulated alongside new forms of 'fixing' identity and behaviour."[68] This accountability globalism fixed certain non-negotiable elements that served to define the Anglican constituencies allied behind this vision; at the same time, it stressed openness and global flow in other arenas.

One of the most central fixed elements for this conservative Anglican globalism lies in its leaders' conviction that Christian doctrine and morality, as stated in scripture, is normative for all the world's Anglican churches. Conservative globalists reject the liberal idea that tolerance of homosexuality is a cultural value compatible with the Bible's message. Rather, they assert that the Bible provides clear standards for sexual morality, and that these standards apply across all cultures. As one conservative British Anglican put it, "[We] believe that we can grasp Christian truth and that it is universally normative."[69] Conservative columnist Terry Mattingly sums up this negative view of the diversity globalists' arguments for the acceptance of homosexuality: "Africans and Asians stressed that they welcome diversity, especially in culture, worship, and church leadership. . . . But they clearly consider diversity a bad word, when applied to basic doctrinal issues such as biblical authority, the Resurrection, or defining the sacrament of marriage."[70] Thus the diversity globalist argument for the tolerance of homosexuality on the same basis as tolerance for various cultural differences within a diverse global community is met by a frank refusal of this logic: the issue of homosexuality is a matter not of acceptable cultural differences, but of unacceptable straying from the gospel.

There is nonetheless some room for the perspectives of different cultures in the conservative globalist view, in the idea of "intercultural" engagement with scripture. For the evangelically minded conservatives in the North and their Southern allies, part of the value of intercultural Anglican relationships lies in the possibility of helping one another understand the gospel more clearly, free of cultural blind spots and biases. One statement to this effect comes from the Dallas conference, when American conservatives and their new allies were just beginning to formulate a

shared vision of global Communion. A document summarizing one Dallas plenary meeting states: "We are to listen to the [biblical] text not only
in full awareness of our own context, but also in relation to the response
of others in their contexts. Thus inter-cultural engagement of our reading
of scripture in the global church is most important."[71] The conservative
British evangelical and South American primate Maurice Sinclair elabo-
rates this idea: "Every culture can contribute understanding of the Gospel
and every culture can distort the Gospel. From our different situations
and cultural backgrounds we need to help each other and correct each
other. . . . The wisdom for guiding our churches must be Christianly
cross-cultural."[72]

Interestingly, superficial similarities exist between this idea of cross-
cultural correction and liberal/moderate globalists' interest in encounter
with diversity. For example, American presiding Bishop Frank Griswold
has argued that Christians around the world "need one another" in order
to discover God's "mutifaceted" truth.[73] Likewise, the Virginia Report on
unity in the Communion, a moderate source, states: "The life of the
Church [in a particular province]. . . . would . . . be helped and challenged
by the contemporary Church in other places, and use the experience of
other Christians as a way of discerning truth within the ambiguities of
local tradition and culture."[74] Thus Anglicans across the spectrum argue
for the value of letting local understandings of the faith be challenged by
other Christians' ideas and experiences.

Yet the core assumptions underlying these ideas are fundamentally different. Liberal and moderate sources tend to emphasize the need for Anglican churches around the world to "seek" and "discern" truth together.
These liberal/moderate statements carry the implication that cross-cultural contact relativizes and broadens local concepts of Christian faith
and life. Such sharing thus leads Christians into a deeper, more engaged
collaborative search for truth, rather than necessarily clarifying Christian
truth in any immediate way. Scriptural truth, for liberals and moderates,
is not something fixed but can be fruitfully opened to global flows. In
contrast, for conservatives, cross-cultural "help and correction" make the
truth more clear by revealing the essence of biblical orthodoxy, free of
cultural biases. The global component contributes to the clarity of knowledge of scriptural truth.

In the conservative globalist vision, scriptural norms should rule the
global church—and so should Lambeth's resolutions (or at least the resolution on human sexuality). Northern conservatives' arguments for global
accountability included an insistence that the sexuality resolution, though
technically nonbinding, should exert a powerful pressure for conformity
on the Communion's provinces. Adherence to the conservative viewpoint
of the sexuality resolution represents another fixed aspect of this glob-

alism, important both because of the resolution's support by a global majority and because the resolution expresses Northern conservatives' understanding of scriptural truth regarding human sexuality. The global web of mutual accountability among Anglican provinces, in this view, should take its power from its accord with both scriptural morality and the widespread political will conservatives believed was revealed in the Lambeth sexuality vote. In the words of American bishop Bertram Herlong, "[Lambeth resolutions] represent the mind and heart of the whole of the church. Any provincial church that ignores or belittles them or disregards them is consciously turning its back on the mainstream of the Anglican Communion."[75] According to accountability globalists, the Anglican Communion's diverse local churches should hold one another accountable to scriptural and Lambeth-validated norms.

In arguing for such global mutual accountability, conservative globalists explicitly argued against the one comfort liberal Anglicans took from Lambeth: the non-binding nature of its resolutions. Northern conservatives asserted that provincial autonomy and a local orientation within the church are the way of the past, and that the Communion has entered an era of global interconnectedness.[76] While fixing their global vision on a particular understanding of scriptural sexual morality, these conservatives also opened up the politics and authority structures of their parishes, dioceses, and provinces, and their own senses of place, membership, and identity, to global flows—through calls for new forms of cross-cultural relationship, for transprovincial solidarity, and for intervention from overseas Anglicans. Conservative-leaning bishop Charles Jenkins of Louisiana wrote after Lambeth, "We are challenged to find a new way of being the Anglican Communion. The old way of being the church, with a high degree of provincial autonomy and a trust in ways English, is no longer viable."[77] Conservative American commentator Richard Kew described the new global interconnections that make inter-Anglican accountability necessary:

> We can no longer either act or make major decisions in isolation from the rest of the Anglican family. . . . Lambeth illustrated that in the global village that has fully emerged only since the last Lambeth in 1988, there is an interconnectedness that far transcends nation, tribe, race, or tongue. From our parishes to our national churches we are now enmeshed in a thickening web of relationships, and whereas the miles once isolated us from one another, those relationships now require an accountability to which we are unused.[78]

Echoing many of Kew's points, Ugandan bishop Henry Orombi summed up the new Anglican accountability to a reporter at Lambeth: "Bishops in America are one part of the Anglican Communion. Whatever they do should be found acceptable within the wider church. If U.S. bishops are ordaining homosexuals is it for the U.S. or the wider church? We are not local priests, we are global priests."[79] For supporters of the sexuality resolution, its passage represented the triumph of the universal over the particular, the global over the local.

ENACTING THE CONSERVATIVE GLOBAL VISION

The accountability globalism articulated by Northern conservatives and some Southern sympathizers following Lambeth rests on the concept of worldwide interprovincial accountability to fixed scriptural norms, clarified through intercultural correction, supported and enforced by a global orthodox Anglican majority. This vision contrasts sharply with liberal/moderate diversity globalism, in which the primary ideal for international communion is diversity in unity, understood as sharing Christian fellowship across differences in culture, experience, and belief. These visions differ and even clash in many of their implications, but it is significant that they are both undeniably global visions. Diversity globalism explicitly seeks to reduce Northern cultural hegemony and global dominance (though its effectiveness at doing so in practice has been debated). As for accountability globalism, critics of this movement have doubted the depth of Northern conservatives' openness to new global influences and identities, suggesting that their globalism is only rhetoric and that their true stance is reactionary and antiglobalist. It is true that the ideal of global openness and equal power is perhaps not fulfilled by inter-Anglican alliances for orthodoxy, since American leaders and American problems still play disproportionate roles in determining how these alliances spend their collective time and energy. Chapters 6 and 7 address some of the other ways familiar patterns of North/South interaction and power imbalance recur, even in the context of these innovative transnational relationships.

Nonetheless, accountability globalism is a true globalism. The intentionality of Northern conservatives in seeking out global relationships, even placing themselves under Southern leaders and allying themselves with Southern churches, belies critics' suspicions. This is no veiled antiglobalism or reactionary vision, in which the older authority structures of white male Euro-American dominance are reestablished to maintain order in an increasingly complex worldwide organization. Instead, this conservative vision embraces the diversity and complexity of the contemporary world. As James Thrall writes, "if the conservative coalition at Lambeth was holding onto a status quo, it was the status quo of a particular ideology drawn from a particular understanding of Christian scripture and tradition," and not the status quo of a particular political order in which power belongs to white Europeans and Americans.[80] Rather, the vision of accountability globalism calls for power to shift away from traditional centers and to locate instead in a worldwide network of church leaders united in their commitment to Anglican orthodoxy. New, global patterns of discipline are envisioned in the service of correction, help, and, above all, accountability among Anglican churches around the globe.

Furthermore, far from reacting against the greater cross-cultural interconnectedness of the (post)modern world, these Northern conservatives, before, during, and since Lambeth 1998, have actively developed relationships with Southern Anglicans in order to pursue their vision of global Communion founded on biblical truth. When the passing months made it clear that the Episcopal Church would not change its direction with respect to homosexuality, American conservatives reached out to their global allies once again. A coalition of American conservative groups (including the AAC, FIF-NA, Ekklesia, and First Promise) under the name Association of Anglican Congregations on Mission, or AACOM, sent out a petition in January 1999. The petition appealed to all the Communion's bishops to intervene in ECUSA on behalf of American conservatives.

The full title of the petition makes its purpose quite clear: "A Petition to Orthodox Bishops of the Anglican Communion for Protection of Orthodox Anglicans in United States until the Episcopal Church of the United States is Reformed or Replaced as a Province of the [Anglican] Communion." The petition asked the orthodox bishops of the Communion to protect orthodox Anglicans in the United States, and also to play a direct role in the reformation or replacement of the Episcopal Church:

> The revisionists control ECUSA's national governing bodies and most of its major dioceses. They cannot be persuaded to change their teachings or be dislodged from their positions of power by the orthodox minority within ECUSA. [This] emergency can be resolved only by the Primates' Meeting, or its individual members, causing the reformation of ECUSA or the replacement of it with a continuing Episcopal Church as the province of the Anglican Communion in the United States.[81]

The petition included 145 pages of supporting documents, including post-Lambeth letters from a number of American bishops stressing that they did not feel bound by the Lambeth sexuality resolution, and the texts of a few counter-Lambeth resolutions that had already passed at the annual conventions of several Episcopal Church dioceses. These documents served to illustrate that the Episcopal Church had long been out of line with the (newly established) Lambeth position on human sexuality, and that this was not likely to change in the aftermath of Lambeth—at least not without significant outside encouragement.

One response to this petition was the meeting in Kampala in November 1999. That meeting, however, was only a first step in Southern Anglican leaders' process of deciding how to respond to American conservatives' renewed pleas for assistance. New experiments and new solutions lay ahead for American dissidents and their Southern allies in the post-Lambeth 1998 years, especially in the many transnational connections that developed as these constituencies enthusiastically used the global frame in innovative and surprising ways to define not only the Episcopal Church but even themselves.

CHAPTER FIVE

"At Home in Kigali": Transnational Relationships and Domestic Dissent

ST. TIMOTHY'S Wednesday night house church group meets in the immaculately furnished home of an elegant couple in their sixties, on the outskirts of this small southeastern town. On a warm autumn evening in 2001 I turn into the development, roll down my car window to punch in the entry code, and follow the winding tree-lined avenue back to their driveway. I'm welcomed warmly by the gathered group, thirteen besides myself. I've been coming regularly to this house church for weeks, intending simply to learn more about the spirituality and community of St. Timothy's, but tonight's conversation will bear more direct relevance to my questions about what this church's relationship with Rwanda means to its members. In the course of the evening's conversation, participants' reflections on a recent presentation on the Rwandan church turn into a spirited discussion about whether the United States should have intervened in Rwanda to stop the 1994 genocide. One member, commenting on the congregation's increased awareness, talked about how she didn't pay much attention to the genocide at the time. Jack, an ex-military man more aware of U.S. foreign policy, recalled wondering in 1994 why the government intervened in Bosnia and not in Africa, where, he says, one battalion could have stopped the killing. He suggests an answer: "Because they [Rwandans] weren't white Europeans."

Esther, an occasional member and perhaps less attuned to the growing interest in and sympathy for Africa among her fellow parishioners, spoke up to argue that we were right not to intervene. In explaining her point of view, she twice referred to the violence between "the Hutus and the Tutus." The second time, Jack and another man simultaneously corrected her, quietly but firmly: "*Tutsis.*" The rest of the group argued, politely, with her position. One woman raised humanitarian issues: as Christians, how can we stand by and watch mass murder? Esther defended her position, insisting that the United States should only intervene where it has national interests. Other group members pointed out that the United States has not followed this policy even-handedly, and that it was actually involved in Rwanda in 1994 through the presence of UN troops.

During this discussion I was scribbling so frantically in my notebook that my consultants paused to tease me about it. I was fascinated to find myself in a roomful of socially conservative, nonacademic, white Americans, nearly all of whom were expressing views about the failure of international responses to the Rwandan genocide that were the same as those of my professors in the notoriously liberal academy. By their own admission, few, if any, members of St. Timothy's had held these positions or knew much about Rwanda at all as little as a year previously. In mid-2000, however, St. Timothy's formed an alliance with the Anglican province of Rwanda through the intermediary organization Anglican Mission in America. Since then, St. Timothy's as a community had moved from the typical American disinterest in Africa, and from the common social conservative tendency to favor isolationism and American exceptionalism, toward a marked concern for engagement with Africa.

Anglican Mission in America is one of many transnational organizations and arrangements that emerged as some Southern bishops and other leaders responded to American conservatives' pleas for overseas help, as expressed in the 1999 Kampala meeting and the AACOM petition. Such arrangements sought to make concrete the accountability globalist vision described in chapter 4 by developing connections of affinity through which Northern conservatives and their Southern allies would live out their concept of the ideal Anglican Communion. In developing such ties, African Anglicans and Episcopal dissidents have asserted that spiritual affinities, such as their shared concerns about sexual morality and biblical authority, trump geographical distance and cultural difference. They imagine, and seek to create, an Anglican world in which geography has ceased to matter—fulfilling many scholars' predictions about the effects of globalization.

These new transnational relationships, in all their scope and variety, raise another common scholarly question about globalization: whom does it involve? Are only transnational and cosmopolitan elites affected by global flows, or are ordinary folk touched by these developments as well? I return to St. Timothy's to explore these questions in the Anglican context by analyzing the lay-level salience of international connections for African and especially American Anglicans. Given all the high-level meetings already described, does this Anglican globalization involve only elites and those who travel globally? Or does it also affect laity and those who stay in one place? The lively foreign policy discussion at that Wednesday evening meeting indicates that Anglican globalization can have parish-level impact, even though its initiators were mainly priests and bishops. Resituating St. Timothy's from its former place as a member parish of its local diocese to a new "location" as a point in a growing transnational orthodox Anglican network brought this congregation—quite literally—into a whole new world of Anglicanism. As Bishop Thomas told me, as we discussed these new connections from the Ugandan perspective, such Americans now "feel themselves at home in Kigali," the capital city of Rwanda.

ANGLICAN MISSION IN AMERICA: DEVELOPING A PARADIGM FOR INTERNATIONAL ALLIANCES

Anglican Mission in America, the organization through which St. Timothy's forged its African connections, was one of the earliest of the new transnational arrangements to emerge after Lambeth, and for several years was also the largest and most controversial.[1] AMiA began with the January 29, 2000, consecration in Singapore of two American priests as bishops by two international primates. Charles Murphy, head of First Promise and rector of a large South Carolina parish, and John Rodgers, retired dean of Trinity Episcopal School for Ministry and a leader in the AACOM coalition, were consecrated to serve as "missionary bishops" to conservative dissidents in the United States by Archbishop Emmanuel Kolini of Rwanda and Archbishop Moses Tay of South East Asia. Bishop John Rucyahana was also involved with the consecrations and the founding of the new group Murphy and Rodgers were to lead. Many First Promise member parishes and clergy became part of the new church organization headed by the missionary bishops, which came to be called the Anglican Mission in America. First Promise's press release stated:

> The two Bishops will provide pastoral support, guidance, and oversight at the request of clergy and congregations that want to continue in the doctrine, discipline and worship of Christ as the Anglican Church has received them. They will actively seek to plant Anglican missions in areas where there are receptive communities and little faithful witness in the Episcopal Church. . . . The sending of these bishops back to the United States is offered as an interim step in an ongoing effort to lead the Episcopal Church back to its biblical foundations.[2]

AMiA was the first American conservative organization under the authority of foreign primates. The consecrations allowed AMiA members to make a strong claim to continued legitimate membership in the Anglican Communion through their connections with Anglican bishops from outside the United States. As John Rodgers put it, "In Singapore, two archbishops gave their blessing for this work. They have saved [AMiA] from becoming simply another group that has broken away from the Episcopal Church."[3] AMiA's "Six Month Report" quoted Murphy and Rodgers as stating, "It is now possible to remain fully orthodox and Anglican on American soil."[4]

For several months after the consecrations, AMiA developed slowly and under much criticism from friends and foes alike. However, in the late summer of 2000 it was given a much-needed boost by the Episcopal Church's General Convention, the triennial meeting at which matters of Episcopal Church policy and procedure are decided by the House of Bishops and House of Deputies, the latter consisting of elected clergy and lay delegates. The 2000 General Convention, held in Denver in July, passed a resolution dealing with three Episcopal dioceses whose bishops still did not ordain and/or employ women priests. The resolution called for a task force to "visit, interview, assess and assist" the dioceses in their "compliance" with the national canons requiring the ordination of women by September 1, 2002.[5] Unlike Anglo-Catholics, many evangelical and charismatic Episcopalians are not strongly opposed to women priests, but they saw this resolution as precedent-setting liberal coerciveness. Furthermore, General Convention 2000 passed a resolution acknowledging the existence of lifelong, committed, nonmarital relationships within the church, though proposed resolutions permitting same-sex unions were defeated.

Immediately after the Convention, in August 2000, the AMiA "missionary bishops" met with their archbishops in Amsterdam, where they were attending an international evangelism conference. In light of the apparent unrepentant heterodoxy of ECUSA, the bishops were given permission to proceed, "full speed ahead," with recruiting and planting parishes and developing an alternative Anglican province in the United States.[6] In the wake of General Convention and with the new mandate from its overseas sponsors, AMiA received many more inquiries about membership. Its "Ten Month Report" stated, "We were inundated with requests and inquiries from priests, parishes and people."[7] AMiA could boast twenty-one member congregations by January 2001, when I attended AMiA's first "Homecoming Conference" to learn more about this growing organization. Besides one curious anthropologist, those attending this conference, held on the spacious campus of All Saints' Church, AMiA's South Carolina headquarters, included a lively crowd from all over the country, both members of existing AMiA parishes and laity and clergy interested in joining the organization. Some of the parishes that eventually affiliated with AMiA were large evangelical Episcopal churches that had broken away, with most or all of their members, from the Episcopal Church. Others were small congregations of disaffected Episcopalians who had left an existing Episcopal church to form an AMiA parish. Four priests and parts of their congregations joined AMiA en masse from the Diocese of Colorado, which had just hosted General Convention. At least one parish that had left the Episcopal Church several years earlier joined

AMiA, as did a Nigerian Anglican parish in Texas. Leaders and parishes associated with the Reformed Episcopal Church and several other Continuing Church groups also explored collaborating with AMiA. At a service in Colorado in June 2001, amid further controversy, AMiA consecrated four more bishops to serve as leaders for its growing and diverse flock. By 2005 AMiA comprised approximately sixty parishes of widely varying sizes, scattered all over the country, though concentrated in the western and southeastern United States.[8]

AMiA's international solution appeared necessary to many because both domestic and other international solutions kept failing. The ECUSA House of Bishops had been slow to consider arrangements allowing conservative bishops to serve conservative parishes in liberal dioceses, and those bishops did not want to take the risks of transgressing diocesan boundaries without church approval. At the international level, AMiA's leaders had been disappointed by the lack of immediate action at the Kampala meeting. The outcome of that meeting had essentially been a deferral of action until the Primates' Meeting scheduled for four months later in Oporto, Portugal—the first meeting of all the international primates since Lambeth. A letter made public after the Kampala meeting, in which the primates present at that meeting responded to the pleas of American conservative leaders, read in part: "At the forthcoming Primates' Meeting we will inform our colleagues of the intolerable situation that you and others like you are facing."[9] Although the primates also assured American conservatives that "among us are those ready to respond to specific and urgent situations which may arise in the months before the Primates' Meeting," this deferral must have been a disappointment to many Americans. Further, it came on the heels of other similar disappointments. There had been little response to the AACOM petition, in spite of the initial optimism of those who sent it out to the Anglican world.[10] Another meeting in mid-1999 between American conservative leaders and several sympathetic overseas primates had also resulted only in a letter assuring First Promise and their allies that the bishops intended to bring the matter of ECUSA's compliance with the Lambeth sexuality resolution before the Primates' Meeting.

These primates' approach to disciplining ECUSA, a measured, slow approach working through the procedures of official Anglican polity, troubled the more impatient American petitioners and some of their global allies. First Promise leaders had hoped at one point for a new Anglican province in the United States within the year 1999,[11] and now the situation would not even be taken up by the primates until their meeting in March of 2000. These repeated delays and deferrals apparently became too much for Kolini, Rucyahana, Tay, and some First Promise leaders.

Two months after the Kampala meeting and two months before the Primates' Meeting, these few took matters into their own hands.

Instead of waiting for a solution that might have involved more international primates, the Singapore consecrations birthed an immediate solution with the support of only two primates, Tay and Kolini.[12] As two out of only thirty-eight primates in the Communion, and thus as highly influential and visible leaders, their participation was essential to give legitimacy to this endeavor. Indeed, one statement by John Rodgers hints that the main reason for the controversial timing of the consecrations, before the March Primates' Meeting, was the imminent retirement of Archbishop Tay.[13] Tay's successor proved willing to accept responsibility for the consecrations once they had occurred, but might not have been as willing to perform them to begin with. Without an Asian bishop, the consecrations would have lost the appearance of support from the global South, broadly defined—other Asian bishops have not been much involved with Northern dissidents, perhaps because the Asian churches are smaller than the African churches and their leaders hence feel less inclined to assert themselves on a global stage. Efforts had been made to secure a third primate to join in the consecrations, to strengthen their validity. Ugandan archbishop Livingstone Mpalanyi Nkoyoyo apparently refused to be involved, and a Congolese priest I met in Uganda told me that Congolese archbishop Patrice Njojo had been asked to be part of the Singapore consecrations. However, the precipitate nature of the consecrations, before the full gathering of primates had had a chance to discuss the matter in Oporto, apparently discouraged these additional primates from participating.[14]

REACTIONS TO AMiA

Liberal and moderate Anglicans and Episcopalians perceived the Singapore consecrations as an attack, rather than—as their proponents argued—a step toward Anglican orthodoxy and worldwide unity. The archbishop of Canada suggested in a public statement that the Singapore consecrations treated bishops as "intercontinental ballistic missiles, manufactured on one continent and fired into another as an act of aggression."[15] ECUSA primate Frank Griswold reacted indignantly: "I am appalled by this irregular action and even more so by the purported 'crisis' that has been largely fomented by [Murphy, Rodgers] and others, and which bears very little resemblance to the church we actually know, which is alive and well and faithful."[16] The archbishop of Canterbury himself sharply challenged the legitimacy and appropriateness of these consecrations.

Liberal and moderate opponents of the Singapore consecrations questioned how Rwandan church leaders could justify moral attacks on ECUSA, given Rwanda's own rocky moral history of genocide. In response, Kolini, Rucyahana, and their supporters have argued that the 1994 genocide is actually one of the key reasons they felt called to respond to conservative Episcopalians. Conservative Pittsburgh bishop Robert Duncan wrote, in a rare sympathetic response to the Singapore consecrations: "Once [Kolini] said to me . . . : 'At the genocide in 1994, the whole world stood back and no one came to Rwanda's aid. We will never stand back when others are similarly threatened, physically or spiritually.' "[17] Phyllis, a middle-aged housewife and active member of St. Timothy's, expressed the same idea to me: "Archbishop Kolini . . . would never turn his back on anyone as others turned their backs on Rwanda." These statements, and many like them, imply that American conservatives are in the same plight spiritually that Rwandan genocide victims were in physically. Some observers find this frequently invoked metaphor too facile. Daniel, a conservative American priest who is critical of AMiA, cut through the logic of this analogy with one sharp remark during our phone conversation: "The difference is that being a refugee in Rwanda means you had 9 out of 10 family members killed, and in America it means someone raised their eyebrow at you at a cocktail party. . . . They're using the same language, but the context is totally different." Daniel's point is hard to dispute, but nonetheless this potent analogy is well accepted and serves an important end: it glosses the 1994 genocide as a foundation for fellow-feeling between Rwandans and American conservatives, who otherwise might easily be put off from involvement with Rwanda by knowledge of its brutal recent history.

While liberal and moderate Anglicans questioned the moral and political legitimacy of the Singapore consecrations, more damaging criticisms came from fellow conservatives, who questioned their wisdom and timing. Many conservatives believed it was not yet time to abandon the Episcopal Church. Some conservative groups, such as Forward in Faith–North America and the American Anglican Council, had expressed interest in oversight from overseas bishops, but were not ready to make that break. AAC leaders, for example, emphatically did not support the Singapore consecrations and criticized AMiA for giving up on the fight for orthodoxy within the church by leading the orthodox out of the church. As Andrew, an AAC member, told me, "AMiA doesn't help front-line parishes, the parishes that feel most oppressed by liberal bishops; it just facilitates leaving."

Furthermore, other conservatives felt AMiA was not only ill-advised, but hurt conservative's efforts to build support among the primates. An article in *Christian Challenge* gives FIF-NA president David Moyer's perspective: "A majority of primates is required to make any solution 'stick.' "[18] Many felt the Singapore consecrations had scuttled hopes that disciplinary action against the United States might come out of the Primates' Meeting at Oporto in March 2000. Conservatives and liberals alike in the Episcopal Church were sharply aware that the stakes could be high at Oporto; this meeting might well bring the global Communion's anger down on those provinces that had disregarded the main message of the Lambeth resolution on sexuality. A fund-raising letter from Ekklesia Society's Bill Atwood from before the Singapore consecrations illustrates how high his hopes were for Oporto: "Rather than being "just another meeting," this one may well be a turning point in the history of the Anglican Communion."[19]

Conservative Americans and other Anglican leaders felt that Tay, Kolini, Murphy, and Rodgers had violated an agreement made at the Kampala meeting not to take action until the Oporto meeting. For example, conservative archbishop Harry Goodhew of Sydney, Australia, spoke out strongly against the consecrations on the basis of their violation of the Kampala statement: "The reason that I demur from the recent action is simple: in my judgment it was too soon, it had too little support, it was against the spirit of an earlier agreement reached in Kampala by a group of conservative primates and archbishops to take the matter to the Primates' Meeting in Portugal, and it was undertaken in a spirit of secrecy."[20] Similarly, Bishop Ezra, one of my Ugandan consultants, told me: "If you were able to get hold of the resolutions in that Kampala conference, it was clear that consecrating bishops or forming new provinces or dioceses . . . was not the right way to go, but that the Primates, who were going to meet in Portugal at that time, would discuss these matters and give a sense of direction."

AMiA's leaders and supporters argued that the situation was urgent, and that the Kampala Statement had left room for responses to such situations.[21] But other conservatives nonetheless blamed AMiA for the lack of a strong outcome from the Oporto meeting. Faced with the Singapore consecrations—shocking, disruptive, dubiously legitimate—many primates sympathetic with the conservative American cause apparently backed away from confronting the Episcopal Church. Andrew told me, "There are people who I think believe that John Rodgers and AMiA torpedoed the Primates' Meeting of March 2000. If they hadn't done that, we could've gotten the majority of bishops to discipline the Episcopal Church. There are people who believe they destroyed our best chance." One conservative article, "The Primates' Oporto Communique: Warning, or Wimp-Out?," examined the outcomes of the Oporto gathering, beginning with the widespread high hopes for the meeting and detailing the disappointing outcome: a final statement that was weak and unclear in its language, and failed to call ECUSA and other liberal provinces to account. The authors of the article placed a significant part of the blame for this failure on the Singapore consecrations: "There were strong hints . . . that some conservative primates were discouraged from taking a harder line because they did not want to be too closely identified with the anomalous Singapore consecrations in January."[22] AMiA's leaders asserted that the Primates' Meeting probably would not have taken any action anyway, but such assertions won them no friends. Jonathan, a priest involved with the AAC, told me bitterly, "Singapore saved the day for the liberals, without a doubt, conclusively. [ECUSA presiding bishop] Griswold should've sent Tay and Kolini the biggest thank-you ever."

PETITIONS AND LOBBYING GIVE WAY TO NETWORKING

The founding of AMiA forced a shift of direction and strategy for the broader conservative movement in its pursuit of the vision of accountability globalism. This vision could have been enforced through two primary paths. First, accountability could be enforced through the official structures of the Anglican Communion—such as the Lambeth Conference or the Primates' Meetings—if their mandate and powers were extended. Alternatively, these standards could be enforced through more ad-hoc efforts to demand accountability, bishop-to-bishop or province-to-province, through international networks. American conservatives' simultaneous pursuit of both strong disciplinary response from the Anglican Communion's official power structures, and other tactics that bypassed and subverted those same power structures, led one critic of this movement to describe its tactics as "renegade authoritarianism."[23]

Conservative Americans appealed for help from official channels in late 1998 when, frustrated by the Episcopal Church's unwillingness to conform to the Lambeth sexuality resolution, the AACOM coalition circulated its petition requesting intervention in the Episcopal Church by the primates, acting in their official capacity as one leadership body of the Communion. Any response from the primates as a body, or even a majority, would have carried relatively clear legitimacy. The right of the Archbishop of Canterbury or the Primates' Meeting to impose policy on individual provinces is uncertain, but *if* such authority exists within the Communion, then the Instruments of Unity would be the entities to wield it legitimately.

However, the AACOM petition also suggested that the Archbishop of Canterbury or the Primates' Meetings might not be the only possible sources for Anglican legitimacy. The petition implied the possibility of an appeal for help through relationships outside the formal international structures of the Communion in the document's request for assistance from "the Primates' meeting, or its individual members." This phrasing reflects the growing tendency for American conservatives to direct appeals for help to particular sympathetic Anglican leaders, regardless of their location or powers in the worldwide Anglican hierarchy. Such appeals represent the deployment of a different model of Anglican accountability, working through networks rather than through the centralized hierarchy of Anglican global polity. These decentered networks of accountability connect Anglicans and Episcopalians around the globe in networks of affinity, like the one binding St. Andrew's Church in Arkansas and their Rwandan bishop, John Rucyahana.

This network-oriented approach to seeking global Anglican accountability not only is a pragmatic strategy, but exemplifies one of the dominant forms of contemporary social and religious movements and international relationships. The languages of networks, reciprocity, and partnership are widely used by Northern Christians of all persuasions. Words like "connection," "relationship," partnership," and "interdependence" dominate ECUSA documents and materials relating to missions and companion diocese programs. Conservative Episcopalians have drawn extensively on these vocabularies and concepts. When I interviewed Jonathan about the AAC and wider trends in American dissidence, he brought up the "rise of alternative networks" within today's Anglican Communion, with "provinces making connections with other provinces on bilateral or multilateral forms." Such alternative networks of affinity serve both of the primary goals of American conservatives: connecting them with other Anglicans who share key convictions, and striking out against the perceived heterodoxy of most Episcopal Church authorities, thus embodying the ideals of accountability globalism.

While the AACOM petition sought intervention primarily through official means, the 1999 Kampala meeting exemplifies the networking approach to international accountability. At that meeting, which had such potential to violate official Anglican procedures that it was held in secrecy, American conservatives appealed to a limited number of Anglican primates for help in establishing a new orthodox American jurisdiction. This jurisdiction, as a "visible restraint and warning" to ECUSA, would serve the cause of global Anglican accountability by demonstrating that the Communion would not tolerate persistent departure from scriptural norms.[24] Conservatives hoped the formation of such a jurisdiction would provide the ultimate rebuke to ECUSA by demonstrating that provinces who would not heed Lambeth and the rest of the Communion would find their boundaries violated and their authorities subverted, as the rest of the Anglican world sought a relationship, not with the province's diocesan and provincial officials, but with its dissident conservative minority.

AMiA emphatically did not receive the traditional sine qua non of official Anglican status, recognition by the Archbishop of Canterbury. Instead, Archbishop George Carey, despite his personal sympathy with American conservatives regarding homosexuality and scriptural authority, expressed displeasure with the Singapore consecrations. In a 2001 letter from Carey to AMiA's primatial sponsors, Carey wrote: "I regard last year's consecrations in Singapore as at best, highly irregular, and at worst, simply schismatic." He argued that the provinces of South East Asia and Rwanda had been given no authority "to consecrate bishops for service elsewhere in the world." Archbishop Carey concluded, "Action of this kind takes you perilously close to creating a new group of churches at odds with the See of Canterbury and the rest of the Communion."[25]

In defending their organization, AMiA's leaders and defenders have invoked the network paradigm, deemphasizing Canterbury as a central source of legitimacy and asserting that AMiA was legitimately Anglican through its connections to the Anglican provinces of Rwanda and South East Asia. One speaker at the AMiA Winter Conference in January 2001, for example, told attendees that AMiA was part of a wider movement in world Christianity in which "quality is replacing geographical proximity." Similarly, a guest preacher at St. Timothy's one Sunday told the congregation, "We are all Africans" in a new world in which "relationships trump institutions." These dissidents' descriptions of their network-based politics echo the terms used by scholars of global movements, revealing a self-conscious globalism not uncommon among contemporary activists.[26]

Within the terms of this networked vision, Archbishop Carey's opinion may not matter much. Through these new transjurisdictional networks, relationships indeed trump geography and institutional structures, and the centrality and authority of Canterbury is called into question. David Virtue and Auburn Traycik made explicit reference to this new, decentralized vision of world Anglicanism in an article about the Singapore consecrations:

> Conservatives . . . believe that, after Lambeth [1998], the old dynamic—which insists that a new U.S. province will not be recognized by Canterbury—will be overcome by the new, in which recognition will be determined by the response of the larger Communion, especially the global South, now Anglicanism's center of gravity and pivotal to the orthodox turn at Lambeth 98.[27]

Similarly, John Rodgers stated in an interview about AMiA: "I do not think the fact that the Archbishop of Canterbury is evaluating the validity of our consecrations is a threat. . . . I am not aware that the Archbishop of Canterbury has jurisdictional authority in these matters; I believe that belongs to the respective Primates."[28] AMiA's leaders thus asserted strongly that other Anglican archbishops can bestow Anglican legitimacy on parishes in the United States. Lacey, a petite woman in her sixties and a member of St. Timothy's vestry, spoke to me vehemently regarding the legitimacy of AMiA's membership in the Anglican Communion: "Is not Murphy a bishop of Rwanda? Is not Rwanda a member of the Anglican Communion?" From the point of view of AMiA's supporters, the yes answers to these two questions add up to an undeniable yes to the larger question of whether AMiA is truly an Anglican body.

Such arguments are certainly effective. Few have questioned the fundamental validity of the consecrations, although the consecration of two priests as bishops for territory A, by the archbishops of territories B and C, and without the consent of church leaders in territory A, is at best irregular and at worst totally illegal within the terms of Anglican polity. But although the case was convoluted, it was not entirely clear that the consecrations were so unprecedented and out of line that they could be dismissed. This ambiguity gave Murphy, Rodgers, and their sponsors space to assert the legitimacy of their endeavor. The new bishops and their supporters argued that this new international solution was both necessary and legal in terms of a new, decentered vision of global Anglican polity.

AMiA not only epitomized the network approach to global accountability, it pushed the wider transnational orthodox movement in the same direction. It is impossible to know whether the 2000 Primates' Meeting would have addressed concerns about ECUSA in a way conservatives found satisfactory without the Singapore consecrations as backdrop. It is clear, however, that given those consecrations and the weak outcome of that meeting, other conservative groups increasingly gave up on strategies to reform ECUSA through the polity and formal procedures of the Anglican Communion. After AMiA's founding, conservatives' efforts to pursue both official/hierarchical and unofficial/networked solutions became increasingly unbalanced. From early 1999 on, tactics addressing official Communion structures, like the AACOM petition and other appeals to the primates, have repeatedly failed to bring about significant change.[29] At the same time, network-style tactics have become increasingly central to the activism of Northern conservatives and their allies. Such tactics are not dependent on the consent of the Archbishop of Canterbury or a majority of primates, instead working through individual relationships and alliances. Following the 2000 Primates' Meeting and ECUSA's General Convention, American conservatives increasingly despaired of appeals to formal channels. Relations between other conservative groups and AMiA worsened during this period, when a number of parishes left conservative Episcopal dioceses for AMiA.[30] Yet at the same time AMiA's strategy of seeking connections with particular overseas leaders willing to extend protection or support began to seem like the only way forward for many conservative Episcopalians. The bottom-up, hierarchy-dodging AMiA paradigm increasingly appeared less and less a violation and a fluke and more and more the wave of the future

Variations on the AMiA Paradigm

By dint of the involvement of two primates, the confrontational nature of its founding, and its relatively large size, AMiA is easily the most visible and controversial example of transnational networking by Southern leaders on behalf of beleaguered conservative Northerners. But AMiA is not by any means the only example of such intervention. Other relationships founded on the same general principles as AMiA's are less organized and official, not necessarily requiring parishes to declare their separation from their Northern provinces. Compared with AMiA, most of these other actions are either on a smaller scale, involving only one parish and/or only one overseas bishop; of shorter duration, involving one or several short-term visits; or less controversial, as in situations where the local Northern bishop tolerates the arrangement, making it less of a violation of Anglican order and collegiality.

Although AMiA is the clearest example of transnational Anglican oversight, the other varied arrangements along the same lines carry just as much significance, if not more. These other arrangements demonstrate that AMiA was not simply the brainchild of a few frustrated and pugnacious Anglican leaders, but is instead only one indication of a much wider trend in world Anglicanism, manifest in many other sites and forms. Gerald, a retired conservative Episcopal bishop, summed it all up during my phone interview with him:

> It used to be something that no one would have thought about. A new series of circumstances . . . has really produced this kind of out-of-the-box thinking. And none of it is really against the rules. The rules never anticipated such arrangements. . . . For many of us these foreign jurisdictions are theologically more nearly where we were when we were ordained, and where the Episcopal Church was. . . . There are many of us who are trying to find creative ways forward that think about the church in different terms than the simple legal and geographical terms that we've always understood.

Other cases where Southern bishops are tending to American parishes differ in important ways from that of AMiA, but they serve many of the same functions, such as enabling disaffected parishes (or as one Ugandan described them to me, "aggrieved churches") in the United States to feel connected with sympathetic bishops in other parts of the world and to obtain sacramental services (such as confirmation and ordination, which require a bishop's presence) that they cannot or will not receive from their own ECUSA bishop. One example, from the many I have heard and read, of dissident Episcopalians' expressions of pleasure regarding these more amicable nongeographic relationships comes from the Rev. Martyn Minns, rector of the conservative evangelical Truro Episcopal Church outside Washington, D.C., who told the *New York Times Magazine* (reportedly "with glee"), "I spend more time with bishops in the global south than with the bishop of Virginia."[31]

Ugandan Bishops in Transnational Relationships

Most Ugandan bishops, like their Rwandan colleagues, were critical of the Episcopal Church's disregard of the Lambeth sexuality resolution. Still, they did not look favorably on actions that might damage relations with ECUSA or the rest of the Communion, and saw the Singapore consecrations as the wrong approach. Bishop Ezra told me that he and his brother bishops in the Ugandan church understand that ECUSA has problems, but as a senior and influential bishop in the Church of Uganda, he was unwilling to add any complications to his province's load: "For us, and most of the bishops in Africa, we say that we see the problem there, but we shouldn't intervene, we shouldn't go to consecrate a bishop there. . . . We have many problems; we don't like to add another problem." Many Ugandan Anglicans expressed concern about the ways the Singapore consecrations and AMiA threatened the authority structure of the Anglican Communion. Stephen, a Ugandan priest in his sixties who serves at a Kampala-area cathedral, responded to my question about his views of the Singapore consecrations: "Personally I wouldn't support it. Because it contradicts the authority, the common communion, for what the Communion stands for. . . . I think there is a sense of indiscipline." Jonah, a priest and teacher at UCU, also implicitly criticized the "indiscipline" of AMiA with this rhetorical question: "How would Kolini feel if some of his parishes went under the Archbishop of Uganda?"

Several consultants stressed to me that an African leader should be officially invited before playing any role in another province. Richard, who is an official in the administration of the Province of Uganda and is thus very conscious of relations with other provinces, told me about his concerns that AMiA and similar arrangements were too invasive. He observed, "When the church was starting here, the King of Buganda invited missionaries. I think if this has come up as a need, I expect that the church in England or the church in America would make some invitations for our people to go and evangelize." Likewise, Michael, a young priest studying at UCU, told me firmly, "I do not believe in a transfer of responsibility for Christian leaders in the U.S. to Christian leaders in Africa. . . . An exchange of personnel should not be exercised in rebellion and rejection."

These hesitations notwithstanding, some Ugandans do feel that bending rules and transgressing boundaries might be justified. I interviewed Aaron, a priest from southern Uganda, in the offices of the international evangelical organization for which he works. As a touring preacher, he is well aware of the differences among Anglican provinces, and believes the situation in North America may demand boundary-crossing of some sort:

> You have some congregations where individuals are really looking for sound Christian leadership. And I know two bishops, mine inclusive, who have been asked by some congregations in North America to offer their episcopal oversight. They hesitated, of course, because of the political reasons and practical implications. . . . [But] I think the idea of geographical respect is likely to be violated for the sake of spiritual intervening in a situation which has gone out of control.

Bishop Ezekiel and his colleague Bishop David, two of the Ugandan church's most outspoken critics of the Episcopal Church, agreed with Aaron, stating that they could see the need for African bishops to intervene and care for American parishes. Bishop David, who heads a Kampala-area diocese and has traveled to several meetings with American conservatives, made an interesting analogy with the missionary period in the church in Africa in arguing that such actions are a reasonable response to the situation in the Episcopal Church today:

> If our brothers in the North cannot get help from their church, which is subjugating them . . . I don't know, probably I wouldn't go, but I support those who can at least go and give them some support. . . . [But] why can't Christians say now, if we want to go and evangelize a group of unbelievers, let's send there bishops? Let's consecrate bishops? That's what they did here in Uganda. When they consecrated the first bishop, they didn't first come here and ask the pagans, should this be your bishop? They consecrated him in England, and he came here as bishop of Uganda. . . . So when Christianity is dead in a place, the missionaries can go, and the missionaries don't have to get permission from the people to be evangelized. . . . So we can consecrate bishops and send them to pagan North America.

Bishop Ezekiel, a recently retired bishop who spoke out against homosexuality at the time of Lambeth 1998, likewise states that such actions are warranted under current conditions:

What these Rwanda people and Asians have done is a real break-through. They are doing something which is extraordinary. Because in normal terms, you do not breach [the Communion]. But they are saying, God is calling us to do the extraordinary. . . . OK, personally, would I do it? I think maybe no. Maybe no. Because the Anglican Communion, I like it. . . . I'm naturally unwilling to lose my membership, to break away, and I still value my fellowship. And so if I'm going to tamper with my relationship with my church, my Anglican church, then I would have to think twice. But if somebody has done it, I don't want to say he has done the wrong thing.

These two bishops both raise the possibility of taking drastic actions themselves and express some sympathy and support for the Church of Rwanda's intervention, but they also both ultimately come to the conclusion that, most likely, they themselves wouldn't actually do anything so drastic ("probably I wouldn't go," "I would have to think twice").

However, although even these outspoken bishops would hesitate to intervene in the Episcopal Church as dramatically as did Kolini and Rucyahana, many Ugandans welcome the idea of bringing an orthodox African witness to the Northern churches. Ugandan and other African Anglicans share American dissidents' hopes for a more networked Anglican world. Numerous Ugandans told me that exchange and reciprocity should characterize contemporary and future missions work. Jonah, a Ugandan priest, told me, "We are at a time when we should have missions from both ends." Bishop Thomas described to me a globe in which Christians travel anywhere to share their faith with one another: "The time is now for us to cross-pollinate one another as the Anglican Communion. . . . The West come to the South, the South go to the West, West go to the East, let's move around, let's influence each other!"

Almost unanimously, Ugandan church leaders and laity told me that AMiA was too confrontational, too schismatic, too disruptive—in short, nothing they would have done or wanted their bishops to do. At the same time, the vast majority of Ugandans I spoke with expressed enthusiasm for having stronger relationships with Northern provinces and having African leaders more actively involved in Anglican Communion affairs. Some Ugandans find these ideas appealing because they believe more mutual engagement among Anglican churches and provinces will be beneficial for all involved. African leaders who take on such alliances often gain enhanced opportunities to obtain resources for their dioceses, as we shall see in chapter 7. Many are also concerned by what they hear about the moral condition of the Northern churches, and are eager to see African leaders help by preaching and evangelizing in the North. Some of the same Ugandan leaders who expressed aversion to AMiA have been willing to participate in less dramatic relationships along the same lines. These informal, often temporary relationships draw relatively little controversy and thus are easier for African bishops to enter into. For example, Bishop Mark told me "it would be difficult" for him to become the bishop of one American parish which had asked for his help, but that visiting and ministering to that parish and others was "no problem":

> If they asked me when I was already with them to confirm, I would confirm. I would confirm. If they asked me to administratively or pastorally link up, like Kolini has linked up, then I would not find it easy to make as a decision personally, for reasons like, if we are making a decision to offer any pastoral concerns for the church in America, it should be made [in the Ugandan House of Bishops]. . . . [But] to go and minister to them, oh, yeah, definitely. That's no problem there. I don't find that difficult.

I present here four examples of situations in which disaffected Northern parishes have sought and received the support and help of obliging African bishops, as part of the Northern parishes' efforts to avoid and protest ECUSA's leadership. My list is by no means exhaustive, and focuses on the actions of Ugandan bishops, but these relationships give some sense of the wider development of the networking approach to conservative globalism exemplified by AMiA.

St. Andrew's, Destin, and Christ Church, Grove Farm

St. Andrew's Church, Destin, Florida, joined AMiA in 2000. Like many other evangelical and charismatic Episcopal parishes, its members felt alienated from the Episcopal Church and sought more orthodox leadership. Unlike many of AMiA's other parishes, however, St. Andrew's had a preexisting relationship with an African bishop, Bishop Wilson Turumanya of Bunyoro-Kitara diocese, Uganda, whom parish leaders had met at the 1997 Dallas conference. When St. Andrew's rector, Michael Hesse, visited Bunyoro-Kitara diocese to teach about charismatic practices, he and the other parishioners with him became convinced that they were not the only ones with spiritual gifts to share. Alan, a leader in that parish who spoke to me by phone about his church's African relationships, explained to me that they "simply started to consider the numbers." There are 20,000 Episcopalians in his American diocese, and 300,000 Anglicans in the city of Hoima, Uganda, alone, with many more in the rest of Turumanya's diocese. Alan quipped, "Who needs to be missionaries to whom?" At St. Andrew's request, Bishop Turumanya sent two of his staff to spend four months as missionaries in Destin, preaching at area churches and evangelizing in neighborhoods. Religion journalist Gustav Niebuhr writes, quoting Hesse's description: "'[The missionaries] made a striking sight, riding bicycles around an overwhelmingly white community where most people drive.'"[32]

Connection with Ugandan Christians was a source of inspiration for St. Andrew's congregation as its sense of connection with the Episcopal Church was weakening. Alan explained that, though the church's formal affiliation is now with the Province of Rwanda through AMiA, they maintain an active relationship with Turumanya's diocese. Alan observed that joining AMiA "made sense to people" and "wasn't a step into space," since Rwandan Anglicans are "next-door neighbors" of Uganda. For members of St. Andrew's, joining AMiA was not just an escape from the Episcopal Church but a way of intensifying already-significant relationships with African Anglicans.

Turumanya's relationship with another American parish, Christ Church, in Grove Farm, Pennsylvania, is another cross-provincial connection illustrating the development of a new sense of Anglican identity based on perceived like-mindedness rather than on geographical proximity. Christ Church is an Anglican-rooted, nondenominational church whose leaders and members left the Diocese of Pittsburgh in the mid-1990s. The diocese's evangelical bishop, Robert Duncan, wanted to keep the new church grounded in the Anglican Communion and contacted Turumanya, who had studied at TESM and had connections in the area. Turumanya agreed to ordain an assisting priest for Christ Church, thus taking partial oversight of the parish.[33] Although Christ Church is not an Episcopal parish, Turumanya's involvement there fits the pattern of connecting evangelical Anglicans in this country with Anglicans in Africa, this time with the mediation of a sympathetic Episcopal bishop.

Both Duncan and Turumanya see this arrangement as not merely an isolated accommodation but an indication of wider trends and greater things to come. In a letter to Christ Church, Turumanya wrote, "I am sure that we can establish a history-making arrangement between Christ Church and Bunyaro-Kitara, one that may point the way for other churches to remain within the worldwide Anglican fellowship without compromising their biblical beliefs." Duncan, for his part, offered an analogy with the abolition of parish boundaries in the Episcopal Church some sixty years ago. "People seem to be better served by being in the congregation that better feeds them spiritually, not just the church that happens to be in their neighborhood." Today, Duncan predicted, "jets may do to diocesan boundaries what automobiles did to parish boundaries"—by enabling parishes to belong to church networks that best "feed them spiritually," rather than the church body within whose geographical boundaries they are located.[34] Duncan's vision epitomizes the postnational, geography-denying tendencies of contemporary global social and religious movements. Sociologist of religion Peggy Levitt has described this trend in terms applying to current developments in the Anglican world: "Just as decentralized, adaptive modes of production are better suited to meet the challenges of global economic competition, so flexible production and dissemination of religious goods may be better suited to meeting the needs of contemporary religious consumers."[35]

Two Ordinations and a Consecration

A third example also features Ugandan bishops getting involved in American ordinations—this time, because the candidates had trained at a seminary which made it difficult for them to be accepted for ordination by any American diocese. Evangelicals, charismatics, and Anglo-Catholics feel the Episcopal Church has made ordination very difficult for them. Although members of both groups would like to increase their presence (and hence influence) in the Episcopal clergy, Anglo-Catholics feel marginalized by the growing pressure to accept women priests, and evangelical and charismatic Episcopalians feel their views on scripture and morality are unwelcome. Moreover, both groups feel that most Episcopal seminaries have been infected with liberalism and (post)modern theology, which may corrupt orthodox students. At the same time, if those seeking ordination attend one of the two conservative Episcopal seminaries, TESM or Nashotah House,[36] or non-Episcopalian evangelical seminaries like Fuller, they are unlikely to be accepted for ordination by an Episcopal diocese's leadership.[37]

The two would-be priests in this case graduated from the seminary of the Reformed Episcopal Church (REC), a small evangelical Anglican denomination that broke away from the Episcopal Church in 1873 following conflicts between evangelicals and Anglo-Catholics. Bishop Terence Kelshaw, the conservative bishop of Rio Grande, was willing to accept the two men into his diocese, but was unable to ordain them because of their REC credentials. The solution lay in involving a foreign bishop, Bishop Samuel Ssekadde of Namirembe Diocese, Kampala, who happily ordained the men.[38] These American priests have never been to Uganda and do not plan to go. Their peculiar situation, serving American churches under the authority of a Ugandan bishop, makes sense only in the context of the struggle within ECUSA for a sustained conservative presence in the clergy—and the increasing tendency for conservatives to look overseas, and to Africa in particular, for help in that struggle.[39]

Although Ssekadde traveled to Texas to ordain these priests, there have been limits to Ugandan bishops' willingness to be drawn into potentially controversial acts. On the same trip, Ssekadde and several other Ugandan bishops participated in the service of consecration for a new REC bishop. They did not, however, lay hands on him in the rite of consecration itself, although their REC hosts had hoped the Ugandan bishops would lend the unimpeachable apostolic validity of their own consecrations to the new REC consecration. One Ugandan bishop explained to me that he and his colleagues were unwilling to break relations with ECUSA, at least not without consultation with the Ugandan House of Bishops: "We can't do it without sharing it with our brothers." Still, by responding to the REC's invitation, and by ordaining the Texas priests, these bishops transgressed boundaries and challenged conventional procedure in order to aid American conservatives and, in the process, raise the profile of the Ugandan church in this bold new transnationally networked Anglican world.

GOOD SHEPHERD, ROSEMONT, AND ALL SAINTS', WYNNEWOOD, PENNSYLVANIA

Bishop Charles Bennison of the Diocese of Pennsylvania is engaged in perpetual conflict with a half-dozen conservative parishes, mainly Anglo-Catholic in orientation, who do not accept his authority as bishop because of his liberal social and theological positions. African bishops have gotten involved in these conflicts in at least two cases. The first case involves the parish of Good Shepherd, Rosemont, and its rector, David Moyer, who is also actively involved in oppositional politics within the Episcopal Church as the head of the conservative Anglo-Catholic organization Forward in Faith–North America.[40] In November 2000, Moyer hosted three overseas primates at Good Shepherd for an international confirmation service. One of the visiting primates, Maurice Sinclair, explained the rationale for the visit: "[We are doing this] to provide a pastoral visit with the provision of the sacrament of confirmation as a response to the spiritual needs of orthodox Anglicans and to provide tangible evidence of the pastoral care and concern of the wider Anglican Communion for people who are deprived of episcopal ministry that is faithful to the mind of the Anglican Communion."[41] Although Bennison ultimately chose to attend the confirmation service, the service demonstrated Moyer's ability to bypass Bennison in favor of bishops whose positions he found more compatible. Those involved saw it as " 'a symbolic act that demonstrated the solidarity of Anglicans around the world' in the cause of traditional church teaching," and a "signal event of bigger and better things yet to come."[42]

Two years later, Bennison yet again faced a foreign bishop's intervention in his diocese—this time in the parish of All Saints', Wynnewood. The priest at All Saints', Eddy Rix, is a Canadian Anglican who, according to David Virtue, "was originally ordained in the Diocese of Lusaka [in Zambia, southern Africa] because no bishop would ordain him in Canada because of his opposition to women's ordination." Bennison had formally inhibited Rix—that is, forbidden him from acting as a priest in the diocese—because Rix was violating church rules by preaching and celebrating the Eucharist in the diocese without Bennison's permission.[43] Rix's bishop, Bernard Malango of Lusaka, held an ecclesiastical trial of Rix on these charges before sympathetic Zambian church officials, who sentenced him only to a private admonition from his bishop. Malango then sent Rix back to his American parish to keep ministering there— apparently beyond the reach of Bennison's discipline, since Rix's Zambian bishop was pleased with his conduct.[44] He remained on the staff at All Saints'.

The arrangement between Rix and Malango is particularly illustrative of the way appeals to external authority move these conflicts into a gray area in which it is unclear what is and is not permissible. As Bishop Gerald, quoted earlier, put it, "None of it is really against the rules. The rules never anticipated such arrangements." The policies and structures of the Anglican Communion don't give clear guidance regarding, for example, whether a priest under the authority of an African bishop may legitimately serve an Episcopal parish against the will of the local Episcopal bishop, or if not, how the American bishop should deal with the situation. The networking approach pursued by American conservatives and their Southern allies is potent precisely because it subverts—without clearly violating—established order, polity, and geographical boundaries.

SOUTHERN INTERVENTION IN OTHER NORTHERN PROVINCES

ECUSA is not the only Anglican province to be faced with the complex challenges of international interventions. In the spring of 2000, St. John's, Kidderminster, a conservative parish in the Diocese of Worcester, England, invited a retired Ugandan bishop to perform a confirmation service in their church in place of their own English bishop, whom the congregation regarded as insufficiently orthodox. In 2002 a number of parishes in the Canadian diocese of New Westminster broke away and sought international help after the diocese voted to permit the blessing of same-sex unions.[45] These churches, calling themselves the Anglican Church in New Westminster (ACiNW), rejected an offer from the Canadian House of Bishops of an "episcopal visitor," a bishop who would serve orthodox parishes under the authority of the diocese's liberal bishop.[46] Instead the churches appealed for assistance from beyond the Canadian church.

In making the case for international assistance, ACiNW leaders argued that their problems were not merely a local conflict between several parishes and their bishop, but one manifestation of global issues within the worldwide Communion: "The crisis in this Diocese is not the result of a minor theological disagreement that has led to chilly relations with our local bishop, but . . . threatens to break communion between our Diocese and a number of provinces in the worldwide Anglican Church."[47] The U.S.-based AAC made a similar argument for the global relevance of events in New Westminster in a statement supporting ACiNW: "The recent actions by . . . the Bishop of New Westminster . . . [show] disrespect for the Anglican global community, and . . . what appears to be a 'world be damned' attitude."[48] These assertions of global relevance were apparently substantiated when leaders appearing to represent "global Anglicanism" chose to intervene in the situation. Early in 2004, the primates of Rwanda, Central Africa, Congo, and South East Asia announced that they would offer protection and oversight to the ACiNW parishes.[49] The ACiNW case illustrates that the global relevance of local conflicts has become a key point for intraprovincial argumentation.

THE NETWORK OF ANGLICAN COMMUNION DIOCESES AND PARISHES

The Network of Anglican Communion Dioceses and Parishes is another case of Northern dissidents seeking Southern help. However, the Network is also qualitatively different in important ways, as an umbrella organization that seeks to unite dissidents into one body with the potential to become the new American Anglican province. Although this book's temporal scope is for the most part limited to the 1997–2002 period, the Network is significant enough, as an outgrowth of the trends I explore, to warrant mention. The Network was officially launched on January 20, 2004, in response to Gene Robinson's election and consecration as bishop of New Hampshire in the summer and fall of 2003. Led by Pittsburgh bishop Robert Duncan, the Network is an outgrowth of the American Anglican Council, but also seeks to transcend the AAC by drawing in non-evangelical groups like FIF-NA and Episcopalians previously uninvolved with this movement. The new Network consisted of ten conservative American dioceses and their parishes,[50] and individual parishes from other dioceses, who may "become non-geographic parishes with [Network] dioceses,. . . . [receiving] ministry leadership and spiritual oversight from [Network bishops]."[51] While the "Network" is domestic in character, it is also intended as a locus for international connections. According to the AAC, the Network "gives us a way to connect with those sisters and brothers around the Anglican world and around the ecumenical community who will no longer recognize the current leadership of the Episcopal Church."[52]

By 2006 ambiguity still surrounded the issue of whether the Network's leaders intend the Network to be an orthodox "church-within-a-church," or, as it were, a "church-replacing-a-church." A January 13, 2004, press release from the AAC stated that the organization, in its Network-related activities, was not "gather[ing] together orthodox dioceses to operate independently of the Episcopal Church" but that the AAC "continues to work within the Episcopal Church to advance the realignment of Anglicanism in North America."[53] Alongside such assurances, however, are indications that some see the new Network as the long-awaited orthodox Anglican replacement province in the United States. In a piece entitled "What Is the Network?" on the AAC website, evangelical priest Martyn Minns writes, "Could [the Network] be a replacement for ECUSA—only God knows but we will be ready."[54] Diane Knippers observed that some hope the Network will become "another church (or "province" in Anglican parlance) [which] could be parallel to the Episcopal Church or could replace the existing Episcopal Church. . . . within the Anglican Communion."[55]

Resolution of this uncertainty surrounding the Network's intentions may lie in the Anglican Communion's eventual response to Gene Robinson's consecration and the moves toward officially blessing same-sex unions in the Anglican Church of Canada. By mid-summer of 2006, the slow wheels of official Anglican polity and process were still grinding out a full response. Initially a commission called by the Archbishop of Canterbury examined the state of the Communion and produced a document known as the Windsor Report. The primates, meeting in early 2005, ratified the Windsor Report's call for the American and Canadian churches to explain their actions to the wider Communion and to place a moratorium on public blessings of same-sex unions and consecrations of gay or lesbian bishops unless and until such practices became more widely accepted in the Communion. The Episcopal Church's General Convention of June 2006 responded to these calls by passing resolutions expressing regret for having caused pain to sister Anglican churches and affirming an ongoing commitment to the Anglican Communion; the Convention also called on dioceses to "exercise restraint by not consenting to the consecration of any candidate to the episcopate whose manner of life presents a challenge to the wider church and will lead to further strains on communion."[56] As a next step, the primates were to meet to decide together whether these measures constituted sufficient cooperation with their requests, or, if not, what the consequences would be for ECUSA. Some conservatives in the United States hope that the final outcome of all this may be the expulsion of the Episcopal Church from the Anglican

Communion, which might make it possible for the Network to be fully recognized as the legitimate Anglican province in the United States—a more likely outcome if the Network's leaders play by the rules by functioning within the Episcopal Church in the meantime.

The Network's leaders hope to be granted official status through the centralized, traditional structures of the Anglican Communion. Failing that outcome, however, the support of a number of international primates means that the Network has the potential to pursue Anglican membership and legitimacy through decentralized transnational Anglican networks of recognition and affinity. The new Network has received strong expressions of support from fourteen primates, who have called the new Network a "hopeful sign of a faithful Anglican future in North America."[57] Even if the Archbishop of Canterbury or other Instruments of Unity do not recognize the Network, these and other individual primates may choose to be in relationship with the Network rather than with the Episcopal Church.

The 2004 consecration of Henry Orombi as archbishop of the Church of Uganda provides one example of this possibility. Ugandan church officials disinvited Episcopal bishops who had supported Gene Robinson's consecration from Orombi's enthronement service, instead inviting a delegation from the Network. The politics of welcome at Orombi's consecration suggest one possible further development of transnational networks of connection and belonging, through the complex and fluid politics of invitation, recognition, and denial. By snubbing the Episcopal Church in favor of the Network, the Church of Uganda—and other provinces that have followed suit in various ways—treat the Network as the de facto true Anglican church in the United States. Shared Anglican identity is defined through mutual recognition rather than through membership in the worldwide Anglican polity—in which the Episcopal Church remains the only official Anglican body in the United States.

Proponents of the Network use a new vocabulary for their their ultimate vision: "realignment." For instance, the AAC's information page about the Network is entitled "Road to Realignment."[58] Diane Knippers also used this term in criticizing the Anglican Communion's centralized structure as colonial and "remarkably unsuited for the 21st Century Church," concluding, "I'm increasingly convinced that global Anglican realignment is both necessary and unavoidable."[59] The term *realignment* captures the idea of connection along lines of affinity, whether within or across diocesan or provincial boundaries, rather than connection or belonging through the older Eurocentric structures of the Communion. According to Knippers and others, a realigned Communion would better match the realities of our current global era. "Realignment," though, is more than just a reformulation of the network paradigm. Whereas previous networked relationships could be seen (and were sometimes intended) as short-term emergency measures, "realignment" connotes a permanent reorganization, a new global status quo.

"AT HOME IN KIGALI": AFRICANIST INTERESTS IN A CONSERVATIVE EPISCOPAL PARISH

These connections and organizations raise one of the questions often discussed in the theoretical literature on globalization: whom do processes of globalization actually affect, and how? Does globalization affect everyone, or only elites, migrants, city dwellers, and travelers? John Tomlinson suggests that the key question about globalization is its broader impact on those who aren't "on the move"—how and to what extent globalization transforms localities, "not just occasionally lifting some people out of them."[60] Although the impact of globalization is uneven in its depth and character due to variations in access to communications and transport technology, its processes undeniably do touch those on the "periphery"— even the poorest and most rural.[61] Anna Tsing and Roland Robertson, among others, point out that globalization involves not only concrete participation in transnational flows but also a developing perception of the global scale as a relevant frame of reference for local events.[62] Such globalism may be much more widespread than actual access to the products and flows associated with globalization.

In much of the preceding text, I have described Anglican globalization through the actions of leaders—priests, bishops, and primates. How do laypeople and their everyday parish life fit into this picture of important men and significant events? Alghough the conservative movement is led by a few activist church leaders, ordinary Anglican priests and congregations in both the United States and Africa are also touched, and changed, by these transnational connections and the ideas that accompany them. From a St. Timothy's member who described himself as an African missionary on the basis of the church's link to the Province of Rwanda to a Ugandan Anglican teenager who felt Africans should carry their faith to the rest of the world but wondered whether Americans would respond by wondering, "Where did God find you, when you were sleeping in a grass hut?," Anglicans around the world have been influenced by globalization within their church to reconsider their ideas about and their relationships with one another.

Among Ugandan Anglicans of all ranks and ages, I found widespread interest in the condition of the Northern churches and the Episcopal Church in particular. Long before the Gene Robinson controversy, Ugandan Anglicans heard rumors and stories about the lack of zeal and orthodoxy in the Northern churches. The more international connections intensified, the more opportunity Ugandan Anglicans had to hear bad news about the American church. For example, the students at Uganda Christian University, a broad spectrum of young Ugandan Christians, gathered one week to hear a talk by a guest on campus, an American missionary to Rwanda from St. Andrew's, Little Rock. The missionary mentioned that some African leaders were now taking control of American parishes to protect them from heterodox American bishops. Talking with students afterward, I found that, although such arrangements were unknown to many students, the idea that the American church was straying from the gospel was familiar. These responses represent a microcosm of what I observed in the Ugandan context: Ugandans, like other Africans, cannot help being aware of America. The United States is a world power, and the Ugandan media transmit and discuss its culture, politics, and problems extensively. As circulated texts and stories, international visitors, and their own bishops and priests tell Ugandan Anglicans about developing transnational connections, what they are learning is not awareness of the United States, but a new way of thinking of Africa in relation to the United States. This is the challenging and exciting message that Africa is superior to America in certain ways and that Africans have something to teach American Christians. The next chapter will explore further how Ugandans see Africa in relation to the United States as the power dynamics of the Anglican Communion shift southward.

In contrast, it is common for Americans to be quite unaware of Africa. The question is whether involvement with transnational networks increases conservative Episcopalians' Africa-consciousness. Are these new relationships only tools for evading and aggravating Episcopal Church leadership? Are they primarily about cutting ties, dissociating from the Episcopal Church, with the foreign bishops merely a means to an end? Or do these alliances also involve taking on new international attachments and identities? St. Timothy's offers a case study of processes of discursive and conceptual globalization in one small American community, as its members' involvement with the transnational dissident movement has led them to new views of the globe, Africa, Christianity, and themselves.

On the one hand, St. Timothy's, as an AMiA parish, has a more sustained, official African affiliation than many of the other parishes I have discussed, and might be expected to take its African connections more seriously than non-AMiA parishes. On the other hand, belonging to AMiA also means the congregation's relationship with its African archbishop is mediated by its American bishop. Many non-AMiA parishes have more direct contact with their various overseas patrons and supporters, which might cause these parishes to take their overseas connections more seriously. The degree to which the laity in a given American parish get involved in its international alliances likely depends on elusive variables such as chance and inclination, rather than the type of alliance. The case of St. Timothy's demonstrates that some parishes, at least, take their international affiliations quite seriously and seek to deepen their relationship with their overseas allies.

When I came to the parish, St. Timothy's had been a member of AMiA for about a year. Several months after AMiA's founding, St. Timothy's vestry had voted unanimously to join the new organization, announcing its decision—which was greeted with a standing ovation—at a parish meeting.[63] The church's name was changed to St. Timothy's Anglican Church, Province of Rwanda. The clergy asked their ECUSA bishop to transfer their letters dimissory to the Province of Rwanda—the official procedure for transferring a priest to the authority of another bishop. Their bishop, seeing this move as legitimating AMiA, refused, as have most ECUSA bishops presented with similar requests. Nevertheless, the clergy of St. Timothy's now regard themselves as under the authority of the archbishop of Rwanda, through the intermediary of Bishop Charles Murphy. Although the church building stands where it always has, on a side street in a small southeastern city, the sign on its front lawn proclaims St. Timothy's as a member parish of the Anglican Province of Rwanda (see figure 2).

Around forty members left the congregation in order to remain loyal to the Episcopal Church, and there was a long and difficult lawsuit over the church property (which St. Timothy's ultimately lost, obliging members to build their own new church), but St. Timothy's transition to AMiA was relatively smooth overall. When I came to the church in 2001, I found a flourishing, welcoming, stable congregation whose members looked positively on their AMiA identity. When I asked members of the church about the move to join AMiA, most expressed complete satisfaction with the break from the Episcopal Church. Several described the vestry's decision as an "emancipation proclamation." Annette, an active member and mother of two young children, told me, "I thought, the lifeboat has finally arrived." Frieda paraphrased scripture to praise their new Anglican head: "God so loved the world that he sent the archbishop [of Rwanda]." Allen, a fiftyish former Presbyterian, told me flatly, "I would've left the church if they'd remained in the Episcopal Church." However, though many felt it might be necessary to leave ECUSA, staying within the Anglican Communion was also important. This attachment was especially keen for the parish's long-term Episcopal members, but also for many members from other traditions who had become very attached to Anglican liturgy, like Allen, who spoke to me at length about the strengths he had discovered in Anglicanism.

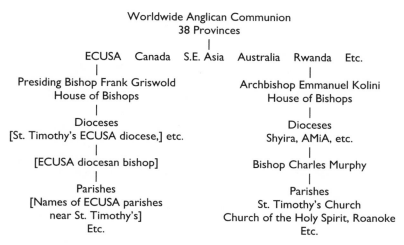

Figure 2. Diagram used to explain the change in St. Timothy's affiliation. (Adapted from a diagram mailed to St. Timothy's members; accessed in private archive.)

Joining AMiA provided a "lifeboat" because it gave this alienated parish a way to continue to claim Anglican identity while breaking from the errant Episcopal Church. Simply leaving the Episcopal Church and becoming, in effect, additional Continuing Churches did not appeal to most churches in St. Timothy's situation. These lively, growing evangelical parishes did not care to identify themselves with the Continuing Church movement, which is mostly Anglo-Catholic in its orientation and which has grown little in its two decades of existence. Joe, the rector, told me simply, "We didn't want to become a Continuing Church." Elmer, Frieda's husband and a lifelong Episcopalian who became convinced the Episcopal Church was off track, still wanted to keep an Anglican identity: "We didn't want to be just fringe lunatics, we wanted to be in an Anglican body." AMiA provided the ideal solution. As the rector of a Florida church which left ECUSA for AMiA stated: "[AMiA] is a God-appointed way out for us, under Anglican authority. We don't miss a beat."[64]

Joining AMiA arguably meant remaining Anglican, but it also meant becoming, at least in name, an African church. St. Timothy's had placed itself under the jurisdiction of the primate of Rwanda. However, St. Timothy's is a long, long way from Africa, and even a few hours' drive from any outpost of African culture more authentic than "The Fun Jungle," two miles down the road, a family amusement park where a giant concrete gorilla guards the entrance and kids ride motorized pink elephants. Most members of AMiA parishes have the average American's minimal knowledge of the global South. Ironically, parish newsletters show that in the summer of 1994, shortly after the genocide in Rwanda, St. Timothy's congregation decided to get involved in supporting refugees. But they chose to support an Eastern European family; the massive post-genocide refugee crisis in and around Rwanda apparently did not come up for consideration.

Seven years later, I found that it was quite common for conversations at St. Timothy's to turn to African religion and politics. The first time I attended the Sunday evening praise and worship meeting, the leader read the group a three-page article about current events in Rwanda, and the rest of the group responded with observations, thoughts, and news items from elsewhere in Africa. By 2001 St. Timothy's was clearly in a very different place, in its collective thinking and its larger loyalties, than it had been in 1994. In joining AMiA and the Province of Rwanda, St. Timothy's not only had taken a convenient road out of the Episcopal Church but had forged a transnational relationship of significant local meaning.

The development of this relationship took time. When St. Timothy's first joined AMiA, members told me they thought little about the African connection, being focused on the escape from conflicts with their Episcopal bishop. As one parishioner told me, "Africa just wasn't on our radar." Others were uncertain about these potential international connections. Arlene told me that her husband, a southerner in his sixties, was initially skeptical because he viewed the church in Africa as a mission field: "Why would they be leading us to a new place?" Some members still seem dubious about the church's African connections. When I talked with Edna and Oliver, an elderly couple who have attended St. Timothy's for most of their lives, and asked them about St. Timothy's African connections, Edna replied, "We're not prejudiced. . . . We needed somebody at that point and maybe the Lord sent [Archbishop Kolini]—I'm that much of a believer." But Oliver added, "I kind of thought we could've found someone somewhere [to help us] without getting into all the troubles Rwanda has." Today some members and leaders at St. Timothy's continue to feel that the connection is mostly significant as an escape. They see their primary involvement as being with AMiA, an American organization in many respects despite its international leadership. A middle-aged parishioner named Morris told me that in his opinion, the Rwandan church just provides St. Timothy's with an authority structure: "More than anything else it means to us that we are no longer associated with the American church."

Nevertheless, after joining AMiA, many at St. Timothy's began to think more seriously about what their connection to Rwanda might mean. Ted described his reaction to affiliation with the Rwandan church: "It was such a wonderful thing . . . I'd never heard of the African church or anything else, then all of a sudden we've got these folks in Africa who are going to take us under their wing. Praise God. I was all for it. . . . They have literally saved us, and we owe them." Andy, a businessman and vestry member, described a similar journey from ignorance to empathy, saying that at the time of the split from ECUSA, "most folks here only knew Africa is Africa, and the people there are dark skinned, and they'd heard about the genocide, but most Americans didn't pay much attention to that." But, he explained, once the Rwandan church helped them in their difficulties, they began to see the Rwandans as human beings and to care about what had happened to them. As Andy suggests, for many people at St. Timothy's, as for the American populace in general, their only association with Rwanda was the genocide—if they even remembered that the genocide in the newspapers in 1994 had taken place in Rwanda. Lacey, a vestry member, told me she'd been dimly aware of Rwanda before, but hadn't taken much interest until AMiA came along. "I remember when the genocide was going on. I can't say I paid much attention to it." She noted that Americans are desensitized to such news, saying that we see Africans killing each other and think, "Ah, they're all cannibals." "And now," she concluded with amazement, "we're under the Province of Rwanda!"

Rwanda and their archbishop are far away, however, and not even easily accessible by e-mail. Having few ways to be in direct contact with their African patrons, members of St. Timothy's tend to take any contact with Africa as a way to relate to the church in Rwanda. One example is the East African Market, a traveling display/sale of crafts mainly from Kenya, Tanzania, and Uganda that comes to St. Timothy's every other year. When I asked about their church's relationship with Rwanda, several parishioners spontaneously mentioned the market as one way they feel they have contact with Africa. When I told Mary, during our interview, that I would be doing fieldwork in Uganda, she immediately told me that her earrings came from Kenya. She went on to point out several other items in her cozy living room that she had purchased at the East African Market over the years—a carved wooden buffalo, a decorative basket. By implication, she presented her attraction to these African objects as part of the positive sense of connection with Africa that has become increasingly central to her own and her church's identity.

Another example of this tendency to relate to Rwanda through any available African contact, regardless of particularities of country or culture, can be heard in members' recollections about John, a young Nigerian priest who spent some time at St. Timothy's about a year before I arrived. John came to the United States to raise money for his ministry with AIDS orphans; St. Timothy's sent him home with two SUVs, six computers, and a great deal more. Many St. Timothy's members mentioned John when talking about what their church's association with the

Church of Rwanda meant to them. One example comes from Lynn, the parish secretary, a woman in her sixties. During a chat one day while I was going through the church's old newsletters at the church office, I told her about my interest in St. Timothy's ties to Africa. She immediately told me how much everyone enjoyed John's presence. She went on to share some more general reflections, saying that she thinks a lot of people "have a wrong conception about Africa as a lot of black people running around," and that meeting people like John and Archbishop Kolini helps Americans realize that Africans are "just like us, or even a little better." This statement captures simultaneously an increased sense of connection and kinship with the church in Rwanda and a sense of the superiority of African Christianity, which is "a little bit better" in purity, zeal, and simplicity. In meeting John and being impressed with his faith and ministry, many members of St. Timothy's increased their regard for African Christianity and found greater meaning in their ties to the Province of Rwanda.

The circulation of stories about Archbishop Kolini also provides parishioners with material for identification with the Province of Rwanda. According to one often-recounted narrative, an American bishop told Archbishop Kolini at Lambeth 1998 that if Kolini supported conservative dissident groups in America, then that bishop's diocese might not be able to send any more funding to the Church of Rwanda. The punch line is Archbishop Kolini's reported reply: "You're threatening me with poverty?" The implication is that poverty might not be a very intimidating threat for a churchman who grew up as a refugee and began his career as a schoolteacher teaching under a tree, because there was no building. (These details are also part of the folklore about Archbishop Kolini circulating at St. Timothy's.) The frequency and pleasure with which St. Timothy's members refer to this story suggest their identification with its message. They see their parish as a plucky underdog that has taken an unpopular stand without fear of the financial consequences. This story tells them that Kolini is the right leader for them—brave, orthodox, and uncompromising—and at the same time encourages them to live up to his courageous example in their own congregation's ongoing legal and financial struggles.

A Journey to Rwanda

John's visit to St. Timothy's was an important step in that congregation's process of learning to value their connection with African Christianity, but a trip to Rwanda undertaken by three members of the congregation sparked even more extensive rethinking of assumptions. This collective and individual rethinking demonstrates that globalization, as represented by the transnational Anglican dissident movement, is not simply Westernization, a one-way process in which the Southern partners take on the culture and ideas of Northerners. Instead, the people of St. Timothy's were influenced by their Rwandan allies to adopt new ways of thinking and talking, indicating that such global relationships have effects in both directions.

About a month after my arrival in the parish, three members of the congregation—Paul, Sarah, and Henry—traveled to Rwanda to see the country for themselves. The trip was a personal, rather than a parish, initiative, but it was wholeheartedly supported by the parish as a way to strengthen the church's relationship with its Rwandan sponsors. The St. Timothy's trio spent two weeks in and around Kigali, Rwanda, under the care of Archbishop Kolini. They toured prisons, orphanages, churches, and genocide sites; preached at church services and spoke at formal dinners; conversed with their archbishop and other Rwandans; and returned home full of experiences to share with the rest of the congregation.

Preparing for this trip involved an intense period of learning about Rwanda for the travelers themselves, including engagement with the academic literature on Rwanda's history and politics. But the whole congregation experienced intensified learning about Rwanda by participating in preparations for the trip and especially by hearing about the journey afterward through a number of sermons, special presentations, and discussions. Through these experiences, parishioners learned more about Rwanda's history, society, ecology, and Anglican church.[65] Even more important than such factual learning, however, was the process of learning to rethink common American assumptions, mostly negative, about Africa. For this congregation, this process could be plainly observed as the travelers' retelling of their experiences and impressions caused many to revise their initial assumptions about the character and power dynamics of their church's relationship with the Province of Rwanda.

In many respects the image of Africa that the travelers gained through their trip conformed to common views of Africa as a continent in crisis, and of Africans as noble victims, joyful and hospitable in spite of their hardships. More will be said of this complex of ideas in the next chapter. Here it suffices to say that this was the Africa the travelers from St. Timothy's expected to see, and to an extent, this is the Africa they talked about when they came home. Sarah described the brilliant smiles on the faces of "children who have nothing." Playing back from his PDA a digital recording of Rwandan children singing at a praise and worship meeting, Paul summed up this vision of joyful Africa: "You've never heard children sing until you've been to Africa, you've never seen children dance until you've been to Africa; and you've never heard drums played until you've been to Africa. People there know how to sing and dance and play the drums."

In other respects, however, their visit fundamentally challenged the travelers' preconceptions about their church's relationship with the Province of Rwanda. Before the trip and while the travelers were away, the ways people at St. Timothy's spoke about their relationship with Rwanda reflected the familiar tropes of missionary and aid relationships. Initially the people of St. Timothy's assumed that this relationship was characterized by a sharing of faith and of material goods which moved primarily in one direction: from North to South. Despite the fact that St. Timothy's acknowledges an African as its archbishop, older habits of thought about Africa as a missionary destination kept reemerging in talk about the trip. And although the travelers were quite definite that their visit to Rwanda was not a mission trip, the classic missionary language of bringing the light of the gospel into the world's dark places was often used to describe the journey, by the travelers and others. For instance, Paul told me in an interview before he left, "Somebody needs to go into that dark place, from the outside, with the light of Christ. Sometimes you can rebuke the Devil from outside, but sometimes you have to put your *body* there—and Rwanda, Africa, is like that."

After the trip, however, the travelers' talk showed that they had come to see Rwandan Christians as their equals, or even superiors, in faith. Talking with their fellow parishioners after the trip, the travelers stressed that, far from being missionaries, *they* came away blessed by the Rwandan Christians they encountered. Paul described the experience this way: "We were surrounded by Spirit-filled, born-again Christians, and they recognized us as brothers and sisters." Sarah concluded: "We didn't go there to bless them. We went there to get blessed. I felt like they taught me so much more than I could give them." Their experiences thus helped to cement the idea of Africa as a Christian continent among St. Timothy's members.

Perhaps an even more surprising lesson for the people of St. Timothy's was that their financial superiority was not the immediate focus of their relationship with Rwandan church leaders. Before and during the trip, the talk of the travelers and other St. Timothy's members revealed strong shared assumptions that the purpose of the trip was, as it was described at the commissioning service for the travelers, to "survey the spiritual and physical needs of our brethren there and come home and report if there are ways St. Timothy's can help." This stress on finding ways to help the Rwandan church, spiritually and especially materially, was common in talk about the Rwanda trip. At one Sunday service, Joe directed the congregation to pray for the travelers, because "they're seeing things they've never seen before, ministering in a land of desperate needs, and we want them to come back and tell us what we can do to help our brothers and sisters in Rwanda."

Yet in spite of expectations that the group would use this trip to assess the Rwandan church's needs, no list of requests was presented upon their return. The travelers had been moved by the poverty they encountered in Rwanda; Sarah half-joked that the experience made her want to sell everything she owns, live in a tent, and send all the money to Rwanda. But their Rwandan hosts hadn't overtly asked for material help. Instead, as the travelers explained, the Rwandans had stressed to their American visitors that gifts should flow out of an established relationship—and thus that establishing a relationship was the first priority. Paul told the congregation about realizing, toward the end of the visit, that "they're not asking for a hand up, they're not asking for a handout—they're just glad we're here. . . . When we'd ask them, What can we do?, they'd say, 'You've already done all you can just by coming here.'" Henry likewise told a house church group, "They really are not so much interested in what you can do for them or give them as in who you are." He concluded that because they spent most of their time just sharing stories with Rwandan Christians rather than canvassing needs and planning charitable gifts, "by American standards, our trip was entirely wasted. By their standard, it was a great success." Sarah added, "We'd rather use their standard!"

Thus instead of the expected appeals for orphanage roofs, prison clinics, and cattle and bicycles for rural clergy, the travelers came home with nothing to present to their fellow members but their own experiences and reflections—and the promise that the relationship would continue to develop. This new perspective on the relationship—that sending money and gifts was not the primary or defining goal—was absorbed and pondered by other members of the congregation. Sam, an active member in his early thirties, described the parish's earlier assumption that it would be able to help Rwanda as "American arrogance," when in fact, he said, "it turned out that the Americans were the ones blessed by the trip, leaving Rwanda with nothing." Ryan and Nancy, a fortyish couple, spoke to me about what St. Timothy's and the Province of Rwanda have to offer each other. Ryan told me, "[Archbishop Kolini] doesn't want our money. They want to teach us more about humanity. . . . They could give us something that we're perhaps a bit lacking in, and we could hopefully help them out where they're lacking. I think it could be a tremendous opportunity to send financial resources that they've never known." Nancy chimed in: "But they don't necessarily want—well, to some degree. . . . " Ryan replied: "It's not the reason for being, but they would obviously welcome. . . ." These last two trailing and awkward sentences point to a struggle to reconcile their previous assumptions—that sending financial resources would be central to St. Timothy's relationship with the church in Rwanda—with the new perspective they learned from the travelers: that material gifts are needed and "welcome," but are not the primary focus of the relationship—the "reason for being."

After hearing from the travelers, members of St. Timothy's began to think and talk about the possibility that, despite their lack of wealth and education, the impoverished people of Rwanda might have much to offer and teach *them*. Sam told his house church group that while setting his clock forward for Daylight Savings Time, he had been thinking about a quotation from Archbishop Kolini that the travelers had shared: "Americans have watches; Africans have time." Sam described himself as seeing American life anew: "We don't have time." When I asked Ted about what African Christians and American Christians have to offer each other, his answer showed that he had been reflecting on the travelers' accounts: "The Africans are relational. They are not goal-oriented, they are people-oriented, and it's the focus of their lives. . . . whereas Americans are goal-oriented, job-oriented, task-oriented, and we have lost a lot of our sensitivity and a lot of our ability to be givers that the Africans have retained." These laypeople, through their church's connection with the Province of Rwanda, were coming not only to think of Africa in new and positive ways but also to look more critically on their own way of life as Americans.

Through the travelers' sharing of their experiences with the rest of the congregation, many at St. Timothy's began to describe the Rwandan church as a source of spiritual wealth, rather than primarily as a destination for sharing material wealth. One outcome of the travelers' journey was, indeed, the establishment of a parish fund for buying materials to build churches in Rwanda. But beyond this tangible level of continued relationship, St. Timothy's congregation has come to take pleasure in its association with the Church of Rwanda, especially now that the association has become a concrete relationship. Sarah remarked to her house church group on how much joy she now takes in writing "Anglican Province of Rwanda" on her donation checks to the church. She said, "That used to be an abstraction. It no longer is. Being a part of the Province of Rwanda is a very special gift." The parish's collective education about Africa has brought many members through much of their initial ambivalence about associating with an African church and to a point of embracing it as a gift.

St. Timothy's global ties have had a clear impact on the congregation. Even though only a few members have actually traveled to Rwanda or met Rwandan Anglican leaders, a much larger number have been influenced by the teaching and conversation surrounding the Rwanda trip as well as by other sources of information, and have begun to think differently about Africa, America, and themselves. Their African ties are no longer an abstraction but part of their shared self-concept as a global parish, a group of people with meaningful and mutual connections with Christians in Africa and around the world.

Looking Ahead

The conservative globalist discourse became much more than talk as, beginning in 1999, Northerners and Southerners together built relationships making manifest this vision of global ties of mutual accountability and belonging. In describing several such relationships, I have indicated the scope and variety of this movement. In recounting how such a relationship is experienced in one American congregation, I have suggested the depth and breadth of lay involvement in these developments. These varied globalist projects, unfolding over several years, have increasingly tended to follow the network or realignment model. Many have lost patience and faith in the possibilities of remaking the Anglican Communion through its existing structures into a more unified and doctrinally controlled body. These developing networks of affinity, which are particular connections between individuals, parishes, dioceses, and provinces, instead bypass and even subvert the centralized, nested geographical authority structure of the Communion. It remains to be seen whether the total "realignment" of the Communion into networked clusters of Anglican bodies defined by affinity rather than by geographic proximity will come to pass. What can be said with assurance is that the innovative pattern of networking undertaken by the Episcopal dissident movement and their overseas supporters has come a long way from its first manifestation at St. Andrew's, Little Rock. Today many believe that such networks will become, functionally if not officially, the new organizing structure of the whole Anglican Communion.

In the development of these North/South alliances, we see that conservative convictions can motivate proactive engagement with globalization, shown in this case in the formation of a transnational movement that challenges geographic distance and cultural difference in order both to develop global affinities and to undercut the authority of national bodies like the Episcopal Church. This perspective casts into question interpretations of recent Anglican Communion events that rely too heavily on the global-shift narrative. Southern and Northern Anglicans did not simply discover each other as ready-made allies, already fighting similar battles. Instead, at the instigation of a small group of innovators, Northern and Southern leaders came together, developed a common agenda, negotiated common strategies (with mixed success—note most Southern primates' slowness in responding to American conservatives' call for intervention), and eventually found a wide variety of mutually beneficial ways to work together for change in the Episcopal Church and the worldwide Communion.

In chapters 6 and 7, I examine further how these relationships function, especially for the African partners. I analyze some of the frictions and mismatches between Northern and Southern allies, thereby further questioning the presumed naturalness of these North/South alliances. Although that analysis reveals some of the limits of the transformation wrought by these new relationships, those limitations do not negate the real and transformative impact of this globalization process. Many conservative Episcopalians have genuinely come to see the world in a new way, with greater interest in the global South and greater respect for the wisdom and resourcefulness of Southern Christians. At the same time, Southern clergy and laity have a new sense that their witness and ministry are needed and desired by powerful, wealthy, and sophisticated Northern churches. The juxtaposition of these changes with more conservative and constraining dynamics in these relationships illustrates the mixed quality of the processes of globalization, which overturn some patterns and reinforce others. Yet for all these ambiguities, these alliances remain strong, a testimony to the determination of Southern and Northern Anglicans committed for differing reasons to the same goal—a new kind of global Anglican belonging.

"Who Wants to Be in the Ugandan Communion?" Perceptions of African and American Christianity

EARLY IN 2004 I witnessed a fascinating conversation on an e-mail list for dissident Episcopalians. On January 26 a listmember, "Faithful Follower,"[1] wrote in to express pessimism about whether any acceptable solution to the Episcopal Church's erring ways would be forthcoming from Anglican Communion leadership: "The Continuing Churches are beginning to look pretty appealing to me. . . . If [Anglican Communion leadership in] Canterbury is going to posture with no real backbone behind their words, of what use are they? And who wants to be in the Ugandan Communion? We're Anglicans, not minions of the late Idi Amin." Several listmembers replied promptly to Faithful Follower's rhetorical question about Uganda. David wrote in under the subject line "Who wants to be in the Ugandan Communion?" to say, "I wouldn't mind a bit. I had been hoping to see a Ugandan Anglican Church spring up here in Boston and I would be there in a minute!" Another member, Frank, told Follower: "Actually, I would have no problem in the Ugandan Communion, or the Nigerian Communion or the Southern Cone Communion, etc. . . . I think your mention of Idi Amin is not really fair to all the Orthodox Christians in Uganda or elsewhere in Africa, Asia or Latin America." Others responded by pointing out the persecution Ugandan Anglicans had suffered under Amin.[2] George wrote in with a recollection:

> I remember back in the late 70's, a seminary student from Uganda . . . [came] to our Church to talk about the persecutions of Christians in Uganda. He told us of Idi Amin's troops coming to Christian Churches on Sunday morning, standing at the back door and screaming at the parishioners standing inside something to the effect of, "Sit down for Allah and live . . ." and then start shooting about waist high with automatic weapons. Next time you are in church, standing for a hymn, glance over your shoulder and imagine a dozen soldiers there with AK-47's preparing to shoot you because you are a Christian! So who wants to be a Ugandian [*sic*] Anglican-Christian??

Rather than seeing Amin as weakening the legitimacy of Ugandan Anglicanism, George believed that the suffering Ugandan Christians experienced under Amin's regime strengthens that church's claim to moral authority. Another member supported this point by posting a biography of Ugandan Anglican archbishop Janani Luwum, who was martyred in 1977 for standing up to Amin.

The conversation, however, was not over. A sympathizer with Follower's position, "Ever Anglican," replied to Frank: "Knock yourself out, then. There is a reason we are Anglican . . . we're NOT Ugandan, Kenyan, Ethiopian, or anything else. The last time I checked, we derived our traditions from ENGLAND. Besides . . . I'd look stupid in African garb. I'm out." In another post, Ever Anglican asserted: "I hardly think the Third World churches should be our role models."

But Faithful Follower and Ever Anglican were clearly in the minority. In one of two long, reflective posts that seemed to conclude the conversation, Anne posted an indirect reply to Ever Anglican:

> It's funny; until Ever Anglican spoke up I had not seen anyone except members of the loony Left take a dismissive attitude towards the Global South. . . . In fact, one of my great comforts of late has been to see how eager my father, a senior citizen Southern gentleman, is to see the African bishops get a good firm hand on ECUSA. . . . If you want to see genuine faith in action, the genuine work of God, look at people who have known real poverty, danger, and suffering—people who may risk their lives for the gospel. There are such people in Africa. . . . If we pray very hard and God has mercy on us, perhaps we will be blessed to come under their authority and teaching.

In another summing-up message, Leslie offered these comments, criticizing some orthodox Anglicans for their unwillingness to accept African leadership:

> I've heard or heard of several good orthodox folk making comments like this, e.g. "I couldn't imagine being under the Bishop of *Nigeria.*" . . . This is racist and unchristian in the extreme. . . . If and when the Anglican Communion splits, it will be interesting to see how many "orthodox" folks will leave for other communions or stay in the rump ECUSA and Church of England simply because they could never imagine being under the spiritual authority of someone from Uganda or Nigeria. We could do worse, folks—and have.

These postings closed the conversation, with the vision of African Christianity as strong, courageous, and worthwhile affirmed over ideas about African Christianity as alien, corrupt, and inadequate.

The spreading of positive images of African Christianity evident in this conversation was also observable at St. Timothy's during my time there. That congregation's experience of finding an alliance with an African church first thinkable, then desirable, involved more and more members' coming to see African Christianity as a positive model. At one house church meeting I attended, a relatively new member of the church questioned the church's African connections. She noted that she "didn't know much about Africa," but described it as "a place not known for its Christianity." Frieda, an older member, replied crisply, "Now it is," and told the newcomer that there are more new Christians in Africa every day than anywhere else in the world. Some members of the congregation described to me their own journeys from bigotry to affirmation, showing that a positive valuation of African Christianity has become a central value for this movement. What is the content, and what are the implications, of this new vision of Africa?

SHARED VISIONS OF AFRICA?

American conservatives often assert that the moral center of world Christianity has shifted toward the global South, an argument allowing Northern dissidents to claim that they are aligned not only with a global majority but also with the wave of the future, the up-and-coming Christian world order. Exchanges like those on the e-mail list and at the house church meeting show that such views are not yet fully established among conservative Episcopalians, but they continue to spread. African Christianity is often described by proponents as the epitome of the good elements of Southern Christianity—both because African Anglican leaders have been so active in dissident politics and because African Anglicanism appears to Northerners to best fulfill positive images of Southern Christianity, owing to the growth of African churches and the poverty and suffering of many African Christians. A high opinion of African Christianity has virtually become part of the orthodoxy to which conservative Northern Anglicans adhere. Abner, a lay member of one Ugandan bishop's staff who possesses substantial experience with American/Ugandan church relations, put it eloquently: "You in America are saying, 'The God of the black backward African is still alive!' "

Ugandan Anglicans generally share this positive view of African Christianity, seeing their churches as stronger and more orthodox than most Northern ones. Such views are particularly salient in light of ongoing debates about Christianity's place in modern Africa. The association of Christianity with colonialism continues to be a critical issue for African theology and biblical interpretation,[3] a fact which became apparent to me when I presented an early draft of this chapter to a small audience of Ugandan scholars in Kampala and a solid half-hour of the subsequent discussion revolved around whether there can be a truly African Christianity. The increasing politicization of Islam, elsewhere in Africa if not yet in Uganda, has made questions regarding the legitimacy of Christianity as an African religion even more pressing. In many African contexts, Muslim leaders have tried to position Islam as the more authentically African alternative to Christianity, cast as the "white man's faith." Ugandan Christians assert the validity of African Christianity by arguing that Christianity has always been an African religion—frequently pointing out, for example, that Jesus spent his childhood in Egypt. Another way Ugandan church leaders defend their faith is by arguing that Southern Christianity is stronger, purer, more scriptural—in short, better—than Northern Christianity. These arguments are implicit in Ugandan preachers' frequent use of anecdotes about Northern Christianity's decadence, drawn from personal experience, rumors, newspaper accounts, and Northern conservative sources. For example, in one sermon I heard a Ugandan priest speak about seeing, in New Zealand, a live broadcast of "Bob and Dick being married by an Anglican priest!"[4] Questioning the orthodoxy of Northern Christianity serves as a way for Africans to speak about the goodness of African churches, in spite of their missionary past and present weaknesses.

The pervasive assertions of the positive value of African Christianity, among both American and Ugandan Anglican clergy and laity, illustrates that this movement's globalizing work has effects far beyond those immediately involved. The allies' actions and arguments have spread their vision of the Anglican globe as increasingly dominated by orthodox Southern Christianity widely among their constituents and observers. In this case, the effects of globalization on worldview and self-image are emphatically not limited to leadership and travelers. These shared concepts of Africa are relevant, as well, to another set of questions about globalization, concerning its capacity to transcend cultural difference and geographic distance. American conservatives have developed a view of African Christians as fundamentally akin to them in faith perspective, despite the two groups' obvious differences. Examining how this positive concept of African Christianity functions in these relationships involves evaluating the effectiveness of this attempt to erase difference in the interests of transnational orthodox Anglican solidarity.

Observers and scholars of globalization also often query whether new global flows can create radically new forms of transnational relationships, or whether new flows merely follow old paths and reinforce old asymmetries, albeit in new vocabularies and forms. Involvement with this globalizing movement moves American conservatives toward new positive views of Africa and leads African Anglicans to a new view of Africa's role and power in the worldwide Communion. I explore here the extent and limits of this transformation in participants' understandings and in the real-life dynamics of these innovative North/South relationships. Discourses used by both Northern conservatives and African Anglicans to describe and explain their alliances reverse the negative terms of common images of Africa in many respects; yet on a deeper level, they reinscribe dualisms of North/South imagery that date back to the colonial era's harsh inequalities and clear North-over-South hierarchy. The way that inequalities in the distribution of wealth shape Anglican transnational alliances will be set aside until chapter 7.

When African Anglicans' own vision of their churches do not correspond with Northern conservative discourses, these discourses can constrain mutual understanding. Though sharing a high view of African Christianity, many Ugandans seem to balk at fully accepting a view of world Christianity divided between a decadent, immoral North and a vibrant, faithful South. Their own experiences as Southern Christians lead them to more moderate views. For example, Richard, a member of the Ugandan church's provincial staff, told me a recent visitor with an evangelical Episcopal renewal team had said to him, "The U.S. is a mission field because people are not taking scripture seriously, there is high moral decay." Reporting this, Richard added reflectively, "Though that is in Africa too, and people are drifting from the church." Ugandan Anglicans' doubts and questions represent a critique of common images and assumptions, demonstrating that African Christians themselves do not uniformly share positive views of African faith. These Ugandan Christians' reflections on Southern Christianity reveal not only their discomfort with the mismatches between such images and the realities of their church but also their recognition that even positive Northern views of Southern Christianity can carry forward the regressive terms of older discourses, reversing the valuations but perpetuating the terms of colonial language about Africa.

The Anglican Church in Uganda is an excellent site in which to examine African Christians' ideas about African and American Christianity. Much as Africa often stands as the epitome of Southern Christianity, Uganda not infrequently is cited, by both Americans and Ugandans, as an exemplar of African Christianity. Next to Nigeria, the Church of Uganda is the largest province in Africa and thus, arguably, the second largest in the Communion.[5] The Church of Uganda is estimated to have perhaps 7 million members, between 20 and 25 percent of Uganda's population (compared with around 2.4 million Episcopalians in the United States, less than 1 percent of the population). The Church of Uganda's size and influence in its own national context and in relation to other Anglican provinces make it one of the sites where Northerners would expect positive images of African Christianity to be most fully realized.

"Black, but Faithful"

American conservatives' development of positive ideas about their global allies involves struggling with race and racism. White racism against blacks is an inevitable factor when the almost exclusively white members of the American dissident movement are brought into connection with, and sometimes under the authority of, black African bishops. The dissident networking movement is to some extent concentrated in the American South, a part of the country with a reputation for deep-seated racism, making it all the more remarkable to many observers that these churches are willing to associate with black African church leaders. In fact, as the debate chronicled in e-mails indicates, seeking to confront and transform others' racism has become an important part of this dissident movement's agenda.

Brad, a thirtyish father of two and a loyal member of St. Timothy's, told me that while traveling by plane, he overheard two women nearby talking about St. Timothy's and describing the church as intolerant and homophobic, then remarking, "They're under some African people, of all things!" Brad confronted the women, telling them it was bigoted to think that someone from Africa is "the wrong color or too dumb and not capable of presiding over an American church." In telling this story, Brad described these women as an example of what's wrong with the whole Episcopal Church: ECUSA leaders talk about intolerance, but *they're* the bigoted ones, because they assume Rwandans, "who've been through more in one day than we do in our whole lives, and who they [Episcopalians] have never met," can't be in charge of an American church. Brad told me he's heard of people in his ECUSA diocese's leadership using the word "junglebunnies," and he argued that ECUSA embodies the American conceit that "we're more advanced than everyone else." For Brad and others, St. Timothy's relationship with an African bishop is seen as proof that its members aren't just conservative bigots (who presumably wouldn't like gays *or* Africans) but are in fact righteous Christians who have conquered prejudice, while holding on to the essentials of the faith. Further, the two women in this story are generalized into "typical Episcopalians" and used as evidence that the Episcopal Church is not the tolerant institution it claims to be, but is actually in the wrong on all counts—both in its tolerance of homosexuality, which should *not* be freely accepted, and in its *in*tolerance of Africans, who *should* be accepted and indeed honored.

As Brad's story demonstrates, some conservatives express their antiracism by arguing with the perceived racism of liberal and moderate Episcopalians. However, as in the 2004 e-mails, working to eradicate racism among fellow orthodox Episcopalians is also a priority. Not surprisingly, no one at St. Timothy's told me that they themselves objected to African connections for racist reasons. But leaders at St. Timothy's assured me that they had lost a few members, and had serious conversations with a few more, because the idea of being under a black archbishop was hard for these members to swallow. Similarly Leslie, in the post quoted above, recalls having heard several orthodox Episcopalians express discomfort at being under a Nigerian bishop—a sentiment Leslie identifies as racist.

Where such racism is overcome, members of this movement express joy and triumph. Anne, in her post, writes of her happiness at seeing her elderly southern father's excitement about African church leadership. She implies that this excitement over black leadership is a breakthrough for him, a man who is a product of the segregated South. The focus of these conversations is overcoming racism toward Africans, not African Americans, and St. Timothy's—a white congregation in a largely-white community—offered little opportunity to observe how these new commitments play out in race relations closer to home. But the stated ideal for these conservatives is the end of racism in both domestic and international contexts. Paul, a leader at St. Timothy's, told me that as a southerner who grew up in the still-segregated 1950s, he had to overcome his own inherited racism as St. Timothy's moved toward relationship with an African bishop. Today he is one of the church's strongest advocates for overcoming racist patterns of thought. He told me that when St. Timothy's first affiliated with AMiA and put "Province of Rwanda" on the church's sign, some parishioners complained. He mimicked these parishioners' complaints, and his response: " 'Do we have to put that up there? They're black!' 'Yeah, but they're faithful!' " He seeks a transformation at St. Timothy's in which the members' old racist ideas are replaced by new ways of thinking about Africans as "black, but faithful."

"THE GOD OF THE BLACK BACKWARD AFRICAN IS ALIVE!"

Racism is only part of what dissidents have to overcome in arriving at a positive evaluation of African Christianity. Images of Africa absorbed by most Americans from the media, schools, and even literature are laden with racist ideas.[6] But elements besides blackness alone also play a role in Americans' negative perceptions of Africa. Colonial ideas of Africa as uncivilized, savage, and dependent upon outside help remain strong in American thought. The news stories and images of Africa that Americans hear and see almost uniformly focus on crisis and need. Such sources perpetuate ideas of Africans as lawless and brutal, riven by tribal hatreds, unable to run their own societies, desperately poor, and superstitious or fundamentalist in matters of religion. Conservative Episcopalians, in seeking to re-imagine Africa, are also engaging with this collection of images and discourses.

Postcolonial scholar Roxanne Lynn Doty, in her 1996 book *Imperial Encounters*, argues for the need to attend to practices of representation in North/South relationships—that is, the ways people talk about and understand the North, the South, and their differences. These representations are centrally important in defining roles, relationships, and practices in North/South relationships of all kinds.[7] Doty points out that these representations are asymmetrically controlled and produced primarily by Northerners. "The issues and concerns that constitute these relations occur within a 'reality' whose content has for the most part been defined by the representational practices of the 'first world.'"[8] Doty sees great continuity in the basic pattern of these representations or discourses, many of which have roots in colonial discourses and practices. For example, she calls attention to the numerous binary oppositions "that we routinely draw upon and that frame our thinking," such as "developed/underdeveloped, 'first world'/'third world,' . . . modern/traditional."[9] These binary oppositions serve as hierarchies, with the South associated with the weaker or devalued term.[10] Similarly, literary scholar David Spurr offers an analysis of "rhetorical modes, or ways of writing about non-Western peoples," which he has found both in colonial-era texts and in contemporary journalistic and other accounts of the non-Western world.[11]

These representational themes, even when used quite differently than in historical colonial discourses, replicate the logic of those discourses and implicitly perpetuate colonial patterns of privilege by defining the North as the superior partner and by constraining the terms and possibilities for relationship. Even though many Americans may have consciously turned away from stereotypes about Africa with roots in colonial discourses of African tribalism, primitivism, superstition, and so on, these ideas still shape current Northern Episcopal conservative (as well as moderate and liberal) ideas about African Christianity. Furthermore, even the new positive concepts of African Christianity are highly stereotyped. Intensified relationships with the African churches may have changed Americans' views of those churches, but few Episcopal dissidents have had extended direct contact with African churches. As a result, normative understandings of African Christianity circulating through the movement tend to shape dissidents' thinking, since they have little opportunity to develop independent judgments. In spite of the increase in global consciousness among these allies, the physical distance separating Northern and Southern constituencies remains significant, limiting mutual understanding in these relationships to the application of stereotypes, even if positively valued ones.

THE SPIRITUAL SOUTH?

One of the major themes of colonial/postcolonial discourse is the trope of idealization. Spurr argues that idealizing the culturally "other" (in this case, people of the global South) serves the rhetorical and perhaps emotional needs of Northerners troubled by their own society.[12] For them, the other represents the good things lost in modern Northern society, things that might be reclaimed if Northerners emulate the other's desirable qualities. Additional themes can also be discerned, but all the discourses examined here constitute an overall idealization of African Christianity, which plays a central role in Anglican conservatives' criticisms of ECUSA and Northern Anglicanism in general. Conservative dissidents point to the orthodoxy, zeal, and other desirable traits they perceive as characterizing the churches of the global South, and seek to bring that moral force to bear in transforming the Episcopal Church.

This idealization of Southern Christianity, contrasted with Northern Christianity, is frequently articulated by both Americans and Africans in terms of the "exchange" model or discourse, introduced earlier. The exchange referred to is essentially the idea that Africans (or Southerners in general) should share their spiritual wealth with Americans (or Northerners in general), while the latter share their material wealth and related assets (such as management and technological skills) with Southern churches. This model was invoked by many of my consultants, both Northern and Southern. Jonathan, who has been involved with the AAC's developing international relationships, told me, "Exposure to the 2/3 World evangelistic ethos is helpful [for Americans]. We get a spiritual benefit, if you like. In return for which, we are comparatively rich and are able to offer material support." Members of St. Timothy's voiced similar ideas. Andy told me, "I see both helping each other. The U.S. has been undernourished spiritually because we've been overnourished materially."

Many Ugandans also described ideal North/South church relationships to me in terms of the exchange model. Robby, a young church musician, had little knowledge of Communion politics but willingly shared his views on the Church of Uganda as we sat on the steps of Namirembe Cathedral. When I asked him for his thoughts on relations between African and Northern churches, he told me, "As in most cases, they [Northerners] assist us in sponsorships, [and] the Anglican bishops of Uganda can assist with spiritual matters." Abner, drawing on his own experiences with inter-Anglican partnerships, observed:

> There are things we lack here, and there [is] . . . something lacking in America. I think there is a general feeling that the Gospel is very needed in America. . . . So whenever some American friends come, they feel

that when we go [to America], we can also help them to share the message for Christ. . . . And when we reach there, the Americans also feel that we are really poor here. When we share [about our faith in America], we say, "This wealth, what about sharing it with African brothers and sisters?"

The exchange model appeals to Africans in part because it offers a clear avenue for Southern reciprocity and relational equality, through the giving of spiritual aid in return for material aid. While Northerners offer practical assistance to poor Southern churches, Southerners are eager to help re-evangelize notoriously secularized Northern countries. As in the rhetoric of neoliberal global economics, each region is envisioned exporting what it has in plenty, trading those goods for what another region can readily provide. Northern conservatives' recent success in building and maintaining relationships with Southern Christians may be at least partially attributed to the possibilities for mutuality that Southern Anglicans find in Northern conservatives' guiding discourses, as compared with these of Northern moderates or liberals who have less-developed ideas regarding Southern Christianity's strengths.

African Christian Spiritual Capital

Examples of exchange language from texts and interviews make clear the ways in which the American and African churches are characterized. The American church, and Northern churches in general, have "material wealth," "material abundance," "financial resources to bestow," "opulent parish budgets," and "people with training in leadership and management," to share with their African brethren. In contrast, the African churches have "more fundamental faith," "spiritual enrichment," "wealth of spirit and soul," "personal values," "the Word of God wholesale," and "people with very, very enthusiastic faith" to export for the benefit of Northern Christians. Such statements about the strength, orthodoxy, and vitality of Southern Christianity often include implicit or explicit arguments about *why* Southern Christianity possesses such a high degree of what one Ugandan priest called "spiritual capital." Members of the e-mail list I watched cited the suffering and endurance of Ugandan Christians under Idi Amin's regime to argue that Ugandan Christians are actually much more faithful than American Christians. Similarly Philip, a British priest I interviewed in Uganda, told me that African preaching carries a special message to Northerners because of the "authority of [Africans'] poverty, of their suffering, of their experiences." Conservative-leaning Kentucky bishop Don Wimberley, writing about the Southern impact at Lambeth, likewise argued that the Southern churches have "earn[ed] the moral right to speak," through their members' experiences of poverty and suffering. In these and countless similar examples, Northern Christians offer explanations of the sources of Southern, and especially African, Christian moral authority or spiritual capital, which they argue obligates Northern Christians to listen to African Christian voices.

Five basic explanatory concepts are commonly cited to justify African Christian moral authority: *youth*, *zealousness*, *numbers* or *growth*, *suffering*, and *poverty*. Each of these concepts emerges from talk about the moral authority of Southern and especially African Christianity. Ugandans often question these images of the African church, sometimes even as they invoke them. Through an exploration of American concepts or images of African Christianity, and Ugandan Christians' reflections on those images, I offer yet another image of one African provincial church: optimistic yet uncertain of the future, confident of its orthodoxy but sharply aware of constraints on its mission.

YOUTH

Northerners and Southerners often explain the differences between the Northern and Southern churches by pointing to the greater youth of the Southern churches, many of which were founded within the past 150 years. This youthfulness has been cited disparagingly by some Northerners, unhappy with the growing influence of African Christianity in the Anglican Communion. Bishop Spong's infamous remarks just before Lambeth 1998 present one such example. In a similar vein, a liberal-leaning American bishop whom I interviewed by phone about conflicts with conservative parishes in his diocese told me that the Episcopal Church differs from other Anglican provinces because it is a "historically advanced culture": "It sounds pejorative to say so, but there are pre-Enlightenment, Enlightenment, and post-Enlightenment societies in the world. . . . The differences between us and the African churches are partly due to this."

Many others, however, Northerners and Southerners alike, use the youth of the Southern churches not to describe them as immature or lacking in understanding, but to explain their perceived superior "spiritual capital"—their greater purity in faith. Philip, the British priest, found hope in the same "pre-Enlightenment" character of Southern Christianity that the American bishop found troubling:

> [Uganda] has never been through the whole both scientific and urban revolution of human life which the West has known. . . . The sense of

God is still very strong here. . . . I am hopeful that Uganda and Africa and Asia will have a lot to teach the rather self-confident scientific world-view which hit Europe so hard over a long period, but which the Church of Uganda has not yet encountered, fully.

Northern conservatives also often uphold the youth of these churches as a factor accounting for their zeal. As one example, an article in a British paper praising the conservative Lambeth sexuality resolution carried the bold headline, "It's the Church's Children That Have Kept the Faith."[13] The young churches of the Communion, recently graduated from mission status, are seen as now holding fast to true Christianity and striving to keep the rest of the Communion on track.

Youth as a characterization of peoples and institutions in the global South has a history in colonial discourses. Throughout that history, youth has been described sometimes as a negative or limiting factor, sometimes as a positive and inspiring characteristic. What has not changed is the binary opposition between the youthful, inexperienced South and the older, experienced, wiser (if sadder) North.[14] Dipesh Chakrabarty has noted the way such talk places Southern societies in a realm of unreadiness or immaturity, temporally dislocated from the contemporary or modern Euro-American world.[15] This perceived separation is about not just time but also knowledge and understanding. Bruno Latour observes that people who understand themselves as modern see themselves as separated from those they define as nonmodern not by "a certain number of centuries" but by "epistemic ruptures."[16] The Northern clergy quoted above express this view. For these Northerners, looking "back" on the allegedly pre-Enlightenment, presecularization Southern societies is often associated with nostalgia and longing. Spurr notes that a colonizing power often sees colonized territory and people as an image of its own immature self, and that "nostalgia for the lost innocence and harmony of [earlier, simpler] Western life" is often part of this perception.[17] In describing African Christianity in terms of youth, Northern Christians are articulating long-held ideas about the relative advancement of Southern and Northern societies and cultures.

Despite the colonial associations of the discourse, Ugandan church leaders, too, sometimes speak of the youth of the African churches as a source of strength. One Ugandan churchman told me, "The church is relatively young in Africa. . . . And that purity, that newness is still there. . . . And that's why the church is still growing in Africa. So that may be an area where the African church may be helpful [to the Northern churches]." Ugandans stress that the youth or newness of their church does not mean it is immature; rather, their descriptions liken the church to a young adult, newly mature and vigorous. Abby, a divinity student at UCU, told me: "The West is being victim of a lot of technological achievements . . . [and] losing the flavor of Christianity, while for us, we are maturing in Christianity. We are at a certain advanced level of Christianity."

Ugandans sometimes explicitly contrasted their church's youth with the Northern churches' age. Bishop Ezra pointed to old age as the problem with the church in the North: "We [think] that the church in the West is suffering from the problems of old age. You see, old age—when you become very old, you become behaving like a baby. Of course you are still ahead of us, you are very brilliant—we are talking generally. . . . Of course you still have people who are theologically far ahead of us and so on. But in terms of faith, you know, sometimes when you get old, you get tired, you begin to do things—you know?—you no longer do things the way you used to do them. So we thought maybe they have problems of old age."

Some Ugandans turn arguments about their church's youth into reproaches to Northern Christians for straying from the gospel message. They argue that the African churches have kept to the faith the missionaries brought, while the Northern churches who originally sent those missionaries have strayed from orthodox faith. Obadiah, a young priest I met on the campus of UCU, told me, "Apart from those deviations of culture, us in Africa had taken [the faith] as it came from the [Church Missionary Society]. So when changes come, we think, what, are we to change the message now?" The idea that Africans have kept the missionaries' faith while the Northern church has strayed into error is often connected with the need to re-missionize the North. Miriam, a young western Ugandan divinity student at UCU, put it this way: "Maybe there is a need . . . for us to go [to America] and say, 'you see we have been taught this and that, but now we can't bear the new teaching.'" This idea is shared by American dissidents. Several members of St. Timothy's commented to me independently that they found it ironic that Americans and other Northerners had taken Christianity to Africa long ago, and now Africans were bringing it back to Americans.

In this compelling vision for African self-esteem, shared by Ugandans and Americans alike, the youthful African churches are repositories of orthodox Christian faith and will come forth to renew the rest of the world. Yet a few Ugandans hinted at ambivalence about this idea. Instead of seeing African fidelity to the faith received from the missionaries as laudable, they wonder—with some humor, but with an underlying seriousness—whether they've just been suckers all along. Prudence, a divinity student, commented on seeing Northern bishops engaging in behaviors which many Southerners regard as inappropriate for Christians: "It is shocking for us to see a bishop drinking alcohol, because we will feel they were telling us lies." And Michael, commenting on the differences between the Northern and the African church, remarked, "Many people on your side have gone a long way to analyze the issues, while for us we are being kept in the myths [while] you may have disproved it." These rare but provocative examples in which Ugandans wonder if they've been lied to or left behind by Northerners, carry echoes of some Northerners' negative views of Southern Christian youth, defined as naiveté or ignorance. The comments also may indicate these African speakers' awareness of the ambiguity of the identification of their church and nation with youth. But these hints of uncertainty aside, most Ugandans join Northerners in accepting and sometimes propounding the idea that the African church's youth gives it strength and orthodoxy that raise its "spiritual capital" well above that of the Northern church.

ZEAL

A second, related explanation for the high level of African Christian "spiritual capital" is that African Christianity is more zealous (or enthusiastic or committed). Phyllis, a parishioner at St. Timothy's, shared with me her feelings about the parish's relationship with the Province of Rwanda: "From everything that I have heard and read, and what I heard from the people who went over there, shows what Godly people they are, and how much they love the Lord." Mary, an American missionary with ties to the dissident movement, remarked to me, "So many people in America have just been in the church and they haven't had a chance to see a living, vibrant faith." The contrast, implicit or explicit, is with an image of Northern Christianity as shallow, over-theologized, and dull. Ugandans often voice similar views of the zeal of the African church in general, highlighting qualities of commitment and enthusiasm for a simple, essential gospel message. A Church of Uganda official told me, "[I don't] mean that [the Church of Uganda] has been perfect . . . but at least you can see that there is vitality. And I attribute this to building our faith, and rooting our faith, on scripture."

This discourse too is rooted in colonial ideas about Africans. Doty notes the endurance of Northern representations of Southern peoples as emotional and passionate rather than rational.[18] Christine Heyrman, writing about the beginning of the Bible Belt, notes that American whites have long held views of African Americans' religion as "distinctive" from white religion, particularly in its "zealous" character, which some eighteenth-century observers attributed to black Christians' ignorance and illiteracy.[19] Such evaluations were easily transferred to African Christians. Despite the origins of these ideas, however, Ugandan and other African church leaders often take them up, not only to describe the strength they see in their own churches but also to criticize the North. Charles, a Ugandan priest, told me, "Our church in Uganda is a very joyful church. . . . Our church celebrates a lot. Our church is a vibrant church. American churches, very few are." Jean-Paul, a Rwandan priest studying at UCU, commented that he believed American priests and parishes wanted to be attached to African bishops because they were lacking something at home: "Maybe it's the spiritual flavor, the charisma, which may be being lost in America, with priests and bishops drying up and preaching eloquent sermons without spiritual flavor, without prayerful healing." The African church, he explained, has leaders with spiritual vigor who can pray for the sick or cast out demons: "[African leaders] have a stronger charisma. Churches in Europe or the U.S. may be lacking that."

Several of my African consultants suggested that the simplicity of the gospel message, as preached in African churches, could help account for African zeal. Stephen, a Ugandan priest, told me: "Some of the problems the American church is facing are too intellectual to make sense to the African mind. [Africans'] concern is, are their sins forgiven? Are they going to heaven? . . . To get divided over whether—like over the Trinity, over these doctrine issues—that doesn't concern them. They have enough faith." Bishop Ezekiel told me, "We are a church close to that of the New Testament, Acts, in Africa. And that's why the sophisticated academicians in the West call us primitives, because we tell them that Jesus is the Lord and He saves." Stephen attributes the identification of Africans as "primitives" to Northerners, while the bishop voices a view of the African church as unintellectual; but both use these ideas to critique the "sophisticated academicians" in the North who are so wrapped up in complex theological issues and so distant from a living and lively faith.

Other Ugandans, however, spoke of a darker side to the simplicity and enthusiasm of African faith, noting that constraints on the African churches, such as limited opportunities for training, may partially account for African Christians' focus on a basic gospel message. Aaron, a Ugandan priest and evangelist, pointed out, "The American church leader is on average a college graduate, but here in Africa we can't raise enough leaders of that caliber. So we just get some intermediate training and give them basic training in pastoral work and ordain them." And Ghanaian scholar and churchman Kodwo Ankrah, who lives in Uganda and occasionally teaches at UCU, noted in a lecture in his Theology and Development seminar: "Nowadays they in the North would like more preachers from here, more missionaries, because we are more dynamic, maybe because we are more ignorant—[laughs] and haven't studied theology, so we say something new!" In his ironic play with the notions of African ignorance and dynamism, Ankrah is aware of the double edge of such characterizations of African Christianity. The limited opportunities and resources available to African preachers may be the very thing that attracts Northerners to such preachers. Nonetheless, double-edged in its implications though it may be, the image of African zeal and simplicity in faith and preaching provides Ugandan Christians with another ground for raising questions about the quality of Northern Christianity, and thus Northern Christians' right to lead in the worldwide church.

NUMBERS

Some other Northern arguments for African spiritual capital are less popular among Ugandans and other African Christians. One of these is what I will call the "Numbers" argument, which essentially states that the much-celebrated rapid growth of African churches gives them moral authority. The idea of a global North-to-South demographic shift in world Christianity, or at the very least in world Anglicanism, is not new. Scholars such as Andrew Walls, David Barrett, and John Pobee had noted the shift in worldwide Anglican numbers long before Lambeth 1998, by which time it had become a truism that the majority of the world's Anglicans now live in the global South.

Evangelical Anglicans in both the North and the South interpret the numerical growth of the Southern churches as evidence that they are preaching the gospel effectively and earning God's favor. The shift in numerical dominance within the Anglican Communion is thus elided with the idea of a shift in the location of moral and spiritual authority within the Communion. The parts of the Communion where Anglicanism is growing fastest—usually generalized as Africa, Asia, and Latin America—are thus also described, often in the same breath, as the parts of the Communion where the gospel is preached most zealously, where orthodoxy is most secure and doctrine most pure. One of innumerable examples comes from the Ekklesia Society's literature: "The growth and vitality of the church, especially in the third world is one of the greatest success stories of the [Anglican] communion, and is an inspiration to the rest of the church. It is especially true in the light of the poverty, famine, injustice and war which is afflicting many of the very areas where the church is growing most dramatically."[20]

Northern conservatives, in arguing that African churches' moral authority arises from their numbers, begin from the idea of rapid church growth in Africa. This idea is quite generalized, since not all African Anglican provinces are flourishing; but in general most scholars of world Anglicanism agree that recent African church growth has far outpaced growth in Northern churches. Northern conservatives interpret this growth as giving legitimacy to African churches according to two rationales. First, they assume the African churches must be doing something fundamentally right to be growing, just as the Northern churches must be doing something fundamentally wrong to be shrinking. Second, by a vaguely democratic logic, they argue that since the African churches are now much the largest in the Communion, they should have a correspondingly strong voice in its activities, even to the point of being empowered to impose orthodoxy on errant Northern provinces.

AMiA's home page illustrates Northern conservative views of Southern church growth: "Christianity is spreading faster than at any time or place in 2000 years. Yet this extraordinary growth is not taking place in the United States where many of the mainline denominations are losing members. . . . Rather, the Christian church and specifically the Anglican church are booming in places like Africa and Asia."[21] Robert Miclean raised similar arguments in a talk about Lambeth:

> Despite persecution, starvation, and government repression, people are coming to Christ in record numbers. The Church is experiencing phenomenal growth in Africa and elsewhere. There are now more Anglicans in Nigeria than in Canada and the United States combined. Most of them are orthodox in theology and evangelical in fervor, which accounts for the growth in membership. The growth of the faithful Church of Christ in the two-thirds world should give beleaguered Episcopalians in the United States rejuvenated hope in our sovereign Lord.[22]

This example makes explicit the assumption that growth is an indicator that a church must be doing things right (orthodox theology, evangelical fervor). Nigeria is not the only African nation to be singled out. In one AMiA newsletter, an article on Rwanda noted, "The church is growing rapidly. It is not unusual for Rwanda bishops, overseeing nine dioceses, to confirm hundreds of people at a time."[23] And when conservative Episcopal scholar and AAC member Stephen Noll moved to Uganda to take charge of Uganda Christian University in 2000, he stated in a sermon marking his departure, "We're not going to a virgin jungle nor evangelizing a pagan people; in fact, Uganda is one of the most Christian countries in the world today."[24]

Numbers arguments are heard in Uganda and elsewhere in Africa, too. Aaron, talking about why African evangelists like himself are in such demand in the North, put the case clearly:

> Of course, the numbers now. The numbers of Christians in Africa are many. . . . [Numbers] give authority and credibility. It's something to do with spiritual capital, really. That explains the enthusiasm and the zeal which the African leaders have, because they have a base. They are

not ashamed. It has to do with conviction and confidence. When you are a minority, your confidence is not the same as one who is in the majority. Numbers are critical.

Bishop Thomas spoke in similar terms about the authority African bishops like himself possess because of "sheer numbers" and the "red-hot experience" of being part of a rapidly growing church: "I think that . . . African and Asian bishops made a very important contribution [at Lambeth 1998]. But of course this is partly due to the fact that that is where, Africa and Asia, is where the Christian church is growing."

As Bishop Gerald, an American conservative leader, described it to me, AMiA and other conservative organizations are "using the great asset of the tremendous amount of numbers that are behind an orthodox witness from Africa" to give strength to their side in conflicts within and among Northern churches. However, while Americans assume rapid church growth translates directly into moral authority for the African churches, Ugandans' reactions to such growth figures (and to their own experiences of church growth, or the lack thereof) are more mixed. They question whether high membership numbers and rapid growth rates necessarily correlate with deep faith and solid orthodoxy, as Northerners often imply. In fact, Ugandan Anglicans frequently express ambivalence and concern about church membership numbers. The predominance of nominal Christians or "churchgoers" (people who seem to perform all the outward actions of Christian life without any deep faith) and worries about how to reach such people came up repeatedly in my interviews with Ugandan Anglican bishops, priests, and laypeople. In contrast to Noll's approving description of Uganda as "one of the most Christian countries in the world," Ugandan preachers not infrequently describe Uganda as a "Christian country" with bitter irony. An elderly Ugandan evangelist, preaching on the UCU campus, observed, "If you listen to the radio, you find Satan is robbing the world. People defile children, school fees are stolen, and people call this a Christian country?" In another sermon, a different preacher admonished his listeners for their recalcitrance in faith: "This is not the first time you've heard this. . . . The gospel has been preached here in Uganda for over 100 years now." Uganda's relatively long history of Christianity, and the large proportion of the population (around 70 percent) who claim to be Christians, seems to these preachers to be belied by the practices of the populace.

Several Ugandans suggested to me that the very pervasiveness of Christian institutions, ideas, and symbols in Uganda's public sphere might account for the shallowness of many people's faith. Robby shared his opinion with me:

Most schools begin with prayers in the morning, and so on and so forth. So the influence of Christianity is actually big. Only that like all human beings, some people are Christians, you know, superficially. They are not deeply rooted in their faith. That's why you hear of things like, you know, in some offices you find embezzlement of funds, you meet people in the streets who are thieves, you hear of prostitution, you know. I mean, people who do these things are not pagans. They are Christians.

A few Ugandans even offered the observation that though sincere Northern Christians were no doubt fewer in number, they were probably more committed, since the strong social norms in favor of Christianity in Uganda encourage nominalism. Bishop Ephraim observed: "The people in America who go to church are really devoted to that church, because it's not the norm now in America to go to church. . . . In our context, . . . the majority will go to church, because if you don't go to church you cannot answer the question, 'Why didn't you go to church?' Because they are going to ask you."

During my interviewing in Uganda, I found that Ugandans often described their church, and Christianity in Africa in general, as broad but shallow. Nelson, a sixtyish Ugandan priest serving a Kampala-area parish, observed to me that Africa is "a continent where you have 20,000 people coming to the Lord every single day, according to statistics." Yet, he went on, there are wars here, violence, dirty cities, HIV/AIDS, and poverty. "What's the problem? Christianity here is a mile long but an inch deep; it has quantity rather than quality." Alexander, a UCU professor, commented, "If Rwanda is 90 percent Christian, why the genocide? Christians must not condone evil," and concluded, likewise, that African Christianity is "an ocean wide and an inch deep." The same phrase is often used to describe Christianity in the United States by those, including conservative Episcopal dissidents, with doubts about the strength and sincerity of American faith. Americans and Ugandans thus share similar perceptions of the depth or quality of faith in their own churches and countries.

This parallel takes on some irony in light of the ways American conservatives fetishize African faith and church growth. American conservatives, despairing of their own churches and convinced that the size and growth rates of African churches prove Africans are preaching the gospel and following God's will, seek help from African church leaders. But at the same time, Ugandan Anglicans are lamenting the situation in their churches, worrying endlessly about how to deepen the faith of nominal Christians and encourage right behavior among committed Christians. In Uganda, besides hearing such concerns voiced in interviews, I witnessed them made manifest in a virtually endless cycle: parish and campus Mission Weeks; crusades and evangelistic campaigns in towns and villages; Bible studies, fellowships, and other discipling opportunities; and sermons preached in Anglican churches urging the congregation members to truly give their hearts to God. All these events demonstrate the concern of many church leaders and members about the quality of Christian belief and practice in their church and their country.

Many lay and ordained leaders in the Church of Uganda are even more troubled by the question of whether the numbers in their churches are growing at all. When I interviewed Bishop Abel, seeking his recollections of Lambeth 1998 and his thoughts on the characteristics of Northern and Southern Christianity, he spoke to this question on the basis of his own experience and the information gathered in a census effort with which he was involved:

> Some people have thought there is a strengthening of the Gospel in the South, and that then it is flowing North. Personally I don't see it that way. What is flowing is the forces of liberal theology, washing away the evangelical South. . . . In the South, we are struggling to hold our own. . . . Pentecostal churches are growing here, but it's "transfer growth" from other churches, not [growth which makes inroads into] Islam or traditional religions. . . . People "converted" now were converted from a "dead" Christian upbringing in the Church of Uganda or wherever. And the Church of Uganda itself has fewer members now than ten years ago. Everyone thought, ten years ago, that the [Church of Uganda] had about one-third of the population. Now, after a census in 2000, they found the Church of Uganda is at 20 percent.

Two Northern missionaries working in Uganda also commented to me on the apparent lack of growth in the Church of Uganda. Like some of the Ugandans quoted here, they were struck by the disjuncture between the Northern rhetoric and what they saw on the ground in Uganda. One of these, a British missionary named Cyril, talked with me about one parish Mission Week we had both attended. He remarked on the post–Mission Week announcements that ninety-one people had been saved. He pointed out that probably relatively few (if any) of those who came forward at the daily altar calls were actually new converts. The sermons preached at these events explicitly invited not only new converts but also those seeking recommitment to Jesus Christ, or a new level of faith, to come forward, and a good number of those who did so probably fit into one of the latter categories. Yet once Mission Week was over, as this missionary noted with some cynicism, the number ninety-one was treated as the number of those saved at Mission Week. Cyril saw this as indicative of a widespread manipulation of numbers to make it seem African churches are growing much more than they may actually be. He recalled viewing a video produced by a Northern missionary agency about the growth of the church in the developing world, which mentioned in passing the vital faith and countless conversions happening every day in Uganda. Cyril told me, "I saw that and I wondered to myself, 'Do they mean the Uganda in East Africa?'"

In addition to the consultants, both Ugandans and Northerners in Uganda, who directly questioned whether the Church of Uganda is growing, many more expressed anxiety about church growth indirectly, by voicing worries about how to make the Church of Uganda into an institution that can capture and engage the younger generation—essentially anxieties about whether the church is even capable of sustaining its current membership. This issue came up, one way or another, in the majority of the interviews I conducted in Uganda. In contrast to the confidence in Southern Christian faith that Northerners often express, Ugandans do not generally find reassurance in their church's numbers. When a Ugandan does comment on the numerical strength of African Christianity, often in the next breath he or she questions the significance of those numbers in terms of real Christianity, wondering whether the African churches' size and growth really represent strong faith—or whether growth can truly be seen in particular African Anglican churches at all.

Such worries about growth in the Church of Uganda do not invalidate general assertions that Anglicanism is growing in Africa, since other Anglican provinces, or other Christian groups in Uganda, may well be growing at impressive rates. What is significant here is that Northern Anglicans generalize what they hear about African church growth to apply to all the African Anglican churches. Accordingly, they ascribe to all those churches the qualities of vitality, orthodoxy, and enthusiasm that they assume this growth implies. By this logic, the Church of Uganda (or Rwanda, or Kenya) must be growing, because it's an African church and the African churches are growing; and it must be vibrant and orthodox and strong in faith, because those are the qualities that make churches grow.

SUFFERING

A fourth argument often made by Northerners praising African Christianity is that the suffering presumed to characterize African life gives moral authority or spiritual capital to African Christians. Such arguments are heard from Northerners on both the liberal and the conservative ends of the spectrum. For example, in one pre-Lambeth issue of the conservative-leaning *Church of England Newspaper*, one piece on African bishops was entitled, "Why It Is Vital to Listen to Suffering," while another article quoted the liberal-leaning primate of ECUSA, Frank Griswold, saying:

"In the suffering of fellow Anglicans there is an incredible testimony to their faithfulness and also an indictment of some of our western selfishness and self-concern."[25]

The presumption seems to be that having to cope with high levels of suffering and life-or-death situations makes African Christians bold and uncompromising in their faith. For example, in 1998 David Virtue wrote about Rwandan bishop John Rucyahana's controversial involvement with St. Andrew's, Little Rock: "Such is the freedom a Christian can know when looking into the face of death—and laughing."[26] One moderate American bishop commenting on Lambeth 1998 argued that suffering gives moral authority:

> This change of [the Anglican Communion's] voice [to the Third World] is not just about the demise of First World supremacy in the Anglican Communion. It is about earning the moral right to speak. We heard countless stories in our small group Bible studies about provinces growing even when spiritual affluence is accompanied by material poverty. . . . We heard personal stories of great suffering. . . . All of this made me realize . . . that when faithfulness to Jesus Christ costs everything you have, then you become a more legitimate voice.[27]

Northern Christians interpret images of Southern suffering through traditional understandings of the suffering of Jesus, attributing to Southern Christians a Christlike authority and wisdom. However, the value placed on suffering by American Christians also reflects their sense of the banality and ease of their own lives. The moderate bishop's statement just quoted implicitly contrasts Third World poverty and pain with First World affluence, and finds greater legitimacy in the former. Mary, an American missionary to Uganda, made this point when she spoke to me about suffering and authority: "The cost of commitment is so much greater in those times of crisis, and that speaks to people in our complacent society . . . I definitely think anyone who's been through a great tragedy has a platform for speaking in a way that people who've just been breezing through don't have."

This argument illustrates the trope of aestheticization, described by David Spurr. Spurr argues that Northerners' relative privilege, and their distance from Southern populations, allows Northerners to view Southern suffering as an aesthetic quality, moving and ennobling.[28] Americans' distance from African suffering is evident in generalizations that suffering and risk characterize all African lives. It is of course true that many African Christians (for example, in parts of Nigeria and Sudan) do face persecution for their faith, and that many others (for example, in northern Uganda, Liberia, or again in Sudan) must contend with the realities of war and oppression as part of the conditions of their daily lives. These realities should not be belittled, but generalizing these specific situations to an overall image of suffering Africa has the effect of reducing the significance of specific situations. Such universal suffering appears insoluble and therefore inevitable, so that all Americans can do (perhaps all they need do) is to admire the noble faith of those suffering Africans. The invocation of African suffering, cited in such generalized ways and tied to idealizations of Africans, can become a sentimental cliché, which Spurr argues is one common result of the aestheticization of suffering.[29]

Besides homogenizing the specificities of violence, disease, and privation in Africa into a generalized and aestheticized image, the rhetoric of suffering Africa is problematic because it can make Africans appear, to American eyes, as fundamentally "other"—different from Americans in experience, thought, and motivation. Northern journalistic writing seems often to assume that "human chaos and disorder are somehow a natural condition of the Third World," rather than tracing these conditions to histories of colonial abuse and mismanagement, economic and environmental exploitation, and the many other factors extrinsic to these nations that have played some role in their past and present troubles.[30] Rather than seeing Americans and Africans alike as situated in a complex and interrelated world system in which one's privilege is often related through twists and translations to another's disadvantage, Americans are wont to see the world as divided between North and South, each world region with its own characteristics and issues. Africa's problems thus appear intrinsic to Africa and Africans.

This "othering" effect of ideas of pervasive African suffering, besides blinding Americans to the North's past and continuing complicity in much of the suffering in contemporary Africa, also hides the many commonalities that American and African Christians may share. The daily lives of many of the Ugandan Christians I met are dominated, not by overwhelming suffering and risk, but by some of the same concerns shared by middle-class Americans: the costs of education, the trials of finding satisfactory employment, maintaining harmony in family life, caring for the aged and the young. Certainly there are important systemic differences in average risk (of AIDS or malaria infection, of traffic accidents, and so on) and in average standard of living between Ugandans and Americans, but few of the Ugandan Christians I met described their lives or the corporate life of their church communities as characterized by constant suffering and risk.[31] If anything, Ugandan friends and acquaintances tended to understate their troubles and difficulties, focusing instead on positive aspects of their lives—friends, faith, opportunities, and hopes.

In my experience, the suffering argument is rarely made by Africans. One notable exception is the tendency for Rwandan leaders (like their American allies) to use the 1994 genocide as a source of legitimacy for their controversial actions in challenging the Episcopal Church. Apart from such cases, few Africans seem interested in making a case for suffering as a source of strength or legitimacy for their church; at least, I did not hear many such arguments. One of the younger theology professors at UCU, James, who received part of his training in the United States and thus has some firsthand familiarity with American talk about the African churches, was one of the only Ugandans who mentioned such an argument for African Christian authority. He did so, however, only to refute it, specifically challenging the idea that the Rwandan genocide bestows moral authority upon Rwandan church leaders: "The whole mission [of Anglican Mission in America] is being built on the question of moral purity. . . . [Yet] I can see that the basis of the mission is shaken. What moral authority does the archbishop of Rwanda have to challenge moral problems in North America, when they are killing one another here? What is the moral authority that is there?"

James is nevertheless an exception in his pointed comment. Usually Ugandans are less direct in expressing their unwillingness to have the strengths of their church attributed to the sufferings of its members. For example, many Ugandan church leaders articulated anxieties about whether illness, joblessness, and other desperate circumstances were encouraging Ugandan Christians to go to "witch doctors" or traditional healers, because they feel the church can't solve their problems. The current trend for Anglican parishes to offer healing services is one response to this perceived failure and to leaders' concerns about whether people's suffering actually weakens the church. But Ugandan unwillingness to attribute their church's strengths to suffering may go beyond simply not finding the argument convincing. Africans are aware that much of the rest of the world perceives the African continent as in a constant state of crisis. They may be hesitant to strengthen that image by talking much about suffering themselves.

POVERTY

Like the suffering argument, the poverty argument is frequently used by Northerners describing Southern faith. This argument assumes that, having little material wealth, Africans value money and possessions less and place their hopes in God instead. Many Northern statements about the African church carry this argument implicitly in contrasting the material poverty and spiritual wealth of the African churches. For example, one Sunday morning at St. Timothy's, the rector reported on the progress of the members then traveling in Rwanda:

What [the travelers] will find in Rwanda and in Africa is that those who have not been blessed with the world's goods tend to turn to the things of God more easily than those who have been blessed. The poor seem to turn to God more easily. They don't have all the stuff we do to depend on. It is easier to be spiritual when you're poor. It is more difficult when you are rich in material things.

Such arguments are grounded in part in Christian understandings of the teachings of Jesus. Some of Jesus' statements, such as his saying that it is easier for a camel to pass through a needle's eye than for a rich man to enter the kingdom of God (Matt. 19:24), are widely interpreted as judgments on the rich or on the spiritual implications of wealth. Idealizing discourses about poverty and spiritual purity also have strong precedents in colonial discourse.

Some Ugandans agree with these Northern arguments that poverty makes faith strong in Uganda and in Africa in general. Several Ugandan Anglicans I interviewed pointed out the low pay for Church of Uganda clergy as one way in which poverty creates more commitment, arguing that if priests' salaries do not provide a comfortable livelihood, the people entering the ministry will do so out of a strong commitment to preaching the gospel and serving the people. Jeremiah, a young priest from southern Uganda studying at UCU, when I asked him what the African church has that the West doesn't, told me:

> I think there is now more commitment. Ministers here are less paid and sometimes go without pay for six months, but they keep preaching. A minister's house isn't nice, and he doesn't have much help, but he will preach the gospel even in such conditions. You find a minister here, a reverend, he has no means of transport. I think you are seeing, they are [walking] from here to there, to preach the gospel. . . . So that [degree of] commitment is lacking in some people coming from your area.

I met many Ugandan clergy, not to mention lay church leaders, who were deeply committed to their work and who lived in quite modest conditions. But, as Stephen, an experienced parish priest, explained, low clergy pay may also discourage some good candidates from entering the ministry, weakening the church overall. Further, as Obadiah, a priest in a poor small-town church, noted, the lack of resources in the Church of Uganda may also mean that its clergy and other officials are more tempted to abuse their positions for financial gain: "Some people actually encroach on some funds of the Christians, like donations, because they are not satisfied with what they get." The church's poverty may cause a temptation for some even as it breeds firmer commitment in others.

Although poverty may arguably produce stronger clergy, its impact on lay members is even more debatable. Northerners' poverty arguments imply that poverty creates more commitment among all Southern Christians. The Ugandans I met did not seem to share this view. Instead, many talked about how widespread poverty tends to weaken, not strengthen, Christian faith. At the same time the church's limited resources, while perhaps selecting for more committed clergy, also limit the capacity of the church to provide for its members' many needs and lift them out of the oppression of poverty. Jonah, a theology professor, told me flatly, "When people are poor they can't truly worship God. They're in bondage to their economic limitations and are unable to worship. 'What do we worship God for?' People can begin to ask these questions." William, a Ugandan church official with a broad knowledge of both his own province and Anglican Communion affairs, expressed concern about the frustration and lack of faith that poverty may produce: "Sometimes people can become frustrated because of poverty and other backwardness, he can't afford to pay fees for the children, he says, 'Aaah, there is no God after all.'" A common theme in interviews with Ugandan church leaders was the need for the church to engage in holistic ministry, meeting people's material as well as spiritual needs, since so many Ugandans struggle with poverty, lack of infrastructure, illness, and other difficulties, and the government has few resources to offer. Church leaders feel the pressure to respond to all these needs, but their resources, too, are sharply limited. Aaron put the problem poignantly, saying that the church cannot do Christ's work if it is unable to feed, to heal:

> If children cannot go to school, or if children are very hungry, or malaria is still tormenting people, we don't preach the live Christ. You see the point? So we still have that challenge of preaching the Jesus who is a healer, who is a giver of life, who can feed the hungry. . . . So that is the challenge we have in [this church]. . . . The gospel must be holistic. Development must be integrated with spiritual issues. That's the challenge which we have.

Poverty is seen as inimical to Christianity because it leads to temptations to steal, because it breeds hopelessness and cynicism, and because it weakens the church's ability to minister fully to its people. Several Ugandans also expressed concern that poverty may lead to moral compromise, as Christians may be lured away from the right path by the promise of wealth. One Ugandan told me, "With a hungry person you can almost do what you want."

That the idea of poverty creating strong faith may be not only incorrect, but dangerous, was pointed out to me by James, the skeptical theology professor:

This idea of the fervency of African Christianity coinciding with crisis in Africa. . . . I'm saying, the Western churches are trying to . . . link the two and romanticize [poverty]. And I'm saying, in my view, that the two are not connected. Although certainly you cannot deny the fact that one is impacting on the other, but it is not on the side of strength. In other words, if the African church, with its faith, had enough resources, it would do more than it has done. That is what I would be arguing strongly for. . . . This romanticization is more or less saying, Make the African church more poor to be more faithful and be more fervent! If these Africans lose their poverty, they are also likely to lose their faith! . . . And you see, that one is also dangerous. It is a dangerous attitude. Because even in the question of partnership, there will be [Northern] people who will say, "OK, let us protect the faith of this African. If he becomes more affluent, he will lose his faith." So there is a fear that the true partnership of the West and Africa will spoil the African church. Make it more affluent, and weaken it.

I have no evidence that romanticization of African Christian poverty has led any potential Northern partners to hold back in their relationships for fear of corrupting the faith of poor African Christians. But, as James observed, it does follow logically that if one believes strong Christian faith in Africa is intimately bound up with poverty, then one may worry that greater wealth might weaken that faith. In spite of Ugandan Christians' many ambivalences about the ever-multiplying aspects of Northern influence evident in their society, very few would want Northerners to withhold involvement or investment in Uganda for the sake of the purity of Ugandan faith. One aged Ugandan clergyman and scholar, Reverend Francis, told me that he, too, worries that Ugandans' faith may weaken as they become wealthier: "Poverty and hardship strengthen Christian faith. . . . We have seen, in Uganda, some people that are very committed when they're poor, but as they come up in the world, they weaken in faith. They are overtaken by a spirit of self-sufficiency—'I can do it all without God.'" But he went on to note that he saw a rich nation which is truly Christian when he visited Korea some years ago. The implication of this observation about Korea, I suspect, was that he would take his chances on Ugandan Christianity if the country could somehow become wealthy. Likewise, Abner spoke of the value of exchanging Southern spiritual wealth for Northern material wealth without any apparent concern that receiving Northern wealth would weaken Southern faith: "When we share [about our faith in America], we say, 'This wealth, what about sharing it with African brothers and sisters?'"

Few who have lived in Africa would dispute that poverty (unlike suffering) profoundly shapes daily life for the vast majority of Africans, though that poverty is of widely varying degrees and types.[32] People who live with such an intimate awareness of poverty—their own, their neighbor's, their relatives', their congregation's—may be less inclined to see it as a significant benefit. Instead of glorying in their purifying poverty, Ugandans long for a sound financial base for their church so they can make the gospel tangible by feeding the hungry, tending the sick, and educating the young. While Northerners talk glowingly about the spiritual wealth of those who have nothing, these Southerners wonder, sadly or cynically, why people who have nothing would adhere to a faith that cannot change their lot.

Convinced that poverty is more of a liability than an asset for their church, yet also believing their church to be stronger in faith than the Northern churches, Ugandans explain that gap by focusing attention on Northern affluence. They argue that Northern wealth and technology have made Northerners overly reliant on themselves and their possessions, so that they no longer rely on God. The question, my Ugandan consultants suggest, is not why the Ugandan church is strong, but why the Northern church is weak. And in explaining that weakness through the corrosive effects of wealth, they also, implicitly or explicitly, call on Northerners to share their wealth and thereby restore their own faltering faith.

Nelson, who spent a year assisting at a parish in England some years back, suggested to me one reason for the difference between the Ugandan and Northern churches is that Northern society is so affluent, and there are few challenges there: "The tendency to take life easy is high. . . . 'Give us this day our daily bread' does not make sense in the UK, because there is plenty of food." Similarly, Bishop Ezra explained why he feels it's "high time for African missionaries to . . . evangelize the churches in the West":

> People here, someone, if they go to Kampala, when he goes on the main road, a friend comes, and then just gives him or her a free lift to Kampala. Because someone prayed in the morning in his house, in his bedroom, he will think that, "Oh, the Lord really replied [to my prayer]." But for you people in the West, [you have] about two cars in the garage! Your fridge, they're full of cookies, full of chicken and all that. Then people begin questioning, people in the West questioning: "What do we pray God for? Cars are here, money is here, and other things are here." But that, as much as you have that wealth around you in your homes, in your households . . . , you are contented with all the wealth, riches you have accumulated, people in the West. That is one of the key problems, why you are faced with a lot of misbehavior.

In Ezra's view, plentiful food, other material goods, and the corresponding convenience in daily life are strongly linked to America's weak faith.

In addition to this critical judgment of the relative wealth and materialism of Northern societies, some Ugandans go beyond criticism and feel compassion for the problems of wealthy Northerners. Tobias, a Ugandan priest on the staff of UCU, told me, "Terrible is the whole war you fight with materialism in your country. Materialism there is almost similar to our spiritual darkness here. Ours is obvious; yours is very subtle. And so you find that a Christian has to struggle with those things." Richard, a Ugandan provincial official, observed: "I think the problem with the Western churches is prosperity. Material prosperity is a real problem, while the church in Africa is struggling with scarcity. That is easier to deal with than prosperity . . . [M: Spiritually speaking.] Yes. It's tough to manage riches. It's much easier to manage poverty. That's a problem." These leaders suggest that the challenges of materialism—self-reliance, greed, complacency, and so on—are more subtly damaging to Christian faith than poverty. In feeling compassion for the spiritual difficulties that wealth entails, Ugandans can look on their Northern Christian brethren with pity rather than envy.

Many Northerners, of course, agree that wealth carries great spiritual dangers, and that American society, for one, is far too materialistic. Members of St. Timothy's, a parish tending toward the upper middle class, often spoke about the negative effects of wealth on their own faith. For example, the rector observed in one sermon, "This congregation is in the top 1 percent in the world. . . . The problem with wealth and stuff is that it deflects us—it takes energy, it takes time." During one house church meeting, Lacey joked about the difficulty of spreading the gospel in a country so afflicted with "affluenza." These and other instances point to the fact that St. Timothy's is a community struggling with the faith implications of its own wealth, in the face of the poverty of their Rwandan allies and many other peoples around the globe and in their own city. At St. Timothy's, the result of the congregation's thoughtful self-examination, inspired by the economic gap between its wealth and its Rwandan partners' poverty, was the organization of a fund-raising project to buy building materials for churches. These efforts are appreciated, but the project does little to confront or address the unequal global distribution of wealth and power.

The relatively modest engagement with African poverty in a parish like St. Timothy's is undoubtedly due in part to evangelical Christians' preference for interventions focused on individual transformation, and relative disinterest in systemic solutions.[33] But the way American conservatives (and, indeed, many moderates and liberals) tend to view African poverty also reduces the sense that a response is needed. James, quoted above, suggested that Americans might hesitate to help Africans for fear that the Africans' faith would be weakened. Even without conscious concern about "spoiling" Africans, however, the Northern idea of African poverty as romantic and productive of strong faith creates a sense that Africans are well-off as they are.

David Spurr examines how Northern discourse often idealizes Southern poverty in ways that reduce or eliminate any sense of obligation on the part of the Northern observer. He brings out these points in his examination of Dominique Lapierre's novel about Calcutta, *The City of Joy*. Spurr writes:

> [Lapierre] helps to manage symbolically the human crisis of the slum dwellers by showing that they have taken the spiritual path out of their misery. . . . The "joy" of Calcutta thus serves to compensate for the great inequality between the Third World and the modernized West; it enables a Western audience to feel compassion and even to see the poor of that other world as living out the realization of some of the West's most ancient ideals.[34]

The idealization of poverty frees the comparatively wealthy Northerner from any sense of guilt or responsibility. Spurr describes Lapierre's work as "a deflection from politics": such idealizations deflect Northerners from engaging with the established patterns of power that create and perpetuate Southern poverty. Spurr observers that aestheticizing poverty isolates images of poverty "from the relations of political and economic power that provide a more meaningful context for understanding poverty [such that] poverty [appears] . . . unrelated, except for purposes of dramatic contrast, to the prosperity that thrives on other shores."[35] Some conservative Episcopalians have learned, through their engagement with Southern allies, to think more critically about economic globalization, the history of colonialism, and American privilege and power. But even those who question the conditions and origins of African poverty still tend to share in the general Northern idealization of it, a perspective that differentiates them from most of their African allies. Spurr notes, "The power to perceive poverty as aesthetic value is a privilege not granted to the poor"—or their ecclesiastical representatives.[36]

Bishop Gerald, a conservative Episcopal leader with his own Southern connections, criticized AMiA for not taking its African allies' perspectives on wealth seriously: "The Africans say, 'No, [doctrine] is not your problem; your problem is materialism, your problem is the whole Western way of life, you do not understand.' 'Well, we don't want to hear that'—because the AMiA crowd is as wedded to the high-style American-style way of life as anything else. So we're not hearing their critique of the economic issues and all the rest." One example of such critique comes from the international confirmation service in Rosemont, Pennsylvania, at which Congolese archbishop Njojo preached on American materialism, saying: "Some want to buy a new car every year. God would like to teach us how to help other people."[37] Njojo's sermon points provocatively to the expectation or hope among Southern bishops that the wealthy American conservatives who are lately inspired to seek relationship with them will also be inspired to balance the material disparities between Northern and Southern churches. Yet to date, while AMiA and other Northern partners have been generous in their giving, engagement with the political and economic issue of changing global disparities in wealth has not become a central issue for this movement.

MISSIONS FROM THE ORTHODOX SOUTH?

One corollary of the American conviction of high African Christian spiritual capital is the idea that missionization needs to shift directions from its traditional North-to-South pattern to one of South-to-North. Differences between American and African perspectives emerge in relation to this idea as well. The idea that Southern Christian leaders may have vital spiritual gifts for Northern churches is not an innovation of the late 1990s, but this idea seems to have gained significantly in popularity and salience since then. An increasing number of Northerners and Southerners, ranging from conservative evangelicals to mainstream and liberal Christians, believe that the Northern churches need the witness of Southern Christian missionaries. Even the CMS, the great British missionary society that once sent missionaries all over the world, has begun to bring "mission partners" from Asia and Africa to serve as missionaries in Britain.[38]

Not surprisingly, disaffected conservative Episcopalians are eager proponents of Southern missions to the North. The idea that Southern Christians have the potential to restore orthodoxy in the Anglican Communion's Northern provinces has been an underlying theme in many of the actions and statements of conservative Episcopalians since the Dallas conference. AMiA, for example, bases its self-understanding partially on the South-to-North missions idea, as its name suggests—Anglican Mission in America. AMiA's website presents the idea of reversal of missions: "For decades, the American church sent missionaries to Africa and Asia. Now, Africa and Asia have reached out their missionary arms to embrace Anglicans in America."[39] I heard this view echoed many times at St. Timothy's, as members talked about AMiA and the Province of Rwanda. AMiA's advocates see this organization as bringing to life the vision of re-evangelization and renewal of Northern Christianity by zealous and orthodox Southern Christians. This understanding is not diminished by the fact that belonging to AMiA is no guarantee that a parish will have any actual contact with African Christians; in several instances, I heard

AMiA's members and leaders simply define themselves as missionaries on behalf of their Southern Christian sponsors.[40]

Many Ugandans agree strongly that the time has come for missions to flow from South to North. Nelson offered me this unsolicited observation: "I would plead that it is high time for African missionaries to leave Africa and go and evangelize—again!—the churches in the West." Sending African missionaries to Europe or the United States is a not-infrequent topic in the Ugandan newspapers. A 1998 article entitled "Africa Evangelizes Europe" approvingly described the missionary work of one African-initiated church, the World Trumpet Mission: "In the 19th century, Christian missionaries traveled from Europe to Africa bringing the message of salvation. The story has now changed and Africa is taking the gospel of Jesus to Europe. . . . Today, African evangelists are calling upon the Europeans to 'arise and shine' and return to their heritage as a Christian nation."[41] Several Ugandans told me that Uganda, in particular, has a missionary calling to the rest of the world, because it was a center of the East African Revival. Watching television one evening, I saw a broadcast of a local praise service that began with a screen showing a map of the world, with arrows going out from Uganda to other countries: the United States, South Africa, Sweden, and many more. This image captured the idea voiced by many Ugandans: that the spiritual vitality of East African Revival–influenced Ugandan Christianity demands that Ugandans share their faith with the world.

Other Ugandans, however, voiced uncertainty regarding how realistic or even desirable it would be to shift the primary direction of missionary movement to South-to-North. When that idea came up in the course of my interviews or informal conversations with Ugandan leaders and laypeople, they often spoke of doubts regarding whether Ugandan Christians were really equipped to act as worldwide evangelists. Three common concerns were the readiness of Southerners to confront Northerners, the lack of funding for Ugandan missionary work, and the question of whether Northerners would accept Southern missionaries. These concerns again reveal the enduring significance of difference (in cultural standing and confidence) and distance (in the need for funding for missionary travel) in transnational inter-Anglican relationships, despite of activists' globalizing efforts to minimize such separating factors.

Several Ugandans suggested to me that the thinking of Southerners accustomed to receiving missionaries, rather than sending them, can present challenges to South-North missionization. When my husband told our friend Samuel, a young UCU law student, about my research on American parishes with African bishops, Samuel responded with amazement: "That's like a father having a child, and then turning around and calling the child the father!" Several Ugandan church leaders spoke about such patterns of thought as a challenge to be overcome, if South-to-North missions are to thrive. Richard, a provincial official, told me that his church needs to develop more confidence in its own strengths, in order to share them with the North: "For a long time the church in Africa has been looking to the West to model the faith, because of the thinking we got from the missionaries. . . . Now we are facing the challenge of turning and realizing, what do *they* want from *us*?. . . . The Church in Africa should develop the confidence to feel we have something to offer the Western world."

Even if Ugandan Christians develop such missionary confidence, sending missionaries to the North will remain difficult. The problem of dependency and insufficient funding was brought up by several Ugandans whom I asked about the desirability of African missions to Northern churches. In his UCU seminar on Theology and Development, Kodwo Ankrah noted that many Africans are now in the North preaching the gospel, but concluded, "the problem that keeps the South from sharing what it has is money," since there are no wealthy mission agencies to send forth African evangelists. Jeremiah, a young priest and UCU student, argued that the African churches need such a mission agency, though he pointed out humorously that the funding would have to come from the North: "One hundred years of the church in Africa, [and] we need to have a missionary society, because we don't have any which can go there. And if we need to have that program, we shall still be dependent on the West!" Inherent in Jeremiah's quip is his knowledge that obtaining Northern funding for anything in Africa is difficult at best.[42]

Even when funding to support Southern missions to the North can be obtained (for instance, in new CMS programs bringing African evangelists to Britain), the financial imbalance between North and South remains a problem, because Southern evangelists' poverty undermines the effectiveness and freedom of their witness. Several of my consultants noted this problem. For example, Jonah, a UCU theology professor, bemoaned the dynamics of a situation in which a British diocese had paid for a Ugandan priest to come serve as an evangelist. Jonah was troubled that the Ugandan's home diocese hadn't been able, or hadn't bothered, to contribute any money to the evangelist's travel costs, "just to show he is our missionary." As it is, the evangelist is in Britain only at his host diocese's discretion, and Jonah worried that this would cause him to water down his message for acceptability, rather than preaching freely as the Spirit calls him. South-to-North missions cannot truly parallel North-to-South missions, because of the inequality in resources for the missionary endeavor, rooted in global inequalities in wealth distribution.

Concerns about funding relate closely to concerns about the acceptability of African evangelistic preaching to American and European ears. If

African evangelists are usually able to reach Northern audiences only with substantial Northern funding, then if Northerners reject the Africans' message, the whole mission collapses. Several of my consultants expressed doubts about whether Northerners would feel African evangelists had anything to tell them. When I asked Bishop Ezra about sending missionaries to the West, he said the Church of Uganda is trying to do so, but observed: "To send a missionary to someone who is proud, he will say that, 'No, I don't like your missionaries, I don't need your service!' It's difficult. Sometimes they say, 'You are primitive, you don't know what you are talking about, you are backward!' It is difficult, but we need to send missionaries there." Christina, the nineteen-year-old daughter of a UCU professor, made the same point when I asked her about the possibility of African missions to the United States:

> I don't know how people in America . . . respond to the Africans. Do they give much attention, or do they not? Because I have heard some of them do not like black people. Secondly, they also don't think we have houses like this one. They think we live in the bush. If we go to a place where somebody has never seen a brown person and he thinks we are acting like monkeys and we try to preach the word of God. . . . they would just say, "Where did God find you, when you were sleeping in a grass hut?"

Both a senior Church of Uganda bishop and a young laywoman thus expressed the general Ugandan awareness that Africans lack credibility in the global North.[43] Ugandan Anglicans know that, whatever positive notions about Africa may circulate in some Northern Anglican circles, many Northerners still see Africa in terms of primitives sleeping in grass huts.

"But Tell Us about You!"

While Ugandans voice ambivalences about the logistics of African missionization in the North, many Northern dissidents express great enthusiasm about bringing African priests and evangelists to preach to Northern Christians. In a commentary on Lambeth 1998, conservative commentator Todd Wetzel wrote, "God is no longer asking [Northerners] to speak to, much less preach at, the Two-Thirds World. The time has come for them to listen and, yes, be converted by a more vibrant Christianity that the Holy Spirit is blowing toward our shores."[44] It is not uncommon for African preachers to visit American or other Northern congregations. Many African clergy and bishops have opportunities to visit and preach abroad—whether guest preaching while studying abroad, exchanging visits with a companion parish or diocese, or otherwise making some sort of preaching tour. For example, the (nonsectarian but largely Anglican) African Evangelistic Enterprises agency sends preachers to the United States and the UK on a semiregular basis. Such visits are not limited to conservative or dissident parishes, though such parishes are often particularly eager to host an African preacher.

Despite American enthusiasm for African preaching, tensions do sometimes arise on these occasions. Sometimes African desires to preach the gospel come into conflict with American aestheticizations of African poverty and suffering, and the Americans' corresponding interest in hearing about how awful things are in Africa. Such conflicts came to light in several stories I heard from Ugandan consultants, and one I read, about Africans preaching in the United States. These stories follow a pattern in which the American parishes (mostly moderate and liberal, but also sometimes conservative) seem to view their visitor as a representative of a continent in crisis. The visitor, however, views himself as a guest preacher, come to share the gospel.

Most of these stories describe facing resistance when preaching in the United States (or sometimes the UK). Kenyan bishop Alexander Muge's visit to a liberal Episcopal congregation provides an example. At dinner with his American hosts before his appearance at one particular church, Muge was asked what he thought about homosexuality. Muge described the results in a written account (widely circulated among American conservatives):

> I told them I was going to preach to the congregation of St. Luke's on the very issue that we were discussing; that I planned to tell them it is evil for people who call themselves Christians to practice homosexuality. The canon and the rector instructed me not to mention anything concerning homosexuality because the national church had suspended consideration on the issue, and to bring it up would be a violation of the rule. I insisted that the Spirit of The Lord was leading me to speak on Sodom and Gomorrah, and there was no way I could restrain the Spirit of God. The rector finally told me that if that is what I was going to preach on the subject of homosexuality, I should not proceed to the church. I told him I accepted this. I was turned away from preaching nothing but the true Gospel of our Lord Jesus Christ![45]

Bishop Ezra gave me another perspective on encountering resistance, telling me how his hosts sometimes try to limit his message—not only in the case of homosexuality but with other issues as well:

> You know, sometimes when you are going to preach, they ask you not to mention this one. For instance, homosexuality. When you go to those

churches, sometimes they say, Don't talk about homosexuality! Don't talk about homosexuality! Or stealing. Don't talk about stealing!. . . . And sometimes when they know that you are going to talk about that one, they don't allow you in their churches to speak. They say, "OK, now we don't need your sermon, please."

I asked how he handled those situations, and he explained, "Sometimes what we do, . . . we don't talk about them. We talk about us. We give them testimony. . . . For the testimony, they can understand, they can hear, they can listen. But when you talk about other things, they say, 'Mmm-mm! We don't like that one.'" In his (extensive) experience, shifting the message from exhortation to testimony usually made his hosts more comfortable.

Stories of such encounters are often told with a moral: in spite of the unpopularity of the preacher's message, a few people were moved by what they heard and changed their lives—proving the visiting preachers were right to preach as they did. Stephen, a Ugandan priest, reflects on his visit to a Chicago-area Episcopal church: "The pastor told me in the vestry, 'I hear you have been talking about sin. We don't dwell too much on sin here.' And I was hearing him saying, 'If you could change your subject. . . . ' And I said, 'Well, if I can't preach on sin and its remedy, then I have no message for the day, in which case, Pastor, you can take over and I will sit in and do whatever else.'" He was allowed to preach after all, and when he made an appeal for conversions at the end of his sermon, "nine people came to the Lord." Bishop Thomas likewise spoke to me about his experience of preaching an unpopular message with surprising success, as demonstrated by reactions afterward: "After I preached, as people were coming out of the church, they were shaking my hand and saying, 'Thank you for saying what you have said, because people in this country don't say it, and we know this could be the true Christian faith, we know this to be the foundation of our church, and we want to hear people who speak like you have done.'"

If many American Episcopalians show some reluctance to hear the particular Gospel message their African visiting preachers feel called to preach, then what do they want to hear from their visitors? The American tendency to focus on (and idealize) African problems is evident here: what the Americans want to hear about, often, is what's wrong in Africa and how they can help. Bishop Ezra, after explaining that he often falls back on giving testimony, talked about reactions to his preaching among Americans: "When you start preaching to them and say that, 'Now, you are doing this one, . . . you shouldn't do like that one,' they say, "My friend, that's not your business. That's our business. *But tell us about you.*'" He explained how he responds to those "Tell us about you" reactions by giving his audience what they want and presenting programs in his church that need funding: "Sometimes when you know that these people are not interested in [your preaching], you just go ahead with your program. Sometimes you have a program, like a water sanitization program—we need to raise funds to provide water, good water, to the community. We have children, street children. . . . We want to build a house for those abandoned children."

Sharing their church's needs, talking about orphans or water sanitization or whatever the pressing project may be, has its advantages. Americans are often generous in response to such appeals. Cecil, an Anglican layman who has spent several months in the United States as a missionary, visiting evangelical and mainstream Episcopal churches, commented on the tendency of American churches to want to hear about Africa's challenges. "At times we would be invited to share the political and economic situation, so that people get to understand . . . how we live, and yet in a Christian way. . . . Some of the American friends would very much listen, wanted to hear how we relate with life as Christians in such conditions." Thus inspired by accounts of African Christian hardships, Americans are quite responsive, as Cecil could testify: "They were very very very enthusiastic, and they helped us. . . . When I went to these churches, I came back with $19,000. You know, they have . . . to give, because they know to whom they are giving." Hearing personal accounts of problems and possible solutions in one African diocese encourages American benevolence, as Cecil discovered.

Not all Ugandan leaders are resigned to Americans' tendency to be more open to pleas for funding than to preaching. While Bishop Ezra takes such situations in stride and uses the opportunities to get help for his own flock at home, Bishop David expressed indignation about such situations:

> Sometimes, when I went to a church [in the U.S.], they wanted me to speak about the orphans here. I told them, "I can't come from Uganda and I talk about the orphans. I come from Uganda, I come with a message. I'll preach, and after the preaching, when there is time, we can talk about orphans." So they wanted me—"Bishop, you talk about"—in the pulpit!—"talk about the orphans." I said, "My friend, traveling from Uganda and I talk in the pulpit about the orphans? I want life! I want to share my story, the story of the African church, the Ugandan church, with you here!" They don't want to hear, some of them.

Bishop David insists that the story of the Ugandan church is not the same story as the story about orphans he's being asked to tell; that the "story of the African church" is a story about life, not suffering and death. On a similar note, Matthew, a priest and UCU professor who has spent time studying and preaching in the United States and the UK, commented to me that he is troubled by some African bishops who do take advantage of Northern interest in African problems in order to fund-raise: "When I was in the U.S. I was very cross with many bishops who used to come with pictures [of starving children] to raise money, swollen bellies, running noses." Bishop David's and Matthew's remarks reveal these Ugandan Christians' recognition that the down side of giving the American audience what they want to hear by talking about Africa's needs is the reinforcement of the idea of Africa most Americans already carry: as a place of continuous crisis, overwhelming poverty, and suffering.

THE PERSISTENCE OF COLONIAL CONCEPTS

What are the implications when Americans, despite all their interest in and concern for the African church, continue to perceive it through images of starving children? There are starving children in parts of Africa, and hungry children in many more parts, and most African bishops would not mind help feeding them. But the Ugandan Christian leaders and laity I met do not care to be seen through the same lens, as an infantilized figure characterized primarily by need and the outstretched hand. For Africans to participate in the continuing definition of Africa as primarily a site of lack and suffering is to accede to American perceptions of Africans as profoundly different from Americans, because of Africans' presumed daily experiences of poverty and suffering. Underlying that American perception is the even more insidious idea that perhaps all Africa's problems point to some even more fundamental difference: perhaps Africa is constantly in crisis because Africans are less civilizationally advanced, less rational, more prone to atavistic hatreds and violence. The image of Africa in perpetual crisis, for white Americans, may have subtle or not-so-subtle resonances with racist thought. In addition, this image of Africa demonstrates the limits of the transformative potential of processes of globalization in this case. As it plays into North/South interchurch relationships, this image of Africa in crisis perpetuates an essentially colonial relationship, in which Northerners share the assets and benefits of their civilization in order to provide for, heal, educate, and lift up their perpetually needy Southern brethren.

Increasingly dominant views of African Christians as spiritual authorities represent a significant step away from the negative and blatantly racist ideas about Africans that are still in circulation—including in the words of some liberal Episcopal bishops following Lambeth 1998. Theodora Brooks, an African priest working in the United States, commented on the persistence of such negative ideas in a letter to her diocesan newspaper shortly after Lambeth:

> Years ago, Africa was always referred to as the "Dark Continent." Artists created buffoonish characters in their attempt to portray the people of this continent. Writers, historians, anthropologists, etc. used choice words such as "natives," "barbarians," and "savages". . . . [Some bishops' negative] remarks about Africans only confirm what Africans have always known; that people have yet to erase the image of Africans that has been passed down to them.[46]

But while some liberal Northern church leaders have described African Christians as superstitious, ignorant, and opportunist, conservative Northern church leaders describe them in glowing terms as defenders of true Christian faith and prophets of a new global revival. Have those who describe the Southern churches as superior in faith finally transcended or "erased" those inherited negative images of Africa? Have new global relationships, and a new global vision, transformed these old patterns and ideas?

Descriptions of African Christians as simple, pure, zealous, enthusiastic and noble in suffering and poverty provide more empowering terms for North/South relationships than some of the alternatives. But they do not escape the terms of earlier, negative discourses about Africa and Africans. Instead, they idealize both African faith and African problems, as well as reinscribing colonial ideas about Africans' otherness in time (the church's youth), thought (simplicity and enthusiasm), and experience (suffering and poverty). Conceiving of African Christians as people of pure and simple faith invokes concepts ultimately derived from older and negative views of Africans as childlike, primitive, and uncivilized. To be sure, these negative images have now been turned on their heads to become idealizations, but the fundamental idea of African otherness carries on unimpeded into the new, romanticized images. Roxanne Doty concludes, after examining the persistence of colonial patterns of thought into contemporary North/South relations such as foreign aid practices: "[These texts] attest to the power of earlier representations, the continuity amidst discontinuity. They form a sort of cultural unconscious that always comes back to the presumption, generally unstated, especially in more recent texts, of different kinds of human being with different capacities and perhaps different inherent worth and value."[47]

Besides perpetuating constraining colonial images, idealizations of African Christianity arguably serve Americans better than they do Africans, by allowing African Christianity to serve as an illustration of conservatives' values in the context of Northern conversations and debates. Visions of African Christians as "noble savages" lend moral authority to the conservative side in moral debates within Northern Anglicanism today. Indeed, the argument over orthodoxy and sexual ethics in the Northern church is often now phrased as an argument over the value and character of African Christianity: whether it is pure, traditional, inspired (so we should listen to the Africans) or ignorant, premodern, fundamentalist (so we need not listen to the Africans).

If the rhetoric of idealization that many Northerners apply to African Christians echoes colonial rhetoric, even in a globalized era of improved communication and renewed mutual relationship, what does that mean for the African church leaders and others who must negotiate this rhetoric in the process of interacting with Northern Christians? In such North/South relationships, Africans must deal with and, to an extent, deal in the images, roles, and discourses that make up Northerners' perception of African Christianity. The pressures felt by African preachers in American parishes point to the ambiguous position of these leaders. Is it better, more tolerable, more advantageous to go along with the American idea of Africans as people characterized by constant suffering, poverty, and need—or to go along with the corresponding American idealization of Africans as pure and zealous gospel preachers? Most Ugandan preachers I interviewed seemed to prefer the latter, but hinted in various ways that this is no ideal position—not least because it feeds into a romanticization of poverty and suffering that most Ugandans find nonsensical. Still, African Christians who interact with Northern Christians must negotiate the latter's imaginings of African Christianity, until and unless they develop relationships that transcend these tropes and stereotypes.

VISIONS OF AFRICA: PRIDE OR SHAME?

As for the American partners in these newly forged North/South Anglican relationships, traces of older negative images of Africa still haunt them as well. Positive visions of Africa, as part of the new conservative globalism, may increasingly permeate Northern Anglican dissident groups, but are still unusual in Northern societies. Some members of St. Timothy's, for example, continue to struggle with the negative associations of blackness and Africanness for outsiders seeing or visiting their church. Continuing ambivalence about St. Timothy's African associations were manifest in a debate over whether to include the name "Rwanda" on a new sign for the church, to be placed on the outskirts of town. This dispute flared up at a vestry meeting—ironically, immediately after one member, Paul, had given a presentation on his visit to Rwanda. It had been decided at a previous meeting that the sign would read, "St. Timothy's Episcopal

Church, Anglican Mission in America." Paul objected strenuously to this text, saying he wanted the sign to include, "Province of Rwanda." Joe, the rector, explained the earlier decision to leave out the African designation: "We didn't want to [include Rwanda]," he said. "It's a confusing thing and it brings about a conflict for some people." Another vestry member said, "Let's not put up anything we're going to be ashamed of." Paul replied heatedly, "Well, I'm not ashamed of the Province of Rwanda." Further discussion followed, but it was clear that the decision on the text was final. This brief debate ended as Joe reminded Paul, "The other thing [meaning Rwanda] just creates some problems for some people." Paul answered, "Well, I think they need to live with that problem." But, outnumbered, he let the issue go.

The sign was printed with no mention of Rwanda—a decision that surprised me as much as it did Paul, given the burgeoning enthusiasm in the parish for relationship with the Anglican church in Rwanda. But the leadership at St. Timothy's, while believing themselves to have transcended their racism and their previous negative ideas about Africa, are still keenly aware that the average unchurched American, those whom they hope to attract and bring to Christ, may not be so liberated and well informed. In spite of most members' pleasure in knowing about and identifying with their archbishop and his church, St. Timothy's leaders were hesitant to face the stigma that they fear association with Africa may carry in the wider world. Breaking from the Episcopal Church is one thing, but publicly identifying yourself as an African church is quite another, in a society in which most people still see Africa as the "dark continent," rather than as a source of gospel light.

CHAPTER SEVEN

Integrity for Sale? Money and Asymmetry in Transnational Anglican Alliances

THE FOUNDING of Integrity-Uganda, the Ugandan branch of the advocacy organization for gay, lesbian, bisexual, and transgender Anglicans, was marked only by a press release from sibling organization Integrity-USA in mid-2000 and passed unremarked in the Ugandan press. But given the controversial character of Integrity-Uganda, it could not long operate undercover. Early in 2001, news of the organization's existence broke in Uganda. The *Monitor* and *New Vision* were kept busy through the following months with updates, commentaries, interviews, letters, and editorials about the controversial new Anglican organization. Integrity-Uganda is the only African chapter of Integrity, founded in the United States in the 1970s.[1] From the first announcements about the Ugandan group, controversy centered on its association with Integrity-USA. In February 2001, the Ugandan House of Bishops described Integrity-Uganda as an outside plant: "This organization is a move by gays and lesbians from the United States which want to establish their root on the continent of Africa to be headquartered in our own country, Uganda."[2]

In contrast, Integrity-Uganda's leaders maintained it was an indigenous organization, responding to local needs. They acknowledged association with Integrity-USA, but insisted their American allies provide only encouragement. In Integrity-Uganda's first public statement, a response to the House of Bishops, it described itself as a local initiative: "We wish to respond to a Press release of the House of Bishops of Church of Uganda . . . which condemned the good efforts of our organization as an outlandish feature from the Episcopal Church in the USA. We want to make it categorically clear that Integrity-Uganda is not an alien influence from the West. It is simply a local initiative borne by a strong need amongst Anglicans in Uganda."[3]

In spite of such assertions, however, Ugandan church leaders and Ugandan press coverage cast Integrity-Uganda as an effort by American gays to spread homosexuality in Uganda. Negative evaluations of Integrity-Uganda have particularly focused on Bishop Christopher Ssenyonjo, a retired bishop and counselor involved with the group. Most Ugandan criticisms of Integrity-Uganda and Bishop Ssenyonjo claim that Ssenyonjo "sold out" to American gays, accepting money and support from Integrity-USA in exchange for propagating homosexuality in Uganda. This view of Integrity-Uganda rests upon the idea, often expressed by Ugandan journalists and church leaders, that homosexuality itself—and/or the ideology that it is an acceptable "alternative lifestyle"—is something entering Uganda from outside, something literally "outlandish."

Ssenyonjo and the organization's other leaders, including Frank and Edward, introduced in chapter 3, were accused of compromising their culture and abetting corrupting foreign influences, and for the basest of motives: greed. In newspaper reports and interviews, the most common explanation given for Ssenyonjo's involvement with Integrity-Uganda was that he was frustrated by his reduced income upon his retirement, due to minimal pension provisions in the Church of Uganda, and sought to make money by ingratiating himself with an American activist group. For example, when asked to explain Ssenyonjo's stand in a 2001 press interview, Archbishop Nkoyoyo offered this explanation:

> It is poverty. He is going against his conscience because of the meager pension . . . he gets. This is a man who used to earn sh700000–sh800000 [$440 per month] on top of driving a Mercedes Benz, servants, a house and food. So when a chance to earn an extra coin shows up, he takes the opportunity. . . . So the church needs to provide better pensions if our clergy are going to retire honourably.[4]

The archbishop concluded by exhorting Ugandans to "brace themselves for old age."

Many Ugandans share this interpretation of Ssenyonjo's motives. Ssenyonjo and other Integrity-Uganda leaders deny that they are propagating homosexuality in Uganda in order to make money, and argue that their work is motivated by concern for an oppressed minority group. In one newspaper article, Ssenyonjo explained how he came to feel sympathy for gay Ugandans: "After my retirement, I set up consultation and counseling services. . . . During my counseling sessions, some homosexuals came to me. . . . I realized that they were a group of frightened people who needed counseling and assurance of the love of God."[5] In another article, Ssenyonjo responded to his accusers directly: "I am not doing this ministry for the sake of money, though I trust that God will not allow me to starve. Some people have been accusing me of being money hungry. I am not."[6] But such denials have not lessened the suspicions of church officials and the Ugandan public that the leaders of Integrity-Uganda allowed themselves to be "bought" by American favors to take up the gay cause.

"Money Is Muscle"

Integrity-Uganda's encounter with these suspicions is only one of many cases in recent contentious Anglican Communion politics in which money has been a central issue. Northern liberal and conservative activists and leaders have repeatedly accused one another of using money to influence Southern Anglicans; Southern Anglicans have argued for their own freedom from such influences, but questioned other Southern leaders' incorruptibility. Andrew, an American conservative leader, told me that in order to understand new transnational alliances, I needed to look at the role of money—ranging from out-and-out corruption to the ways decisions are subtly influenced by the availability of funds. AMiA bishop Chuck Murphy himself pointed to the power of money in current international Anglican politics in a press interview soon after his consecration: "If you make the decision to . . . go over the heads of . . . the Episcopal Church . . . to get leadership, you'd better have some money. Money is muscle; it makes things happen."[7]

An examination of questions of money, influence, and power in North/South Anglican relationships again raises the issue of whether globalization is primarily Westernization. I have argued that these alliances cannot be reduced to simple ideological colonization of the Southern partners. Yet financial pressures to conform to Northern expectations, though they may not compromise Southern Anglicans' independence, certainly complicate it. In addition to the Westernization question, this chapter also speaks to the potential of this conservative Anglican globalism to transform established patterns of worldwide Northern dominance. Those involved in these alliances frequently assert that they are creating new kinds of global relationships that escape past patterns of Northern cultural and economic domination and that will help initiate a new era of mutuality or even Southern dominance, free of past inequalities. The profound asymmetry in wealth between Northern and Southern partners, however, makes it difficult, if not impossible, to consign financial considerations to irrelevance. The difference in the way money matters for American and African Anglicans creates a disjuncture in how these Anglicans talk about the role of money in these relationships. In terms of inequalities of wealth and corresponding disparities in power, the global order created through these innovative relationships, as in the world in general, tends to follow patterns of Northern privilege and power established during the colonial era. The potential of this new global vision and its advocates to create a radically new Anglican world order is constrained by the realities of global inequality, played out more or less overtly in the dynamics of these alliances.

MONEY MATTERS: NORTH/SOUTH DIFFERENCES

Accusations about the exercise of influence through financial power permeate debates in the Episcopal Church and Anglican Communion today, especially with reference to relations between Northern and Southern Anglicans. Americans and Ugandans have very different perspectives and sensitivities on these issues. For the American partners, despite the salience of their international relationships, their primary focus of conflict remains the American church situation. In this context, both the liberal and the conservative sides have sometimes positioned themselves as advocates for the disadvantaged around the globe; both sides have also sometimes implied that their opponents are using disadvantaged peoples in order to bolster their party's position in intra-Episcopal politics. These accusations of manipulative, neocolonial influence-wielding carry particular weight in light of the general endorsement, by liberals and conservatives alike, of the idea of a new global era characterized by the full, free participation of the formerly colonized provinces in Communion affairs.

American conservatives' and liberals' mutual accusations of financial coercion of Southerners shed some light on the role of North/South alliances in Northern debates. In Uganda, accusations about monetary influence function very differently, intersecting with issues of need, dependency, and postcolonial ambivalence about Northern power. My Ugandan sources include interviews, fieldwork data, and assorted documents, while in examining Northern debates, my sources are largely texts expressing the views of leaders and commentators. These textual sources are readily available to Episcopalians of all persuasions, and have shaped many people's perceptions of current Anglican conflicts. The fact that these texts largely present leadership views should thus not be taken as indicating that lay Episcopalians do not share these views. In discussing my research with liberal and moderate Episcopalians, I have heard many voice the same suspicions as the leaders quoted in this chapter, that money is at the root of alliances between Northern conservatives and Southern Anglicans. Such accusations demand an examination.

It is true, of course, that money itself, and not only suspicion about the use and abuse of money, permeates relationships between Northern and Southern Anglicans.[8] Here I am less interested in the actual movements of dollars than in the way money, and the power it represents and bestows, is a factor in the ways people describe, experience, worry about, and negotiate evolving North/South relationships in today's Anglican Communion. I thus seek, to paraphrase novelist John Crowley, to examine not the impact money has on these relationships but the impact that the *notion* that money has an impact on these relationships, has on these relationships.[9]

LIBERAL ACCUSATIONS: NEOCOLONIAL CHICKEN DINNERS?

Northern liberals and some moderates have argued that Northern conservatives exploit Southern Anglicans by using their material advantages to attract Southern supporters. They describe Northern relations with Southern Anglicans as economically and politically exploitative and neocolonial. They view these alliances as founded on power relations that allow the Northern partners to use the Southern partners' statements and actions to serve Northern agendas—thereby extending, rather than reversing, Northern global hegemony. Liberals rarely accuse their opponents of flat-out bribing or buying votes from Southern Anglicans. Instead, they suggest that American conservatives have found so many willing Southern partners because of the Americans' ability to offer various forms of support, including paying their Southern partners' travel expenses to bring them to meetings to be informed, persuaded, and equipped to fulfill Northern ambitions.

One such case dates from Lambeth 1998, when many liberal leaders and activists were highly suspicious of the activities of Northern conservatives, especially those based at the Franciscan Study Centre, a building rented by a coalition of conservative groups to provide resources for bishops from poorer provinces. One American priest who was present at the Conference argued that the "stigmatization" of homosexuals was "eagerly encouraged by a very active group of American conservative propagandists with lots of money to spend who occupied a command center in one of the residences of the campus [the FSC], fomenting and encouraging this movement of collective blackmail."[10] Archbishop Holloway, primate of the Anglican Church of Scotland, spoke out soon after the sexuality vote to complain about Northern conservatives' activities at Lambeth: "There was a lot of American money from a very traditionalist diocese and a lot of entertaining of bishops from the two-thirds world. What [conservatives] have done is, having failed in their own Church at home, they have hired the opposition from abroad."[11]

Besides making this bald accusation, Holloway is often named as one source (along with Episcopal bishop Barbara Harris) of accusations that conservatives bought the loyalty of Southern bishops with meals held at the FSC—sometimes described as barbecues, but most infamously named "chicken dinners."[12] A July 2003 article by conservative British Anglican reporter Andrew Carey, son of the former Archbishop of Canterbury and author of the controversial pre-Lambeth article on Bishop Spong, summarizes the implications of the "chicken dinners" accusations: "Evangelicals were accused of buying the support of the developing world. The memorable phrase 'chicken dinners' still describes the literal beliefs of some fundamentalist modernist bishops who apparently believed that African church leaders would sell their soul for an evening barbecue."[13] Carey's account demonstrates how "chicken dinners" became conservative shorthand for the racism and insensitivity of liberal "fundamentalist modernists"—by which he means those committed with fundamentalist zeal to a modernist approach to Christianity.

Meals were held at the FSC for various bishops and other Lambeth attendees. But Holloway's and others' remarks imply that these meals went beyond mere hospitality, and should be seen as an effort to persuade Southern bishops to support the Northern conservative agenda. These and other Northern liberals make the case that Northern conservatives bought the loyalties of Southern church leaders, or at least used financial and material incentives inappropriately in persuading Southerners to take up their issues, especially homosexuality. Such suspicions are probably strengthened by conservatives' history of explicitly using money as a tool or weapon in intra-Episcopal conflicts. Episcopal churches are required to contribute funds to their dioceses, and dissident churches have often chosen to withhold those funds as a protest. A mid-1990s conservative Episcopal slogan was "Stay [in the church]. Don't pay. Don't obey. Pray." In a 2003 article David Virtue expressed confidence in the power of money as a weapon for conservatives: "[Withholding funds] is the last bastion of hope the orthodox in ECUSA has to get back at the liberals and revisionists."[14]

Furthermore, it is true that conservative evangelical Episcopalians' alienation from the Episcopal Church has corresponded with an intensification of their engagement with the African church. This intensification, in turn, has often resulted in financial, technological, and other material advantages for the African individuals and church bodies who choose to be so engaged. American conservatives no longer see North/South relationships as simply a way to minister to needy Christian brethren, but now view such ties as a way to be in relationships of solidarity and mutual support with like-minded orthodox Christians—an understanding that encourages greater engagement and often greater generosity. To offer just one example, following Gene Robinson's consecration, some dissident parishes expressed the intention to stop giving money to the Episcopal Church entirely and devote all the withheld funds to mission and development work in Africa.

This intensification of relations between American conservatives and various Southern allies has led some liberal and moderate Episcopalians and Anglicans to accuse American conservatives of colonizing Southern Anglicans by using material inducements to appropriate Southern numbers, voices, and moral authority. Episcopal priest and scholar Ian Douglas described contemporary Anglican Communion politics in these terms in an influential article entitled "Lambeth 1998 and the 'New Colonialism.'" Douglas begins with a general critique of the continuation of colonial patterns of power in the Anglican Communion:

Nations in the southern hemisphere are still subject to the economic, political, and military whims of the industrialized West. This "new colonialism" infects all international conversations today and Lambeth is not immune from such pressures. . . . The 1998 Lambeth Conference is vulnerable to the new colonialism in which players from Western industrialized nations, with their sophisticated communication, control of the media, and deep pockets, continue to have a disproportionate amount of control over the lives of sisters and brothers in Africa, Asia, Latin America and the Pacific.[15]

Douglas's critique of Anglican neocolonialisms encompasses both the Northern left and the Northern right, but he goes on to criticize conservatives in particular, noting the way American conservative groups appropriated the outcomes of the 1997 meeting in Kuala Lumpur in a manner "not wholly dissimilar" from "the mining and export of raw materials from the south for the benefit of the West's industrial machine in the colonial era."[16] Douglas argues strongly for an essentially neocolonial view of relations between Southern Anglicans and Northern conservative Episcopalians. Other liberal leaders and commentators, like Bishop Holloway, explicitly identify Northern economic power as the central tool of such exploitation.

For many liberal Northerners, who are unwilling to believe that Southern Anglicans have turned against them on their own initiative and are deeply suspicious of their Northern antagonists' newfound solidarity with the global South, the view that these South/North alliances amount to the buying of Southern loyalties both makes sense of perceived betrayals and also defuses their impact. If these alliances are seen as founded on economic exploitation, Southern Anglican leaders' activism no longer appears as independent justification of Northern conservatives' positions by the majority of Anglicans in the global South. Rather, it appears as merely the result of Northern conservatives' using their economic advantages to hire allies. From this viewpoint, Northern conservatives' discourse of "global shift" seems a cynical fiction and these North/South alliances appear instead as a form of neocolonial domination and exploitation.

CONSERVATIVE RESPONSES: LIBERAL RACISM AND CONSERVATIVE LIBERATION

In response, American conservatives argue that they themselves, far from colonizing Southern Anglicans, are actually helping liberate them from racist Northern liberal domination. In the case of the FSC, conservatives insisted the operation there was only an effort to extend hospitality and assistance to Southern bishops, not to buy their loyalties. One piece in the post-Lambeth issue of *Encompass*, the AAC's newsletter, refuted the "chicken dinners" idea and instead asserted conservatives' solidarity with Southern Anglicans: "Most [FSC] sessions included a buffet or dessert. This habit of feasting gave some small-minded opponents the opportunity to say we had influenced bishops with 'chicken and sausages.' The feasting was a sign of the truly cordial relations we have developed over the years with Third World churches."[17]

Northern conservatives not only defended themselves, but went on the offensive. During and after Lambeth, conservative print sources tended to play up liberal accusations about the FSC, and to use these stories as an opportunity to point out the racism implicit in liberal leaders' assertions that Southern bishops were swayed by wealthy Northern conservative lobbyists. One conservative American priest complained about accusations of bribery in a letter published in *Encompass*:

> I am deeply grieved to learn that there are post Lambeth rumors and accusations of bribes to the third world bishops. I wonder why the voice and opinion of the third world bishops have upset us so much in the West. Have they not listened and obediently followed our decisions and interpretations for many centuries? Do we want them to be subservient forever? Will we not have a grace to respect the dignity and the voice of those who are not as affluent as we are in the West? It looks as if we measure their integrity with green dollars. They may be poor, but not lacking integrity.[18]

Similarly, Bill Atwood of the Ekklesia Society, writing well after Lambeth, sharply criticizes liberals: "As the only person who hosted a chicken dinner at the 1998 Lambeth Bishops Conference, let me say that pejorative characterizations by Western leaders of bishops from the two-thirds world as people without conviction who are easily swayed are racist and imperialist."[19] This quotation, and the Carey quotation about chicken dinners, both date from mid-2003, a full five years after Lambeth 1998. Conservatives' continued references to "chicken dinners" and related liberal accusations suggests that they feel that this issue serves them more effectively than it served their liberal critics, by enabling them to assert, and attack, Northern liberal racism.

In addition to accusing Northern liberals of racism, conservatives argued that the FSC, rather than being a site of Northern neocolonial activity, aided in the decolonization of world Anglicanism. Conservative leaders and commentators described the FSC, using terms like "resource" and "facilitate," as an endeavor to serve and inform Southern church leaders, empowering them to have their say at Lambeth 1998. A *Christian Challenge* article refuting liberal allegations cited "the FSC effort to resource and network global South bishops at Lambeth, particularly to help them make sense of the Conference's western procedural and theological nuances."[20] Conservatives argued that the FSC's activities helped level the uneven playing field of global Anglican politics by providing Southerners with the same preparation, communications, and lobbying resources that Northerners have had all along. Jonathan, who was familiar with the FSC facilities through his involvement with the AAC, told me, "We've never felt it was our job to put an agenda forward, but to work to give voice to [Southern] Anglican leaders."[21]

The liberation of Southern Anglicans with which American conservatives are concerned is not only ecclesio-political but also economic. Rejecting accusations that they are abusing money in their alliances with Southerners, conservatives charge that, in fact, Northern liberal church leaders have long used money manipulatively in their relations with the Southern churches. They argue that the Northern provinces have historically prevented Southern leaders from disagreeing with them over doctrinal orthodoxy and other matters by keeping them subjected through the provision of funding for Southern church programs. Bishop Gerald shared his observations on the power dynamics of the Communion, telling me that the attitude of many Northern liberal leaders is, "We're all equal [in the Anglican Communion], but we [in the North] are more equal because we have more money." He described the Episcopal Church as "abusive with its economic power," manipulating the Primates' Meeting and other international Anglican bodies. Arlin Adams, a layman writing for a conservative e-mail list, leveled similar charges at Archbishop of Canterbury Rowan Williams, who is widely regarded as liberal in his theology and social positions and thus is distrusted by many conservatives. In this 2003 satire, Adams attributed the following thoughts about an upcoming visit to West Africa to Archbishop Williams:

> Good grief, I've got to visit some of those awful fundamentalist provinces this summer, and it doesn't look good for the prospect of buying them off with funding, unless everybody will just shut up about this stupid sexuality thing. . . . Hey, perhaps I can send in [Anglican Consultative Council head Canon John Peterson] with a pocket full of walk around money . . . and he can throw money at them before I arrive, and then they will be happy to see me.[22]

Adams suggests that Williams and, by extension, other Northern liberals believe they only have to spread cash around to make friends in Africa.

Liberals view the years since Lambeth 1998 as an era of Anglican neocolonialism characterized by Northern conservative exploitation of Southern Anglicans while conservatives see a new, decolonized global era, in which the events of Lambeth 1998 and Southern intervention in the

Episcopal Church show that Southern Christians have thrown off the yoke of past economic domination in order to stand up for orthodoxy, even under threat of sanctions. David Virtue expressed this view in 2000: "It is . . . apparent that money will not be a big enough inducement to . . . keep ECUSA in the [Anglican] club, nor will the African bishops care one jot if that is the case. They have lived without [money] for centuries and they will go on living without it."[23]

Bolstering such Northern conservatives' arguments are instances in which funding has apparently been cut or shifted away from Southern provinces involved in oppositional politics in ECUSA. One example concerns Trinity Church, Wall Street, a large and wealthy Episcopal church in downtown New York. In mid-2001 this church decided not to renew funding for a theological education program it had been funding in the Church of Rwanda. A notice on Trinity's website explained that this cut was related to Rwandan bishops' "actively working to promote schism" in the Episcopal Church.[24] American conservatives' regard for their Southern allies was further increased by Rwandan leaders' refusal to be cowed by the loss of funding. Members of St. Timothy's spoke often and proudly of Archbishop Kolini's courage in the face of economic coercion, and AMiA's newsletter carried an appeal for member parishes to contribute to the theological education fund, reciprocating their Rwandan archbishop's assistance to them.

Another case of alleged attempted liberal coercion involves Bishop Ronald Haines of Washington, D.C., and Ugandan bishop Eliphaz Maari. Shortly before Lambeth 1998, Bishop Maari had spoken with Bishop Haines to seek funding for Uganda Christian University, which Maari then headed. Haines wrote to Maari shortly after Lambeth, expressing his and his diocese's dismay over the Lambeth resolution on sexuality, and seeming to link this with the possibility of providing funding to UCU:

> The gay and lesbian community [in this diocese] has been particularly graced with the gift of generosity. That leads to some of our present difficulty. One gay person said to me, "If I am an abomination, is my money also abominable." As a diocese we would like to be in greater partnership with brothers and sisters in Africa, but for the present time we have a considerable impediment presented by the Lambeth decision. . . . We sincerely want to be in partnership, but there is no way we can be in partnership without gay and lesbian people being involved in our side. . . . Your insight would be greatly appreciated.[25]

Haines's letter was widely interpreted by Ugandans and American conservatives as an attempt to use funding for UCU as a carrot to persuade Maari to recant his Lambeth vote for the sexuality resolution. This case, which received considerable publicity in American conservative circles and the Ugandan church, strengthened the perception in both contexts that American liberals use their wealth to coerce compliance with their agenda. As with the Trinity Church case, Northern conservative coverage informed readers how to contribute directly to UCU. In documenting such cases, American conservatives applaud Southerners' courage in resisting perceived financial coercion; in responding to the resulting financial needs, conservatives fill out their self-appointed role as facilitators of economic liberation and decolonization of the Anglican global South.

Thus in the realm of interprovincial funding relationships, as well as in the realm of Communion politics, conservative Northerners argue that they and not their liberal opponents are the ones truly liberating Southern Anglicans from domination and marginalization. They view the strengthening of relations between Northern conservatives and Southern Anglicans as the result of a process of decolonization, enabling true affinities to surface, not the result of a process of neocolonization (as some liberals would argue) that creates the appearance of solidarity where none truly exists. The alliance between Northern conservatives and Southern Anglicans at Lambeth is described as an overturning of colonial patterns and structures, as the newly minted allies work together to thwart the agendas of the liberal and moderate Anglican leaders who hold most of the institutional and financial power in the Anglican Communion.

WE ARE ALL ANTI-IMPERIALISTS

Anthropologist Scott Morgensen has noted the popularity of rhetorics of anti-imperialism in the contemporary world. Nearly everyone wants to liberate the oppressed, empower the marginalized, and fight imperialisms of every form.[26] His observations are easily applied to disputes among Northern Anglicans, in which both conservatives and liberals position themselves as liberating Southern Anglicans from neocolonial domination. Both liberals and conservatives described Lambeth 1998 as positive evidence that the old colonial structures of the Anglican Communion were finally crumbling. Ian Douglas and Kwok Pui-Lan evaluate Lambeth in such terms in their 2001 coedited volume, *Beyond Colonial Anglicanism*: "Lambeth 1998 signaled for all that the colonial structures of the first two hundred years of the Anglican Communion were giving way to something new."[27] In a similar vein, conservative commentator Doug LeBlanc has written that Lambeth 1998 meant the death of "the days of cultural imperialism."[28] Diane Knippers offered this optimistic evaluation, in 2004, of the potential for reshaping the inherited English-centered, colonial structures of world Anglicanism.

Right now, the determination of who is in and who is out of the Anglican Communion rests with the Church of England, most specifically
the Archbishop of Canterbury. . . . Much of the joint work of Anglicanism goes forward through the London-based Anglican Consultative
Council. Archbishop Drexel Gomez of the West Indies is blunt about
the problem. "Many of our brothers in the global South resent that the
minority North still controls the Anglican Communion and sets the
agenda for meetings," he said this month. . . . "There is the feeling that
although we people of color are present, we are not fully accepted." In
short, Anglicanism retains a 19th Century colonial structure. . . . The
post-colonial churches are coming of age. Something new is coming.
American Episcopalians, both liberal and conservative, can only watch
and wait.[29]

Both conservatives and liberals in the global North voice eagerness to
witness—and, if possible, to facilitate—the rise of a transformed global
order, in which the North no longer sets agendas or determines outcomes.
All these declarations, however, raise the question of how the economic
and political realities of North/South relationships in the contemporary
Communion relate to this talk of liberation and equality.

GIFT OR COMMERCE IN NORTH/SOUTH RELATIONSHIPS?

Northern debates over who is liberating and who is obstructing liberation
amount to efforts to purify Southern positions and actions from the taint
of Northern patronage. Seeing Southern positions as "pure" in this way
requires acknowledging the monetary and other material resources that
undeniably flow along lines of affinity between Northern and Southern
Anglicans. Cleansing Southern activism from suspicions of Northern influence requires that these material flows must be clearly defined as free
gifts, and not as elements of exchange relationships in which Southern
Anglican leaders speak and act in order to obtain material benefits.

Drawing on the work of Marcel Mauss, I argue that these Northern
debates over money and influence represent a contentious effort to maintain two cultural categories, commerce and free gift, as separate and mutually exclusive.[30] As Mauss argued in the essay translated as *The Gift:
The Form and Reason for Exchange in Archaic Societies*, modern European capitalist thought has created, and tries to maintain, a clear distinction between these two kinds of activity, commerce and gift—a distinction
unknown to most of human history and most human societies. Mary
Douglas, in her introduction to the 1990 edition of *The Gift*, summarizes

this distinction as "the idea that commerce and gift are two separate kinds of activity, the first based on exact recompense, the second spontaneous [and] pure of ulterior motive."[31] The idea of the free gift, according to Mauss, is an innovation of capitalist societies, in which commercial exchange has become the dominant form for the transfer of property and the practice of gifting has become marginal to the economic structure. The notion of the free gift, the wholly disinterested, generous transfer of material goods from one person to another (who incurs no obligation to reciprocate), is a concept that could only exist in the interstices (birthdays, wedding showers) of a capitalist society, an economy founded on monetary exchange rather than on the systems of reciprocal gifting that constitute foundational economic practices in most non-Western societies. Mauss further observes that a clear differentiation of gift and commerce is difficult to maintain, even in the capitalist cultures that believe in the distinction. The gift/commerce distinction, like other modernist dichotomies, requires maintenance and policing (or purification) in order to keep the terms distinct and thereby make it possible to interpret relationships and determine obligations.

Northern debates over the role of resource flows in North/South inter-Anglican alliances represent a contentious mutual policing of the boundaries between the categories of commerce and gift. Each side accuses the other of transgressing that boundary by claiming to give freely while actually conducting commerce by demanding a return on its investment from Southern Anglicans (support, intervention, or strategic silence). At the same time, players on each side tend increasingly to give to (or withhold gifts from) Southern partners along lines of affinity (or antagonism) defined by Northern church conflicts. This giving and withholding strongly suggests, though Northerners may be unwilling to admit it, that such gifts are not wholly disinterested but are often entangled with inter-Anglican political loyalties.

The debates between Northerners over these issues boil down to one key question about the involvement of Southern leaders in Northern church disputes: Are they, or are they not, doing it for money? Significantly, this question presumes a strong gift/commerce distinction. Either the statements and actions of Southern leaders are purely independent and autonomously undertaken, and any corresponding material benefits are truly free gifts; or the statements and actions of Southern leaders have been influenced or elicited by the judicious application of material resources and should be seen in terms of the give-and-take of commerce—meaning they carry little moral weight, having been "bought." Mauss argues that this strong gift/commerce distinction is ideological and discursive, rather than descriptive of social realities. The distinction becomes even more problematic in the Ugandan context, which is less thoroughly penetrated by capitalist ideology and where issues of gift and exchange are complicated by colonial history and contemporary dependency.

"AFRICANS JUST WANT WHAT THEY SEE ON TV": CULTURE AND POWER IN UGANDA

One day, about halfway through my stay in Uganda, I caught a lift across the UCU campus with Reverend Francis, an elderly Ugandan priest and professor. As we drove, I asked him whether he'd ever been to the United States. He explained that he had spent a sabbatical with a church in the northeastern United States a couple of years ago. His bishop, Reverend Francis explained, had been worried because Francis didn't yet have any arrangements for a retirement home. Since retirement provisions are minimal in the Church of Uganda, clergy do their best during their careers to scrape together the resources to make their own retirement arrangements. It is especially important to build a home for use after retirement, when the Church of Uganda no longer provides housing—or, as Reverend Francis put it, "you may become destitute." Such preparation is often aided by friends and supporters in the United States or the UK. Reverend Francis had made few such connections and his bishop was anxious to give him such a chance, because his retirement was quickly approaching. The bishop accordingly found him a parish exchange opportunity, which had the desired effect. With the aid of his American friends, he now has a half-completed retirement home, though some of the funds have also gone to pay medical bills for himself and his wife.

Hearing this story, told offhandedly and apparently with no intent of arousing sympathy, brought home to me the extent to which ordinary Ugandans depend on the largesse of Northerners—not only as members of a debtor nation needing loans and grants from wealthier nations and international organizations to finance its day-to-day operations, and not only as members of a church that is frequently only able to meet people's needs through the generosity of various NGOs, but even as individuals whose connections with potential donors, or lack thereof, can make or break their chances of a comfortable life or a peaceful and timely death. Such dependence is perhaps the most significant way that Anglican globalization has an impact on those who never travel global networks themselves. Even if an individual never leaves her village, the connection her bishop, her priest, or she herself makes with Northern Anglican bodies or individuals may bring her a new school or church building, a rainwater tank, a milk cow, help with school fees, or other resources. Given these realities, Ugandans are much more sensitive to the meanings and implications of receiving gifts or of being dependent than are the largely middle-class Episcopalians who toss around accusations of bribery and vote-buying in their disputes over doctrine and morality.

In the last chapter I contrasted the Northern tendency to romanticize Southern poverty with Ugandan attitudes regarding the effect of poverty on the Church. Many Ugandans argue against the idea that poverty strengthens their church, seeing it instead as a liability—not least because it may make them vulnerable to accepting donations with strings attached,[32] tempting them to compromise their own culture, values, or goals. Poverty thus creates a situation in which the intrinsic and extrinsic attractions of outside goods, resources, and ideas are always in tension with desires for independence and self-determination and with mistrust of outsiders' motives and values. These tensions are manifest in Ugandan society in a complex ambivalence toward external influences and goods.

Things Northern (and especially American) undoubtedly exert a powerful attraction on many Ugandans. A friend's favorite café in downtown Kampala had a huge mural of the characters from the American televison series *Friends* painted on the wall, the movie theaters in Kampala show American blockbusters, and the markets are full of second-hand Gap clothes and knock-off "Nike" gear. Everyone we met seemed to want to go to America, even those who harbored deep reservations about American culture and power. Yet even while Ugandans idealize the North and desire its ways and commodities, they also often express mixed feelings about, or resistance to, Northern influences. This can be seen, for instance, in public calls for selectivity about what Uganda takes in from outside. A speech delivered on behalf of President Museveni at the consecration of a bishop I attended included this exhortation to selectivity:

> Internet Cafes are the new craze of our youths and they are spreading in the urban centers and this is good. However I am appealing to the church to reach the youth to guide them on what is of use and on what is morally debasing and to avoid what is morally debasing. We cannot prevent progress but at least we should guide our youth to absorb what is useful and discard what is not.[33]

In classes at UCU, students often talked of their concerns about Northern influences on Ugandan society. In a discussion on the morality of pastors, one student remarked that cohabitation "is coming to such a peak that even clergy are going into that," and observed, "the church has to find a way not to copy foreign cultures that are coming in, and remain Bakiga or a Baganda or whatever." But a student behind me whispered to a friend that Ugandans have to allow some of their culture to be transformed: "You must be *selective*."

Attractions to and ambivalences about Northern influence are inflected by a sharp awareness of the marginal position of Uganda, and Africa in general, from the viewpoint of Northern culture, politics, and economics. To take one minor but telling example, several Ugandans told me of their indignation at the practices of British Air, which has the interiors of its airliners sprayed with an insecticide before takeoff on Uganda-to-UK flights. Fred, a UCU professor, described the practice to his African Theology class: "The minute they get to Africa, they [British Air staff] begin spraying, because they don't want cockroaches." British Air may have solid epidemiological reasons for the practice, but it sends a clear message to the mainly African travelers in the cabin that they must be fumigated and decontaminated before touching clean European soil. David Spurr notes that "the fear of contamination that combines images of social and biological disorder" has a place in the rhetoric of debasement of colonized places and peoples: "The association of the Third World with epidemic disease is epidemiologically sound, but metaphorically loaded."[34] Ugandans' complaints about being sprayed by British Air, and many similar comments and quips, reveal a keen sense of being seen as inferior and unimportant by the dominant political and economic powers of the world. This awareness only heightens the tension between attraction and aversion to Northern things and Northern ways.

These tensions and desires are matters not only of culture, identity, and style but also of economic resources and dependency. The *mivumba* debate in Uganda provides one trenchant example of the entanglement of cultural and economic issues. The vast majority of Ugandans wear Northern-style clothes, most of which are actually used clothes from North America and Europe.[35] These used clothes, known as *mivumba*, are by far the cheapest clothes in Uganda; in addition, they are valued for being "really" Northern, not local or Asian copies of Northern styles. The *mivumba* phenomenon extends far beyond clothing: used vehicles, appliances, and other second-hand consumer goods flow into the global South. But the practice of importing other people's castoffs is controversial. In May 2002, near the end of my time in Uganda, a furor erupted in the Ugandan papers over a proposal by President Museveni to dramatically raise taxes on *mivumba* goods, with the intention of stimulating domestic industry and raising national self-esteem. Museveni's idea drew some support, but also sharp criticism. Newspaper features, and friends who talked with me about the issue, argued that most Ugandans couldn't afford anything more expensive than *mivumba*. Those who could afford a respectable wardrobe at current *mivumba* prices might only be able to manage one or two suits of clothes at higher prices, and this would in fact *lower* self-esteem, and hurt job prospects as well.

Is it more desirable to live as second-class citizens wearing castoffs in a Northern-dominated global culture and economy? Or is it better to shut that door and struggle for self-sufficiency and self-esteem, quite possibly at the cost of living with far fewer consumer goods? In Fred's African Theology class at UCU, a student spoke up to praise Museveni's 1980s plans for a closed-border, produce-what-you-consume Uganda. Fred responded by challenging the student: "OK, but this guy [another student] is wearing jeans from London, and he wouldn't have bought them if they said 'Ggulu' on them." Ggulu is a town in northern Uganda, a war-ravaged part of the country looked down upon by southern Ugandans. Fred went on to condemn the reluctance of Ugandans to turn away from outside goods: "The problem is with *us*. . . . When something is given free, it may be very expensive in the long run. How long are we going to beg?" In the *mivumba* debate, as in many other contexts, the weak Ugandan economy and the relative poverty of most Ugandan people add urgency and complexity to key cultural, aesthetic, and identity questions—in this case, what people wear and what that says about their place in the world.

CULTURE AND POWER IN THE CHURCH OF UGANDA

In the life of the Church of Uganda, debates and tensions over Northern influences are similarly entangled with matters of resources and power. One important context for understanding Ugandan Anglicans' ambivalences regarding Northern influences is the ongoing debate over whether Christianity can ever truly be African, given the colonial history of the church. These questions of Northern influences in the church and the Africanness of African Christianity are evident in the tension between renewal and indigenization, two major liturgical trends in the Church of Uganda today. As we saw in chapter 1, many Ugandans see renewal as coming from the North. Some worry that, in the words of Rev. Stephen, renewal is "eroding a bit of our cultural witness to Christ." In particular, renewal trends in worship are associated with Northern Pentecostal television shows widely shown in Uganda. Robby, a young Ugandan Anglican who leads a youth choir at Namirembe Cathedral, summed up television's influence: "Automatically everyone is looking toward that. Africans don't know what they want; they just want what they see on TV."

Indigenization,[36] on the other hand, involves conscious efforts on the part of church leaders to shape Anglican worship to reflect more thoroughly the cultural context of Uganda, recovering and incorporating Ugandan aesthetics which in many parts of the country had never been integrated into Anglican worship. Alexander, a young theology professor and one of many advocates of indigenization on the UCU faculty, told me he would like to see more "liturgy rooted in cultural expressions of our people." The idea is that Ugandan Christianity would thrive and grow if it were more culturally appropriate. Robby told me that he, too, supports indigenization, because, as he put it, "The African beat is different from the Western beat." Indigenization has some commonalities with renewal; both movements involve less use of inherited Anglican liturgical texts, greater freedom in prayer, more lively music, and the use of more instruments. In contrast to renewal, however, indigenization involves use of local languages instead of English, use of traditional Ugandan instruments instead of Northern electronic instruments, use of music based on traditional local tunes and rhythms rather than Northern-style praise choruses, and revising liturgical texts rather than moving away from formal liturgy altogether. Renewal and indigenization co-occur to some extent; for instance, many worship music teams mix Ugandan local-language worship songs with Northern praise songs in their repertoires. But though strongly supported by provincial leaders (not least the archbishop of Uganda), indigenization is not spreading through the Church of Uganda as rapidly as the renewal trend. In spite of Ugandans' worries about Northern influences in church and culture, Northern cultural capital still exerts a powerful pull.[37]

Like these two liturgical movements, many of the pressing issues in the Church of Uganda come down to questions of Northern influence—the tension between attraction to Northern cultural products transmitted by the media, markets, and visitors, on the one hand, and the desire to reclaim and revalue "local" ways associated with a particular ethnic group, Uganda as a whole, or the entire continent of Africa, on the other. These issues are complex, and made more so by the church's dependence at all levels on outsiders' financial support for its ministry. Many Church of Uganda leaders told me they feel called to "holistic ministry," meaning they seek to meet the many material, as well as spiritual, needs of church members. These needs include clean water, education, agricultural development, and much more, since the Ugandan state provides little such assistance. Church leaders believe their church has a mandate to respond to a much wider range of needs than an American church would, but the Church of Uganda also has far fewer resources at its disposal than most established American church bodies.

In following the holistic ministry mandate, the Church of Uganda is dependent upon its leaders' abilities to attract outside resources and on outsiders' willingness to help. Abner, a layman who has been involved in North/South church partnerships in his diocese, explained to me that American help for Ugandan needs flows naturally out of amicable relationships: "The whole thing revolves around who is your neighbor. You must feel for a friend. . . . We know we are all [equal]. But . . . there is more wealth in the States than in Africa. There is no question about that. So normally [Americans] have a heart to ask what they can do, you know, to help. And normally they share." However, as the word "normally" hints, such relationships cannot be depended upon; the American partners' interests or fortunes may change and funding may be cut—or never granted to begin with. Several Ugandans complained to me about the inadequate support they feel their church gets from the larger Anglican Communion. Samuel, a young Anglican layman, told me, "I think today the donations from you people are minimal." Some Ugandans I talked with contrasted the Anglican situation with the Pentecostal churches, since many of the larger Pentecostal parishes receive considerable support from Northern sponsors, or with the Roman Catholic establishment, also believed to be more responsive to African needs.

Ugandans are thus in a complex position with respect to attitudes, styles, and other cultural influences that enter their society and their church from the North, a position that is further complicated by the economic positions of Uganda as a nation, the Church of Uganda as an institution, and many Ugandan individuals and families. Ugandans' dependency on donations, loans, and other forms of support from outside the nation and, usually, outside the continent raises the stakes on matters of culture and choice. The Northern way of acting, dressing, or worshipping frequently appears cheaper, more remunerative, or otherwise advantageous. The complicating effects of differential material advantages on cultural and religious choices have deep roots in East Africa's missionary history. Robert Strayer notes that, in colonial Kenya, joining a mission community and taking on the missionaries' ways became "an important means by which subordinate peoples could tap the resources of their rulers."[38] In many respects, positive relationships with Northerners remain such a means today.

Because of all this, Northern accusations about the role of money in North/South relationships cut to the heart of Ugandans' predicament. From the Ugandan perspective, there is no way to purify North/South relationships of material elements, because there is no way for inequalities of access to resources not to be at issue in these transnational Anglican interactions. Both Northerners and Southerners in such relationships may strive not to make money the central issue, but money is never irrelevant. Gerald, a conservative-leaning Episcopal bishop with experience in mission and development work in Africa, gave me his perspective on why some African leaders choose to join forces with American conservatives: "Their primary concern, I think, is to build the liaisons, both organizational and economic, that are going to be able to help solve some of their problems over there, which are primarily economic." Although Gerald's views exemplify the strong tendency to assume North/South relationships are fundamentally about money, his statement is based on his own work in Africa and friendships with African Anglicans. His view is supported by the frequency with which Ugandans mentioned the needs of the Church of Uganda (and the wealth of the American church) in interviews and conversations with me during my fieldwork in Uganda.

Given the politically charged nature of North/South Anglican alliances in the Communion today, the twin threats of financial inducements and financial sanctions are constantly in play as Southern and Northern Anglicans work toward a more influential and autonomous role for the South in Anglican Communion affairs. Anthropologist Erica Bornstein has argued, on the basis of her study of child sponsorship relationships, that transnational sponsorship relationships may create a sense of transcending difference and distance to create intimacy and equality. But she also observes that at the same time such relationships have other, less positive effects: they reinforce the Northern and Southern partners' experiences of the economic disparity between them and can raise anxieties about neocolonial exploitation.[39] On much the same note, Kathryn Sikkink has concluded, "Foreign funding is both a lifeblood and a major source of asymmetries of power within transnational networks."[40] In the North/South relationships I examine here, and indeed at every step on the path toward a postimperial global Anglicanism, Northern advantage and Southern need and dependency are reinscribed, with mixed results for North/South mutual understanding and Southern self-determination.

In renegotiating their role in the larger Anglican world, Southern leaders must constantly deal with Northern bids (sometimes quite literally) for their support, friendship, or silence. Such bids are hard to disregard, given the economic needs that relationships with Northerners can fulfill, but can also be hard to accept, depending on the conditions explicitly or implicitly attached. How do Southern church leaders deal with these constraints and demands, this ongoing tension between their needs and desires for equal, free, and sincere relationships with Northern Christians, for resources to support their ministry, for greater power in world Anglican politics, for autonomy, for self-respect?

Assistance and Autonomy in Relationships with Northern Conservatives

Both Northern liberals and conservatives have, by their words and actions, implied that Southern church leaders could be convinced through financial persuasion to support Northern claims and agendas. Such accusations are considerably more challenging and insulting for African and other Southern bishops than for the Northern parties who aim them at each other. Not surprisingly, many Ugandans I spoke with did not want money to be (or appear to be) the *central* concern in the formation and maintenance of North/South relationships. They are uncomfortable with being perceived as acting or speaking solely to attract or oblige donors and sponsors.

A conversation I had with Aaron, a Ugandan Anglican priest and international evangelist, is telling in this regard. When we met, he had just written to several American parishes (on the advice of an American colleague) to explore the possibility of partnership relationships:

> Very recently I wrote to about twenty-five pastors of the Episcopal Church. . . . I was writing to them to say, Look, I would like to establish some kind of contact so you can visit us, so we can visit you, as Episcopalians in the Communion. And only one has replied so far. He thought I was asking for money, which I wasn't. I was asking for camaraderie, I was asking for fellowship. . . . I am saying to them, we need to visit one another. You come to Africa, see how we do things, and we come there and we see how you do things, and we get mutually carried by each other's faith and way of doing things. But this gentleman replies and says—he may have thought I was asking for money, which I wasn't at all. I mean, eventually the question of finances will come in, but that was not the immediate thing.

The "question of finances," as Aaron noted, will inevitably arise, as it does in most North-South relationships. After all, few Ugandan dioceses can afford plane fares or other practical necessities for building relationships. But Aaron was both insulted by the presumption that financial interest was his primary motive in seeking to establish these relationships and discouraged by the fact that the American priest perceived his overture in that way.

To answer such suspicions, Southerners tend to stress the agency of the Southern partners in North/South alliances and their ownership of their positions and actions. African leaders assert that they support what they support (and reject what they reject) on their own initiative and for their own reasons, and that what they gain or lose from their stands is incidental. They thereby reaffirm the gift/commerce distinction, and assert that any North/South transfer of resources is (or should be) a matter of *free gift*. George, a conservative bishop with close ties to the American dissident movement, spoke to me about the funding he receives from Northerners impressed by his bold actions: "I don't want anybody to think I'm doing what I'm doing because I want [my American allies] to support me. . . . What I am doing is not for support, material. No, it's for the glory of our Lord Jesus Christ." George states firmly that while his actions on behalf of American conservatives may *attract* material support, they are not done *for* material support.

Other African leaders have asserted similar positions with respect to the resources they have received from American and other Northern conservatives. In particular, Africans who took advantage of the opportunities provided by Northern conservatives before and during Lambeth 1998 contend that their support for the sexuality resolution was unrelated to their appreciation of those opportunities. As I argued in chapter 3, Southern bishops were for the most part predisposed to share the conservative American position on homosexuality. The Dallas and Kampala meetings and other pre-Lambeth preparations funded and organized largely by Northern conservatives, however, had an undeniable impact, by convincing Southern bishops it was necessary to speak out on that issue and by helping them with the procedural skills to do so.

Unlike Northern conservatives themselves, who in talking and writing about the Dallas conference, the FSC, and other Lambeth strategizing tended to downplay their role in encouraging and equipping Southern bishops, the Ugandan bishops I interviewed freely acknowledged that Northern conservatives helped them to prepare for the sexuality debate. Yet these African leaders were very clear that Northern conservatives' help only went so far. They answer the charge that they have been pawns for Northern conservatives by arguing that Northerners showed them how to put across their views effectively, but did not determine or shape those views. With respect to the Franciscan Study Centre in particular, Bishop Abel assured me that the resources provided there were only to help Southern bishops understand "the process of Lambeth," and not to influence their views:

> [The FSC facility] was helpful in that it helped some of the people who had never been at Lambeth to know the dynamics of Lambeth, the dynamics and process of debate, and motions, and being focused. . . . I would here dispel what we used to hear, the fact that some of the times the African bishops used to meet in that center, that they were being bribed, that they were being lobbied to support certain motions. No! . . . I was there, and I saw what was happening. It was mainly fellowship and networking, making friends and getting exposed, as I said, to the process of Lambeth.

Many Ugandan leaders stressed that Northern conservatives helped them know how to manage Lambeth debates. Bishop Mark, describing Lambeth 1998, told me that conservative Americans at the FSC helped the Africans "so that when we are in plenary, we are smart and we can talk to the point." Bishop Ezekiel agreed that conservative Northerners'

efforts to prepare Southern bishops, through various pre-Lambeth conferences and the activities of the FSC, helped him and other African bishops
not to "be led astray by the very clever debates that the [liberal] American
bishops will offer during Lambeth, and not understand the background
information of how those debates would be." He concluded, "We appreciated [conservatives' efforts] very much."[41] Richard, a provincial official, described the pre-Lambeth meetings as "a time of sensitization, of
organization . . . to prepare people." Bishop Ezra, when I asked whether
the pre-Lambeth meetings helped African bishops, told me that the meeting simply brought African leaders together to "get one voice"—but that
the Americans didn't "add another thing" to what the Africans already
believed on sexuality and other issues.

In presenting such a view of pre-Lambeth meetings and Lambeth itself,
these African leaders implicitly and sometimes explicitly reject the view
that the assistance and resources provided by Northerners shaped their
views or bought their support. More generally, like Bishop George, Southern church leaders may acknowledge that their relations with conservative
(or other) Northerners often result in various forms of assistance, but
clearly assert that their positions and actions are independent of Northern
influences—are, in effect, the cause and not the outcome of Northerners'
increased engagement. This position insists on the purity of Southern
Christian convictions and the integrity of Southern Christian agency in
the face of Northern conservatives' evident increased investment in relations with Southern Christians.

INDIGNATION AND TEMPTATION IN RELATIONS WITH NORTHERN LIBERALS

In situations where Southern leaders' positions correspond with the desires of Northern allies, then, Southern leaders stress African agency and
independence, naming the associated material benefits of their alliances as
free gifts flowing out of relationship, not given in exchange for Southern
support for Northern positions.[42] In contrast, when Northern interests
are perceived as offering inducements to take positions that most Ugandans see as unacceptable, Ugandans voice condemnation of the Northerners for exerting coercive pressure, and sanction members of their own
church and society who appear tempted or subverted.

Ugandan leaders react sharply to perceived attempts to influence their
church to conform more closely to the beliefs and attitudes of Northern
liberal Christians. These reactions reflect their anxieties about the vulnerability of their church and society to corrosive outside influences. Bishop
Ephraim told me indignantly, "The bishops in America are using money

as bait, which is wrong!" Bishop George talked with me about Bishop Haines's letter to Bishop Maari, concluding that Africans had better remain poor and faithful than accept funding with conditions attached: "Some [American leaders] are just political and punitive, pejorative, derogative. Some tend to think that if they don't relate to us, we shall be choked and starved, we shall have to beg because we are too poor, we can't do without their money. . . . I cannot betray the Lord Jesus Christ because I want money." Nelson, a priest in the Church of Uganda, remarked on the Haines–Maari case as well, and raised the issue of the needs that can create temptation—but that also make it more imperative that African leaders resist.

> It is unfortunate that such a thing is going on in the body [of Christ— that is, the worldwide Church]. And [African bishops] also don't have a moral right to receive such assistance, if it is on those terms. . . . Of course the pressure is there. The needs are clear, and the money would be useful. But they are now in that dilemma. Is it a question of receiving money from any circle? They would go to Saudi Arabia and get money from Muslims, and they probably would get more money! So they have a problem of faithfulness and the reality on the ground.

Ugandan church leaders like Bishop Maari are indeed faced with a "problem of faithfulness and the reality on the ground": how to remain faithful to their convictions and values as Ugandan Christians while at the same time negotiating the reality that, because the Church of Uganda depends on outsiders' assistance, it must sometimes deal with and in outsiders' values and agendas. Precisely because these issues of dependency, choice, and conscience are so commonplace, protecting Ugandan convictions and culture is important—as evident in the strong negative reactions expressed by Ugandan church leaders to outsiders who seem to be attempting coercion or bribery, and insiders who seem to have been coerced or bribed. These reactions are all present in the case of Integrity-Uganda, to which I now return. Examination of this case, however, reveals more than just condemnation; it suggests also that Ugandan Christians possess a stronger sense than most Northerners of the ambiguity and complexity of *gift*, including a greater awareness of the obligations of reciprocity.

"IF MONEY IS THE MOTIVATION, WE ARE ALL TO BLAME"

The vociferous and widespread negative response to Integrity-Uganda, and particularly to Bishop Ssenyonjo's role, exemplifies Ugandan anxieties about their church's poverty-induced vulnerability to outside influences.[43] To most Ugandans, Ssenyonjo appears to have sold out to a foreign agenda, an action that demands a harsh response because it undermines the appearance of African incorruptibility. Ssenyonjo's support for Integrity, Ugandans fear, demonstrates that Africans can be "bought" and even persuaded to support homosexuality, which many Ugandans see as alien and/or shameful. The lively discussion in the Ugandan newspapers about the role of Northern money in the founding of Integrity-Uganda reveals concerns about where poverty (and greed) might lead Ugandans.

Some of this conversation has involved the same distinction between commerce and gift that preoccupies Northern liberals and conservatives in their mutual casting of aspersions. In contrast with the language of gift used for Northern conservatives' provision of resources to their African allies, in the case of Integrity-Uganda, in which the Northerners involved are advocating a position regarded as fairly radical by most Ugandans, Ugandan leaders and commentators condemned the organization as a transgression into the realm of commerce. From this perspective, Ugandans reacted harshly to Integrity-Uganda in part because of African church leaders' sharp awareness of their material and economic vulnerabilities; they felt the need to censure those who appeared to have betrayed that vulnerability by sliding down the slippery slope of dependency, selling off their good names for American favors.

The treatment of Integrity-Uganda and its leaders, however, has another aspect that reveals the interpenetration of gift and commerce in Ugandans' lived experiences of North/South relationships. Despite public condemnations, the Ugandan church and Ugandan society have been rather restrained in their treatment of Integrity-Uganda. Ssenyonjo's involvement, once it became common knowledge, did cause a rift between him and his church and disrupted his livelihood and relationships. Numerous church and civic leaders had harsh words for him, which were eagerly quoted in the papers. The Church of Uganda banned Ssenyonjo from functioning as a bishop, a hardship because he had previously earned some supplementary income by helping out Namirembe diocese bishop Samuel Ssekadde, who is vehemently opposed to homosexuality. The young priest Frank and his family also suffered socially and economically from the church's displeasure and the public's negative attention. Yet in spite of the undeniable negative impact of their involvement, neither Ssenyonjo nor the group's other leaders have been jailed or physically harmed. Moreover, Integrity-Uganda's leaders told me that many church colleagues' private reactions have not been as harsh as their public statements. As of summer 2003 there had not been a strong enough consensus in the Ugandan House of Bishops to defrock Bishop Ssenyonjo.[44]

Paradoxically, at least to western eyes, this degree of quiet tolerance or restraint may also be due to Ugandans' awareness of their vulnerability to economic influences. I first arrived at this interpretation when it dawned upon me that many Ugandans seem relatively untroubled by the idea that Ssenyonjo took up the homosexual cause for money. The first few times I heard someone say of Ssenyonjo, "We suspect he is only doing it because his pension is small," or words to that effect, I heard it as an additional insult: not only is he betraying Ugandan faith and culture, but he's doing it for money! My reaction was informed by my own culturally conditioned acceptance of a strong commerce/gift distinction, with its correlate that any position taken for monetary gain does not have the legitimacy of a position freely taken. Eventually I came to hear not only the words of such remarks but also their tone and context, and I understood that these statements were intended as mitigating explanations for Ssenyonjo's actions. Enlightened, I realized that most Ugandans find it easier to accept, tolerate, and even excuse Ssenyonjo and others for becoming involved with Integrity-Uganda for reasons of material gain, rather than for becoming involved out of an inner conviction that Integrity-Uganda's cause is right. Jeremiah, a young priest studying at UCU, told me, "People are suspecting that [Ssenyonjo] did it to secure his retirement package," then went on to say, "Still, people were devastated, people even cursed him." The word "still" reveals that the idea Ssenyonjo "did it to secure his retirement package" reduces the magnitude of his crime.

Most Ugandans would rather think that Ssenyonjo "sold out" than that he was convinced of the need for Integrity-Uganda's work. This fact says less about how hard it is for Ugandans to imagine other Ugandans supporting homosexuality than it does about how easy it is for Ugandans to imagine other Ugandans changing their tunes to please potential Northern donors. In spite of Ugandan leaders' public condemnation of Ssenyonjo for allegedly following the logic of commerce into a position out of line with Ugandan mores, Ugandans also talk about Ssenyonjo's error as if it falls on a continuum with other familiar and comprehensible behaviors. Ugandans' experiences with North/South relationships and dependency have kept them keenly aware of the ambiguity of gift in such relationships, and the rarity of the truly free gift.

The "free gifts" of sponsorships, materials, funds, and expertise, regularly given to Ugandan individuals and churches by a wide range of Northern sponsors, allies, and admirers, almost always carry some conditionality or expectation of reciprocation—even if only the expression of gratitude that acknowledges the Northern partners' understanding of their role. For both Northern and Southern partners, such gifts are not free, but a complex hybrid of gift and commerce. As Mauss wrote concerning the traditional mode of reciprocal gifting, "just as these gifts are not freely given, they are also not really disinterested. They [are] . . . not only made with a view of paying for services or things, but also to maintaining a profitable alliance."[45]

The material correlates of North/South relationships are not separable from the relationships themselves. They are part of the terms of relationship. This reality seems more easily recognized and more readily acknowledged by Ugandans (and perhaps by Africans in general) than by Northern partners, who may be more invested in the idea of the "free gift" and who also, as the primary givers, are freer from the obligations of reciprocity their Southern partners must negotiate. Usually such obligations can be managed without much difficulty or compromise on the part of the Southern leaders involved. The fear lurks among Southerners, however, that the temptations of such relationships and the exigencies of Southern needs may lead some into relationships involving actions or positions that their coreligionists and countrymen see as beyond the pale.

Ugandan discourse about Integrity-Uganda places Bishop Ssenyonjo and Integrity-Uganda as extreme cases of a situation many share and everyone understands: that of balancing one's own needs and convictions against donors' agendas. I heard Ugandans' familiarity with the idea of economic persuasion in my consultants' many remarks about Integrity-Uganda that assumed a link between the rise of homosexuality as an issue in Uganda and the economic vulnerability of the Church of Uganda. For example, Nelson, a Ugandan priest, explained to me that people were bitter about Ssenyonjo because they feared Integrity-Uganda might be "a beginning": "People have a feeling that the West, by having resources, may try to introduce these values in a tricky way. People are poor, it is hard to say no, so the faith may be diluted."

Two statements from Integrity leaders also make the point that Ssenyonjo's case attracted so much attention and censure, not because it was atypical, but because it was so very typical. Frank told us that Archbishop Nkoyoyo had been in the United States when the news about Integrity-Uganda was breaking in Uganda. Frank said that in many of the American churches the archbishop visited, people said, "We hear you're harassing sexual minorities in Uganda!" When Archbishop Nkoyoyo tried to downplay Integrity-Uganda's significance by saying that Bishop Ssenyonjo was only involved with Integrity to get money from Northerners, according to Frank, Nkoyoyo's American hosts asked him, "And what are *you* doing *here*?" Similarly, Bishop Ssenyonjo in an article in the Ugandan newspaper *New Vision* article from May 2001, pointed out that he is not the only Ugandan bishop to receive funding from abroad.

> I have great sympathy for those people who say I am looking for money in crusading for the gay populace in this country. This is not true. Instead I can cite many bishops in the Church of Uganda who are being paid by the gay folks and have still failed to provide a support system

for the gay community here. Others are still paid by the conservative sources to make sure there is no gay support in our Church—and these are responsible for the propaganda in the media. So if money is the motivation factor, then we are all to blame in some way.[46]

These Integrity leaders have an interest in justifying their own actions, since Integrity-Uganda does receive some financial support from Integrity-USA and other Northern supporters. Nevertheless, their point is significant. Many Ugandan church leaders and others receive (or seek) outside funding and could be vulnerable to the same charges of soliciting American support, and even of taking actions or making statements to increase the likelihood of attracting such support. Indeed, one of my consultants told me that his bishop, who has developed strong relations with conservative Episcopal evangelicals in the course of pursuing renewal in his own diocese, has been accused of "selling the church" by some of his members—perhaps those unhappy with renewal-related liturgical changes, or simply suspicious of the prominent involvement of outsiders in their diocese. Integrity-Uganda is not alone in raising suspicions that Ugandan church leaders have compromised in order to attract and secure American attention, friendship, and funding.

"BEGGARS HAVE NO CHOICE"

The ideal of North/South relationships founded on the "free gift" principle—mutual fellowship and unconditional sharing of resources—was reportedly put into words quite bluntly by Archbishop Nkoyoyo at a dinner held during Louie Crew's 2001 visit to Uganda as a member of the Episcopal Church's Standing Commission on Anglican and International Peace with Justice Concerns. Crew, who founded Integrity-USA, wrote in his account of his trip that the archbishop told the Western delegation, "You need to understand me quite clearly. . . . We believe it is your Christian duty to support us with your money, but we don't want you to bring your issues here."[47] This your-money-not-your-issues standard may be an attractive ideal for many Ugandans, but most realize that it will rarely be the reality, and that their acceptance of outside support will often leave them open to pressures to take up the agendas of their donors—whether tolerance of homosexuality, particular forms of democratization, free trade, women's rights, or other ideological programs.

The issues raised by the formation of Integrity-Uganda thus relate closely to poorer countries' general position of dependency on foreign aid and foreign political will. An article in *New Vision*, entitled "Ssenyonjo May Yet Have the Last Laugh," examined the link between dependency and homosexuality.

> They say beggars have no choice. Homosexuals may soon be able to
> flex their economic muscle to developing countries. . . . There is a say-
> ing, which goes something like this: He who pays the piper calls the
> tune. This is an apt reminder to nations like Uganda, which receive
> foreign aid from developed nations like the USA and Canada. By ac-
> cepting the said help, you lose some autonomy. . . . [The] changes
> sweeping across North America, Europe and Japan where gays and
> lesbians are now accepted as part of life, will soon cut a wide swath
> through Africa. . . . [because] most African countries are dependent on
> foreign aid for development assistance . . . [and] donors are increas-
> ingly demanding certain returns from the recipients. For instance, polit-
> ical democratisation is now one of the conditions for receiving aid. . . .
> No doubt, the time will soon come when homosexual issues will be on
> the table too. If it comes to pass, such a demand will be quite simple:
> Change your views and laws about homosexuals or forget about the
> goodies that we promised you last year.[48]

This writer articulates a keen sense of Uganda's social, political, and economic vulnerability to the demands or conditions of donor countries and
other "development partners." The agendas of such partners are difficult
for Ugandan organizations, religious or civil, to resist. Sounding fatalistic
rather than alarmed, William, a Ugandan priest familiar with Anglican
Communion power dynamics, predicted to me that pressure from donors
and the influence of the mass media would inevitably cause homosexuality to become accepted in Uganda:

> As the world becomes a small village, and TV and information becomes
> very easy to attain, you have all these pressing pressures, and some
> promoters of the homosexual agenda are very political. . . . The general
> [Ugandan public] does not accept it yet. [M: You used the word "yet."
> Do you think that it will become accepted?] Well, a lot of things are
> becoming accepted. . . . People don't want to spend their energies stop-
> ping something that doesn't concern them . . . [and] legislation in the
> local countries is very much influenced by international pressure groups
> that appear as NGOs.

Integrity-Uganda is thus alarming to Ugandans partly because it appears
as the vanguard of a movement, a new wave of economic and cultural
colonialism in which the values of Northern NGOs and other donors will
be forced upon Southerners as conditions attached to the aid they need.
Bishop Ssenyonjo's involvement with Integrity, though tacitly tolerated,
is vocally condemned as a warning of what could happen to any Ugandan,
given how often Ugandans face such dilemmas as individuals, in their
churches, and as a nation.

NEGOTIATING RELATIONSHIPS IN AN UNEQUAL WORLD

As I indicated earlier, one of the most common questions asked about developing North/South Anglican alliances is whether Southerners are engaged in these alliances primarily for reasons of material gain. When first writing this chapter, I kept catching myself trying to evaluate that question. As I worked with my data, however, I found myself increasingly intrigued by the pervasiveness of financial considerations in inter-Anglican relationships. Accusations about the role of money are so common that there is no way to judge whether material considerations played a greater role in one relationship or another, or to judge when that role was significant enough to cross some fine and shifting line and be named as bribery or coercion. In fact, my analysis led me to the conclusion that the significance of questions about the role of money in particular situations pales when compared with the larger issue of the drastic economic inequality that fundamentally shapes the dynamics, and constrains the possibilities, of these relationships. From the Ugandan perspective, and likely from the perspective of the poorer Anglican provinces in general, the question of money in North/South relationships is not a question of which Northern bidder will win Southern loyalty and support by providing the biggest check to pay school fees and buy water tanks. Rather, the question is how to make the best of whatever opportunities can be found to build and strengthen relationships with Northerners (which relationships may, or may not, produce school fees and water tanks), while at the same time negotiating the web of conditions and expectations surrounding such relationships so as to best maintain the integrity of one's faith, values, and practices.

This position of material disadvantage has a profound impact on Southern Anglican voices—not only in how they are heard and regarded, but in what Southern Anglicans may choose to articulate to begin with. The increasing entanglement of North/South inter-Anglican relationships with conflicts among Northern Anglicans has sometimes resulted in the redirecting of material benefits away from connections that have become colored by these antagonisms (as in Trinity Church's cutting funding for theological education in Rwanda) and toward new lines of affinity (as in some conservative parishes' redirection of funds from ECUSA to African mission partners). Ugandan Anglicans I interviewed seemed ambivalent about this trend toward Northern investment in North/South relations only along lines of doctrinal or moral affinity. These church leaders knew that their conservative Northern allies are a minority in the Northern church and that most of ECUSA's leaders are moderate or liberal in their theological, social, and political views. The Episcopal Church is one of the wealthiest provinces of the Anglican world, and the Church of

Uganda, like other African churches, has long depended on relationships with Episcopal churches and the fellowship and funding that those relationships entail.

Such dependency means that, in cases when there are moral and doctrinal differences between donors and their African partners but neither the donors nor the press make an issue out of those differences, African church leaders may choose not to make an issue of those differences themselves. Three Ugandan bishops I spoke with suggested that they were willing to be in relationship with liberal Episcopal leaders and dioceses, as long as the Episcopal partners did not place conditions on them or make their differences an issue (as Bishop Haines had, in his letter to Bishop Maari). Several other Ugandan church leaders told me they had friends and partners in various camps within the American church, and wanted to keep it that way, without permitting U.S. intrachurch conflicts to disrupt their transnational relationships. Further, during the course of my own fieldwork, I observed that very few Ugandans pressed me about my own convictions. Most simply chose to assume that I shared their views on important matters, rather than get into conversations that might prove awkward for all parties. Although my position as a researcher differs in significant ways from that of a visiting Northern church leader seeking to establish some form of interchurch relationship, this sort of "don't ask, don't tell" policy may be widespread in North/South interactions.

Given the real and sometimes challenging differences between American and African Anglicanisms, many Ugandan leaders in such relationships thus follow a policy of tact and pragmatism within the limits of conscience. In the cases of the Franciscan Study Centre and Integrity-Uganda, Northern support probably did not persuade African leaders to take new positions, but may have encouraged them to be more outspoken on matters of shared concern. In other situations, when African leaders' views conflict with those of Northern partners or potential partners, African leaders may find themselves in a position where it is most polite, and pragmatic, to hold back their views.

The view that African leaders sometimes choose tactful silence was articulated by West African Anglican primate Robert Okine, in an interview with David Virtue exploring why South African bishops voice liberal views on homosexuality.

> "You don't bite the hand that feeds you," said Archbishop Robert Okine, Primate of West Africa. "The South African churches have been given millions of dollars from U.S. dioceses and the U.S. National Church to fight apartheid and support women's ordination. They were easily manipulated to support liberal values because of American money. . . . We Africans have a sense of appreciation even when we

disagree with a person. . . . Some bishops cannot distinguish between exploitation, and under duress, because of the people they serve and the poverty they see every day they can be bought."[49]

Okine implies that the South African bishops may secretly hold negative views of homosexuality, but express approval because of the funding they have received from the American Episcopal church. Like some of the remarks about Bishop Ssenyonjo, Okine's remarks about South African bishops are derogatory, suggesting that these bishops have allowed themselves to be "manipulated" and "exploited." The point of the criticism seems to be, however, not that South African bishops have received funding from America, but that they have allowed that funding to influence them too much. Further, Okine includes himself in one statement: "We Africans have a sense of appreciation even when we disagree with a person." His phrasing leaves open the possibility that, in comparable circumstances, he, too, might choose to express appreciation rather than voice his disagreements and disrupt a relationship.

DISPARITIES IN WEALTH: PURIFICATION AND PERSISTENCE

My examination of these various cases suggests that money issues are so pervasive and complex that the either/or, commerce versus gift perspective prevalent in Northern (and some Southern) rhetoric is untenable. Purifying money from the ideological, cultural, doctrinal, and practical issues with which it is perennially entangled is all but impossible. This work of purification is equally difficult and contested whether the goal is to purify money from ideological conditions, as when Archbishop Nkoyoyo called for the North to give money without issues, or to purify ideological positions from the taint of money, as in the expressed desire of both Northern liberals and conservatives to hear a Southern voice free from the taint of monetary influence. The persistence of rumors of bribery and coercion in the cases I have mentioned shows that it has never been possible to eliminate suspicions that hopes of monetary gain have influenced Southerners by tempting them to speak or to be silent on particular issues.

The impossibility of separating monetary aid from less tangible obligations, from the African point of view, was dramatically evident in the decision of the Council of Anglican Provinces of Africa at its April 2004 meeting to refuse funding from the Episcopal Church following the November 2003 consecration of Gene Robinson.[50] This decision was based on a strong perception that accepting ECUSA's money implied acceptance of its actions. Archbishop Akinola of Nigeria stated after the meeting, "We will not, on the altar of money, mortgage our conscience, mortgage our faith, mortgage our salvation."[51] The Church of Uganda has been prominent in enforcing this decision on itself, refusing funding from Episcopal Relief and Development, United Thank Offering, and other charitable organizations within the Episcopal Church. Archbishop Henry Orombi described these actions as "walking in light regarding our financial accountability"[52]—implying that the church's financial ties must be closely examined in light of its moral commitments, to ensure that the church is not "accountable" to any donors whose beliefs were not acceptable.

Many Episcopal Church individuals and agencies were willing to continue their giving, even to African provinces whose leaders had condemned ECUSA. For example, in June 2004, suffragan bishop Catherine Roskam of New York, who supported Robinson's consecration, was raising money for the training of clergy wives in Uganda. Archbishop Orombi wrote to her refusing the offered aid, explaining:

> I am sure that . . . you are motivated by genuine concern for the difficult circumstances that pastors' wives experience in Uganda. That is not a bad thing, but the situation is overshadowed by your support for the same-sex agenda of ECUSA. . . . I want to say it with sadness and deep regret that we cannot receive any financial support from you and your diocese. To do so would . . . imply that we are willing to accept what you have come to believe.[53]

Although the cases and data I have drawn upon predate this strong stand on Orombi's part, the general situation I have described provides essential background for understanding this dramatic decision. Orombi's refusal of aid from ECUSA, despite his church's many needs, makes it clear that he and his fellow African leaders have little faith that such gifts can ever be truly free. Even if the American donors believe or assert that their gifts have nothing to do with persuading African provinces to accept ECUSA's stand on homosexuality, African leaders feel they cannot take that risk. The only way to be absolutely certain that no influence is occurring is to cut financial ties entirely; the only purification possible of these long-established donor relationships is that of eliminating them entirely. This move has the additional effect of resolving some of the tensions inherent in the situation of the African churches, desirous of self-determination but also long dependent on outsiders' assistance and agendas. African leaders described their rejection of American funding as a difficult but salutary move toward independence. Archbishop Orombi called Gene Robinson's consecration "a wake-up call on our part to find ways to sustain ourselves honourably," and Akinola told journalists about the African bishops' decision, "If we suffer for a while to gain our independence and our freedom and to build ourselves up, I think it will be a good thing for the church in Africa."[54]

The difficult choices made by these African leaders demonstrate, once again, that as long as economic inequality characterizes North/South relationships, it will remain nearly impossible for Northern and Southern partners to trust themselves or their colleagues to speak and act entirely from their convictions. Wherever North/South relationships exist, there is inevitably room for dispute over the role of money. Is the financial support offered by Northern partners a mere side effect, a "free gift," a natural and spontaneous outcome of positive engagement between Northern and Southern partners? Or does the prospect or reality of financial support have a motivational effect, intentional or unintentional, in leading Southern leaders to be more sympathetic to potential Northern partners? The reality of the role of money in these relationships lies somewhere between these two poles, in the unmarked territory between commerce and gift. Nonetheless, offers, refusals, accusations, and denials continue to circulate.

In spite of the expressed desire of both liberals and conservatives in the global North to bring about a new global era in which the Southern churches participate in the Communion on their own terms, the relative wealth of the Northern churches continues to shape North/South relationships within the Communion. Southern Anglican moral dominance, so eagerly advocated by Northern conservatives, is balanced against, and limited by, continued Northern Anglican material dominance. Even these innovative alliances between Northern conservatives and Southern Anglicans, in which the Northern partners explicitly seek equality and reciprocity, are often described in terms of the exchange of financial and spiritual benefits, making it clear that the partners' positions are not equivalent. The Northern partners inevitably possess the greater ability to circulate information and people, convene meetings, and set agendas. Anglican conservative globalism, though it has indisputably brought about new relationships between Northern and Southern Anglicans, remains limited in its ability to create new *kinds* of relationships, less constrained by the too-familiar patterns of Northern power.

CHAPTER EIGHT

The Next Anglicanism? Conclusions and Implications

THE COLLABORATIVE ACTIVISM of American conservatives and Southern Anglican leaders has brought the Anglican Communion into the Episcopal Church to an unprecedented degree. Conflicts over doctrine and morality within the Episcopal Church have been effectively globalized, so that they are now widely seen as of global, rather than domestic, scale and significance. The Northern and Southern allies accomplished this globalization through their use of discourses asserting the relevance of the global Communion, and through projects that, by linking American dissidents with Southern leaders and churches, appear to instantiate the global relevance of Episcopal Church debates. As one observer describes it, "the international mechanisms of the Anglican Communion—its annual Primates' Meeting, the decennial Lambeth Conference of Bishops, and the See of Canterbury itself—have been injected into an historically local and national battle against [the Episcopal Church's] mainline leadership, creating a new terrain of conflict, mobilization, and leverage."[1]

This North/South movement opposing Episcopal Church policies is both conservative and globalist, challenging the assumptions of many scholars of global movements that globalism and progressivism are intrinsically linked. Simon Coleman, in his study of globalization among Swedish Pentecostals, has noted such thinking and argues that "tribalist" movements, that is, conservative movements reaffirming particular identities and worldviews, can be actively globalist in their outlook and activities.

> [Scholars of globalization are] correct to see the reassertion of neo-tribalism as inherent within the global circumstance, and it is true that such a reaction may come from people who feel left out of the cosmopolitan ecumene (or who object to its existence in the first place). As we shall see in the case of charismatic Christianity, however, it is possible to regard a rhetoric of "tribalism" as positively and actively seeking to redefine the global condition, and not simply as a defensive reaction in relation to it.[2]

The movement I have depicted here, like Coleman's Swedish Pentecostalism, is not merely a defensive reaction but positively and actively seeks to redefine global Anglicanism in terms of decentered networks of accountability and shared doctrinal orthodoxy, protected and enforced by the leaders of the Anglican global South. In the process, the Northern partners in this movement have come to a new awareness of the globe and their privileged place in it, while the Southern partners have acquired new networks, new tools, and a new enthusiasm for bringing their perspectives and concerns to a global stage—all developments that ought to inspire the most principled progressives. The redefinitions of the Anglican Communion and of North/South relationships undertaken by this movement have not, perhaps, been thoroughgoing; I have shown in chapters 6 and 7 how older patterns of Northern domination are perpetuated and produced within this movement. Nonetheless, the vision is undeniably globalist, and the living out of the vision may be no more flawed than that of many leftist globalisms—which are often just as much shaped by Northern money and agendas, and just as prone to the temptation to romanticize Southern peoples and treat them as "other" in movement rhetoric.

Furthermore, the globalization produced by this orthodox Anglican movement is not limited in its impact to leaders and activists, nor is it merely a process of Westernization, an exporting of American conflicts to Southern locales. This movement's globalizing work has shaped the thoughts and lives of Anglican clergy and laity around the world, from the middle-class white Americans of St. Timothy's who now regularly discuss news from Africa to the Ugandan laity who now see their church as challenging Northern global dominance, and whose new cows, coffee fields, or church buildings may result from the generosity of Northern conservative partners. As for the question of Westernization, it is true that this movement is not wholly successful in erasing differences, distances, and asymmetries between the partners. The financial dominance of Northern partners means that North/South relationships develop at the will of Northerners, constraining Southerners' autonomy. Meanwhile, the language associated with the global-shift vision, of the orthodox and vibrant South, obliges Southern Anglicans to negotiate their newfound position of moral authority in terms of images of Southern Christianity that are not of their making. The dominance of homosexuality as an issue in these relationships is also undeniably reflective of Northern concerns, and the increasing salience of this issue in the Southern churches further illustrates the influences of the Northern media, NGOs, and religious groups in inciting and shaping public debate in many African countries.

Northern domination, however, is not the only dynamic at work in these relationships. The balance of power between these Northern and Southern allies is shifting and complex. African Christians' responses to homosexuality are not dictated by Northerners, but reflect African contexts and concerns. Nor has the flow of ideas in these inter-Anglican alliances been only one-way. American partners have taken up some South-ern concerns—note the growing interest in African politics among St. Timothy's parishioners. These alliances have also facilitated Southern leaders' access to the tools and platforms they need to voice their positions to the Anglican Communion, and have undermined the Northern-based authority structures of the Communion. Some effects of this movement thus look more like "Southernization" than Westernization.

The best conclusion may be that in Anglicanism, and in globalization more generally, both Westernization and de-Westernization (or "South-ernization") may take place simultaneously at different levels or locations. For example, taking up the American debate over sexuality (Westerniza-tion) may give African leaders the opportunity to speak for their churches on an international stage (de-Westernization). Assessing Lambeth 1998, scholars Ian Douglas and Julie Wortman raised the question of whether the past few years had finally seen the ascendancy of a truly postcolonial and decolonized world Anglicanism, in which Southern Anglicans play their full and rightful role alongside their Northern colleagues, or whether the Communion remains dominated by Northerners who are trying to "manage diversity" by determining the manner and implications of in-cluding Southern Anglicans.[3] The globalization of the Anglican Commu-nion in recent years involves both processes. Northerners, both liberal and conservative, have tried to put forward their own visions of diversity, capturing their understanding of what it means to include Southerners. Still, even in the midst of all these Northern agendas, Southern leaders have managed to speak out and increase the influence of, and interna-tional attention to, their churches.[4] The useful question about globaliza-tion processes and projects is not simply whether they spread Western/ Northern hegemony, but which aspects of Northern hegemony are being spread and which are being limited or reversed. The movement I present here reaffirms Western hegemony at certain points, but also challenges and unsettles it in numerous and important ways.

The bias toward the Left in the scholarly literature on global move-ments reflects scholars' interests more than it reflects the true range of global movements in the contemporary world. Conservative movements, like the global orthodox Anglican movement, Coleman's Pentecostals, and many others, can and do think, talk, and act globally. A conservative agenda or cause is not necessarily incompatible with a global outlook, especially if the conservatism in question is ideological or religious (rather than ethnic or regional) and therefore easily taken up by constituencies around the world. Conservative movements may easily be "reactive" in their core values and motivations—their content, in James Peacock's ter-minology—and at the same time use innovative, even revolutionary glob-alizing tactics and pursue counterhegemonic globalist ideals.[5]

The implications of this reality are many. To begin with, the possibility of conservative globalism should cause progressive activists and academics alike to reexamine their thinking. Conservative globalist movements confound assumptions about progressivism and conservatism. In the Anglican Communion, for example, who has made the most progress toward decentering traditional authority structures? Is it the largely white Anglican liberals who eagerly affirm racial, cultural, and sexual diversity? Or is it the broad coalition of American, European, African, Asian, and Latin American Anglican conservatives who support an essentially heterosexist and patriarchal understanding of biblical morality? Delinking globalism from progressivism also leads to a new appreciation of the independence and agency of Southern allies in Northern-headed or -initiated movements. In this era of generalized anti-imperialism and multiculturalism, Northern leaders and activists of all stripes are eager for Southern allies. As analysis of this Anglican movement shows, progressives cannot take Southerners' loyalties for granted; Southern actors' local concerns and critical perspective on Western culture make them as likely to sign on with conservative Northern causes as with progressive ones. Finally, recognizing the reality of conservative globalism is crucially important for our understanding of the global present and future. The contemporary movements that are busy forging transnational relationships and identities, developing common global agendas and perspectives, and shaping global civil society are not exclusively progressive. Scholars, activists, and members of the communities touched by such movements will understand globalization better, and engage with it more effectively, if they recognize the important role of globally engaged conservative movements in today's world and tomorrow's.

DISCOURSE AND POLARIZATION: PHILIP JENKINS'S THE NEXT CHRISTENDOM

One group of Northerners well aware of the potential of conservative globalism is found in the Episcopal Church. Thanks to the proactive globalizing of American dissidents and their Southern partners, moderate and liberal Episcopalians with any awareness of Communion affairs (a rapidly growing number, as the denomination's conflicts draw increasing attention from the media and incite discussion in congregations) now see conservatism and globalism as linked—perhaps even exclusively linked. This view is strengthened by the currency of the global-shift model, which depicts the world as divided between the revisionist and secularized North, and the zealous and biblicist South. The idea of a global Anglican backlash, spearheaded by righteous Southern leaders against the Episcopal

Church and other errant liberal Northern provinces, had become widely accepted among conservative Northerners and many Southern Anglicans when I completed my fieldwork in June 2002. A few months later, the publication of Philip Jenkins's book *The Next Christendom* and his re-lated article in the *Atlantic Monthly* strengthened the legitimacy of the global-shift vision among its proponents and propelled it into much wider circulation among liberal and moderate Episcopalians.[6] In these pieces, Jenkins argues that Christianity in the global South is growing, conserva-tive, and assertive, and will increasingly be the force with which Northern religious and political leaders must reckon.

Jenkins's work drew wide attention in the secular media. Ian Douglas notes in his review that "the public imagination [was] captured" by Jen-kins's ideas.[7] Journalists and Jenkins himself often positioned his argu-ment as *the* explanation for the increasing involvement of Southern Angli-can leaders in the Episcopal Church and the Anglican Communion. His *Atlantic Monthly* article cited Anglican Mission in America as an example of the rise of Southern Christianity. In one feature on National Public Radio, Jenkins was explicitly positioned as the expert explaining the phe-nomenon of American Episcopal parishes reaching out to African church leaders. These media sources brought the idea of a North-to-South shift in global Anglicanism to a wide range of interested moderate and liberal Christians and secular observers, and in particular to a wider Episcopal audience—those who don't read David Virtue or the *Christian Challenge*, but do read the *Atlantic Monthly* or listen to NPR.

Jenkins accurately observes that American Christians have not tradi-tionally paid much attention to Christianity in the rest of the world.[8] However, the eager audience for his work in Episcopal lay and clergy circles—conservative, moderate, and liberal—demonstrates the new ur-gency with which Episcopalians are today seeking understanding of their Southern coreligionists. Jenkins's conclusions were read by both conser-vative and moderate/liberal Episcopalians as historicizing, explaining, and generally naturalizing the growing trend for Southern Anglican lead-ers to speak out against the Episcopal Church. However, different constit-uencies had different reactions. For conservative Episcopalians and some globally aware moderate and liberal Episcopalians, Jenkins's work ap-peared not as a new set of ideas but as a scholarly explication of what they already perceived as the emergent condition of the worldwide Anglican Communion. For liberal or moderate Episcopalians who were relatively unfamiliar with these ideas about global shift in the Anglican Commu-nion, Jenkins's work appeared as a warning call, bringing threatening trends to their attention. I first heard about Jenkins's work through the buzz of conversation in my own (liberal-leaning) Episcopal parish, where one member who had recently read Jenkins's article told me gravely, "It sounds like we're entering a new Dark Ages."

While liberals and moderates received Jenkins's conclusions with trepidation, conservatives responded to his work with excitement and pleasure, finding in his account an apparently independent and objective justification for their optimism regarding the southward shift of moral authority in world Christianity. Jenkins's focus on the growing numbers and growing influence of Christianity in the global South, and his characterization of Southern Christianity as a monolithic, conservative, zealous force, accorded perfectly with the ways many conservative Episcopalians and Anglicans were already speaking about Southern Christianity. As a result, Jenkins's work was repeatedly cited by American conservative Episcopalians and their allies. In July 2002, acclaimed British evangelical theologian Alister McGrath, addressing a worldwide conference of evangelical Anglicans, cited Jenkins:

> What will the future of the Christian faith look like? A recent highly-acclaimed study by Philip Jenkins paints a picture which many western Christians need to heed. . . . Jenkins shows that the churches that have grown most rapidly in the global south are far more traditional, morally conservative, evangelical, and apocalyptic than their northern counterparts. . . . Might not the rise of Anglicanism in the developing world represent a judgement of the complacencies of western Anglicanism?[9]

In December 2002, David Virtue similarly cited Jenkins's ideas in describing an emergent shift in world Anglicanism: "Jenkins argues that Americans are all but unaware of what is one of the most important shifts of the twentieth century—the explosive growth of Christianity in the Southern Hemisphere. His book . . . reveals to the world that Christianity in its orthodox and evangelical form is alive and well and flourishing like streams in the desert in Africa, Asia and Latin America.[10]"

Jenkins was invited to address the December 2002 meeting of the U.S. Anglican Congress, a group of conservative Episcopalians and Anglicans, and the January 2003 AMiA Winter Conference, where he spoke on "the opportunities of the changing balance of world Christianity."[11] One conservative priest, writing about the AMiA conference, makes it clear why Jenkins is so popular among dissidents who place their hopes in Southern intervention in the Episcopal Church:

> The primary thesis of [Jenkins's] book is that the churches of Asia, Africa, and Latin America are becoming the center of Christendom. This is happening because Southern Churches proclaim a dynamic, living gospel, a faith badly needed in the countries of the Northern Hemi-

sphere. AMiA believes this, and for that reason, invited Philip Jenkins to speak at their conference. In fact, AMiA itself is a mission of the Diocese of Rwanda [*sic*], a missionary outreach of the African Church.[12]

Jenkins's significance for conservative Northern dissidents is best summed up on the "Endorsements" page of the website of one AMiA parish. The final name on the list of those endorsing AMiA is that of Philip Jenkins; the text beneath his name reads, in part:

> The Anglican Mission in America is part of the global expansion of Christianity that is rooted in what is being called the "global south": Africa, Asia and South America. Professor Philip Jenkins, from Penn State, tells this story in his book "The Next Christendom". . . . While [Jenkins] is not a spokesperson for the Anglican Mission, his research and insights are helping many to understand the exciting things happening in global Christianity.[13]

Indeed, Jenkins's writing spread the global-shift thesis to a wide range of Anglicans and Episcopalians as an explanatory framework for developments in the Anglican Communion.

Jenkins's timely formulation was again widely circulated in the summer and fall of 2003 during the much-publicized controversy over the election, confirmation, and consecration of Gene Robinson, an openly gay and partnered priest, as bishop of New Hampshire. Conservative Episcopalians and other Anglicans cited Jenkins's findings on weakening Northern Christianity to explain the Episcopal Church's actions, and described the rising South as their source of encouragement and hope in this time of crisis, as in these quotations from an August 2003 meeting of American conservatives:

> [Conservative evangelical] Bishop Robert Duncan. . . . [believes that God may be acting] on a global scale: casting down the mighty institutions of the West and raising up the embattled and often despised Christians of the Southern Hemisphere. . . . "When Philip Jenkins, author of *The Next Christendom*, says 'Christians are facing a shrinking population in the liberal West and a growing majority of the tradition Rest,' I know what he means. I've seen it in my lifetime," [TESM Dean Peter] Moore said.[14]

The popularity of the "Next Christendom" thesis provides a partial explanation for the extensive press coverage of the Robinson controversy in secular sources. Jenkins's thesis places this story of conflict within a relatively small mainline denomination into a frame of global religious and even political salience. In one revealing example, an editorial in the

Dallas News covering the August 2003 meeting of conservatives was entitled, "Looming Schism: Anglican Split Is Between First, Third Worlds."
This writer invokes Jenkins in explaining why current inter-Anglican conflicts are of wider relevance.

> The lobby of a Dallas luxury hotel filled with Anglicans isn't many
> people's idea of a revolutionary cell, but that's exactly what it is. The
> conservative Episcopalians gathering here this week to protest the na-
> tional church's approval of an openly gay bishop aren't merely disgrun-
> tled traditionalists. They may be on the losing end of this particular
> issue within the Episcopal Church, but their meeting is worth consider-
> ing in the context of a worldwide struggle that may transform Chris-
> tianity in this century. We won't take sides here, but we do urge you to
> pay attention, because what's happening in Dallas is momentous. It has
> attracted the attention, and engaged the passion, of Anglican leaders
> throughout the Third World. This is neither solely an American nor
> solely an Anglican concern. As one veteran church journalist put it on
> the eve of the conference, "What we're seeing here is Philip Jenkins's
> thesis in action."[15]

Thus as inter-Anglican controversies evolved through 2002 and 2003,
Jenkins's formulation of the "global-shift" idea became, for Northern
Episcopalians, Anglicans, and outside observers, the essential explanatory
model for these controversies and their wider implications. This process
represents the intersection of two large-scale trends: the liberal/conserva-
tive polarization of American Christianity, and the rising visibility and
influence of Southern Christianity. The result of this intersection is that
Americans' and Africans' ideas about growing Southern Christianity increasingly conform to the pattern, and are laden with the content, of
American cultural polarization.

THE NEXT ANGLICANISM? HOW EPISCOPALIANS READ PHILIP JENKINS

Episcopal dissidents' reading of Jenkins's work is open to question, or
at least revealingly selective. The view of Jenkins's work as independent
confirmation of trends in world Anglicanism carries an interesting circularity, because—as a footnote in his book reveals—Jenkins was first inspired to develop his thesis about North/South Christian divisions and
struggles while observing the events of Lambeth 1998. Thus Jenkins, in
a sense, was in his book presenting the global-shift concept, elaborated
and thoroughly footnoted, back to the conservative Anglicans who inspired him to begin with.

This circularity is not the only incongruity in conservative Anglicans', and others', adoption of Jenkins's work as justification for Anglican developments. Jenkins's main focus is actually geopolitical; he seeks to improve upon Samuel Huntington's "clash of civilizations" thesis.[16] The main thrust of Jenkins's argument is that global conflicts between fundamentalist Muslims and Southern Christians will increase throughout the next century, but this thesis is largely ignored by Anglican readers. The conflicts that interest these readers are those between Northern and Southern Christians—to which Jenkins does give considerable attention, but which are not his central theme. American readers also tend to ignore Jenkins's cautions about the anomalous religious character of the United States. Jenkins points out the persistent strength of American Christianity, and argues that the United States sits somewhere between the extremes of the Christian South and the secularized North, best epitomized by western Europe.[17] However, nearly all Episcopalians and commentators who invoke Jenkins's thesis in relation to Episcopal and Anglican affairs treat the United States, and the American Episcopal Church, as perfect examples of the weakening and secularization of Northern Christianity that Jenkins describes.[18] Along the same lines, American conservatives assume the Southern Christian conservatism Jenkins describes corresponds with their own, though Jenkins cautions that Southern moral and political positions do not line up neatly with Northern conservatism. Generally speaking, Northern Christians tend to read Jenkins's account of Southern Christianity to accord with their own hopes or fears.

Jenkins himself was likely unsurprised that conservative Episcopalians and other observers of the Anglican global scene took up his writings to support their own global ideologies. He notes that Northerners project their own ideas and desires onto the rising Christian South, and argues that contrary to such projections, these changes will not perfectly fulfill any Northern dreams or agendas:

If in fact the global South represents the future, then it is tempting to claim that one's own ideas are more valid, more important, because they coincide with those of the rising Third World. For the Left, the rise of the South suggests that Northern Christians must commit themselves firmly to social and political activism at home, to ensuring economic justice and combating racism, to promoting cultural diversity. Conservatives, in contrast, emphasize the moral and sexual conservatism of the emerging churches, and seek to enlist them as natural allies. . . . For both sides, the new South is useful, politically and rhetorically. Even if an activist holds an unusual or unpopular position, it can be justified on the basis that it represents the future: if they wait long enough, they will be vindicated by the churches of Africa (or Asia, or Latin America).[19]

In looking at the global South, conservative Episcopalians have often seen their own dreams and desires mirrored back at them. These Northerners have articulated their expectation that Southern Christianity will meet all their needs and settle all their conflicts by rising to power in the Anglican Communion, rescuing and justifying Northern conservatives, and restoring the fallen Northern churches.

Are these globalizing North/South alliances best understood as an outcome of the heralded rise of Southern Christianity to rebuke the errant North and hold its churches accountable to the gospel—with the help of a few like-minded Northerners? By this logic, alliances between Northern conservatives and Southern Anglicans would be explained by a natural correspondence of interests between Southern Christians and disaffected Northerners who reject revisionist trends in the Northern churches. Talk about these alliances often describes them in such terms, as founded on and embodying some essential similarity, and the success of these alliances may indeed be partially explained by important similarities between the Southern and Northern partners. Despite significant contextual differences, most Ugandan church leaders do share an evangelical sense of identity and attitude toward scripture with conservative Episcopalians, and many also share a renewal orientation in worship. True, Ugandan Christians also share aspects of their faith and thought with many Northern liberals, such as commitments to economic justice and developmentalism. However, most Ugandan Christian leaders seem to perceive themselves as having more important concerns in common with Northern conservative evangelicals. In part this is because Northern liberal Christianity is identified with the cultural currents of modernity, individualism, and sexual liberation that Ugandans see as threats to their own values, and in part because Ugandans' own biblical convictions predispose them to see a shared focus on scripture as more important than a shared focus on, say, international debt.

Any explanation of these alliances on the basis of some natural convergence, however, can only go so far. Although Southern Anglicans and Northern dissidents do share some orientations, many of these shared perspectives, such as concern about the Episcopal Church's position on homosexuality, have been developed in and through their growing alliances. The strength of these relationships owes more to motivation and opportunity than to preexisting, natural affinities. Northern conservatives have been highly motivated to seek out relationships with Southern Anglicans in recent years. This zeal springs from their strong sense of alienation and disempowerment in their own churches and their desire to connect with potentially like-minded Anglicans elsewhere, both for the sake of gaining rhetorical and practical resources for domestic debates and for the sake of the sense of connection itself—Northern conservatives often express joy at feeling solidarity with Anglicans around the world.

Where Northerners seek to build North/South relationships (and it is, almost always, Northerners who have the resources to establish or maintain such relationships), Southerners usually welcome opportunities to engage, for reasons arising out of their own contexts. Ugandans describe North/South relationships as desirable for the sake of fellowship and the sharing of faith and experiences. They also often mention the much-needed material resources that tend to follow the lines of such relationships. Further, Ugandans describe such relationships (for example, in the context of preparations for Lambeth 1998) as providing them with opportunities and resources to assert Southern voices on a global stage.

These relationships and their cooperative activism are successful because they serve the needs of Northern dissidents, while also giving Southern leaders opportunities to preach their convictions and advance their churches' interests. The global-shift narrative, however, has the effect of rendering invisible the collaborative work of these constituencies, and especially the active role of Northerners in propelling Southern Anglicanism to the fore in contemporary Anglican Communion debates. In so naturalizing the global South's rise, the global-shift vision masks persistent inequalities in power and influence within the Anglican Communion—and perhaps makes substantive change even more difficult.

GLOBALIZATION AND DISSENT

The global-shift narrative, in short, does not capture the complexity of the Anglican Communion's current global dynamics, nor of the North/South activist alliances that have become so influential. Yet despite (or perhaps because of) the complexities and ambiguities of the situation, the global-shift, North versus South vision has taken a firm hold and become ubiquitous in writing about the Episcopal Church and Anglican Communion. The logic of the vision is simple and therefore attractive, regardless of whether the rising South is perceived as savior or menace.

Still, for all its apparent discursive power, it remains unclear whether the global-shift thesis will ultimately produce what it describes. Up until the controversy over Bishop Gene Robinson, these connections had had relatively little direct effect on Episcopal Church policies, and even in the current post–Gene Robinson disruption, it remains unclear whether a substantive split and realignment of the global Anglican Communion will occur, not withstanding the apocalyptic North/South rhetoric surrounding this controversy. American conservatives have been repeatedly disappointed by the slow response from the primates, who, three years after Robinson's consecration, have not yet asked ECUSA to leave the Communion. Should the Episcopal Church be disrecognized by the Communion, the Network of Anglican Communion Dioceses and Parishes is positioned as a possible new American Anglican province. It is impossible to say, at this moment, how much the established polity, policies, budgets, and relationships of the Episcopal Church will ultimately be affected by reactions (negative or positive) to the consecration of Gene Robinson. Nor is it at all clear whether the predicted "realignment"—stemming from the dissociating and renetworking currently under way in the Episcopal Church and wider Communion—will result in a new global configuration conforming to the model of North/South split, with the Communion broken into a small, liberal Northern Anglican body and a large, orthodox, evangelical Southern body embracing like-minded Northern Anglicans.

Whatever dissociations and divisions may occur, however, the Anglican Communion's recent history can be interpreted as a story of coming together as much as a story of coming apart. Many speak of current controversies as if they were tearing up an established, settled way of being a global Communion, but even the short history I offer here casts that view into doubt. In many respects, the controversies of recent years represent in themselves the working-out of coexistence as a global Communion. As I showed in chapter 2, becoming a postcolonial, multicultural Communion characterized by the full participation of all provinces became an active project of the Communion leadership only in the 1960s and 1970s. The ideal of being a *global* Communion, with a high degree of interconnectedness and mutual awareness, is newer still, dating back perhaps to the mid-1990s.

These trends amount to a sort of "shrinking" of the Communion—a process similar to the "shrinking of the world" often identified as a significant aspect of globalization, as the mass media, electronic communication, rapid international travel, and other intensified forms of global connection increasingly bring events in one locality to the consciousness of people elsewhere, enabling almost immediate reactions.[20] The relevance of this phenomenon for the Anglican Communion is that "global Communion" is not only a relatively recent term in Anglican vocabulary but also a relatively recent reality. Since the mid-1990s the Communion's provinces have experienced a significant increase in the degree and speed of mutual knowledge, thanks both to the increasing penetration of the electronic media and to the efforts of Anglican leaders eager to increase inter-provincial awareness—whether the e-journalists of the Anglican Communion News Service or American dissidents seeking overseas Anglicans' sympathy. As the 1960s-era CBS commentator Eric Sevareid put it, "Now, with the highly-developed arts of mass communication and mass transportation, we can misunderstand each other faster and more deeply than ever before."[21] The controversies, tensions, and discoveries of affinities, differences, and antagonisms with which the Anglican Communion is currently struggling have much to do with its member provinces simply learning more about one another—and finding that they don't, after all, have as much in common as they had assumed in the days when all they knew was that they shared a liturgical heritage and an allegiance to Canterbury. One conservative leader, Bill Atwood of the Ekklesia Society, almost suggested as much in an article on the 2003 Primates' Meeting responding to Gene Robinson's election. Atwood wrote about the ways Anglican leaders around the world have gained in knowledge about Episcopal Church policies in recent years, and concluded, "Information has overcome disbelief and has given way to outrage."[22]

This intensified flow of information goes a long way toward accounting for strong global reactions. At a recent Episcopal diocesan convention, a conservative speaker arguing for proposed resolutions that would censure the Episcopal Church for consecrating Gene Robinson stated, "Regardless of how you feel about [homosexuality], the facts speak for themselves in that the scope of reaction from the world-wide Anglican Communion is bigger than to any previous division in the American church." He intended to imply that the degree of international response indicates that homosexuality is more damaging than any previous controversial issue. However, the intensified response he observes likely has more to do with increased awareness on the part of Southern church leaders (as Atwood hints) than with the intrinsic character of homosexuality as an issue.

The Anglican Communion's current struggles may then be a matter of global communion being, not torn apart, but examined more fully for its implications and desirability. This conclusion is supported by the mandate of the Lambeth Commission, the special committee established to address the consequences of Gene Robinson's consecration. This commission was charged, not to debate homosexuality, but to explore questions of polity, relationship, and accountability, namely "issues of process . . . , the nature and purposes of Communion, the obligations of Communion, authority, [and] the role of the instruments of unity in preserving fellowship."[23] Archbishop Robin Eames, primate of Ireland and convener of the Lambeth Commission, has raised the question of whether, given the increased diversity and increased mutual awareness within the Communion, some moment of crisis, division, and reevaluation was inevitable—whether precipitated by the issue of homosexuality or by something else entirely.[24] The current "crisis" in the Anglican Communion may fundamentally be the result of increased global connectivity that is forcing the Communion's member churches to come to grips with what exactly they mean by "global Anglicanism."

IMPLICATIONS OF THE GLOBAL-SHIFT VISION

If the Anglican Communion stands at a critical moment of increased mutual knowledge and reevaluation of the nature of Anglican unity, the global-shift discourse as applied to world Anglicanism takes on a troubling significance. This vision of a polarized Christian world, and the activist transnational alliances that have propagated it, has profoundly shaped the rise of global consciousness among Episcopalians and perhaps other Northern Anglicans. Conservatives have brought their global vision of activist orthodox Southern Christianity into the consciousness of the larger Episcopal Church by soliciting the involvement of Southern leaders and discursively using the moral authority of those leaders to attack the Episcopal Church.

This entanglement of conservative dissidence with global awareness has created a difficult situation in the Episcopal Church today, as reactions to idea of the rise of Southern Christendom fall out along the lines of conservative/liberal polarization within American society. Conservative Episcopalians see the rise of Southern Christianity primarily as an opportunity, while moderate and liberal Episcopalians increasingly regard Christianity in the global South as a threat, and the possibility of global relationships as limited to conservatives. When I talk with moderate and liberal Episcopalians about my research, I frequently hear responses like, "I had never thought much about the rest of the Anglican Communion until all this came up," and, "Is it really true that African Anglicans are so conservative?" Such comments and questions show that for many Episcopalians, growing consciousness of the rest of the Communion has coincided with a growing perception of the global South as conservative and judgmental.

Concern about Southern Christians' impact on American mainline churches is not limited to the Episcopal Church. Jenkins's work raised these issues for Northern Christianity in general, and leaders in other American mainline denominations have been watching Episcopal and Anglican conflicts unfold with curiosity and some anxiety. Other American Protestants mulling over the rise of global South Christianity may be seen in a recent edition of *Pulpit & Pew*, a publication of the Lilly Foundation, in which Methodist pastor and professor William Willimon comments that Southern Christianity "is both an inspiration for and a judgment upon declining European and North American Christendom."[25] Baptist leader Chad Hall notes that American leaders need to decide "whether to brace for these shifts [in the locus of world Christianity], embrace these shifts, or do both."[26] These leaders express ambivalence about the potential impact of Southern Christianity on Northern churches. At the Louisville Institute annual seminar in January 2004, one of my colleagues explained that he and others were interested in my work because they want to know if what is happening to the Episcopal Church will happen in their churches, too. Will the integration of formerly marginalized groups become tied up with divisive moral issues in other denominations as well? Few other American denominations have the international scope of the Anglican Communion, but some have substantial Southern immigrant membership; the composition of their churches is shifting dramatically even in the domestic context. Hence the salience, for other Northern Protestants, of the questions of difference, inclusion, and division with which the Episcopal Church and Anglican Communion are struggling.

Because the prevailing global-shift vision presents Southern Christianity as a threat to most mainline Northern churches, many liberal and moderate Episcopalians and other American Protestants are becoming simultaneously more aware of Christianity in the global South and more likely to cede the possibilities of relationship with Southern Christians to conservatives. Retreating from the multiculturalist dreams of diversity globalism, they pull back into a defensive posture, anxious to protect their churches from Southern influences. Likewise, Southern Christians, though always somewhat more globally aware than Northerners, have grown in awareness of their Northern coreligionists—getting much of their information from Northern conservatives. In Uganda I received many "Is it true. . . ?" and "I have heard . . . ?" queries about whether the Northern church is really as liberal as it's made out to be. Anglicans North and South have gotten the message that Northern and Southern Christianity have little or nothing in common.

This increasing polarization is evident in the ways Southern Anglicanism is invoked in the Episcopal Church. One effect of the interpenetration of North/South Anglican politics and left/right Episcopal politics is that Episcopalians' talk about their own church often involves discussion of Southern Christianity. At a recent diocesan convention, debates over resolutions dissociating the diocese from Robinson's consecration, proposed by the diocese's conservative minority, were couched in terms of the impact of that consecration on the Episcopal Church's relations with the worldwide Anglican Communion. One conservative accused the Episcopal Church of violating relations with African churches, and another insisted, "This is not about homosexuality, but about unity and amicable relations within the worldwide Anglican Communion." For liberals and moderates at the convention, conversations about ECUSA's political and moral stands likewise often took place through talk about relations with Southern Anglicans. Some diocesan leaders publicly affirmed their own positive relations with particular Southern leaders, challenging conservatives' claims that the Episcopal Church's policies have injured such relationships. Other Episcopalians questioned the importance of relationship with Southern Christians. In response to conservatives' talk about relations with the African churches, I overheard two attendees discussing the quality of African Christianity. One passed on some stories he had heard about the corruption and patriarchalism of one African church; his neighbor observed, "They're just not where we are." Some Episcopal liberals and moderates thus reassert their relationships with Southern Christians; others downplay the value of such relationships. In either case, however, liberal and moderate Episcopal leaders' ideas about Christians in the global South, and the desirability or possibility of relationship with Southern Anglicans, have been deeply marked by the global-shift vision and the North/South alliances that appear to substantiate that vision by bringing Southern Anglicans to challenge the American church.

Anglicans and Episcopalians increasingly see the Anglican Communion in terms of binary oppositions—liberal/conservative, North/South—even though these simple categories are inadequate for describing the reality of Northern and Southern churches and Christians. Yet if Anglicans increasingly act out their global relationships on the basis of assumptions that Southern Anglicans have an inherent affinity with Northern conservatives, this global vision of North/South division will nevertheless become more and more descriptive of relational realities. Although Southern church leaders are keenly aware of their members' many locally unmet needs and of the marginalization of Southern Christian voices, and thus are eager for North/South relationships that bring resources and opportunities, they have become more guarded about accepting offers of relationship or support from the North, fearing that ideological strings are attached. Meanwhile American liberals and moderates, who control a vastly disproportionate amount of the worldwide Communion's funding, may hesitate to seek out or maintain relationships of companionship, exchange, and mutual support with Southern Anglicans, fearful that Southern Christians are uniformly hostile to nonconservative Northern churches. As Willis Jenkins notes, such withdrawal on the part of the American or other Northern churches contributes to "a Communion-wide environment of distrust, suspicion, fear, and alienation."[27]

The Northern liberal/moderate majority and Southern Anglicans, rather than welcoming this new era of greater interconnectedness with enthusiasm and goodwill as the globalist discourses of Lambeth 1998 urged, are increasingly suspicious of each other. Diversity globalism, the vision of celebrating difference within community so often invoked at Lambeth 1998, has taken a beating and faces stiff competition from the accountability globalist vision, in which the orthodox South demands Northern conformity to particular moral rules—a vision bearing implications of inevitable conflict and irreconcilable differences.

Some Episcopal leaders and commentators continue to argue for alternative global visions. For example, in his review of Jenkins's *Next Christendom*, Ian Douglas explicitly countered Jenkins's globalist vision with one of his own:

> If there is a crisis in world Christianity, it is not between an old Christendom of the West and a new Christendom of the South but rather between an hegemonic, monocultural expression of Western Christianity and an emerging, multicultural global Christian community embodying radical differences. The emergence of the diverse voices of Christianity in the Third World is not "the next Christendom" but rather a new Pentecost. . . . God's ongoing intervention in the world is being made real in the many tongues and cultural realities of a new Pentecost.[28]

Douglas argues for a radical diversity globalism, one that does not merely appreciate difference but welcomes its transforming impact. He asserts that what American Christians should feel, in gazing upon the rise of Southern Christianity, is wonder and excitement about radically new possibilities—not fear about being overrun by judgmental fundamentalists.

The potential for Episcopal liberals and moderates and their colleagues in other Northern churches to feel this kind of excitement about Southern Christianity may appear to have been foreclosed by the close ties between American dissidents and many Southern leaders. These alliances, and their work of globalization in bringing the Anglican Communion into the Episcopal Church, have made it seem that the rise of the global South can only mean greater strength for Northern conservatives. The global-shift model supports this view by naming Southern Christians as uniformly conservative and thus as natural allies for Northern conservative dissidents. All of these factors may lead Northern liberal and moderate Anglicans to conclude that there is little space, and little hope, for them in the global Communion today. Anglicans, Episcopalians, and observers all need to recall, however, that the connection between conservatism and globalism is no more intrinsic and necessary than that between progressivism and globalism. The alliances currently so influential in Communion politics are not the result of some exclusive affinity between Northern conservatives and a monolithic, orthodox Southern Christendom. Rather this unlikely and remarkable coalition has been painstakingly built across profound differences in culture and experience, with the parties' commonalities constructed as much as discovered. Tracing the history of this movement has been a process of "writing against globalization": not taking globalization for granted, but analyzing the processes and projects by which these allies wove global networks binding local and national Episcopal Church conflicts to bishops and provinces all over the world.

Recovering the contingency, the noninevitability, of both dissident North/South alliances and the globalization they have produced has important implications. First, the close relations between Northern conservatives and many Southern Anglican leaders and churches do not mean that other North/South inter-Anglican relationships have become impossible. The polarization of the Anglican Communion may have advanced far enough to limit such possibilities, but not to eliminate them. Not every Southern Anglican bishop, parish, and individual wants to choose sides in Northern debates, or would choose the same side as those whose involvement I have explored. Further, Northern dissidents cannot take their overseas allies for granted; these relationships will require ongoing serious attention to their Southern partners' needs and concerns in order for Southern leaders to remain willing to invest time and energy in Northern church disputes. A second and related point is that the image of the global South projected by the North/South dissident movement does not capture the reality of those continents and churches, as my partial portrait of the Church of Uganda indicates. The leaders and members of the Episcopal Church and other denominations will meet the changes of this new era differently, depending on the lens through which they view the global South—as a monolithic, threatening entity, or a complex and diverse set of places and peoples with their own concerns and perspectives. I hope that my writing against globalization will reopen the possibility of curiosity, excitement, and even optimism about the opportunities and challenges of the changing geography of worldwide Christianity.

Notes

INTRODUCTION: A COMMUNION IN CRISIS?

1. In her comprehensive review of official Episcopal Church actions regarding homosexuality, found in the appendix of *To Set Our Hope on Christ: A Response to the Invitation of Windsor Report P135*, Pamela Darling notes that by early 1994 a teaching document prepared by the House of Bishops suggested "an open attitude toward sexuality in general, and homosexuality in particular," 97 (New York: Office of Communication, Episcopal Church Center, 2005), www.episcopalchurch.org/documents/ToSetOurHopeOnChrist.pdf (accessed May 2, 2006). Chapter 1 includes further discussion of the Episcopal Church's engagement with progressive issues since the 1950s.

2. Philip Jenkins, *The Next Christendom: The Coming of Global Christianity* (New York: Oxford University Press, 2002), 4, 7, 14.

3. Anna Tsing, "The Global Situation," *Cultural Anthropology* 15, no. 3 (2000): 330.

4. Ibid., 337.

5. Zsuzsa Gille and Sean O Riain, "Global Ethnography," *Annual Review of Sociology* 28 (2002): 271–95; Susan Brin Hyatt, "Writing against Globalization," *Anthropological Quarterly* 75, no. 1 (2001): 205–12.

6. Jonathan Xavier Inda and Renato Rosaldo, "Introduction: A World in Motion," in *The Anthropology of Globalization: A Reader*, ed. Inda and Rosaldo (Malden, MA: Blackwell Press, 2002).

7. See, for example, John Tomlinson, *Globalization and Culture* (Chicago: University of Chicago Press, 1999). The question of the newness of globalization has preoccupied some globalization scholars. The general consensus seems to be that while humans have always circulated culture, commodities, and genes, there is both a quantitative and a qualitative difference in the developments of recent decades.

8. Ulf Hannerz, "Cosmopolitans and Locals in World Culture," in *Global Culture*, ed. Mike Featherstone (Thousand Oaks, CA: Sage Publications, 1990), 237.

9. Tomlinson, *Globalization*, 37–40.

10. Peter Beyer, *Religion and Globalization* (London: Sage Publications, 1994), 92.

11. Manuel Castells, *The Power of Identity, vol. 2: The Information Age: Economy, Society, and Culture* (Malden, MA: Blackwell Publishers, 1997), 21, 25.

12. Ibid., 66, 109.

13. Benjamin R. Barber, *Jihad vs. McWorld* (New York: Ballantine Books, 2001). Another area of scholarly focus on global religion is the religion of migrants and diasporic populations. Peter van der Veer, for example, in a chapter examining Indian religious nationalisms, argues that "these movements do not resist globalization but in fact embrace it." His account of the globalism of these

movements, however, is limited to their efforts to involve diasporic Indians. Such scholarship focuses on a limited aspect of globalization—the ties connecting diasporic populations with their homeland—and does not engage fully with the question of how a conservative religious movement can embrace global diversity and openness. Peter van der Veer, "Religious Nationalism in India and Global Fundamentalism," in *Globalizations and Social Movements*, ed. John Guidry, Michael D. Kennedy, and Mayer N. Zald (Ann Arbor: University of Michigan Press, 2000), 315–38.

14. See, for example, Guidry, Kennedy, and Zald, *Globalizations and Social Movements*, and Jackie Smith and Hank Johnston, eds., *Globalization and Resistance: Transnational Dimensions of Social Movements* (Lanham, MD: Rowman and Littlefield, 2002).

15. Simon Coleman, "The Faith Movement: A Global Religious Culture?," *Culture and Religion* 3, no. 1 (2002): 6.

16. James Peacock, *Global Identity in the U.S. South* (Athens: University of Georgia Press, in press).

17. Ekklesia Society, "Rationale for the Ekklesia Society," Ekklesia Society home page, www.ekklesiasociety.org (accessed August 5, 1998).

18. Hyatt, "Writing against Globalization," 206–7.

19. Tsing, "Global Situation," 328.

20. Simon Coleman, *The Globalisation of Charismatic Christianity* (Cambridge: Cambridge University Press, 2000), 6.

21. Hilary Cunningham, "The Ethnography of Transnational Social Activism: Understanding the Global as Local Practice," *American Ethnologist* 26, no. 3 (2003): 583.

22. Deborah G. Martin and Byron Miller, "Space and Contentious Politics," *Mobilization* 8, no. 2 (2003): 143–56.

23. Gille and O Riain, "Global Ethnography," 284.

24. Tsing, "Global Situation," 329; Gille and O Riain, "Global Ethnography," 283.

25. Coleman, "Faith Movement," 11.

26. Jenkins, *Next Christendom*, 2. See chapter 8 for more on Episcopalians' adoption of Jenkins's work.

27. See Miranda Smith, "Church Battles, Culture Wars: The Case of the Episcopal Church" (MA thesis, University of North Carolina, 1999).

28. For details regarding the growth of Southern Christianity, see Jenkins, *Next Christendom*, and Timothy Samuel Shah, "The Bible and the Ballot Box: Evangelicals and Democracy in the 'Global South,'" *SAIS Review* 24, no. 2 (2004): 118.

29. A related case in the Church of England at about the same time resulted in similar controversy, but a different outcome. Canon Jeffrey John, a gay man with a partner, was nominated to serve as suffragan bishop of the Diocese of Reading. Following an outcry from evangelicals in the Church of England and Anglican leaders around the world, John withdrew his name from consideration. James Solheim, "Openly Gay Priest in England Withdrawing from Appointment to Episcopate," *Episcopal News Service* 2003–157 (July 3, 2003).

30. David C. Anderson, "A Place to Stand," American Anglican Council (2003), http://www.americananglican.org/News/News.cfm?ID=798&c=21 (accessed March 24, 2004).

31. Colleen O'Connor, "The Anatomy of Schism: A Battle of Biblical Tyranny," *Everyvoice* (2003), www.everyvoice.net/modules.php?op=modload& name=News&file=article&sid=272 (accessed October 11, 2003).

32. David Virtue, "Wrenching Split in Fabric of Communion if Primates Don't Act," *Virtuosity Digest*, October 11, 2003, archived at http://www.virtueon line.org/portal/index.php.

33. Willis Jenkins argues that the vehement response to Robinson's consecration from Southern bishops owes much to the Episcopal Church's disengagement from global mission in recent decades, with the result that few liberal and moderate Episcopal leaders and laity have a grounded sense of how to engage in shared mission across difference (297). Jenkins's argument complements my own, which focuses on the increased engagement of conservative Episcopalians during the same time span. Willis Jenkins, "Episcopalians, Homosexuality, and World Mission," *Anglican Theological Review* 86, no. 2 (2004): 293–316.

34. See especially George Marcus, *Ethnography through Thick and Thin* (Princeton, NJ: Princeton University Press, 1998).

35. Gille and O Riain, "Global Ethnography," 286–87.

36. Ulf Hannerz, "Several Sites in One," in *Globalisation: Studies in Anthropology*, ed. Thomas Hylland Eriksen (Sterling, VA: Pluto Press, 2003), 18–38.

37. Lewis C. Daly, "A Church at Risk: The Episcopal 'Renewal Movement,'" *IDS Insights* 2, no. 2 (2001): 3.

38. I have not given UCU a pseudonym because it is so well known in many circles as a significant site for North/South connections that I thought it impossible to describe it adequately while still disguising its identity. Further, UCU is not institutionally involved in contentious politics in the same way that St. Timothy's is, and thus requires somewhat less ethnographic protection. I have treated its staff and students with the same level of anonymity that I have given my American consultants.

39. The only patterned difference I observed was in degrees of awareness; people farther from the central urbanized region were generally less exposed to news or rumors about Episcopal Church or Anglican Communion events.

40. I was on a first-name basis with most of the priests and laypeople among my consultants in both the United States and Uganda. With some priests and most of the bishops I interviewed, I actually addressed them by their title and surname. Finding Ugandan surnames difficult to fabricate, however, I have chosen to use first names for all my pseudonyms.

41. Hannerz, "Several Sites," 34–35.

42. Faiz Ahmad Faiz, *The Rebel's Silhouette: Selected Poems* (Amherst: University of Massachusetts Press, 1991), xi.

43. Talal Asad, "The Idea of an Anthropology of Islam," Georgetown University Center for Contemporary Arab Studies Occasional Paper Series (Washington, DC, 1986), 17.

CHAPTER 1. RENEWAL AND CONFLICT: THE EPISCOPAL CHURCH
AND THE PROVINCE OF UGANDA

1. Frank S. Mead, *Handbook of Denominations in the United States* (1951; Nashville, TN: Abingdon Press, 1990), 100–101; *Lesser Feasts and Fasts* (New York: Church Publishing Company, 1998), 392.

2. David L. Holmes, *A Brief History of the Episcopal Church* (Valley Forge, PA: Trinity Press International, 1993), 104. For a comparative anthropological perspective on the doctrine of apostolic succession, see Nancy Jay's work on sacrificial patrilineages. Jay, *Throughout Your Generations Forever: Sacrifice, Religion, and Paternity* (Chicago: University of Chicago Press, 1992).

3. Asad, "Anthropology of Islam," 14–15.

4. Anglican Communion News Service, "The Revd Ian T. Douglas Upholds Importance of the Anglican Communion," ACNS 3628 (October 16, 2003).

5. Elesha Hodge, "Accidental Missionary," *Christian History* (Fall 1997), http://www.ctlibrary.com/ch/1997/56/56h040.html (accessed March 24, 2004).

6. Holger Bernt Hansen, *Mission, Church, and State in a Colonial Setting: Uganda, 1890–1925* (New York: St. Martin's Press, 1984); W. B. Anderson, *The Church in East Africa* (Dodoma, Tanzania: Central Tanganyika Press, 1981).

7. Louise Pirouet, *Black Evangelists: The Spread of Christianity in Uganda, 1891–1914* (London: Rex Collings, 1978), 195.

8. Ibid., 16.

9. The term "fundamentalist" is often used to describe the African Anglican churches as a negative label intended to denote an intolerant and unreflective attitude toward Christian morality and biblical authority. However, no one in the groups I studied, in Africa or the United States, self-identifies as fundamentalist, nor is the term analytically applicable. Generally speaking, fundamentalists tend to take strongly literalist positions on biblical meaning and a more separatist position relative to the wider society. Both the American and the Ugandan Anglicans discussed here are better described as evangelical, by virtue of their moderate literalist stance on Biblical authority and orientation toward engagement with society. For one explanation of the difference between evangelicalism and fundamentalism, see Robert Woodberry and Christian Smith, "Fundamentalists, et al.," in *Annual Review of Sociology*, vol. 24 (Palo Alto: Annual Reviews, 1998), 25–56.

10. Pirouet, *Black Evangelists*, 22–23.

11. Kevin Ward, " 'Obedient Rebels'—The Relationship between the Early 'Balokole' and the Church of Uganda: The Mukono Crisis of 1941," *Journal of Religion in Africa* 19, no. 3 (1989): 194–227.

12. Kevin Ward, "Same-Sex Relations in Africa and the Debate on Homosexuality in East African Anglicanism," *Anglican Theological Review* (Winter 2002):1, http://newark.rutgers.edu/~lcrew/homosexualityAfrica.html (accessed January 13, 2003).

13. Holger Bernt Hansen and Michael Twaddle, eds., *Developing Uganda* (Athens: Ohio University Press, 1998); Arne Bigsten and Steve Kayizzi-Mugerwa, *Crisis, Adjustment, and Growth in Uganda* (New York: St. Martin's Press, 1999); Susan Dicklitch, *The Elusive Promise of NGOs in Africa: Lessons from Uganda* (New York: St. Martin's Press, 1998).

14. The naming of the American province as "Episcopal," rather than "Anglican," reflects in part the assistance of the Scottish Episcopal (Anglican) church in its founding and in part the unpopularity of the term "Anglican," meaning "English," during the period after the American Revolution. One parish leader at St. Timothy's, after reading over parts of this manuscript, pointed out to me that St. Timothy's had broken only from the Episcopal Church in the United States; since the Province of Rwanda's official name is L'Église Episcopal au Rwanda, they actually still belong to an Episcopal church.

15. Timothy L. Smith, *Revivalism and Social Reform: American Protestantism on the Eve of the Civil War* (Gloucester, MA: Peter Smith, 1976), 29–30; William Syndor, *Looking at the Episcopal Church* (Wilton, CT: Morehouse-Barlow, 1980), 76.

16. Allen C. Guelzo, *For the Union of Evangelical Christendom: The Irony of the Reformed Episcopalians* (University Park: Pennsylvania State University Press, 1994). Although this historical influence on the church is undeniable, Guelzo's diagnosis of an "Anglo-Catholic hegemony" might be questioned in recent years. Strong Anglo-Catholics tend to oppose the ordination of women and have thus felt increasingly marginalized in the Episcopal Church since the 1970s.

17. Holmes, *Brief History*, 92.

18. I suggest that "traditionalist" is a better description of Episcopal attitudes toward the liturgy than "conservative," because most Episcopalians in the church today value keeping to Prayer Book liturgies but accept the 1979 version of the Prayer Book and welcome some degree of liturgical flexibility, especially if those changes are seen as a restoration of ancient church practices or as borrowing from elsewhere in world Christianity.

19. Holmes, *Brief History*, 162.

20. Mead, *Handbook*, 104.

21. Holmes, *Brief History*, 148–49.

22. David E. Sumner, *The Episcopal Church's History: 1945–1985* (Wilton, CT: Morehouse-Barlow, 1987), 161.

23. Holmes, *Brief History*, 175.

24. Ibid., 177.

25. Ibid., 176.

26. Kit Konolige and Frederica Konolige, *The Power of Their Glory: America's Ruling Class, the Episcopalians* (New York: Wyden Books, 1978).

27. Wade Clark Roof and William McKinney, *American Mainline Religion* (New Brunswick, NJ: Rutgers University Press, 1987).

28. Robert Wuthnow, *The Restructuring of American Religion: Society and Faith since World War II* (Princeton: Princeton University Press, 1988); Charles Y. Glock, "The Churches and Social Change in Twentieth Century America," *Annals of the American Academy of Political and Social Science* 527 (1993):67–83.

29. The term "practicing" is used by some who believe homosexuality is sinful, capturing their belief that some people do have innate homosexual urges but that acting on these urges nevertheless goes against scripture.

30. Holmes, *Brief History*, 165.

31. Ibid., 157–58; Sumner, *Episcopal Church's History*, 3.

32. Holmes, *Brief History*, 167–68.

33. Ibid., 172.

34. See Donald S. Armentrout, *Episcopal Splinter Groups: A Study of Groups Which Have Left the Episcopal Church, 1873–1985* (Sewanee, TN: School of Theology, University of the South, 1985).

35. Guelzo, *For the Union*, 4.

36. John M. Krumm, *Why Choose the Episcopal Church?* (1957; Cincinnati: Forward Movement Publications, 1996).

37. Sumner, *Episcopal Church's History*, 154–55.

38. Ibid., 154–55.

39. A detailed history of General Convention actions concerning homosexuality may be found in the appendix of *To Set Our Hope on Christ: A Response to the Invitation of Windsor Report* P135.

40. Holmes, *Brief History*, 170–71.

41. Guelzo, *For the Union*; Roger Steer, *Church on Fire: The Story of Anglican Evangelicals* (London: Hodder & Stoughton, 1998): 347.

42. Sumner, *Episcopal Church's History*, 123.

43. "Evangelical Fellowship in the Anglican Communion," EFAC website (1999), http://www.episcopalian.org/efac/articles/efachst.html (accessed August 26, 2005).

44. Daly, "Church at Risk," 5.

45. Steer, *Church on Fire*, 359.

46. Ibid., 347.

47. Ibid., 363.

48. Ibid.

49. All of the organizations listed here are headed by bishops or priests, and most, though not all, influential leaders in this movement are ordained. The relatively low representation of lay leaders probably reflects the reality that in the Episcopal Church in general, and perhaps especially in its Anglo-Catholic and evangelical wings, it is easier to command respect and marshal resources as an ordained person.

50. Steer, *Church on Fire*, 365.

51. Jack H. Taylor, Jr., "Episcopalians United Is Operating Illegally," n.d., http://andromeda.rutgers.edu/~lcrew/eurrr_illegal.html (accessed August 5, 1998).

52. Episcopal Synod of America, "Episcopal Synod Rejects Court Decision," ESA website (1996), http://www.episcopalsynod.org (accessed July 31, 1998).

53. PECUSA is an older name for the national Episcopal Church, which dropped the use of the word "Protestant" in 1964. Because the national Episcopal Church's headquarters are in New York City, the church was only incorporated in the state of New York. Taylor, "Episcopalians United."

54. James Solheim, "Dispute over Use of Church's Name Moves toward Resolution," Episcopal News Service (1999), http://arc.episcopalchurch.org/ens/99-2285.html (accessed March 24, 2004).

55. Asad, "Anthropology of Islam," 16.

56. See Faye Ginsburg, *Contested Lives* (Berkeley: University of California Press, 1989).

57. The high visibility of a few liberal leaders who are outspoken on this issue may account for conservatives' tendency to describe the church as having been hijacked by liberal leadership. Interestingly, according to one account of conflicts within the Presbyterian church, the conservative evangelical movement in that denomination uses similar language, describing itself as "a popular rebellion from the pews against a tyrannical and elite denominational leadership and its supposedly 'secular humanist' . . . agenda," a rhetorical move which the (liberal) author of this account refers to as "pseudo-populism" (Daly, "Church at Risk," 4). However, such discourses should not be dismissed entirely as mere political rhetoric, for though some conservative Episcopal leaders may use such rhetoric strategically, many conservative laity with little involvement in the church's polity may believe their church to have been taken over by tyrannical liberal leaders.

58. For example, lay deputies elected by their home parishes (for annual diocesan conventions) or dioceses (for the national-level, triennial General Conventions) play a significant legislative role in church affairs.

59. David Helminiak, *What the Bible Really Says about Homosexuality* (1994; San Francisco: Alamo Square Press, 2000): 26–27.

60. Steer, *Church on Fire*, 362.

61. As in the broader social-political debate over homosexuality, much conservative Episcopal discourse is focused on male homosexuality, which seems to incite a greater reaction than lesbianism from most who oppose the tolerance of homosexuality.

62. Constance Sullivan-Blum, "'The Two Shall Become One Flesh': Why Same-Sex Marriage Threatens Evangelical Christians" (paper presented at the biennial meeting of the Society for the Anthropology of Religion, Providence, RI, April 2002).

63. Kit Kincade, "Who Is 'Defending Tradition'?: The Controversy within the Episcopal Church," *Louisville Courier-Journal*, October 12, 2003, http://www .courier-journal.com/cjextra/editorials/for-3-kincade1012–9299.html (accessed October 15, 2003).

64. Anderson, "A Place to Stand."

65. Asad, "Anthropology of Islam," 15.

66. Catherine Bell, "Performance," in *Critical Terms for Religious Studies*, ed. Mark C. Taylor, 205–24 (Chicago: University of Chicago Press, 1998), quotation at 206.

CHAPTER 2. TAKING AFRICA SERIOUSLY: THE GLOBALIZATION
OF CONSERVATIVE EPISCOPALIANS

1. Sumner, *Episcopal Church's History*, 163.

2. For a number of fascinating essays on American evangelicals' missions-inspired world consciousness, see Grant Wacker and Daniel H. Bays, eds., *The Foreign Missionary Enterprise at Home: Explorations in North American Cultural History* (Tuscaloosa: University of Alabama Press, 2003).

3. The term "Two-Thirds World" refers to the global South and is intended to remind the listener that two-thirds of the world's population live in areas those in the North habitually ignore. Episcopal conservatives' use of this term, along with "global South" terminology, tends to surprise academic readers who expect those terms to be limited to academics and progressive activists.

4. Michael F. Gallo, "The Continuing Anglicans: Credible Movement or Ecclesiastical Dead End?," *Touchstone* (Winter 1989): 29.

5. Steer, *Church on Fire*, 375.

6. Sanjeev Khagram, James Riker, and Kathryn Sikkink, "From Santiago to Seattle: Transnational Advocacy Groups Restructuring World Politics," in *Restructuring World Politics: Transnational Social Movements, Networks, and Norms*, ed. Sanjeev Khagram, James Riker, and Kathryn Sikkink 3–23 (Minneapolis: University of Minnesota Press, 2002), quotation at 19.

7. Deborah Martin and Byron Miller, "Space and Contentious Politics" in Khagram, Riker, and Sikkink, *Restructuring World Politics*, 148–49.

8. American Anglican Council, "Who We Are," AAC website (1996); no longer available online (accessed July 31, 1998).

9. Ibid.

10. Ekklesia Society, "Rationale."

11. John Wall, *A Dictionary for Episcopalians* (Boston: Cowley Publications, 2000), 71–72.

12. Michael Marshall, *Church at the Crossroads: Lambeth 1988* (San Francisco: Harper and Row, 1988), 16.

13. Ibid., 68.

14. Ibid., 95.

15. Ibid., 29.

16. Ibid., 29.

17. Ibid., 96.

18. Ibid., 114–15.

19. Ibid., 149, 255.

20. Lambeth 1998 was also a particularly large Conference because all suffragan bishops (assisting bishops who do not have full charge of a diocese) were invited, with the intent of maximizing the Conference's diversity.

21. Maurice Sinclair, "For the Love of Christ: Reaffirming Anglican Orthodoxy in a Time of Change" (1997), accessed in private archive.

22. Roland Robertson, *Globalization: Social Theory and Global Culture* (London: Sage Publishing, 1992).

23. David Harvey, *The Condition of Postmodernity* (Oxford: Basil Blackwell, 1989); Anthony Giddens, *The Consequences of Modernity* (Cambridge: Polity Press, 1990).

24. Michael Kearney, *Reconceptualizing the Peasantry: Anthropology in Global Perspective* (Boulder: Westview Press, 1996); Arjun Appadurai, *Modernity at Large: Cultural Dimensions of Globalization* (Minneapolis: University of Minnesota Press, 1996).

25. Tomlinson, *Globalization*, 4–7.

26. Hannerz , "Several Sites," 27–28.

27. Tsing, "Global Situation," 345.

28. Clifford Bob, "Political Process Theory and Transnational Movements: Dialectics of Protest among Nigeria's Ogoni Minority," *Social Problems* 49, no. 3 (2002): 399.

29. Ian T. Douglas, "Lambeth 1998 and the 'New Colonialism,'" *Witness* (May 1998): 9.

30. Simon Sarmiento, "Lambeth perspective: Two Kuala Lumpur Statements," Society of Archbishop Justus website (1998), http://justus.anglican.org/newsarchive/lambeth98/sjn16.html (accessed August 28, 2003).

31. Douglas, "Lambeth 1998," 11.

32. Steer, *Church on Fire*, 394.

33. Louie Crew, "The Kuala Lumpur Statement," Anglican Pages (1997), http://newark.rutgers.edu/~lcrew/kuala.html (accessed October 2, 2002).

34. Doug LeBlanc, "The Dallas Statement" (1997), http://members.core.com/~figueroa/dallas.htm (accessed October 3, 2002).

35. Stephen Noll, "The Handwriting on the Wall" (1997), accessed in private archive.

36. Anglican Life and Witness Conference, "Listening Group Reports from Day One" (1997), accessed in private archive.

37. LeBlanc, "Dallas Statement."

38. Ibid.

39. Ibid.

40. For example, the May 1999 edition's Letters pages included thank-you notes from a Singaporean and a Kenyan bishop.

41. William Atwood, "The Primates in Canterbury," *Mandate* (May/June 2002): 14.

42. Sidney Tarrow, *Power in Movement* (Cambridge: Cambridge University Press, 1998), 192.

43. Cunningham, "Ethnography of Transnational Social Activism," 589.

44. Ibid., 596.

45. Kyle Brazzel, "Thomas William Johnston Jr.," *Arkansas Democrat-Gazette*, February 17, 2002, sec. D: 5.

46. "First Promise Gains Strength," *United Voice*, Episcopalians United website (1998), http://www.episcopalian.org/EU/dispatches/promise.htm (accessed September 5, 2002).

47. Robert Stowe England, "First Promise Raises Global Stakes." *Encompass*, April 19, 1998, http://www.episcopalian.org/EU/dispatches/promise2.htm (accessed September 5, 2002).
The group's name is a reference to the Episcopal Church's rite for ordination to the priesthood, in which priests-to-be vow to be loyal to the "doctrine, discipline, and worship of Christ as this Church has received them," and then to "obey [their] bishop" (*Book of Common Prayer* [New York: Church Hymnal Corporation, 1979], 526). The founders of First Promise felt that where these two vows were in conflict, the first must take precedence.

48. "First Promise," *United Voice*.

49. Brazzel, "Thomas William Johnston Jr.," 5.

50. England, "First Promise."

51. Ibid.

52. Brazzel, "Thomas William Johnston Jr.," 5.

53. David Virtue, "East African Bishop Launches Broadside at Treatment by George Carey," *Virtuosity Digest*, January 20, 2003.

54. Quoted in Brazzel, "Thomas William Johnston Jr.," 1.

55. England, "First Promise."

56. Brazzel, "Thomas William Johnston Jr.," 5.

57. England, "First Promise."

58. Ibid.

CHAPTER 3. "WHITE HANDS UP!" LAMBETH 1998 AND THE
GLOBAL POLITICS OF HOMOSEXUALITY

1. Victoria Combe, "Bishops Sway to Beat of Drums in Cathedral," *Daily Telegraph* (UK), July 20, 1998, 7.

2. Peter Moore, "Lambeth '98," *Anglicans for Renewal* 75 (1998).

3. Andrew Brown, "How Fear of Islam Forced the Church to Attack Gays," *Daily Express* (UK), August 7, 1998.

4. Clare Garner, "How I Felt the Wrath of a Bishop . . . as the Church Votes for Gay Ban," *Independent* (UK), August 6, 1998.

5. James Solheim, *Diversity or Disunity? Reflections on Lambeth 1998* (New York: Church Publishing Incorporated, 1999), 63–66.

6. Robert Stowe England, "Lambeth's Plenary Debate on Sexuality" (1998), 5, accessed in private archive.

7. Doug LeBlanc, "Americans Decry Spong's Remarks on Africans," *United Voice*, July 17, 1998, http://www.episcopalian.org/eu/uv (accessed November 2, 2002); Andrew Carey, "African Christians? They're Just a Step up from Witchcraft," *Church of England Newspaper*, July 10, 1998.

8. David Skidmore, "Bishop Spong Apologises to Africans," *Lambeth Daily*, July 28, 1998: 1.

9. "Rants, Raves, and Reflections: What They're Saying about the 1998 Lambeth Conference," *Christian Challenge*, November 1998, 6–9.

10. Moore, "Lambeth '98."

11. Todd Wetzel, "Anglicanism's Tent of Meeting," *United Voice*, July 29, 1998, http://www.episcopalian.org/eu/uv (accessed November 15, 2002).

12. Doug LeBlanc, "Kolini Underwhelmed by Spong's Regrets," *United Voice*, July 31, 1998; http://www.episcopalian.org/eu/uv (accessed August 5, 1998).

13. Larry Stammer, "Anglican Council Draws Cassocks of Many Colors," *Los Angeles Times*, August 3, 1998.

14. Doug LeBlanc, "It's Time to Hear from the South," *United Voice*, July 19, 1998; http://www.episcopalian.org/eu/uv (accessed November 19, 2002).

15. The majority of the resolutions that emerged from this committee work, as is usual at Lambeth, were so uncontroversial that they were passed without debate.

16. Alistair Macdonald-Radcliff, "After Lambeth, It's Time for Change: An Interview with Lamin Sanneh," *Church of England Newspaper*, August 7, 1998, 11.

17. Stephen Noll, in his account of Lambeth 1998, complained, "The predominance of non-white bishops here is striking. Sadly, this predominance is not matched in terms of the Conference leadership, which is largely white and largely liberal theologically." He noted the control of the conference agenda by the Anglican Consultative Council (ACC), and wrote, "In the eyes of many, the ACC (note not AAC!) has been inordinately influenced by the West and the Episcopal Church USA in particular." (Noll, "Diary from the First Week of the Lambeth Conference of Anglican Bishops, July 18–25, 1998," http://www.americananglican.org/Issues/Issues.cfm?ID=89&c=10 (accessed April 6, 2004).

18. As Buchanan's position might suggest, the South African church is an exception to the widespread opposition to homosexuality among African Anglicans.

19. Victoria Combe, "Repent on Gay Sex, Say Angry Africans," *Daily Telegraph* (UK), July 24, 1998, 7.

20. Noll, "Diary."

21. Solheim, *Diversity or Disunity*, 56; Doug LeBlanc, "Homosexuals Speak in a New Venue," *United Voice*, July 31, 1998, http://www.episcopalian.org/eu/uv (accessed August 5, 1998).

22. Invitation to meeting on July 29 (1998), accessed in private archive.

23. "An Evening to Understand More about Homosexuality and the Reality of Change" (1998), accessed in private archive.

24. "Observations on the Politics of Passing a Sexuality Resolution" (1998), accessed in private archive.

25. For fuller accounts of the debate, see England, "Lambeth's Plenary Debate"; Solheim, *Diversity or Disunity*; Noll, "Diary"; and Kim Byham, "A Sad Diary" (August 5, 1998), http://newark.rutgers.edu/~lcrew/kim06.html (accessed October 16, 2003).

26. William Swing, "Bishop Swing's Response," in *Petition to the Primates' Meeting and the Primates of the Anglican Communion for Emergency Intervention in the Province of the Episcopal Church of the United States of America*, Association of Anglican Congregations on Mission (AACOM) (1999), appendix 64, vol. 1 (hereafter cited as *AACOM Petition*); accessed in private archive.

27. Two resolutions (cited in section [g] of this resolution) that would have affirmed the Kuala Lumpur Statement were on the table for discussion the next day, but when they came up for debate, the bishops voted to move on to other business—in effect a decision that Lambeth 1998 had already said enough on the issue of human sexuality. Simon Sarmiento, "Lambeth News," Society of Archbishop Justus website (1998), http://justus.anglican.org/news/sjn17.html (accessed August 12, 1998).

28. "Lambeth Conference 1998: Resolution 1.10 Human Sexuality," Anglican Communion Official Website, http://www.anglicancommunion.org/windsor2004/appendix/p3.6.cfm (accessed July 23, 2006).

29. England, "Lambeth's Plenary Debate."

30. I here temporarily shift from "Northern" to "Western," since "Western" is still commonly used as a designation for Euro-American culture.

31. Tomlinson, *Globalization*, 81; G. Ritzer, *The McDonaldization of Society* (Newbury Park, CA: Pine Forge Press, 1993); Walter LaFeber, *Michael Jordan and the New Global Capitalism* (New York: W. W. Norton Co., 1999).

32. Akhil Gupta and James Ferguson, "Beyond 'Culture': Space, Identity, and the Politics of Difference," in *Culture, Power, Place: Explorations in Critical Anthropology*, ed. Akhil Gupta and James Ferguson, 33–51 (Durham, NC: Duke University Press, 1997).

33. Ibid., 38.

34. Inda and Renato Rosaldo, "Introduction"; Giddens, *Consequences*.

35. Steve Brouwer, Paul Gifford, and Susan D. Rose, *Exporting the American Gospel: Global Christian Fundamentalism* (New York: Routledge, 1996).

36. Joel Robbins, "The Globalization of Pentecostal and Charismatic Christianity," *Annual Review of Anthropology* 33 (2004): 117–43.no

37. Richard Kew, "What's in store after Lambeth?," *Encompass* 2, no. 3 (1998).

38. "Police Warn Martyrs Day Criminals," *New Vision*, June 3, 2002.

39. Ward, "Same-Sex Relations."

40. Ibid.

41. John Kalini, *Namugongo: From Shame to Glory* (Kampala, Uganda: Education Department, Namirembe Diocese, n.d.); Francis Marion, *New African Saints: The Twenty-two Martyrs of Uganda* (Nairobi: St. Paul Publications—Africa, 1985).

42. Ward, "Same-Sex Relations."

43. Elizabeth Povinelli and George Chauncey, "Thinking Sexuality Transnationally," *GLQ: A Journal of Gay and Lesbian Studies* 5, no. 3 (1999): 439–40.

44. Rudolf Gaudio, "Imagined Hegemonies: Gay Imperialism and the Need for Critically Queer Ethnography" (paper presented at the annual meeting for the American Ethnological Society, Providence, RI, April 24–26, 2003).

45. Joseph Massad, "Re-Orienting Desire: The Gay International and the Arab World," *Public Culture* 14, no. 2 (2002): 361.

46. Ibid., 374.

47. Scott Long, A. Widney Brown, and Gail Cooper, *More than a Name: State-Sponsored Homophobia and Its Consequences in Southern Africa* (New York: Human Rights Watch/International Gay and Lesbian Human Rights Commission, 2003), 12–14.

48. Ibid., 24.

49. Ibid., 50–51.

50. Stephen O. Murray and Will Roscoe, eds., *Boy-Wives and Female Husbands: Studies in African Homosexualities* (New York: Palgrave Macmillan, 2001); John Mburu, "Awakenings: Dreams and Delusions of an Incipient Lesbian and Gay movement in Kenya," in *Different Rainbows*, ed. Peter Drucker (London: Gay Men's Press, 2000); Martin Duberman, Martha Vicinus, and George Chauncey, Jr., *Hidden from History* (New York: Meridian, 1990); Mark Gevisser and Edwin Cameron, eds., *Defiant Desire: Gay and Lesbian Lives in South Africa* (Cape Town: Ravan Press, 1995).

51. Ward, "Same-Sex Relations."

52. Titus Kakengo, "Poverty Made Bishop Ssenyonjo Deviate," *New Vision*, n.d., 2001, accessed in private archive. Undoubtedly the AIDS epidemic, which has hit Uganda hard, is part of the context for the adoption of this epidemiological language. However, gays are rarely blamed for the spread of AIDS in Uganda,

since AIDS afflicts such a broad spectrum of the populace (including many children); the American stigma on AIDS as a "gay disease" makes little sense in this context.

53. Massad, "Re-Orienting Desire," 382.

54. "Museveni U-turn on Gays?," *Q Online* (1999), http://www.q.co.za/news/1999/9911/991116-museveni.htm (accessed January 14, 2004).

55. You-Leng Lim, "Homosexuality: How the Economics and Politics of Singapore Have Shaped the Anglican Diocese and Its Role in the Province of South East Asia" (1998), http://newark.rutgers.edu/~lcrew/lenglim2.html (accessed April 6, 2004).

56. Combe, "Repent."

57. "Notice Paper for Plenary Session on Wednesday, 5 August, Lambeth Conference 1998," accessed in private archive.

58. Ward, "Same-Sex Relations."

59. Linda Lilian, "Gays, Just Come Out, Fame Awaits You!," *Monitor* (Kampala), July 29, 1998, 20; "I'm gay! And it's my right to be!," letter to the editor, *New Vision* (Kampala), August 6, 1998, 9; "Good Stand," editorial column, *New Vision* (Kampala), August 8, 1998, 10.

60. Long, Brown, and Cooper, *More than a Name*, 41.

61. Ruth Gledhill, "African Bishops Outraged at Sexual Liberalism," *Times* (UK), July 23, 1998.

62. The influence of missionaries—an explanation offered by some Northern liberals trying to make sense of African Christian conservatism—is often overstated. Ward notes that many Northern liberals have attributed African opposition to homosexuality to the work of the evangelically oriented Church Missionary Society. Ward argues that although this explanation may have some limited value, it both oversimplifies the character and work of the CMS and underestimates the significance of other historical and cultural factors that have shaped the various African churches. Ward, "Same-Sex Relations."

63. I did not seek to air or press my own views on homosexuality during the course of my fieldwork, in either Uganda or the United States. When my consultants asked my views, I shared them. I was interested to find that, among Ugandans, my pro–gay rights position was received with curiosity rather than with hostility. However, I was also interested to note how rarely I was asked about my views. Most Ugandans seemed to assume that my husband and I were the kind of American Christians they were used to seeing in Uganda: renewal-oriented in worship and relatively conservative in moral and theological convictions.

64. Ward, "Same-Sex Relations."

65. Ibid.

66. Robert Lancaster, "On Homosexualities in Latin America (and Other Places)," *American Ethnologist* 24, no. 1 (1997): 193–202.

67. See chapter 7. One interesting side story here is that some liberals recurrently bring up the idea that Africans should accept homosexuality because the Northern churches have tolerated African polygamy. However, this parallel is not convincing to African Anglicans. Most African priests and bishops see polygamy as an unfortunate cultural feature they must respond to pastorally. As one bishop told me, "In the past, we have had weaknesses—say, polygamy—in the South. But

... nobody has ever [said] ... 'Let's go to the North and convince them that they should have more than one wife.' We know it is a weakness—that is not something you would want everybody to get in." Thus African church leaders' views toward polygamy are not analogous to Northern liberals' views toward homosexuality.

68. Ed Stannard, "Sexuality, Debt Loom as Concerns of World Bishops," *Episcopal Life*, November 1997, http://gc2003.episcopalchurch.org/episcopal-life/Content2.html (accessed April 5, 2004); Doug LeBlanc, "Provinces Ready to Confront U.S. Bishops," *United Voice*, n.d., 1997, accessed in private archive.

69. Douglas, "Lambeth 1998,": 11.

70. Todd Wetzel, "There Is No Deadlock," *United Voice*, July 29, 1998, http://www.episcopalian.org/eu/uv (accessed July 31, 1998).

71. Noll, "Diary"; Diane Knippers, "Invitation" (1998), accessed in private archive.

72. Knippers, "Invitation."

73. Robert Miclean, "Restoration and Repentance at Lambeth" (1998), accessed in private archive.

74. Julie Wortman, "Sex, Debt, and God's New Thing," *Witness*, October 1998, 4–26.

75. Ian T. Douglas, "Radical Mutuality Still out of Reach," *Witness*, November 1998, 25. In fact, some African bishops spoke to this explicitly, stating that because homosexuality had become such a prominent issues associated with Lambeth and was hence receiving a great deal of press coverage in their home contexts, they needed a strongly conservative resolution on sexuality to show their constituents and rivals at home that Anglicans were standing firm for orthodoxy.

76. In contrast, some sources, such as English bishop Peter Selby's book *Grace and Mortgage* (1997), argue that the Bible says a great deal about debt and lending practices—quite possibly more than it says about sexual ethics. The reason for greater attention to sexual than to monetary ethics in today's church must, perhaps, be sought elsewhere than in relative degrees of scriptural attention.

CHAPTER 4. FROM AFRICAN/ASIAN JUGGERNAUT TO GLOBAL ORTHODOXY MAJORITY

1. While the liberalism of a few other provinces, such as Canada, New Zealand, and sometimes England, has also been addressed by this transnational movement at times, the focus has consistently been on the United States—in part because most of the movement's Northern members are American and in part because of the United States's general global dominance.

2. Geoffrey Chapman, "Presentation to the Kampala Meeting held by AACOM" (1999), accessed in private archive.

3. Tarrow, *Power in Movement*, 181.

4. Beyer, *Religion and Globalization*, 26.

5. Castells, *Power of Identity*, 114.

6. Doug LeBlanc, "Africans Strengthen Sexuality Resolution," *United Voice*, August 6, 1998, http://www.episcopalian.org/eu/lambeth/chastity.asp (accessed August 12, 1998).

7. Stephen Noll, "Lambeth Speaks Plainly," in *Mixed Blessings: Why Same-Sex Blessings Will Divide the Church* (American Anglican Council, 2000), 30.

8. Douglas, "Lambeth 1998," 11.

9. David Virtue, "South African Bishops out of Step with the Rest of Africa" (August 7, 1998), http://www.prayerbook.ca/cann/1998/pbslam30.htm (accessed April 7, 2004).

10. Elaine Storkey, "Church Turns Its Back on Western Agenda," *Independent* (UK), August 8, 1998, 7.

11. "Review and Outlook: Bruising Bishops," *Wall Street Journal,* August 14, 1998.

12. Jenkins, *Next Christendom,* 224.

13. "Welcome page," Anglican Communion website, http://www.anglican communion.org/welcome.html (accessed September 14, 2000). The photo's caption identified only Carey, but its file name included the word "rwanda."

14. Or, as Uganda's president Yoweri Museveni titled his 2000 book, "What Is Africa's Problem?"

15. Additional resolutions did address other world "trouble spots," including Northern Ireland, Israel and Palestine, and South Asia, Iran, Iraq, Libya, and the Koreas.

16. Jenkins, *Next Christendom,* 203.

17. David Skidmore, "Lambeth Struggles over Homosexuality in Emotional Plenary Session," Anglican Communion News Service LC098 (accessed August 7, 1998).

18. David Skidmore, "Advocates of Homosexuals Dismayed but not Deterred by Sexuality Resolution," Anglican Communion News Service LC101 (accessed August 7, 1998).

19. It is not known how each bishop voted at Lambeth, because this was not a roll-call vote but a show of hands, and press and activists were not allowed in the plenary hall.

20. Jean Torkelson, "Bishop Votes with Church on Gay Rights," *Rocky Mountain News,* August 12, 1998, http://insidedenver.com/news/0812gay5.html (accessed August 12, 1998).

21. Gary Gloster, "Bishop Gloster on the Voting at Lambeth" (1998), http://newark.rutgers.edu/~lcrew/lambeth87.html (accessed February 3, 2003).

22. Richard F. Grein and Mark S. Sisk, "Pastoral Letter, Aug. 31, 1998," in *AACOM Petition,* appendix, vol. 1, 79. Many of my citations in the following pages come from this AACOM collection; however, most of these documents are also available on Louie Crew's comprehensive and useful Anglican webpages (andromeda.rutgers.edu/~lcrew/rel.html).

23. Catherine Roskam, "A Message in the Wake of the Recent Lambeth Conference" (August 18, 1998), http://andromeda.rutgers.edu/~lcrew/roskam01.html (accessed April 7, 2004).

24. Swing, "Response."

25. Frank Griswold, "Presiding Bishop Responds to Newspaper Articles," Anglican Communion News Service 1759 (August 17, 1998).

26. Diane Knippers, "Sex and the Anglicans," *Weekly Standard,* September 7, 1998.

27. Hays Rockwell, "Reflections on Lambeth," in *AACOM Petition*, appendix, vol. 1, 121–24.

28. Swing, "Response."

29. Frederick Borsch, "A Message from the Bishop of Los Angeles," in *AACOM Petition*, appendix, vol. 1, 52–53; Swing, "Response."

30. Swing, "Response."

31. Although this particular idea may have some explanatory value in parts of Africa, such as Nigeria, it does not apply equally throughout the continent. Competition with politicized Islam was not a significant concern for the Church of Uganda, as of 2002.

32. "Scottish Bishop Condemns Anti-gay Vote," *Scotsman* (UK), August 6, 1998, http://www.yahoo.co.uk/headlines/980806/scotsman/scotsman.902408462 .html (accessed August 8, 1998).

33. Swing, "Response."

34. Michael Hopkins, "Lambeth Conference Sexuality Resolution Has No Credibility" (1998), http://www.rci.rutgers.edu/~lcrew/lambeth98/lambeth37 .html (accessed April 7, 2004).

35. James Thrall, "An International Community? The Anglican Communion and the 1998 Lambeth Conference" (Duke University Divinity School, 2000), 20.

36. "Rants, Raves," *Christian Challenge*.

37. Martin Smith, "Martin Smith SSJE on Lambeth," in *AACOM Petition*, appendix, vol. 1, 73–75.

38. Ibid.

39. Borsch, "Message."

40. Charles Moore, "Gay Rights Train Derailed at Lambeth Conference" (1998), http://synod.321media.com/321/articles/read_it (accessed October 3, 2002).

41. LeBlanc, "Africans Strengthen."

42. "Summing up the Lambeth Conference," *Church Times* (UK), August 14, 1998.

43. James Stanton, "Lambeth 98: Scripture Rules," *Encompass* 2, no. 2 (August 1998): 1.

44. Kew, "What's in Store."

45. Knippers, "Sex and the Anglicans."

46. Auburn F. Traycik and David Virtue, "1998: A New Day for Anglicanism," *Christian Challenge*, January–February 1999, 8.

47. Auburn F. Traycik, "Sex Resolution Didn't Need Africans, Bishop Says," *Christian Challenge*, January–February 1999: 16–17.

48. Noll, "Lambeth Speaks," 35.

49. Ibid., 34–35.

50. Many of the 45 abstentions apparently represented people who could not stomach voting for the resolution, but hesitated to vote against it. For example, Frank Griswold, presiding bishop of ECUSA, abstained from this vote, but his personal belief that gay and lesbian persons should be affirmed by the church is well known. Close to 100 of the bishops present at the conference are not accounted for in the vote totals; some of those absentees may also have been, in effect, abstaining from this controversial vote.

51. Solheim, *Diversity or Disunity?* 35.

52. For example, two major commissions, the Eames Commission and the Inter-Anglican Theological and Doctrinal Commission, had examined issues of authority, unity, identity, and relationship within the Anglican Communion since Lambeth 1988 (Solheim, *Diversity or Disunity?*).

53. The position of the Archbishop of Canterbury as head of the church in England goes back to well before the Reformation, but the other three Instruments of Unity have been added through the Anglican Communion's history in response to the Communion's growth in size and complexity. The Lambeth Conferences began in the mid-nineteenth century, spurred by the need to keep in touch and maintain unity across a church now spread throughout the growing British empire. The Anglican Consultative Council was initiated in 1971 "as a representative body of the churches of the Anglican Communion made up [of] equal numbers of bishops, priests, and lay people" (Douglas, "Lambeth 1998," 27). This body would meet regularly in order to be in dialogue and deal effectively with the diversity of the postcolonial Communion. The Primates' Meetings were initiated in 1979 by the conservative-leaning presiding bishop of ECUSA, John Allin, in order to balance the progressive leanings of the ACC (ibid.).

54. Solheim, *Diversity or Disunity?*, 261.

55. Douglas, "Radical Mutuality," 26–27.

56. Alistair Macdonald-Radcliff, "The Primates Follow Up: From Lambeth to Portugal to Kanuga," in *Mixed Blessings*, 38–39. Macdonald-Radcliff also referred to the Primates' Meetings as one of the Communion's "instruments of authority," a telling modification of the more common "instruments of unity."

57. Quoted in Stammer, "Anglican Council."

58. Thrall, "International Community?," 21.

59. There are, of course, Anglican and Episcopal leaders and commentators who articulate and pursue more radical commitments to diversity and its implications. Thrall's criticisms (and Douglas's, to be quoted below) show that some of the Episcopal Church's left-leaning scholars and observers, for instance, find this sort of liberal/moderate globalism superficial and almost as distasteful as any conservative alternative.

60. Ian T. Douglas, "The Exigency of Times and Occasions," in *Beyond Colonial Anglicanism*, ed. Ian Douglas and Kwok Pui-Lan (New York: Church Publishing Incorporated, 2003), 25–46.

61. Grein and Sisk, "Pastoral Letter."

62. Borsch, "Message."

63. Swing, "Response." In the original, the first two sentences of this letter are in emphatic boldface.

64. Fred Ellis and Michael Hopkins, "We're Not Going Back," in *AACOM Petition*, appendix, vol. 1, 42.

65. David Virtue, "Lambeth Outtakes: From My Ear to Yours," *Virtuosity Digest*, August 3, 1998.

66. LeBlanc, "It's Time to Hear."

67. Moore, "Gay Rights."

68. Coleman, "Faith Movement," 6.

69. Colin Blakely, "Editorial," *Church of England Newspaper,* no. 5423, August 7, 1998, 7.

70. Quoted in Solheim, *Diversity or Disunity?*, 229. Doubtless many Southern bishops do feel this way, but the fact that Mattingly and other Northern writers have chosen to use Southern voices to make their arguments is nonetheless significant. These writers realize the rhetorical power of attributing arguments for strict limits on cultural difference to Southern bishops, who belong to cultures which Northerners perceive as "other" and thus as the primary beneficiaries of cultural tolerance. In contrast, Northern conservatives making the same argument could easily be written off as repeating the familiar conservative antidiversity trope.

71. "Listening Group Reports from Day One," Anglican Life and Witness Conference, Dallas, 1997, accessed in private archive.

72. Maurice Sinclair, "Message from Malaysia" (1997), http://trushare.com/25JUN97/JN97SINC.htm (accessed October 3, 2002).

73. Griswold, "Presiding Bishop Responds."

74. Thrall, "International Community?," 27.

75. Ibid., 19.

76. Ibid.

77. "Rants, Raves," *Christian Challenge.*

78. Kew, "What's in Store."

79. Quoted in David Virtue, "Bishops Vote Overwhelmingly for Biblical Standards on Sexuality" (Aug. 5, 1998), http://synod.321media.com/321/articles/read_it (accessed August 5, 1998).

80. Thrall, "International Community?," 18.

81. AACOM Petition, 1999.

CHAPTER 5. "AT HOME IN KIGALI": TRANSNATIONAL RELATIONSHIPS AND DOMESTIC DISSENT

1. The Network of Anglican Communion Dioceses and Parishes, launched early in 2004 and described below, has arguably usurped both these distinctions now.

2. "Press Release," First Promise, January 29, 2000, http://www.firstpromise.org/SPPress1.htm (accessed April 29, 2003).

3. Anglican Mission in America (AMiA), "Anglican Mission in America (AMiA): A Story of Leadership, Faith and Mission" (2001), accessed in private archive.

4. Anglican Mission in America (AMiA), "Six Month Report" (2001), personal collection.

5. David Virtue, "GC2000: the Bonfire of the Sexualities—Part 2" (2000), http://listserv.episcopalian.org/scripts/wa.exe?A2=ind0009b&L=virtuosity&D=1&H=1&O=D&F=&S=&P=295 (accessed April 9, 2004).

6. AMiA, "Anglican Mission."

7. Anglican Mission in America (AMiA), "Ten Month Report" (2001), personal collection.

8. Jan Nunley, "Anglican Mission in America waiting for meeting of Anglican primates in March," Episcopal News Service 2001–16 (January 2001), http://www.wfn.org/2001/01/msg00146.html (accessed April 9, 2004).

9. Kampala Meeting, "A Letter to the Participants and Invited Observers Attending the Group of Primates Meeting Held in Kampala from 16th to 18th November 1999" (1999), http://www.episcopalian.org/cclec/letter-kampala_nov 1999.htm (accessed April 9, 2004).

10. Several primates did respond to the AACOM petition by writing to Episcopal presiding bishop Frank Griswold, who in turn invited them to "come and see" the situation in the Episcopal Church for themselves. Two primates and three bishops accepted this invitation to evaluate ECUSA. Their report on their visit reveals that, having seen the Episcopal Church for themselves, the bishops agreed with conservative Episcopalians that matters were seriously awry, but apparently also found the situation less dire than they had been led to expect and expressed a preference for internal, rather than international, solutions. (Anglican Communion News Service, "An Open Letter from Primates of the Anglican Communion to the Most Reverend Frank Griswold, Presiding Bishop of ECUSA," ACNS 1816 (March 18, 1999); "Come and See" Report (1999), http://www.episcopalian.org/cclec/report-griswold-dec99.htm (accessed April 29, 2003).

11. Doug LeBlanc, "Conservatives Dream of a Global Shift" (1999), http://www.episcopalian.org/eu/uv<langle> (accessed October 2, 2000).

12. Two retired American bishops and a retired South American bishop also assisted in the consecrations, along with Rwandan bishop John Rucyahana; there is a long history of active participation by retired bishops in oppositional politics in the Episcopal Church.

13. David Virtue, "Exclusive Interview with The Rt. Rev. John H. Rodgers" (2000), http://www.firstpromise.org/Consecration/virtuerogers.htm (accessed September 30, 2000).

14. In order to strengthen apostolic succession it is traditional in Anglicanism for at least three bishops to participate in the consecration of a new bishop.

15. "'Irregular Action' among Anglicans," *Christian Century*, February 23, 2000, http://www.findarticles.com/cf_dls/m1058/6_117/60026671/p1/article.jhtml (accessed April 9, 2004).

16. Kathryn McCormick and James Solheim, "Singapore Consecration Provokes Strong Response throughout the Church," Episcopal News Service 2000–030 (May 3, 2000), ecusa.anglican.org/ens/2000–030.html (accessed April 29, 2003).

17. Robert Duncan, "Bishop of Pittsburgh Responds to the Consecration of Bishops Rodgers," Anglican Communion News Service 2025 (February 11, 2000), http://www.anglicancommunion.org/acns/acnsarchive/acns2025/acns20 25.html (accessed April 29, 2003).

18. Auburn F. Traycik, "Dropping Out, Dropping In," *Christian Challenge*, November 2000.

19. William Atwood, "The Ekklesia Society" (January 7, 2000), accessed in private archive.

20. Harry Goodhew, "Statement by Archbishop Goodhew" (February 11, 2000), accessed in private archive.

21. Moses Tay and Emmanuel Kolini, "A Letter from Anglican Archbishops Tay and Kolini to the Archbishop of Canterbury," *United Voice*, May 2000.

22. David Virtue and Auburn F. Traycik, "The Primates' Oporto Communique: Warning, or Wimp-Out?" (March 28, 2000), http://listserv.episcopalian.org/scripts/wa.exe?A2=ind0003d&L=virtuosity&D=1&H=1&O=D&F=&S=&P=327 (accessed April 9, 2004).

23. Daly, "Church at Risk," 4.

24. Chapman, "Presentation."

25. George Carey, "Letter to Archbishops Kolini and Yong" (June 19, 2001), http://trushare.com/75AUG01/AU01CARY.htm (accessed April 9, 2004).

26. Cunningham, "Ethnography of Transnational Social Activism," 596.

27. David Virtue and Auburn F. Traycik, "Stage Set for Creation of Separate Orthodox Province in Anglican Communion" (February 11, 2000), http://listserv.episcopalian.org/scripts/wa.exe?A2=ind9902&L=virtuosity&D=1&H=1&O=D&F=&S=&P=1243 (accessed April 9, 2004).

28. Virtue, "Exclusive Interview."

29. The reevaluation of ECUSA's place in the Anglican Communion undertaken by the primates and Archbishop of Canterbury Rowan Williams following Gene Robinson's consecration led some American conservatives again to place hope in official channels—in particular, in the possibility that the Communion would recognize the Anglican Communion Network, described later in this chapter, as a legitimate Anglican province separate from ECUSA. By mid-2006, however, this had not yet occurred, and many conservatives appeared to be growing impatient once again with the slow pace of Anglican Communion procedures.

30. AMiA, "Ten Month Report."

31. Michael Massing, "Bishop Lee's Choice," *New York Times Magazine*, January 4, 2004, 39.

32. Gustav Niebuhr, "Episcopal Dissidents Find African Inspiration," *New Vision* (Kampala, Uganda), April 22, 2001, 34.

33. Ann Rodgers-Melnick, "Church Links to African Bishop," *Pittsburgh Post-Gazette*, September 27, 1998, http://www.post-gazette.com/regionstate/19980927epis6.asp (accessed April 9, 2004).

34. Ibid.

35. Peggy Levitt, "Redefining the Boundaries of Belonging: The Institutional Character of Transnational Religious Life," *Sociology of Religion* 65, no. 1 (2004): 10.

36. Nashotah House, located in Wisconsin, is Anglo-Catholic in its orientation and much smaller than the evangelical-charismatic Trinity Episcopal School for Ministry.

37. The extent to which conservatives in the Episcopal Church have been excluded by others in the church, or have isolated themselves, is difficult to determine without more focused study. In defense of those who turn away such candidates, one Episcopal priest pointed out to me that evangelical candidates seeking ordination often do not care deeply about the Episcopal Church and the Anglican tradition, per se; he argued that it makes little sense for the Episcopal Church to

invest in training and ordaining people who have, in turn, minimal investment in the Episcopal Church.

38. David Virtue, "Kelshaw Breaks New Ground in Louisiana Ordinations," *Christian Challenge* 38, no. 3 (1999).

39. Alistair Macdonald-Radcliff, who serves as international liaison for the conservative American Anglican Council, was also ordained a priest "on behalf of the Bishop Ssekkadde of Namirembe" (Diocese of Pittsburgh, "June Calendar" [2001]), http://www.pgh.anglican.org/html/calendar/cal_2001/cal_mo_jun_01 .html (accessed August 30, 2002).

40. FIF-NA has been sympathetic to AMiA and the AAC, but has been hesitant to throw in its lot with more evangelically oriented dissident bodies. In 2004 it joined the new dissident Network, but maintains its own distinctive identity as a constituent subgroup. The Anglo-Catholic and evangelical constituencies share negative perceptions of ECUSA, but their concerns are significantly different. The issue of the ordination of women, for example, has often been a major stumbling block in relations.

41. David Virtue, "Visitation in Response to US Pastoral Emergency say Primates" (2000), http://www.concordtx.org/wrldnews/episc2.htm (accessed December 12, 2002).

42. Gustav Niebuhr, "Bishops' Visit Shows Rift Over Episcopal Leadership," *New York Times*, November 25, 2000, A8; Chris Herlinger, "Priests Continue to Challenge U.S. Episcopal Authority," *Christianity Today*, December 14, 2000, http://www.christianitytoday.com/ct/2000/150/44.0.html (accessed August 27, 2002).

43. David Virtue, "Bennison Thwarted Again," *Virtuosity Digest*, January 7, 2003.

44. Ibid.

45. Leanne Larmondin, "New Westminster Synod and Bishop Approve Same-Sex Blessings," Anglican Communion News Service 3029 (June 18, 2002).

46. Anglican Church in New Westminster (ACiNW), "Anglican Diocese of Yukon Supports Bishop" (2003), http://www.acinw.org/articles/AnglicanDio ceseofYukonSupportsBishop.html (accessed February 20, 2004).

47. Anglican Church in New Westminster (ACiNW), "ACiNW Responds to Episcopal Visitor Announcement" (2003), http://www.acinw.org/articles/ RespondstoEpiscopalVisitorAnnouncement.html (accessed February 20, 2004).

48. Anglican Church in New Westminster (ACiNW), "Fourteen Primates Say They Will 'Resolutely Address' New Westminster Blessing" (2003), http:// www.acinw.org/articles/NewWestminsterBlessing.html (accessed February 20, 2004).

49. Anglican Church in New Westminster (ACiNW), "Canadian Churches Offered Temporary Adequate Episcopal Oversight" (2003), http://209.35.87.15/ amia/events_sub.cfm?id=17 (accessed February 20, 2004).

50. The dioceses of Albany, Central Florida, Fort Worth, Pittsburgh, Quincy, Rio Grande, San Joaquin, South Carolina, Springfield, and Dallas. "Membership Directory," 2005, Network of Anglican Communion Dioceses and Parishes,

http://anglicancommunionnetwork.org/membership/parishes.cfm (accessed April 12, 2005).

51. American Anglican Council (AAC), "What Is the Network?" (2004), http://www.americananglican.org/News/News.cfm?ID=934&c=21 (accessed February 2, 2004).

52. Ibid.

53. American Anglican Council (AAC), "Statement by the American Anglican Council on Oversight of New Georgia Congregations by the Diocese of Bolivia" (January 13, 2004), http://www.americananglican.org/News/News.cfm?ID=937&c=2 (accessed February 2, 2004).

54. AAC, "What Is the Network?"

55. Diane Knippers, "What Do Conservative Episcopalians Really Want?" (2004), http://www.beliefnet.com/story/138/story_13869.html (accessed February 20, 2004).

56. Pat McCaughan, Melodie Woerman, Jim DeLa, and Nicole Seiferth, "From Columbus: Convention Responds to Windsor Report's Call for Moratorium," Episcopal News Service, June 21, 2006.

57. Bruce Mason, "Fourteen Anglican Primates Issue Strong Statement of Support for Newly Launched Network of Anglican Communion Dioceses and Parishes," AAC News, February 7, 2004, http://www.americananglican.org/News/News.cfm?ID=968&c=21 (accessed February 20, 2004).

58. Found at http://www.americananglican.org/Team/TeamList.cfm?c=46 (accessed February 20, 2004).

59. Knippers, "What Do Conservative Episcopalians."

60. Tomlinson, Globalization, 9.

61. Ibid., 136; Nestor Garcia Canclini, "Cultural Reconversion," in On Edge: The Crisis of Contemporary Latin American Culture, ed. G. Yudice et al, 29–44 (Minneapolis: University of Minnesota Press, 1995).

62. Tsing, "Global Situation"; Roland Robertson, "Religion and the Global Field," Social Compass 41, no. 1 (1994): 129.

63. St. Timothy's Episcopal Church, AMiA, "Letter to congregation explaining decision to join AMiA" (2000), accessed in private archive.

64. "Anglican Mission in America Gaining Support," Living Church 221, no. 13 (2003): 6.

65. The travelers devoted a good deal of energy in both learning about and teaching about the 1994 Rwandan genocide, probably the biggest stumbling block for Americans trying to relate to Rwanda. In teaching the congregation, the travelers struggled not to view Rwanda as the "other," even as they strove to convey the horror of the genocide. Edward told one audience, "I didn't sign up to be born a white male in North America. That's what God dealt me. If I'd been born a Hutu in Rwanda, what would I have done?" The travelers also presented a hopeful picture; Paul observed that being in Rwanda gave them a chance to "see the mercy and grace of God in the process of healing a nation." Thus the issue of the genocide was handled by trying to explain it historically, and by assimilating it to a vision of Africa as suffering, but always faithful and joyful.

CHAPTER 6. "WHO WANTS TO BE IN THE UGANDAN COMMUNION?"
PERCEPTIONS OF AFRICAN AND AMERICAN CHRISTIANITY

1. All these names are pseudonyms for the posters' user IDs.

2. One of the many and complex patterns of oppression by Idi Amin's regime involved the persecution of Christians in the name of Islam. Kevin Ward, "The Church of Uganda Amidst Conflict," in *Religion and Politics in East Africa*, ed. H. Hansen and M. Twaddle, 72–105 (Athens: Ohio University Press, 1995).

3. Samuel Paul, "Interpretation of the New Testament from the Third World: A Global Perspective" (paper presented at the annual meeting for the American Academy of Religion, Atlanta, November 25, 2003).

4. Theologically, racially, and socially, if not geographically, New Zealand is identified as Northern; indeed, it is one of the Communion's most liberal provinces.

5. Official figures often place the Church of England as the largest Anglican church, with Nigeria and Uganda following. However, the Church of England is an established church, meaning all English people are officially members of the church unless they declare membership in another religious body. Attendance at churches in England is relatively low.

6. For example, Chinua Achebe has argued persuasively that Joseph Conrad's *Heart of Darkness*, widely used in high school literature courses, cements negative images of Africa in Northerners' minds. Chinua Achebe, "An Image of Africa: Racism in Conrad's Heart of Darkness," in *Heart of Darkness: A Norton Critical Edition*, ed. Robert Kimbrough, 251–62 (New York: Norton, 1988).

7. Roxanne Lynn Doty, *Imperial Encounters: The Politics of Representation in North-South Relations* (Minneapolis: University of Minnesota Press, 1996), 4.

8. Ibid., 5.

9. Ibid., 2.

10. Ibid., 92.

11. David Spurr, *The Rhetoric of Empire: Colonial Discourse in Journalism, Travel Writing, and Imperial Administration* (Durham, NC: Duke University Press, 1993).

12. Ibid., 125.

13. Theodore Dalrymple, "Straight and Narrow: It's the Church's Children That Have Kept the Faith," *Sunday Times* (South Africa), August 23, 1998, accessed in private archive.

14. Doty, *Imperial Encounters*, 79–98.

15. Dipesh Chakrabarty, *Provincializing Europe* (Princeton, NJ: Princeton University Press, 2000).

16. Bruno Latour, *We Have Never Been Modern* (Cambridge, MA: Harvard University Press, 1993), 71.

17. Spurr, *Rhetoric of Empire*, 41.

18. Doty, *Imperial Encounters*, 88, 110.

19. Christine Leigh Heyrman, *Southern Cross: The Beginnings of the Bible Belt* (New York: Knopf, 1997), 49.

20. Ekklesia Society, "Rationale."

21. AMiA home page (2003), Anglican Mission in America, http://www.angli canmissioninamerica.org (accessed April 29, 2003).

22. Miclean, "Restoration."

23. "Rwanda: More than a Companion," *Anglican Mission in America Newsletter*, no. 3, October 2000.

24. Stephen Noll, Sermon, St. Stephen's, Sewickly, PA, June 4, 2000, accessed in private archive.

25. Bob Libby, "Why We Americans Appear to Be Arrogant," *Church of England Newspaper*, July 17, 1999, 10.

26. LeBlanc, "Africans Strengthen."

27. "Rants, Raves," *Christian Challenge*

28. Spurr, *Rhetoric of Empire*, 47.

29. Ibid., 53.

30. Ibid., 165–66.

31. The Northern Ugandans I talked with constitute a significant exception, in that they readily spoke about the suffering endured by their communities in the long conflict between the Ugandan government and the rebel Lord's Resistance Army, led by self-proclaimed spirit medium Joseph Kony and known for its brutal child abductions. Many Northern Ugandans are concerned about the lack of international attention to the ravaging of their home region, and eager to spread the word.

32. In Uganda, for example, in much of the country even the poor eat reasonably well, because of the fertility of the soil. But in other respects, these rural populations are dramatically underserved, with limited access to clean water, education, and health care, and constrained by their economic position—for example, pushed into cash cropping and family-dividing migrant labor.

33. Christian Smith, *American Evangelicalism: Embattled and Thriving* (Chicago: Chicago University Press, 1998), 190–94.

34. Spurr, *Rhetoric of Empire*, 134.

35. Ibid., 48.

36. Ibid., 47.

37. Jan Nunley, "Rosemont Confirmation Attracts Opposites in Faith," Episcopal News Service, December 1, 2000, http://www.episcopalchurch.org/ens/ 2000-221.html (accessed August 27, 2002).

38. Diana Witts, "CMS Work Today" (n.d.), www.telegraph.co.uk/et?ac=0 04155897623313&rtmo=VDq6JVqK&atmo=rrrrrrrq&pg=/et/01/1/18/ncrus18 .html (accessed February 8, 2001); Victoria Combe, "Missionaries Flock to Britain to Revive Passion for Church," *Daily Telegraph* (UK), January 18, 2001, http://anglicansonline.org/news/ (accessed February 8, 2001).

39. AMiA, "Anglican Mission."

40. Though AMiA has not made it a goal to bring Southern missionaries to American churches, its leaders feel that the organization nonetheless embodies the idea of South-to-North missionization. In a report on one AMiA parish, Barbara Bradley-Hagerty noted that since joining AMiA, members of this parish see themselves as "Rwandan missionaries" ("Profile: Episcopal Church Debating Surge in More Conservative Evangelicals from Africa," *Morning Edition* (NPR News),

January 27, 2003; *Virtuosity Digest*, January 28–30, 2003). I have heard members of St. Timothy's describe themselves in the same way.

41. Irene Tumwine, "Africa Evangelizes Europe," *New Vision* (Kampala), July 19, 1998.

42. A Ugandan bishop told me a story illustrating the difficulty of matching up African Christians' enthusiasm for missions with the means to support them. He described reading that the CMS was having trouble using up its own missionary budget, and suggesting to a CMS missionary that the organization use those funds to support African missionaries in Europe and other parts of the world. However, as he recounted to me, the CMS man told him, " 'You know, [whispering for emphasis] in CMS, the money which is there has been given by British people for British people also.' " When I asked if he thought this was racism, he replied tactfully that he preferred to see it as "lack of vision."

43. I suspect the rise of e-mail "Nigerian scams" has served to further weaken African credibility in the United States.

44. Wetzel, "There Is No Deadlock."

45. Alexander Muge, "A Tale of Two Cultures," *St. Andrew's Messenger*, St. Andrew's Episcopal Church, Fort Worth, Texas, vol. 10, no. 1 (June 1, 1998), accessed in private archive. The final sentence was in boldface in the original.

46. Theodora Brooks, "An African Priest Comments on Lambeth," *Episcopal New Yorker*, October–November 1998, 3.

47. Doty, *Imperial Encounters*, 162.

Chapter 7. Integrity for Sale? Money and Assymetry in
Transnational Anglican Alliances

1. Integrity-USA, "Integrity Announces Formation of Ugandan Chapter" (2000), http://www.integrityusa.org/gc2000/press/7–7-00b.html (accessed May 4, 2003).

2. Bishops of the Province of Uganda, "Press Release: To the Public and Citizens of Uganda," February 1, 2001, accessed in private archive.

3. Integrity-Uganda, "Integrity-Uganda Chapter Press Release," January 2001, accessed in private archive.

4. Kakengo, "Poverty."

5. Christopher Ssenyonjo, "God Sent Me to the 'Outcasts,' " *Monitor* (Kampala), May 31, 2001.

6. Christopher Ssenyonjo, "I Have Never Been Homosexual," *New Vision* (Kampala), May 9, 2001.

7. Patricia Nakamura, "Pivotal Moment: Bishop Charles Murphy Talks about His Consecration in Singapore," *Living Church*, March 26, 2000, 8.

8. For an overview of the role of conservative foundations in funding the Episcopal dissident movement, see Jim Naughton's article, "Following the Money," a special report from the *Washington Window*, the newspaper of the Episcopal Diocese of Washington, April 2006, http://www.edow.org/follow/ (accessed May 2, 2006).

9. "The truth is so much more interesting: secret societies have not had power in history, but the *notion* that secret societies have had power in history *has* had power in history." John Crowley, *Aegypt* (New York: Bantam Books, 1987), 388.

10. "An Allegation Revisited: Were African Votes 'Bought'?," *Christian Challenge*, November 1998, 9–10.

11. "Scottish Bishop," *Scotsman* (UK).

12. Ruth Gledhill, "Liberal Bishop 'Felt Lynched' in Gays Debate," *Times* (UK), August 7, 1998, http://www.rockies.net/~spirit/united/articles/9808news .html (accessed August 2, 2003).

13. Andrew Carey, "Myths and Rumours," *Church of England Newspaper*, July 17, 2003, 8.

14. David Virtue, "Opening Comments," *Virtuosity Digest* 2003–47, June 23–26, 2003.

15. Douglas, "Lambeth 1998," 11.

16. Ibid.

17. Stephen Noll, "The AAC Team: We Came, We Saw, We Served," *Encompass*, 2, no. 2 (August 1998).

18. Patrick Augustine, "Letter to the Editor on Lambeth," *Encompass*, no date; accessed in private archive.

19. William Atwood, "EKKLESIA General Secretary says sexual compromises undermines evangelism," *Virtuosity Digest* 2003–47, June 23–26, 2003.

20. Noll, "The AAC Team."

21. Several informed liberal observers of the conference agreed that the FSC's activities should be described not in terms of bribery or persuasion, but rather perhaps in terms of facilitation, since African and other Southern bishops were already predisposed to side with Northern conservatives on the sexuality issue. A piece in the conservative publication *Christian Challenge* quoted Dr. Louie Crew, founder and past president of Integrity, stating: "[Conservatives] did not buy votes; instead, they organized coalitions and taught those who already agreed with them how to make the system work for their advantage" ("An Allegation Revisited," *Christian Challenge*). Likewise, an editorial in the left-leaning British paper the *Church Times* raised a pertinent question: "All that the conservative Americans can be accused of is identifying a sympathetic body of opinion and helping it to develop the political skills needed to make itself heard. The process was one of enablement rather than manipulation, and the fact that it needed to be done by the conservatives is another question to be asked of the Anglican Consultative Council, whose job it more properly was" ("Summing Up the Lambeth Conference," *Church Times* (UK), August 14, 1998, accessed in private archive).

22. Arlin Adams, "Unspinning Rowan Williams," *Virtuosity Digest* 2003–47, June 23–26, 2003.

23. David Virtue, "New Center of Gravity is Emerging among Anglican Primates" (2000), http://listserv.episcopalian.org/scripts/wa.exe?A2=ind0011e& L=virtuosity&D=1&H=1&O=D&F=&S=&P=179 (accessed April 10, 2004).

24. Daly, "Church at Risk," 3.

25. Doug LeBlanc, "Is My Money Also Abominable?," *United Voice*, March 30, 1999, http://www.anglicanvoice.org/voice/haines0399.htm (accessed October 9, 2002).

26. Scott Morgensen, "Contesting Indigeneity: Queer and Native Politics of the Sexual and Transnational" (paper presented at Duke University, January 29, 2003).

27. Ian Douglas and Kwok Pui-Lan, eds., *Beyond Colonial Anglicanism* (New York: Church Publishing Incorporated, 2003).

28. Doug LeBlanc, "Where Do We Go from Lambeth?," *United Voice*, October 14, 1998, http://www.episcopalian.org/eu/lambeth/chastity.asp (accessed January 18, 1999).

29. Knippers, "What Do Conservative Episcopalians."

30. Here I am reading Mauss's work through the lens of Bruno Latour's understanding of modernity, laid out in *We Have Never Been Modern* (1993). I am particularly indebted to Latour for my use of the verb "purify" to describe efforts to clarify and separate categories of thought.

31. Marcel Mauss, *The Gift: The Form and Reason for Exchange in Archaic Societies* (1954; New York: W. H. Norton, 1990), vii.

32. One short satirical piece that appeared in a Ugandan paper while I was there quoted an imaginary Ugandan official thanking President Bush for sending Uganda an aid package, but complaining that the aid had all leaked out from between all the strings attached to the package, and suggesting that next time they might try using cellotape instead of string.

33. Yoweri Museveni, "Speech on the Occasion of Dunstan Bukenya's Consecration as Bishop of Mityana," January 27, 2002, personal collection.

34. Spurr, *Rhetoric of Empire*, 88–89.

35. Notable exceptions to Northern clothing in Uganda include the West-African-turned-pan-African tailored styles in African fabrics, worn by some urban young people, and the traditional dress often worn by older and rural people.

36. This term is roughly equivalent to the Catholic concept of inculturation.

37. Interestingly, many supporters of renewal actually describe it not as Westernization but as a kind of indigenization—arguing, for example, that the lively beat and free prayers are more in keeping with the indigenous African spirit. In general, the Ugandans who described renewal as a form of Westernization rather than indigenization were opposed to it. Some of these were pro-indigenization, some were Balokole who prefer their own form of renewal, while some were just ordinary Ugandan Anglicans who want to keep using their familiar prayer book and music.

38. Robert W. Strayer, *The Making of Missions Communities in East Africa: Anglicans and Africans in Colonial Kenya, 1875–1935* (Albany: State University of New York Press, 1977), 59, 158.

39. Erica Bornstein, "Child Sponsorship, Evangelism, and Belonging in the Work of World Vision Zimbabwe," *American Ethnologist* 28, no. 3 (2001): 595–622.

40. Kathryn Sikkink, "Restructuring World Politics: The Limits and Asymmetries of Soft Power," in Khagram, Riker, and Sikkink, *Restructuring World Politics*, 301–18.

41. The only real criticism I encountered came from James, the UCU professor quoted in the previous chapter, who questioned the implications of the fact that so much Northern help was needed for an African voice to be heard at Lambeth: "Since the beginning of the Christian mission in Africa, I think Africans sometimes have not been allowed to articulate their own problems and issues. . . . When you bring this question of the discussion at Lambeth, clearly any contribution which the African church was trying to make was not taken seriously. Either it was brushed off as people being naive, or people who have not sensitized the issues, or people who have been recently converted from heathenism. . . . Even the voice which came out from the African church was channeled through, I think, some of the Western church leaders, . . . the ones who were sympathetic with the African stand. These were the people to articulate, and then [the other bishops] could listen, but not [to] the Africans themselves."

42. In an interesting parallel to these Ugandan leaders' talk about Northern sponsors, David Maxwell examines the spiritual autobiography of Ezekiel Guti, an important figure in the Zimbawean Assemblies of God. Maxwell describes a "parable" Guti tells about his early travels to the United States: "He is offered financial assistance from a white man if he will submit to his authority." Guti rejects the offer; but, as Maxwell shows, his work and ministry are funded to a substantial degree by Northern white donors. However, Guti describes this support positively, as "love-offerings," in contrast to that first offer of assistance, framed as an attempt at coercion. David Maxwell, " 'Sacred History, Social History': Traditions and Texts in the Making of a Southern African Transnational Religious Movement," *Comparative Studies in Society and History* (2001): 502–24.

43. Corresponding to such perceptions, a view of Integrity-Uganda as a fundamentally colonial institution—that is, something imposed on Uganda by outsiders who believe they know better and possess superior political, cultural, and economic power—carries great weight in Uganda, strengthened by the coincidence that Integrity-USA founder Louie Crew was in Uganda on unrelated Episcopal Church business at the time that Integrity-Uganda's first press release was published.

44. Bishop Ssenyonjo was defrocked in March 2006, allegedly because he had founded a new non-Anglican denomination in Uganda, thus violating his ordination vows to the Church of Uganda. Archbishop Henry Orombi's statement on the matter referred to Ssenyonjo's advocacy for gays and lesbians among Ssenyonjo's wrongs, but this advocacy was apparently not the proximate cause for the church's final expulsion of Ssenyonjo. Henry Luke Orombi, "Church Dissociates Herself from Christopher Ssenyonjo," *Virtuosity Digest*, March 29, 2006.

45. Mauss, *The Gift*, 73.

46. Ssenyonjo, "I Have Never."

47. Louie Crew, "Queer Christian on the Road in Uganda," February 24, 2001, http://www.andromeda.rutgers.edu/~lcrew/natter/msg00196.html (accessed March 5, 2001).

48. Opiyo Oloya, "Ssenyonjo May Yet Have the Last Laugh," *New Vision* (Kampala), May 23, 2001.

49. Virtue, "South African Bishops."

50. The official statement from the CAPA meeting stated only that the African provinces would seek to develop their own economic and theological training resources, to reduce dependency on the Northern churches; but many primates stated that this meant, for them, refusing all funding from Northern churches, especially ECUSA. "Statement from the Primates of the Council of the Anglican Provinces of Africa," *Anglican Communion News Service* 3814, April 19, 2004.)

51. Tom Malti, "Churches Refuse Funding over Gay Issue," *Virtuosity Digest*, April 18, 2004.

52. Henry Orombi, "Statement from the Archbishop of the Church of the Province of Uganda" (Sepember 23, 2004), *Virtuosity Digest*, September 29, 2004. "Walking in light" is a phrase associated with East African Revival spirituality, and refers to examining one's own sins and temptations honestly and publicly.

53. David Virtue, "Uganda to Roskam: Thanks but No Thanks," *Virtuosity Digest*, June 14, 2004.

54. David Virtue, "Uganda Primate Says All ECUSA Funding Is Being Rejected," *Virtuosity Digest*, September 7, 2004; Malti, "Churches Refuse."

CHAPTER 8. THE NEXT ANGLICANISM? CONCLUSIONS AND IMPLICATIONS

1. Daly, "Church at Risk," 9.

2. Coleman, *Globalisation*, 59–60.

3. Ian T. Douglas and Julie Wortman, "Lambeth 1998: A Call to Awareness," *Witness*, September–October 1998, 24–25.

4. Recall, for example, the story of Congolese archbishop Njojo preaching on American materialism, at the Rosemont, Pennsylvania, international confirmation service—perhaps a rather off-message sermon from the point of view of American conservatives.

5. Peacock, *Global Identity*.

6. Philip Jenkins, "The Next Christianity," *Atlantic Monthly*, October 2002: 53–68.

7. Ian Douglas, "Book Review: The Next Christendom," *The World & I* (n.d., 2003), http://www.townhall.com/bookclub/jenkins.html (accessed November 5, 2003).

8. Jenkins, *Next Christendom*, 4.

9. Alister McGrath, "A Lecture to the 'Future of Anglicanism' Conference, Oxford, UK," July 8, 2002, http://www.americananglican.org/Issues/Issues.cfm ?ID=401&c=16 (accessed November 4, 2003).

10. David Virtue, "Opening Comments," *Virtuosity Digest*, December 18, 2002.

11. American Anglican Council, "News," 2003, http://www.americananglican.org/News/News.cfm?ID=376&c=21&Type=s (accessed November 4, 2003).

12. Robert Sanders, "A Word from the South," *Virtuosity Digest*, January 21, 2003.

13. Christ the Redeemer Church (Louisiana), "Endorsements" (2003), http://www.ctronline.org/values/Relationships/endorsements.htm, (accessed November 4, 2003).

14. Doug LeBlanc, "What in the World is God Doing?" (August 3, 2003), http://www.anglican.tk/modules.php?name=Content&pa=showpage&pid=265 (accessed February 8, 2004).

15. "Looming Schism: Anglican Split Is between First, Third Worlds," *Dallas Morning News*, October 8, 2003: 20A.

16. For an evaluation of Jenkins's political conclusions, see Shah, "The Bible and the Ballot Box."

17. Jenkins, *Next Christendom*, 103–4.

18. This negative evaluation of American Christianity, in spite of sociological indicators of its continuing strength, is in keeping with the culture of American evangelicals, who tend to see themselves as threatened by and embattled with the forces of secularism. See Smith, *American Evangelicalism*, 20.

19. Jenkins, *Next Christendom*, 13–14.

20. Harvey, *Condition of Postmodernity*; Giddens, *Consequences of Modernity*.

21. Walter Cronkite, "Eric Sevareid," *All Things Considered*, February 12, 2004, http://www.npr.org/news/specials/cronkite/ (sound file, accessed April 10, 2004).

22. Atwood, "Primates in Canterbury."

23. Anglican Communion News Service, "Lambeth Commission Tackles Tensions in the Church," ACNS 3781, February 16, 2004, http://www.anglicancommunion.org/acns/articles/37/75/acns3781.cfm (accessed March 8, 2004).

24. Robin Eames, "Lecture 1: A Growing Reality" (paper presented as the 2005 Sprigg Lectures, Virginia Theological Seminary), *Virginia Seminary Journal* (February 2006): 4–12.

25. Donald Miller, "Emergent Patterns of Congregational Life and Leadership in the Developing World: Personal Reflections from a Research Odyssey" (Pulpit & Pew Reports, 2003, Duke University), 36.

26. Ibid., 31.

27. W. Jenkins, "Episcopalians," 297.

28. Douglas, "Book Review."

Index